D1175181

AGONIES OF THE INTELLECTUAL

Allan Stoekl

gonies of the Intellectual

Commitment, Subjectivity,

and the Performative

in the Twentieth-Century

French Tradition

University of Nebraska

PRESS

Lincoln & London

1992

Library of Congress
Cataloging in Publication Data
Stoekl, Allan.
Agonies of the intellectual: commitment,
subjectivity, and the performative in
the twentieth-century
French tradition / Allan Stoekl.
p. cm.
Includes bibliographical references
and index.
ISBN 0-8032-4215-8 (alk. paper)
1. France –
Intellectual life – 20th century.
2. Philosophy,
Modern – 20th century. I. Title.
dc33.7.S76 1992
001.1'0944–dc20 91-17143
CIP

Publication of this book was
assisted by a grant from
The Andrew W. Mellon
Foundation

*Because he was a priest,
it was easy for him to become
the monster that he was.*

"Chianine," in Bataille's
L'Abbé C.

Contents

Acknowledgments

THIS BOOK could not have been written without the generous aid provided by Yale University, through the Morse Junior Faculty Fellowship. My senior colleagues, Professor Thomas Greene in Comparative Literature, and Professors Peter Brooks, Georges May, and Jacques Guicharnaud in French, were kind enough to support me in my bid for this fellowship.

Thanks also to people who read and criticized early versions or parts of the manuscript, especially Profs. Rodolphe Gasché, Diane Rubinstein, Sara Suleri, Richard Rand, Lawrence Kritzman, and Candace Lang.

Grateful acknowledgment is made to the original publishers of the following portions of this book: "Nizan, Drieu, and the Question of Death," (Chapter 2), published under the same title in *Representations* 21 (1988): 117–45, © 1988 by the Regents of the University of California. Reprinted by permission. "The Performance of Sartré's *Nausea*" (Chapter 3), published under the same title in *The Yale Journal of Criticism*, 1.2 (1988): 1–22. "De Man and Guilt" (Chapter 9), published in part, under the same title, in *Responses to de Man's Wartime Journalism*, ed. W. Hamacher, N. Hertz and T. Keenan (Lincoln: The University of Nebraska Press, 1989): 375–85. "Sur Bataille: Nietzsche in the Text of Bataille," (Chapter 10) published under the same title in *Glyph 6* (Baltimore: Johns Hopkins University Press, 1979): 42–67. Reprinted by permission of the Johns Hopkins University Press. "Hegel's Return" (Chapter 11), published in part, under the same title, in *The Stanford French Review*, 12.1 (1988): 119–28. *The Stanford French Review* is published for the Dept. of French and Italian by Anma Libri, Saratoga, California.

This book is dedicated, with much love, to my wife, Nan Moschella, and to our two cubs, Bruno and Ricky (of "The Bruno-Ricky Show" fame).

Los Robles, March 1991

Abbreviations

Introduction:
The "Ends" of the
Secular Cleric?

RECENTLY many books in the United States have been devoted to the question of the intellectual.[1] It seems as though this figure has long stood at the edge of the grave. Of course his or her death has been proclaimed many times, most recently by Foucault and Lyotard, but those who argue for that death are intellectuals themselves.[2] Is the lamenting for, or championing of, the loss of the intellectual, then, nothing more than a form of narcissism on the part of a small number of self-lacerating, overeducated individuals?

One could respond, sincerely enough, that there is a need for a certain type of intellectual in this country – an intellectual who seems no longer to exist. "Intellectual" is a vague word, to be sure, and one can make of it just about anything one wants: Russell Jacoby, in *The Last Intellectuals*, mourns the loss of a certain type of nonacademic writer, one who is by nature anti-Establishment and whose efforts effectively are read – and are readable – by a relatively large number of nonspecialized, educated readers. That audience, the reviews they read (the old *Partisan Review*, *Hound and Horn*, the old *New Republic*, etc.), along with their favorite writers, are no longer around. Jacoby can find many reasons, all vaguely sociological, for their demise: the decline of bohemia, the leveling effect of consumerism and television, the rise of the mega-university.

Jacoby's nostalgia has to do not only with the intellectual him- or herself, but with a vision of society in which the well-written page and the reasoned argument still count, one in which cultured people who think as individuals can effectively oppose the dead weight of unresponsive government and tyrannical popular culture. If we see intellectuals in this way, as figures of resistance or revolt – and not simply as members of a "new class" of career-oriented

I

technical, bureaucratic, and managerial experts – then we must attempt to see in what ways they have exerted their influence in the United States in the past.[3] Perhaps it is not surprising to note that Jacoby's brand of intellectual has never had a firm social position in this country, that his or her position has always been an extremely marginal one.[4] Even in the glory days (for intellectuals, at least) of the 1930s, "highbrows" were confined to a few eastern cities (from which their influence did not extend), and their function lay almost exclusively in the relaying of, and quibbling with, movements that came from abroad: the *Partisan Review* crowd, after all, even in its anti-Stalinism, was simply echoing, and weakly at that, a debate whose terms were set in Europe.[5]

I sympathize with Jacoby's project, but I strongly disagree with him when he would establish in this country a figure that he claims *once existed here*. Of course we have had, and continue to have, many writers and thinkers who take their cue from abroad, serving mainly to ingest, regurgitate, and then traffic in the work of their European colleagues, now made palatable for domestic consumption. (I myself am as guilty of this as anyone.) But have we ever had a Zola, a Sartre, even a Foucault – let alone a Heidegger? One might argue that only in countries or regions with a strong Catholic tradition of coherent official doctrine – and its implementation by a corps of trained and faithful bureaucrats, a clerisy – does the intellectual have just the remainder of the role exemplified by these figures. In Protestant countries, and especially the United States, the tradition of the authority of anyone and everyone to interpret (correctly) the Bible for him- or herself effectively precluded the formation later of a powerful secular intellectual corps. There may be pragmatists, trained experts and technicians, safely ensconced in government facilities – but not a group of independent but authoritative generalists writing and interpreting for, and read within, the larger public sphere.[6]

One must turn to a country like France where something like Jacoby's phantasm of the intellectual continues to function, albeit feebly. Before we can ask if such a figure can be imported – along with wine and cheese and other tidbits of French civilization – we must try to determine the origin and fate of the intellectual in a country whose republican ideology, to a large extent, is grounded on the necessity of the secular priest as mediator and representative. If we can grasp the how and why of the decline of this figure, then I think we will be in a better position to ask if an American intellectual can be revived, or founded. This last question is not the topic of this book, but I have written the book as a necessary first step to asking the question. For if the notion of the French intellectual is (or has become) radically incoherent – an intellectual who was at least for one fleeting moment seemingly clearly formulated in regard to his or her political, polemical, and representational/representative function – then one is hard-pressed to imagine how the intellectual can be revivified in a country where the role of this figure has never even existed, let alone been clearly defined.

This is not necessarily a cry of despair; if one recognizes, in spite of the history of the impossibility of the American intellectual (as Jacoby has defined it), the necessity of its invention, then that founding act can be posited only in the light (or darkness) of the situation of the French writer throughout the twentieth century. There is no point in simply reenacting positions from the past and from another culture. Instead one must start by following through, if only from a distance, the various movements, the various binds: at the end of this process of personal, political, and social *Bildung* (as Hegel would call it), one at least has a picture (an impossible *Bild*, in effect) of the virulent impasse of the intellectual, which for me is the necessary but painful position of Georges Bataille.[7] Perhaps the American intellectual can avoid simply aping the French by starting off (if only in the circular movement of the return) at the moment of agitation in which the French seem to have stopped, after he or she recognizes how their impasse has come to pass. Perhaps. But it is also possible that this eventual doubling of the French intellectuals' doubling will not, indeed cannot, lead outside itself: the final aping may very well consist only in the repetition of an automutilating agony. I use this last word in its etymological sense: striving, competition, confrontation – but also, as in French, death agony.[8]

One initially turns to France for a coherent model of the intellectual and for a historical overview of its various subsequent avatars throughout the twentieth century. It is generally recognized that France, even today, is a country in which intellectuals, devoted above all to the aesthetic and eminently rational powers of their own language, constitute a *république des lettres* that transcends politics, cultural particularity, and religion and that plays a unifying role within the country.[9] What one anticipates doing is a kind of sociology/intellectual history: the two would, in any case, seem inseparable. One approaches the intellectual as a sociological phenomenon: as a figure, he or she plays a very specific role in relation to state and ideological institutions, the media, the larger reading public, even the church. A sociological study of the various "representative" intellectuals, however, must lead to a project in intellectual history: what did each of these figures stand for, and how did each differ from his or her predecessor and followers?[10] How did each generate the intellectuals who came after – and before? The social history of the intellectual is itself therefore inseparable from the documents in which the figure of the intellectual is posited or elaborated by intellectuals. It is with such writings that I will be exclusively concerned in this book: these writings must be read not as superfluous fragments that simply illustrate an "extratextual" history but as texts whose inner coherence must be evaluated and questioned. Only after this type of reading is carried out can one pose the larger question of the sociology of the intellectual.

But we immediately come up against a difficulty that has dogged much of twentieth-century thought: call it the "hermeneutic circle" or whatever, the problem is that intellectual history is inevitably written by an intellectual – who is therefore writing his or her own history, recounting the stages of his or her own intellectual development, and who is, since those stages are always the fulfillment of a social function, also doing a sociology of his or her own intelligence. There is no position outside of the itinerary of the intellectual's self-formation from which that movement can be evaluated and through which predictions can be made. The position of the writer itself is determined by the end (if such a thing is imaginable or representable) of the movement he or she is charting. But what can a self-formation mean if it is the category of the "self" that has been put in question by recent intellectuals? For that matter, what can a sociology mean if the very possibility of a coherent society has been challenged? And history? If these problems confront us at the end of our journey, how can we confidently anticipate at the outset the simple and harmonious unification of the history (and sociology) of the intellectual with intellectual history as a discipline? How can one carry out a Hegelian project (the formulation of a coherent role – in society and in thought – for the intellectual) in a post-Hegelian era?

While refusing to distinguish the history of the intellectual from intellectual history, we must nevertheless recognize that, rather than finding a perfect dovetailing of commitment, theory, and writing at the end of our trajectory, we may find something very different. It may be only in the first version of the contemporary, twentieth-century intellectual that we can discover at least the fantasy of a perfect match between social function and self-reflexive truth. Or, more precisely, perhaps it is only at the beginning that the intellectual activity, misreading itself, is able to formulate itself as coherent, finished, at an end. That is why I devote the first chapter of this book to the sociologist Emile Durkheim. His project included a formulation of the task of the intellectual that comprehends both public utility and truth (which is also a social truth, or the truth of society). We start out in Durkheim with a coherent definition of the dissident (but constructive and representative) intellectual.[11] For Durkheim, the intellectual is both independent of the coercions inherent in all social groupings, devoted to and following the rules of reason, *and* he or she is fully committed to the implementation of reason in society. Now the truth determined by the intellectual is nothing other than the fact that in all religions – no matter how "primitive" – the force worshiped in ritual, in the periodic incandescence in which people meet and renew their social bonds, is the eminently reasonable drive to be a social being, to derive strength from the community.

4

The intellectual is independent to the extent that he or she is devoted only to reason – to determining the rational bases of society itself – and not to any mystique of nation, religion, race, or clan. And yet the task of the intellectual in its most fundamental sense is religious: the rational roots of all religion, when understood and propagated in the public schools, will serve as the foundation for a secular, republican cult of civic and state duty.

The Durkheimian intellectual could not be more "engaged," more immersed in his or her own community. At the same time, he or she could not be more independent, more devoted to the dictates of reason alone. The intellectual is both a state authority, speaking from within an institution (the university) as a sociologist or anthropologist, and, at the same time, he or she is totally independent, a critical force, even a dissident, who freely writes against abuses of political and cultural power. The sociologist in essence writes his or her own sociology, assigning him or herself a position of authority in respect to the new, secular religion of public morality. Further, he or she posits a kind of universal intellectual history, in which the delusions of all past religions are analyzed and gone beyond. This, in fact, is the ultimate goal of Durkheimian anthropology.

I start with Durkheim because his project is a significant step beyond the earlier Enlightenment tradition of the *philosophe* (Voltaire, Diderot) or that of the nineteenth-century positivist (Comte), despite the fact that in his rationalism and positivism Durkheim obviously owes much to these precursors.[12] Unlike Comte, Durkheim does not attempt to replace a religion of superstition with one of reason. Instead, he recognizes the rational core at the heart of the darkness of "primitive" religion, at the heart of the seemingly irrational. The difference is significant, and it is emblematic, in its rigor, of the typical twentieth-century joining of aesthetics, science, and primitivism.[13] The force of the "primitive" sacred need not be expunged – it need only be interpreted correctly (as "moral enthusiasm"), making use of the appropriate social-scientific techniques. This force will then be at the disposal of the rational and just society. Modernism and its high priest will be generated out of a scientific reinterpretation, and appropriation, of the primitive. The intellectual is now the truth of *all* society; he or she stands for the implementation not only of the reason but also of the moral energy inherent in all human congregations. In fact, in this humanist model the intellectual is the ultimate human subject, serving as the pivot around which all other individuals turn, and through which they know themselves as subjectivities and know their places as social beings as well. The intellectual, through the educative function, makes possible the reproduction of the reasonable civilization (and its institutions) by which people recognize their own healthy energy. The intellectual is a secular priest or priestess celebrating the mass of his or her own representative subjectivity; the anthropological and sociological text of his or her own self-knowledge is the secular Bible; the public school is the secular church; the university is the secular Vatican.

Very early on something went wrong with this model. Indeed Durkheim's own followers, while concerned with questions of social integration and exchange, showed little interest in the master's theories of a republican religion.[14] Those in France after World War I who can be said to have followed Durkheim in his concern with religion were not his students at all but avant-garde writers like Georges Bataille.[15] Durkheim's gesture of recognizing the truth of "primitive" religions, while it may seem a classic gesture of Western ethnocentrism to many observers today (it authorized the colonization, so to speak, of the "primitive" experience itself), nevertheless also made possible a kind of radical inversion of Durkheimian rationalism. Where Durkheim saw a rational secular sacred, Bataille saw an irrational one; Durkheim's secular priest became, for Bataille, a shaman bent not on furthering bourgeois civil society but in sweeping it away in an apocalyptic revolution; the schoolteacher became a pornographer writing of the murderous, erotic frenzy of children – a frenzy directed, as often as not, against a Catholic priest.[16]

It is not enough to say that Durkheim opened the way for Bataille by revalorizing "primitive" religion and, most notably, sacrifice; there was something more. As I attempt to show in the first chapter of this book, Durkheim was never able to exorcise a certain energy or force at work in primitive societies, indeed in their very founding. Of course for Durkheim the moral enthusiasm of the community, reflected upon in moments of ritual, was the very thing that motivated each person's activities in and for the group. One can certainly argue, as Durkheim himself does, that the necessary force is rational, but one can just as easily go in the opposite direction, seeing that the force of the act, while perhaps responsible for the establishment and unification of a coherent society, is also necessarily subversive of a reasonable and knowable collective integrity. If the enthusiasm of "primitive" ritual is seen as not rational but irrational, and not creative but destructive, then a Nietzschean force can be presented that replaces the harmony of a Durkheimian-Hegelian *Bildung*; one can even argue that a strata of Durkheim's text authorizes, indeed mandates, this type of reading. Durkheim's secular priest is threatened by Bataille's shaman *within* Durkheim's own text.

Now I am not arguing that all the authors examined in this book were necessarily influenced by Durkheim, or even that they had read him. I want to suggest only that the kind of synthesis he attempted in and through the figure of the intellectual failed, and that this failure, explicitly or implicitly, is rewritten in all subsequent formulations of the intellectual. One of the basic premises of my book is that French intellectuals after Durkheim were incapable of seamlessly joining the energy of their moral authority – and its instituting violence – with their role as representations (of society) and representatives (of the collective will of the people). Intellectuals are inherently violent, are indeed lost in violence, not so much because they feel compelled to pick up a gun and literally fight – although many of course dream of doing just that – but because they can no longer perfectly fuse, in their own self-conception, or in their activity in the world, their role as active agents on the one hand and as signifiers of the scientific truth of the human on the other.[17] Put another way, the dangerous force of the act of writing or speaking can no longer be cleanly reconciled with the form of representation: an unredeemable violence is lodged in the break that is now the intellectual function.[18]

This fissure results in two radically different types of writing intellectuals – one is devoted to the not necessarily rational force of writing or language itself, the other to the constructive project of representation and communication. This distinction can be linked with the two types distinguished by Roland Barthes: the author and the writer. Barthes's distinction is an absolutely fundamental one; it inherits much from the nineteenth-century distinction between the "political" author (Zola) and the author whose subject is language itself (Flaubert). No doubt the distinction can also be seen well before the nineteenth century.[19] Barthes takes this debate into the twentieth century in a characteristic way, introducing into it a scientific (semiotic, linguistic, anthropological) and rhetorical orientation. The distinction now is not a merely stylistic one but runs much deeper; the very opposition Barthes puts forward presupposes (if only to discount) a hypothetical unity, established under the sign of science, in which a purely formal mechanism (grammar, writing) is perfectly fused with adequate representation. The author, according to Barthes, performs his activity on his own "instrument," language. His action is "immanent in its object": "The paradox is that, the raw material becoming in a sense its own end, literature is at bottom a tautological activity, like that of those cybernetic machines constructed for themselves (Ashby's homeostat): the author is a man who radically absorbs the world's why in a how to write."[20]

While Barthes stresses the labor of the author, it is clear that his or her act is far from the constructive effort by which one (like the slave in Hegel's *Phenomenology*) can constitute one's own subjectivity through the externalization of a formative negativity. The author is lost in tautology, not grounded in self-reflexivity: "the author is the only man, by definition, to lose his structure and that of the world in the structure of language" (AW, 145). The act of the author is the mechanical run-through of linguistic or grammatical structures. Clearly for Barthes neither the content of the author's works, nor the constitution of a putative self through a transitive language, is at stake: instead, the author is characterized by the "cybernetic" movement of language, which is a "power to disturb the world" (AW, 146). But how can one even write of the world in such a context? Doesn't the "world" here imply a transitive function of language that "authorship" precludes? In that case, one can only stress power – or force – of the act of the language-machine incessantly rewriting the traces of the language-machine.

Barthes's writer, on the other hand, writes to communicate; he is a "transitive man, he posits a goal, of which language is merely a means; for him language supports a *praxis*, it does not constitute one. Thus language is restored to the nature of an instrument of communication, a vehicle of 'thought'" (AW, 147).

It should be stressed here, I think, that the communicative role of the writer implies a subjectivity on the part of both the sender and receiver of "thought." In addition, the political task of the writer necessitates, we might say – though Barthes does not make this point – a different model of rhetoric from the one associated with the author: the writer represents, his or her project is elaborated under the sign of reference, or the trope of metaphor, whereas the author acts, or rather he or she is nothing more than the robotic functioning of performative rhetoric, the indefinite proliferation of the speech act.[21]

The duality of this author/writer inevitably follows, I would argue, from the breakup of the coherence of the Durkheimian model of the intellectual – or, put another way, that duality is always already operative in Durkheim, in the tension between the totem as (re)instituting act and the totem as representation (see chapter 1), but it displays itself on the historical and sociological plane only in the years after World War I. We might even say that the most notable aftermath of Durkheimian sociology is the necessity of rethinking, in light of the author/writer split, the sociology of the intellectual. But how can we write of the author as intellectual – a word that after all implies intelligence and thought (which in turn implies communication between autonomous subjectivities) – when the author, as we have seen, may be nothing more than the mechanical eruption of language as act? How can we begin to propose a social role for this figure – in order at least to lay the groundwork for a sociology of the intellectual – if the labor of Barthes's author is radically asocial, the affectless movement of a machine?

Barthes stresses the fact that the author/writer function can never be separated as neatly as he has done: "I am describing here a contradiction which in fact is rarely pure: everyone today moves more or less openly between the two positions, the author's and the writer's. . . . Today, each member of the intelligentsia harbors both roles in himself, one or the other of which he "retracts" more or less well" (AW, 149). Indeed – and this is my argument throughout this book, the principal movement behind each of the chapters – the author and the writer are always caught in a sort of mutual interference: as we will often see, one cannot establish the communication of the writer without some-how, impossibly, basing it on the blind act of the author; conversely, the "author's" violent and repetitious language always struggles against, but de-pends on, a social commitment, a mediating and representative subjectivity. We might say that there is always a minor author in each writer, and vice versa. But this coexistence, if one can call it that, is not a simple historical curiosity, as Barthes at times seems to imply; rather it is the very impossibility of the unity of the intellectual, the rending moment in which the writer would know the author (whose violence is the unknowable) and in which the author would incessantly found the knowledge of the writer (whose knowledge is the neces-sary forgetting of the author's act, even in the depiction of it). Barthes, in stressing the fundamental differences between author and writer, sets the stage for much work to come – such as that of Paul de Man.[22] At the same time, though, in largely attempting to valorize one side over the other (the author over the writer) Barthes is forced to neglect the extent to which the schism he identifies runs through and under much if not all of twentieth-century French writing of and by the intellectual. The author does not supplant the writer; on the contrary, the writer's representation, and subjectivity, is at the origin of the author's act of dispersing the writer.

The first part of my book is concerned with three authors – Paul Nizan, Pierre Drieu la Rochelle, and Jean-Paul Sartre – who may all be considered writers. Indeed much of Barthes's polemic in "Authors and Writers" is directed against Sartre's downgrading of poetry, and his affirmation of prose in the first chapter ("What Is Writing?") of *What Is Literature?* In fact one could even say that Barthes is simply inverting the Sartrean hierarchy established there. Sartre takes aim at the modern author – epitomized by the surrealists – whose work is a self-consuming artifact, a mechanism that destroys nothing less than the distinction between subjectivity and objectivity: "Automatic writing was, above all, destruction of subjectivity. When we try our hand at it, rushes of blood spasmodically tear through us; we are ignorant of their origin . . . ; we must then perceive them with foreign eyes. . . . But the surrealists' second step was to destroy objectivity in turn. It was a matter of exploding the world . . . one had to do one's best . . . to disintegrate particular objects, that is, to do away with the very structure of objectivity in these witness-objects" (WIL, 152).

According to Sartre, the surrealist conflates subjectivity and objectivity (the author's text becomes a foreign production, objects are "witness-objects") only to do away with *both* realms. Needless to say, for Sartre this strategy reeks of bad faith; Sartre would retain a subjectivity that is devoted both to self-reflection and to representation, one that communicates a state of the world and the necessity of changing it: "I shall say that a writer is committed when he tries to achieve the most lucid and the most complete consciousness of being embarked, that is, when he causes the commitment of immediate spontaneity to advance, for himself and others, to the reflective. The writer is, par excellence, a mediator and his commitment is to mediation" (WIL, 77).

The subjectivity of the Sartrean writer thus mediates and represents; at the same time its knowledge is not a pure rationality, one that transcends time and place. "Whatever game he [the writer] may want to play, he must play it on the basis of the representation which others have of him" (WIL, 77). In a clear response to Julien Benda, the author of *The Betrayal of the Clerks* (1926), who argued that the intellectual betrayed his own vocation, his clerical devotion to timeless and transcendent truths, by enlisting in the cause of historically limited projects and politically contingent truths, Sartre maintains that the writer is always immersed in a milieu, and that he or she cannot – and should not – hope to rise above it into some universal, rational, but sterile and meaningless realm: "Can one imagine for a moment that he [the novelist Richard Wright] would agree to pass his life in the contemplation of the eternal True, Good and Beautiful when ninety percent of the negroes in the South are practically deprived of the right to vote? And if anyone speaks here about the treason of clerks, I answer that there are no clerks among the oppressed. Clerks are necessarily the parasites of oppressing classes or races" (WIL, 78).

In passages such as this one we see how Sartre's project constitutes a fragment of the Durkheimian one – not so much a half as a jagged remnant, itself split between the force of a linguistic or semiotic – but also partisan – act and the equanimity of a wholly adequate representation and mediation. Durkheim, like Benda, posited as the project of the intellectual – the secular clerk or cleric – the defense of a timeless truth arrived at through independent and even lonely effort: in Durkheim's case, this truth was nothing other than the fundamental rationality and the potential transparency of the human social group. Sartre, on the other hand, argues against Durkheim and Benda that there is no universal human grouping that transcends regional or local conditions; one is always in a situation, defined by the gaze as well as by the categories of the Other. Hence for Sartre, Benda's cleric is himself already committed, already partisan, even though he might think he represents only abstract truth – and he represents nothing other than the privileges of the elite class to which he belongs.

Sartre, then, recognizes a limited or historicized truth – the bugaboo of Benda – and the violence of its implementation. In this sense he represents a decisive break with the tradition of Durkheim, which at least fantasized a perfect bond between act and representation. But, very much like Durkheim, Sartre would eventually subordinate the force of a (re)founding gesture to the stasis of the signified. In this sense he is fully a Barthesian writer, and he can also be associated with the refusal of the speech (or totem) act and the ultimate

Durkheimian affirmation of a model of reference and conservation. (I use this latter term not in a pejorative sense, but in a technical one: reference entails the transmission or preservation of what is already "there" – in this case the collectivity itself – rather than its founding or imposition.)

For all the authors and writers examined in this book, the sacrificial gesture retains the primordial importance, if not the meaning, accorded to it in Durkheim's anthropology. We have in the tradition of committed literature, espoused not only by Sartre but also by Drieu, Nizan, and many others, the affirmation of both an adequate cognition and of a partisan, necessarily limited (or contingent) truth, one of chancy acts and dirty hands. As I show in the chapters of part 1, the apparent unification of these two (the blind act and reflective cognition) is regularly accomplished, in these committed writers, through the violence of sacrifice. Sacrifice alone allows the community in revolt to represent itself as unified to itself, and to affirm itself through the knowledge of its union against an Other. The sacrificial model was certainly also espoused by Durkheim, but in his writings sacrifice is a fundamentally peaceful rite in which one's gift to the gods, and the reception of riches from the gods (translated into secular terms, one's contribution to the community, and the benefits one receives from the community) are reenacted. Following in the wake of Durkheim, but also attempting to revise his model radically, the committed writers retain sacrifice, but for them it is worthless if it is not violent, brutal, an eruption of an apparently meaningless death into the social group. This shift in emphasis is clearly an indication of the collapse of Durkheim's system, of the failure of a later generation to believe in the wholly adequate translation of limited, violent acts into overarching scientific and moral truths.[23] But for Sartre too the violence espoused by the committed writer, uncompromising as it may be, can and must take on meaning through its interpretation: the victim and his death become metaphors for something else, something larger. Thus the absurdity of the worker Paul's death in Nizan's *Trojan Horse* is overcome when the other striking workers agree to give (or impose on) his death a meaning through the continuation of their struggle (see chapter 2). Sheer contingency is necessary to the social formation, but only when it is recuperated by a constructive, temporal dialectic. The problem, however, lies in this very contingency of violence: for violence to represent, meaning must be arbitrarily, and forcefully, thrust upon it. That in fact is the major violence "behind" the minor, representational (or represented) violence of sacrifice.

My readings of these writers therefore all demonstrate, in one way or another, that this process of the internalization of a radicalized violence (in the subjectivity of the committed writer, who continues to make possible the unification of the group through his or her interpretive practice) is countered by another violence, this one infinitely more resistant. If Sartre would dismiss the automatism of the Barthesian author, he himself nevertheless depends, in his depictions of a sacrificial social grouping (descriptions which themselves are meant to act as motors for a larger, extratextual social unification), on an arbitrary speech act that is fundamentally mechanical, neither subject to the control of human consciousness nor subsumable within a "group in fusion." The late *Critique of Dialectical Reason* (1960), whose central movement recognizes the recalcitrance of the blind and directionless performative precisely by attempting to formulate the "group" through the act's total humanization, runs into difficulties because it fails to recognize that the plenitude of the speech act that guarantees the representation of the group's fusion (and thus its fusion in general) is indistinguishable from the emptiness of the shifter that is associated with the aleatory unification-through-dispersion of the series (see chapter 5). The writer, then, as a committed intellectual, is split, not because he or she is always *dans le coup*, forced to make potentially dangerous, compromising, or traitorous decisions, (that kind of compromise is nothing but an indication of a phantasmic Sartrian machismo), but because, accompanying the "major" function of representation that undergirds the intellectual's activity (he or she represents the masses or some other group, the group represents itself to itself through its proxy, the intellectual, when he or she dies through some sort of sacrifice, etc.), there is a "minor" one – which itself opens the possibility of the representation-function – of the empty, automatic functioning of language on language, the authorless, directionless, and receiverless speech act. (Sacrifice itself should be considered, first and foremost, as a kind of speech act.) In this latter instance, as in the case of the Barthesian author, there can be no question of an originary subjectivity, be it personal or collective.

The author is equally split; but in this case it is not sacrifice as humanistic representation that is undermined by an inhuman act so much as it is a sacrifice of sacrifice itself – the sacrifice of the representation of the human through sacrifice – that is undermined by the return of the social, by the possibility, in other words, of social unification through separation. For this reason it is extremely naive to maintain that the author has in any way supplanted the writer, that the anthropological model, grounded on metaphor or mimesis, has simply been replaced or overturned by a deconstructive problematic of the violence of *écriture*. Such a view entails a fully Hegelian model of temporality, in which one world view simply succeeds another. Equally naive is the position that the performative act is exclusively logically prior to representation, that it always founds and mandates the latter in the act of abolishing it.[24] If the performative can be said only to refound, however, then the "original" foundation is a fiction situated on an infinitely receding horizon; the imposition of force is always both prior *and* belated, always radically different from, and at the same time confused with, representation.[25] Thus one cannot privilege either function of rhetoric, or either concomitant social role of the intellectual: their positions can be said to be reversible (although not necessarily symmetrical). Thinking of the consequences of this reversibility for the intellectual – conceived as both a rhetorical *and* a social function/figure – is by no means an easy task, but one whose difficulty will be exacerbated, I hope, by a reading of my book.

A good example of a theorist of the "intransitive" author is Maurice Blanchot. In writing of the two "slopes" of literature – one the realist type, the other the poetic, Blanchot too, in the essay "Literature and the Right to Death," attempts to revise the distinction and reverse the hierarchy established, in the first chapter of Sartre's *What Is Literature?*, between prose and poetry. And like Barthes, Blanchot recognizes that these two realms, so easily distinguished, nevertheless are always contained in each other: "an art which purports to follow one slope is already on the other."[26] But Blanchot's recognition of this is linked, unlike Barthes's, to a larger (Heideggerian) affirmation of the displacement of traditional metaphysical oppositions (such as inner/outer, inner imagination/external representation, alive/dead, human/inhuman, etc.).[27] This gesture is a characteristic tactic of all the authors (or rhetoricians) who will follow – Foucault, Derrida, and de Man. Thus one of Blanchot's slopes, which is associable with Barthes's mechanized author, "allies itself with the reality of language, it makes language into matter without contour, content without form, a force that is capricious and impersonal and says nothing, reveals nothing, simply announces – through its refusal to say anything – that it comes from night and will return to night" (LRD, 49).

One cannot, however, simply oppose the labor of "meaningful prose" to this "echo speaking on and on in the midst of silence" (LRD, 50), because "realism" itself, attempting to grasp an "imaginary whole" (i.e., a larger meaning or sense) beyond the particular, fragmentary, negations of individual words and concepts (which "separate" and "destroy" particularities in order to know and communicate them [LRD, 48]), leads only to the application of "negation to language itself," and thus to the exhaustion of language "by [its realization] as that totality on the basis of which each term would be nothing" (LRD, 49).[28] In other words, even going down the opposite slope – following Sartre, in effect – leads only to the same movement by which language "comes from night and will return to night," by which "art sets off in quest of a language that can recapture . . . absence itself" (LRD, 51). What apparently is only an "interest in the world" becomes a focusing on "the work of the negative in the world and for the world" – and the work of the negative, death, in and on language itself. (It should be no surprise, then, that Mallarmé comes to represent, for Blanchot, a writer who is on both slopes [LRD, 51]).

Introduction

If an outward-turning prose tends, in Blanchot, to move in and around death itself, it is only a measure of the impossibility literature faces in maintaining distinctions that are generated by the very movement of "death in the process of becoming" (LRD, 55) – the movement, in other words, by and through which literature itself is disclosed. This is not to say that such distinctions are merely forgotten but that they are violated in such a way that they are maintained but also emptied. Clearly sacrifice, of the type we see presented and put to work in writers such as Nizan and Sartre, is a movement of autoreflection by which such oppositions – higher/lower, native/foreigner, progressive/reactionary, etc. – are instituted and maintained. Blanchot's sacrifice, on the other hand, characteristically violates (or sacrifices) this movement of representation to the extent that it transgresses the necessity of a founding transgression. Sacrifice is maintained only in the sacrificing of sacrifice itself. In the essay "The Gaze of Orpheus," Blanchot writes that his version is an "unceremonious sacrifice in which the unconcerned gaze which is not even a sacrilege, which has none of the heaviness or gravity of an act of profanation, returned the sacred itself – night in its unapproachable depth[s] – to the inessential, which is not the profane but rather does not fall within these categories."[29]

The "inessential" does not exclusively fall within the traditional opposition sacred/profane, yet it is the repository of the sacred! We can see how the model of sacrifice – which for the writers was inseparable from the function of language as reference – is revised by an author such as Blanchot. If language is not representational in the simple sense, but only a "force that is capricious and impersonal and says nothing," and if no distinction can be maintained between that force and the more traditional role of writing that would seem to lie in representation (which itself is really only the application of negation to language by language), then it is apparent that sacrifice too can work to install the death of representation in the very mechanism (sacrifice itself) that guarantees the representation of human society and the integrity of the human being in society. The "inessential," intimately tied to an "unceremonious sacrifice," violates the distinctions and representations apparently tied to sacrificial ritual.

By a certain sleight of hand, Blanchot has telescoped the writer into the author; he has also commandeered sacrifice, and made it the "death" of the very distinctions that a representational sacrifice maintains. But this leads to a problem: to what extent are the two slopes, the opposition between author and writer – or between the capricious force of the performative and the serious form of the constative – simply being conflated? Doesn't Blanchot's gesture amount to a forgetting of such oppositions, rather than to their sacrifice (i.e., to their affirmation in the moment of their transgression)? To what extent is the sacred now simply *outside* such oppositions? Such a gesture would amount, finally, only to the full valorization of one category (author) over another (writer), and to the reinstitution of the distinction that was, it seemed, being sacrificed: the figure of the author has now usurped the writer's position, it is now "above" the writer – but the writer in opposition must nevertheless be maintained, if only to guarantee the author's superiority. The triumph of the author means, paradoxically, the maintenance of the writer as the only other option. Will the writer then return as the unassimilable element that violates the security of a sacrifice that sacrifices sacrifice itself? How? Will the inability to retain a simple distinction between author and writer lead to something other than the triumph of the author?

These problems also haunt an important article by Philippe Lacoue-Labarthe, "The Caesura of the Speculative."[30] A consideration of some of the questions it raises may help us answer them. Lacoue-Labarthe, explicitly following Bataille, presents the sacrificial ritual as intimately tied to the foundation of the dialectic, and to speculative philosophy in general:[31] "it has been known . . . for a long time that the dialectic, the *theory* of death, presupposes . . . a *theatre* – a structure of representation and mimesis, an enclosed space, distant and preserved . . . where death in general, decline and disappearance, is able to contemplate 'itself,' reflect 'itself,' and interiorize 'itself.'" (CS, 58).

Lacoue-Labarthe goes on to link this to the fact that "within the earliest stages of absolute idealism there is a quite explicit foundation for the speculative process itself (of dialectical logic), a foundation based on the model of tragedy" (CS, 58); this idealism was dependent on the "philosophical exploitation . . . of the Aristotelian concept of *catharsis.*"

This association of the dialectic with a theatrical-sacrificial self-representation through catharsis is a very important one:[32] it is the model of the formation of the community, of the subject in it, and of the philosophical science that guarantees it (anthropology/sociology), a model that reappears, in one guise or another, in every author I examine in this book. I want to stress, though, that for Lacoue-Labarthe, an "author" writing in the wake not only of Bataille and Blanchot but also of Heidegger and Derrida, this paradigm of sacrifice will itself be sacrificed. And it is here that we see the other fragmentary remain of the Durkheimian intellectual: if writers such as Nizan and Sartre attempted to use sacrifice to ground their versions of revolutionary violence and intellectual subjectivity "in situation," then authors such as Blanchot, Lacoue-Labarthe, and a number of others discussed in part 2 attempt to use the sacrificial model to defuse the entire speculative-dialectical-cathartic structure of sacrifice itself – and the entire scaffolding of metaphysical oppositions with which it is linked. We see this strategy espoused in a straightforward way by Lacoue-Labarthe himself at the end of "The Caesura of the Speculative." Through his reading of Hölderlin's reading of *Oedipus the King*, Lacoue-Labarthe argues that Oedipus was a tragic hero – that he became, in effect, a sacrificial victim – because he attempted to solve a social crisis using a religious mechanism: "The tragic fault consists, then, in the religious and sacrificial interpretation of the social ill. The tragic hero is destroyed, as Schelling said, by his wishing to carry out the ritual and by desiring a "pharmakos" in order to remove the defilement which he imagines to be sacred. . . . He who desires difference and exclusion excludes himself. . . . Tragedy, because it is the catharsis of the speculative, reveals disappropriation *as* that which secretly animates and constitutes it; tragedy reveals (dis)appropriation" (CS, 82).

Self-consciousness – the highest point of the dialectical and tragic movement – is therefore nothing but the awareness of the necessity of the expulsion (the catharsis) of the sacrificial-religious movement that is itself dependent, and based, on catharsis (CS, 81). This, as Lacoue-Labarthe puts it in a very Bataillean formulation, is the "insanity of self-consciousness" (CS, 82), the movement by which the appropriative (mimetic) movement of knowledge is disappropriated through nothing other than the tragic representation – itself a movement of appropriation (mimesis) and catharsis. Little wonder, then, that Lacoue-Labarthe writes, "The structure of tragedy itself becomes immobilized and paralyzed" (CS, 83).

But what is the "religious/sacrificial/speculative" that is being voided in this way by tragedy? Nothing other than the social, the organization of social life through the mechanism of mimesis, representation, catharsis. Lacoue-Labarthe refers to the "catharsis of the speculative" as a "paradox," but he does not follow it as far as he could go. Of course tragedy itself is a social mechanism, one that was first religious and later played (as we know from Aristotle) a social role in its purgation of the spectators' emotions. The real paradox is that if speculation is indissociable from the cathartic mechanism, *then catharsis can purge itself only through catharsis*, through the speculative. Tragic catharsis – is there any other kind, finally? – must purge itself as speculative catharsis; and tragic catharsis itself is then indissociable from the dialectical/self-reflexive (self-representational) philosophical, linguistic, and social function that is supposedly being purged. *Pace* Lacoue-Labarthe, one cannot arbitrarily dissociate "tragedy" from the rest of the sacrificial mechanism; if Bataille has taught us anything, it should be that. The most rigorous purgation of social, philosophical, and religious self-representation leads immediately to the return of that self-representation.

The expulsion of the speculative is only the return of the speculative, through the back door. This movement asserts itself in the texts discussed in part 2 of this book, in the form of the return of a social and even political problem in approaches that had seemingly done away with the writer and his or her naive polemical representations. One cannot posit, as Blanchot does, an "unceremonious sacrifice" that will somehow escape the fundamental social distinctions that are inseparable from ceremony (and, in the end, from metaphysics), such as that between sacred and profane. Oppositions of this sort are not done away with quite so easily. One inevitably rediscovers, then, the double slope of the author and writer together – a movement that Blanchot seemed to abandon when he collapsed writer into author. That collapsing, ironically, only reaffirmed once more the author/writer distinction, by demonstrating the superiority of the author. But, as we will see in the readings of Foucault, Derrida, and de Man in part 2, there is a repetition of the social sphere, and of the writer who would represent it and intervene in it, at the very moment these authors most effectively eliminate these items. Oppositional terms, along with the logic of opposition itself, are emptied out – purged – but this movement only assures their return. Thus the "universal intellectual" in Foucault, the politicized "matter/spirit" opposition in Derrida, the "sacred" in de Man – all these terms are strongest in their resistance at the moment in which their exclusion from the project is most necessary. This return of the political, and its attendant sacrificial and mimetic operations, is the one thing that breaks down the easy superiority of the author over the writer: in this way too the metaphysical opposition between writers and authors that reasserted itself in authors like Blanchot (and in the others I discuss in part 2) is itself transgressed by the return of the speculative and specular model of the engaged writer.

This eruption of the social dimension – the realm of subjectivity, purposeful actions, and so on – in the domain of the author is therefore nothing if not the impossibility of maintaining rigorous oppositions, such as author and writer, speech act and representation. The return of mimesis in the guise of social and political concerns, and the apparent return as well of the validity of oppositions such as writer/author, indicates instead, paradoxically enough, only the breakdown of the stable model of these oppositions affirmed by the author. The two are neither telescoped together, nor are they fused in some higher, dialectical synthesis. They cannot be joined in a self-representation because the representative function of language is itself only a fragment – a slope – of this impossible opposition. Mechanical speech act and human (and humanistic/scientific) representation can never simply be melded in a higher representation: they are not symmetrical opponents amenable to such easy coordination.

And yet each is the adialectical unthought or unthinkable of the other. It matters little, in the final analysis, which slope is major and which is minor; the important thing is that the two are violently tied – and that all the texts we will examine deny this link, in one way or another. The writers – Nizan, Drieu,

Sartre – all attempt a committed writing through a social representation inseparable from a constructive sacrificial model. In a number of different ways, however, this model of sacrifice is always disrupted by the mechanical clatter of the performative. Conversely, our authors – Paulhan, Blanchot, Foucault, Derrida, de Man – would affirm the capricious force of language's echo, its cybernetic and tautological activity, over its speculative, referential, and cathartic tasks. But in this case too, even though major and minor tendencies are reversed, we see the same thing happening: an underside, an unknown or unknowable – which is not *simply* dialectically appropriable – of political and subjective representability that disrupts the smooth operation of the murmur of language.

If we can even write of a deconstruction of metaphysical oppositions, then, it is to be located not in their rigorous "emptying out," their transformation into "phantoms" (Derrida), or in their simple expulsion, but instead in the movement by which those oppositions are reinscribed, the ways in which each figure is nondialectically doubled by its other, in texts that all attempt to work out an inevitably *coherent* figure of the writer or author. Oppositions are violated in the conflict, the incessant mutual implication, of doubles, neither of which can eliminate or appropriate the other. This tension can be rewritten in any number of ways – as political betrayal or impotence, as methodological failure, as cause for despair, or as the final triumph of French Heideggerianism, beyond even the efforts of the French Heideggerians themselves.[33] It can even be presented as nothing more than two fundamentally incompatible sides of rhetoric – the constative and the performative. But each of these characterizations is only a reduction and a forgetting of what is really at stake: in one case the violence of a cybernetic language is reduced to a social formulation (political betrayal, automutilation, etc.); in the other, the political is reduced to the operations of language ("what we are writing about are 'really' rhetorical structures," etc.). Each of these necessary misinterpretations only reestablishes a system of coherent oppositions. The agony of the intellectual that I will attempt to trace in this book – his or her agon, be it a struggle or a death agony – breaks the easy distinctions that ratify the cultural or political hubris linked to the favoring of one slope or the other. If the intellectual today is anything, it is this agony, which, apparently so abstract, is nevertheless a political/sociological phenomenon as well.

A first step on the way to understanding the sociology of such a radically incomprehensible figure can be seen in the case of Georges Bataille. How does one write the doubleness of author and writer? Does one "know" it? Clearly not; yet Bataille, unlike all the other figures examined in this book, does not attempt to conceal or expel one slope or the other. He or, more accurately, his text is not necessarily "aware" of this in a conventional sense – indeed any "knowledge" would signal once again only an overcoming of the duality, its reincorporation in a rigorous and seemingly definitive hierarchy. Rather the duality is exacerbated in a *non-savoir*, a "not-knowing," that is not so much a reflection-upon as a display, an exhibition of some "thing" that may not even be "there"; we as readers are thrust into the position of guilty voyeurs. The political and textual conflict *may be* "out there," in a spectacle we can halluci-nate, gaze upon obsessively, or ignore. The conflict between Nietzsche and Hegel, between textual and political (or postpolitical) communities in Bataille, is elaborated in a number of different series of texts, which both in their style and their content reflect, but also ignore, contradict, and violate each other. Yet we can at no point judge whether this is a "conscious" or "unconscious" project. The Nietzschean authors and the Hegelian writers in Bataille contain, coexist with, and obliterate each other. Bataille is the only "author/writer" who does not attempt to subordinate one function, one figure, one commu-nity, to the other; his works are the crossing point between two mutually exclusive but necessary and mutually implicated intellectuals. That is why my book is, so to speak, written under his sign.

Finally, the figure of the Bataillean intellectual also implies a distinct social function – and a sociology. After we have moved through the impossible *Bildung* implied in my book, perhaps we can go on to consider the sociology that would follow from it. Although I do not attempt such a task here, Ba-taille's attempt at revising Durkheimian sociology in his College of Sociology project might provide some hints in this direction. Above all, Bataille con-siders society and the sacred that motivates it not as a simple coherent unit, but as *double*, split between a "right-hand" sacred of conservation and renewal, and a "left-hand" one of expenditure and destruction.[34] Bataille hints that he would give priority to the left over the right, but clearly the two are inextrica-ble. Similarly, a sociology of the intellectual might consider the potential social or political effects of the doubling of that figure, torn as he or she is between a left-hand side, the violence of the act (the author), and the right-hand side, the constructive labor of representation (the writer).[35]

At the end of the process sketched in this book, we might be led to expect, in good Hegelian fashion, a self-reflection of an intellectual subject who has experienced, and represented, all of his or her preceding avatars. The intellec-tual would negate those earlier versions while also embodying them; his or her final self-knowledge and self-representation would entail a definitive summa-tion (and a definitive recounting), along with a completion of the earlier, necessarily fragmented, positions. My book ends, however, with an inter-pretation of Bataille's rewritings of Nietzsche and Hegel – a "stage" that is out of sync chronologically and whose larger problem defies the possibility of the temporal development of the constitution of an integral intellectual consciousness.

On the simplest level, any attentive reading of Bataille puts to rest the kind of intellectual history that would separate French thought from 1933 on into two periods: first the Hegelian (Kojève, Merleau-Ponty, Sartre), then the Nietzschean (Foucault, Derrida, Deleuze).[36] This type of reading, which perhaps offers to optimists some version of a Foucauldian end of history, is put in question when we recall that Bataille's project from the outset entailed the juxtaposition of these two figures and of their readings in the different strata of Bataille's incompatible texts. Any telos is precluded by an opposition that had all along been stuttering on.

Beyond this, Bataille at the "end" only repeats the situation that we will see, for example, at the end of the chapter on Derrida (chapter 8), where a prominent type of contemporary resistance that opposes Derrida and his reading of Heidegger comes from Luc Ferry, who openly advocates the Sartrean reading of Heidegger. At this point one has the strong, even vertiginous sense of being caught in a vast historical vicious circle, with periods running to the point of exhaustion and then flipping over into the movements that had preceded them: from a Nietzschean Heidegger we will return only to a Hegelian one.[37] But the story here ends with Bataille rather than with Ferry, because in Bataille we are reminded that this flipping is inscribed in each of the texts already, that Nietzsche can be instituted only on the opposing Hegelian slope, that the author is always already locked in struggle – or locked in an embrace – with the writer, and vice versa. In a similar way genres cross and violate each other. It is often held that Derrida is a playful, "literary" philosopher – and that, in contrast, others, like Sartre, are more "serious" (or "rigorous," "limpid," "philosophical," etc.). But our readings of writers like Sartre, or Drieu La Rochelle for that matter, show that their thesis novels are largely incapable of referring to anything other than their own automatic performances; conversely, Derrida's or Foucault's writings prove to be the bildungsroman of the ghost of a subjectivity that refuses to die. The "authoritarian" thesis novel and the irrefutable political-philosophical essay (such as Sartre's *Critique*) are from the outset crossed by frivolous literary play and empty, "fictional" speech acts, while works embracing such speech acts inevitably come to face the repetitious insistence of a coherent and even politicized consciousness.[38]

Of course it will be objected that my choice of authors is arbitrary. Where, for example, is the master thinker of the sacrificial mechanism, René Girard? My answer is that I have not tried to write an exhaustive history of French intellectuals – the very ahistorical and fragmentary nature of my mock history is signaled by the placement of the Bataille chapters at the end of the book. Even the very category "French" is put in question by the inclusion of de Man in my false pantheon (if de Man can be said to be French at all, it is exclusively in his innovative way of rewriting an antihumanist Heidegger). I have tried to sketch out roughly the elements of two versions of the French intellectual in this century, which can also serve as a framework for the analysis of other projects. Thus one can imagine sections on Kojève and Girard in part 1, or Deleuze, Baudrillard, and Irigaray in part 2. With the addition of these authors, however, I think the larger outline would remain more or less the same: the necessity and impossibility, on the one hand, of putting the negativity of sacrifice to work through representation, along with the concomitant institution and valorization of individual or collective subjectivity, and, on the other, of the affirmation of a violence in language, rhetoric, or other sign systems that puts in question the coherence of that subjectivity – and then, finally, the mutual interference of these two models. The reader is free, of course, to continue (or parody) my project by analyzing these authors – but I will refrain from using the tool-kit analogy here, which has recently become so popular, to describe my own work. Texts, after all, are not *just* mechanical devices, and we are not *just* the robots that reassemble them.

What then of the American intellectual? In the opening pages of this Introduction it may have appeared that I was dismissing the possibility of this creature, denying its past and very much putting in doubt its future creation or imposition. Of course it is not as simple as that. One need only read one of Jean Baudrillard's latest books, *America*, to find an interesting take on what is at stake in this discussion.[39]

Baudrillard characterizes American culture as desertlike, a lateral movement or drift somehow analogous to the endless drive through the vast empty spaces of the American Southwest. This movement implies the "deliverance from the social," and the "acceleration of molecules in the heat [that] contributes to a barely perceptible evaporation of meaning" (A, 9). This is a surface movement that is the death of culture, its "zero degree" (A, 78); instead of the movement in depth of European analysis – the excavation or exploration that looks for "hidden meanings" and that tries to open "false bottoms" – in America we have only the space of "mutation" (A, 23) and the entropic drive of the jet engine, always rushing toward "the vacuum in front of it that sucks it forward" (A, 11).

This inexorable onrush of the destruction of signification, the leap of meaning into the void, is demonstrated, for Baudrillard, by the activity of American intellectuals. They are seen either staring at the video screens of their word processors (A, 34–37), or coveting the markers of European culture – art, history, metaphysics, cuisine, the prestige of, and the respect accorded to, the European intellectual (A, 79). Most important, this hunching before the computer screen is a kind of automatic self-reflexivity ("all that fascinates us is the spectacle of the brain and its workings" [A, 36]) that nevertheless "is not narcissism and it is wrong to abuse the term to describe the effect. What develops around the video or stereo culture is not a narcissistic imaginary, but an effect of frantic self-referentiality, a short-circuit which immediately hooks up like with like, and, in so doing, emphasizes their surface intensity and deeper meaninglessness" (A, 37).

We are still in the desert: the horizontal displacement and the Barthesian "zero-degree" of the death of signs is now the short-circuit – or the closed circuit – of a machine: beneath or before the intensity of the onrushing signs lies their demise, the not-knowing of the void somehow contained in the space of the mechanism.

All this starts to look familiar: it is, one could argue, Barthes's "author," caught up, without any admixture of subjectivity, in the cybernetic circulation of signs – and in the concomitant death of signification. Conversely, Baudrillard's "European" is Barthes's writer: the latter above all seeks meaning, and tries to represent, and argue for, historical change. Indeed "the concept of history as the transcending of a social and political rationality, as a dialectical, conflictual vision of societies" (A, 80) is not, Baudrillard argues, that of the Americans; the very achievement of the American utopia, the end of history of American modernity – a state in which radical political or cultural change is inconceivable – has superseded the European model of representation, knowledge, revolution, and progressive change: "We shall remain nostalgic utopians, agonizing over our ideals, but baulking, ultimately, at their realization, professing that everything is possible, but never that everything has been achieved. Yet that is what America asserts" (A, 78–79).

The irony in all this lies in the fact that, if the American utopia somehow supplants a never-completed European history – and if the American surface extinction of signs replaces the dialectical movement of the uncovering of truth and the sacrificial, theatrical exclusion of falsehood – then Baudrillard's own text, which on some level purports to reveal something about America, is itself supplanted by the sheer electrical intensity of the incessant death of language. But that intensity, that act, can be noted only through its representation in Baudrillard's book. In other words, Baudrillard must continue to write *as* a European intellectual when he demonstrates the necessary demise, through the fact of American modernity, of European intellectual subjectivity. America, the death of Europe, can only be known, can only be written, from Europe – by a European cruising through the desert, then (as Baudrillard portrays himself) boarding a jet and returning to Europe and, finally, writing his own death as a person of "culture," of writing.

This self-cancellation of the European cleric is doubled by the fate of his or her American colleague. Baudrillard is not quite right when he portrays the American as nothing more than a blip of energy in a computer circuit – a blip that is, moreover, deluded about its own status. The American is clearly more, or other, than that. If the European can fly to America and impossibly represent the truth of the place – even if this truth is only the end of truth – then the American can fly to Europe and relay European truth through the electronic circuitry of his or her machine. Of course the European would (and does) present the American as nothing more than a failure, a tourist, an unhappy consciousness – but Baudrillard, after all, by his own reckoning, as a European, can write only from within the closed, Hegelian space of authenticity (and he can therefore ultimately judge only the inauthenticity of the Other). How, then, would the American judge (or transmit) the European? The answer to that question, I hope, can be found in the pages that follow.

It is not a question of one model, one territory, one intellectual, supplanting the other; instead, the European (the writer) already contains and knows the hostile and ugly American; on the other hand, the American (the author) shuttles back, forces into circulation, and dooms the dominant but impotent European. Each figure in its autonomy from and refusal of the other is based on, and depends on, that other; implied in each slope is a minor – fatal but originary – version of its opposing number. The American, staring vacantly into his or her machine and tapping out messages that no one will read, is always already caught up in the dynamics of the decline of European political and cultural history; the European, issuing definitive evaluations and predictions, is always already rolling in the desert. Caught in this nonsymmetrical opposition, we can no longer write (of) one side without the other; to that extent, each is the defeat and the affirmation of the other. Perhaps, then, the future "founding" of the American intellectual – the realization or forceful enactment of his or her *Bildung* at the end of a history of versions of the European intellectual – can no longer easily be extricated from the death-in-life of his or her European cousin.

1

Durkheim and the
Totem Act

WE ARE perhaps accustomed to thinking about the French social sciences –
and especially anthropology and sociology – from the perspective of the
1960s: the very different versions of the "death of man" proposed by Claude
Lévi-Strauss and Michael Foucault seem to pave the way for Jacques Derrida's
even more radical questioning. Too often we ignore the larger French context
of the debates, which take place against a background of the powerful model of
a humanistic sociology developed most thoroughly by Emile Durkheim about
the turn of the century.

A reading of Durkheim is important, at least in part because much contemporary theory is often seen merely as a prolongation or perfection of German
philosophy, such as that of Nietzsche or Heidegger. While it is necessary to see
it from this perspective, we must also recognize that much of what has come to
be called "structuralism" and "poststructuralism" evolved as a critique of a very
specifically French humanist and rationalist social science that stresses both the
importance of the autonomous "person" within a powerful state and, at the
same time, an orgiastic sacrificial experience that would seem to challenge, at
least at first, the very existence of that "person." Durkheim's project is un-
doubtedly the most carefully worked out synthesis of rationalism, anthropological humanism, and secular religion to come from France in the twentieth
century. Indeed it is from the bits and pieces of a disarticulated Durkheimian
project that much contemporary work arises: a critical reading of Durkheim is
in fact a necessary condition for the approaches of Georges Bataille, Maurice
Blanchot, Michael Foucault, Gilles Deleuze, and others. Such a reading, even
though never explicitly elaborated by these authors, is nevertheless a crucial,

implied subtext of their writings.[1] In fact their work implies, if only by exclusion, the type of synthesis attempted by Durkheim.

As we will see, Durkheim stresses the rational bases of all religions; the ultimate sacred element is to be found not in a temple or tabernacle, but in the "human person" himself.[2] This "person," precisely because he is not an individual with various selfish peculiarities but instead is what each human being has in common with all others, is both the foundation of all society and its ultimate (sacred) symbol. Indeed the "person" and the "collectivity" are dependent on one another: the collectivity finds its raison d'être in the protection of and reverence for the (nonegoistic) self, and the latter finds his truth in the larger society, because his own activity is literally meaningless unless it refers to, and is directed toward, the betterment of the community. Utilitarianism, pragmatism, the doctrine that a rational ethics is dependent only on individual judgment and perception, all this is necessarily set aside: a person's acts are significant only if they serve to strengthen, advance, or somehow constitute the larger community.

This is a rationalism that nevertheless recognizes the "truth" of all cultures, which they themselves are unable to interpret correctly. Only with the key of Durkheim's work can "primitive" religions be interpreted correctly: the central thesis of *The Elementary Forms of the Religious Life* is that behind every superstition, every seemingly irrational rite or gesture, every form of violence, there is a perfectly rational motive, one that we in modern societies cannot afford to dispense with. The force of orgiastic rites is reduced by Durkheim to moral enthusiasm; gods and totems are nothing but occulted representations of society itself and its ultimate signifier and signified, the abstract person. The foreign, the exotic, the incomprehensible, are subordinated to the domestic, the Western, the logical; in Durkheim's reformulation of modern secular society, the human being is, finally, subject to the community and to the institutions of the secular religion, which are, above all, the public schools and the state. These formations imply an ultimate institutionalized "man": the teacher, the intellectual, the secular cleric – the one who, through an externally imposed discipline, inculcates in the minds of youth, and indeed in the minds of the lay members of the society, the ever-developing, always renewed morality of the sacred person in a reasoned and reasonable community.

Clearly such a doctrine is a response to the demand, in the early years of the Third Republic (and culminating at the time of the Dreyfus affair), for a coherent and egalitarian social philosophy that would serve as an antidote to the authoritarian, militaristic, and Catholic tendencies in French society. By the 1930s, however, in the wake of the war, it became much harder to believe in the saving virtues of republican morality; the College of Sociology, as conceived by Georges Bataille in 1937, had as its mission, not the transformation of sacrificial violence into an "enthusiasm" that was merely an adjunct of a law of reason, but instead the actual liberation of such untamed violence. Bataille still wanted to work toward a scientific understanding of the principles of religion, but those principles – which, explicitly following Durkheim, he saw as the very foundation of society – were themselves now presented as fundamentally irrational. Bataille envisaged a secular cult (founded on scientific principles and modes of investigation) of the irrational, with himself as a lay shaman rather than an intellectual.

Subsequent rewritings of Durkheim have not gone back on Bataille's initial gesture of establishing the priority of "left-handed" elements (violence, sexuality, ecstasy) over "right-handed" ones (order, reason, social hierarchy, and institutionalization) in religious – and hence all social – formations. Critics such as Foucault and Deleuze have posited a kind of anthropology after the "death of man"; the components of social life and ritual in Durkheim's analyses fly in every direction: without a coherent (and repressive) community, person, or state to serve as an anchor for violent religious impulses, the sacred comes to be situated in the very decomposition of a coherent society. Madness, sexuality, deviant languages or writing, individual inventions of desire, remain as always partial repositories of the sacred, writhing fragments left over after the destruction of a conformity that recognizes individuality only in the form of abstraction. Comprehensive institutions such as prisons or school systems are analyzed and criticized for carrying out various formative and disciplining functions that are not that far from those prescribed by Durkheim – and their explosion is mandated. Traditional intellectuals, teachers, authors, inseparable from such institutions, are proclaimed "dead."[3] All people are heterogeneous and definitively marginalized "desiring machines"; their very insides are composed (if of anything at all) of savagely warring eroticized organs.

While we might question the *possibility* of the author who continues to fulfill the officially sanctioned role of the French intellectual while proclaiming his own death, we should nevertheless note that the French anthropological or sociological tradition, even up to the present day, continues to concern itself with specific social questions – with analyses of the community or communities, power, education, the state, the role of the individual – that the German philosophical tradition, at least since Friedrich Nietzsche and Martin Heidegger, tends to avoid. Heidegger, even in his critique of technology, is concerned primarily with clearing the ground for the possibility of thought (of Being). Foucault, on the other hand – and in spite of his obvious debts to Nietzsche and to Heidegger – wants his analyses to be useful for the development of social action, even if that action will have nothing to do with a utopian anticipation of the forms a future culture is to take. In that way, in spite of everything, recent French theory may be more closely tied to the French tradition than to the German; Durkheim too was interested not so much in a philosophical reordering as in a sociological reassessment of the past and future of communities.

One must return to Durkheim, then, certainly not to back him up against recent (and not so recent) French critics who would explode his system, but to read him more carefully than is usually done, and to see in what ways these critics' analyses are mandated by the very text of Durkheim himself.

I

Before proposing a reading of Durkheim, I would like to present in this section a brief summary of the themes and approaches that have proven most important for virtually all the subsequent rewritings of Durkheim. I will purposely set aside the larger problems of interpretation these positions entail, especially those concerning the possibility of reason and representation in the relation between person and community: I will return to these in the second section of this chapter. At this point I want to present only what I take to be the kernel of the thought of a certain Durkheim – Durkheim the rationalist, Durkheim the apologist for such republican institutions as the free citizen, the egalitarian state, and lay education.

Durkheimian sociology is based on the perception that the bases of society are fully rational: even the most "primitive" religions, when properly analyzed, demonstrate the very phenomena that a fully developed, modern secular society *should* possess if it is ever to be instituted. The outward trappings of a non-Western cult (and the social organization from which it is inseparable) may appear irrational, but in fact on a profound level such religions function much more successfully than do those of modern societies, which are much less coherent: the breakdown of traditional values and the refusal on the part of pragmatism or utilitarianism to recognize the basic importance of religion has resulted today only in a sterile individualism, characterized by the anomie that is responsible for the elevated rates of suicide in many parts of western Europe, and by the repressive state that refuses to take into account human rights.[4]

Durkheim therefore writes against a brand of sociological positivism (that of Auguste Comte, above all) that regards religion or "theology" as mere superstition, a stage gone beyond in intellectual evolution. On the contrary, for Durkheim even the "simplest" religions, such as those of the various Australian tribes (most notably the Arunta and the Warramunga) and the North American Indian tribes he studies in *The Elementary Forms of the Religious Life*, contain the fundamental, and fundamentally rational, mechanisms of all social life.[5] This does not mean, of course, that Durkheim would like to see a return to tribal life: the problem with the aborigines, and for that matter with all other religions up to the modern era, is that they do not know *how* they are right.

Durkheim is first concerned with the *force* of the sacred as it is manifested by the totems of clans. Objects, animals, or plants sacred to a tribe seem to embody a kind of electrical charge or force. It is not that people of the Crow clan simply worship their totem animal the crow, or see themselves as crows. Instead, the Crow people share with crows a certain principle, a certain energy. The totem (such as the crow) is only the major "material form through which is represented to the imagination this immaterial substance, this energy diffused through all kinds of heterogeneous beings" (EF, 189).

This force is both physical and moral. Durkheim notes that it can be passed from one object to another like an electric current or like a fluid escaping from "points." The totem object is something like a magnet; when it is broken into pieces each piece retains the full force of the sacred. At the same time, this force is moral: the native has fear and respect for a sacred object, animal, or person. In showing respect for totemic beings or things, the person "has the feeling that he is obeying a kind of imperative, that he is fulfilling a duty." "Moreover," Durkheim goes on to say, "the totem is the source of the moral life of the clan" (EF, 190).

This "power" has as many names as there are peoples: Durkheim singles out orenda (the Iroquois), wakan (the Sioux), and above all mana (the Melanesian islanders) (EF, 193–94). Mana cannot be seen as a kind of deity or supreme being, because it cannot be localized or personified. It can pass, seemingly arbitrarily, from one object or being to another, but it can never be localized in a single one. As Durkheim says of wakan, "[It] is averse to any personification and, consequently, it is unlikely that it has ever been thought in its abstract generality with the aid of such definite symbols" (EF, 196–97). There is no universal mana; rather there is a multiplicity of manas, each of which cannot "extend beyond the clan and the circle of things which are attributed to it" (EF, 196).

Durkheim must now explain why mana is both a moral and a physical force. He does so by noting that the totem is the "flag" of the clan; like a flag, it represents the collectivity itself of which the individual is a member. The native, however, cannot recognize this, since "the clan is a reality too complex for such rudimentary intellects to be able to represent it in its concrete unity" (EF, 220). So the force exuded by the totem is in reality nothing more than the renewed energy that comes to the subject from collective life, and which renews and transforms him. It is from the totem that actions seem to spring, but the force of the totem, which belongs to, or is in contact with, each member of the clan, is nothing other than "the collective and anonymous force of the clan" (EF, 221).

Even though the power of the emblem (for that is what the totem is) – that is, the force that the emblem represents – comes from the outside, its energy is manifested only within each clan member; it is "present and acting within [him], since it raises [him] to a higher life" (EF, 221). The totemic principle is finally nothing other than the clan itself, "thought in a material form that the emblem represents [*que l'emblème figure*]" (EF, 222); primitive thought is incapable of thinking in terms of abstractions, so it represents society's power in the only way it can: through emblems. This is not to say, however, that the force that the totem represents is any less external for all that; "[totems] translate, not the manner in which physical things affect our senses, but the way in which the collective consciousness acts upon individual consciousnesses" (EF, 223). We are moved by what exists outside of us and above us; patriotic fervor, heroic acts in society, all are inspired by powerful symbols and emblems that embody the force of the community itself. The force of the emblem is not merely subjective. Totems are "more or less crude or refined figures and metaphors [behind which] there is a concrete and living reality" (EF, 225). The god, like the totem, is "only the figurative expression [*l'expression figurée*] of society" (EF, 226). And this god is a force when it acts through us, when we are moved by it to do great things. Man as moral force is far from being an abstract representation; when he is inspired by the collectivity, he is suffused with an energy that makes him *ecstatic*. "[A] very intense social life always does to the organism, as to the consciousness, a kind of violence which disturbs its normal functioning; . . . there is perhaps no collective representation which, in a sense, is not delirious" (EF, 227). But Durkheim quickly goes on to note that this is only a "pseudo-delirium," because it is only a manifestation of "ideas" that are founded not in material things, but "in the nature of society" (EF, 228).

It should be clear by now that the "emblem," or "metaphor," that is the totem is more than a merely passive sign that dryly conveys a meaning; it not only represents but it acts when it is internalized – as, for example, when it is eaten – by individuals in society. (The totem thus not only represents the group, it represents mana – in other words, the force of the group, its animating spirit. But in a sense its intervention *is* this force, since by its very imposition the group's "animation" is made possible.) It acts on people to bring them together, to fill them with enthusiasm for the common rituals or activities of the clan – or of the larger civil society which for Durkheim is its modern equivalent. Indeed in many cases the totem is merely a sign – not even a word is some cases – that becomes an act, which serves to unite the group, which enables it to represent itself to itself as a totality: "It is by letting out the same cry, by speaking the same word, by making the same gesture concerning the same object that they are, and feel, in accord" (EF, 230). The totem sign, then, while inhabited by (when representing) mana, is the agent that animates people (that makes *them* represent mana) and that allows them to see themselves as part of a group, to be unified within a group. Its force is that of the image of the group, but it should be stressed that, finally, this energy itself is only part of a much larger representation: in and through rituals, no matter how frenzied, society "becomes conscious of itself," and the totem is necessary for the "continuity of this consciousness" (EF, 231). This is why Durkheim can write of a "pseudo-delirium" which is in the end only a representation of a social idea, founded "not . . . in the nature of the material things on which [totems and the force of mana] are grafted, but in the nature of society" (EF, 228). Force is therefore subordinate to a higher ideal and to a higher, nonviolent, eminently reasonable process of (self-)representation.

It should be stressed, however, that this process is a two-way street; the person is not only inhabited or possessed by the totem and the mana it represents; he or she, in a sense, possesses, or acts on, the totem or the god. The force of society not only comes from the outside; it is generated from within. As much is contributed as is received; in other words, the person is capable of autonomous action.

In an important chapter of *The Elementary Forms*, "The Notion of the Soul" (chapter 8), Durkheim stresses the identity between the soul as it is conceived in "primitive" societies, and mana. Just as the totem represents, as it is infused with, mana (the moral energy of society), so too the soul is a representation – and an individuation – of mana. "The individual soul . . . is the anonymous force which is at the basis of the cult, but incarnated in an individual whose personality it marries; it is mana individualized" (EF, 264). As with the sacred power of the totem, the soul's attributes – its "inner life," mental force, immortality – are attributed by Durkheim to the power of the community, which the person embodies and represents. And just as sacred objects and implements are treated with respect and protected by prohibitions, the soul as well is accorded a sacred status, which survives even the temporal and physical limits of the body (EF, 266). The belief in the permanence of the soul is derived from the apparently eternal life of the group. Since the force of the soul is really nothing other than that of the group, the group's immortality is easily projected onto the person: "Individuals die, but the clan survives. The forces that constitute its life must therefore have the same perpetuity" (EF, 268).

As in the earlier cases of the totem and mana, Durkheim seeks to rationalize "primitive" beliefs about the soul; if the soul's power and sacredness is nothing other than that of society individualized, then the soul, like the totem, is an emblem of the clan. But he goes beyond this: the soul, or the person (as he prefers to call its modern, secular version), is both driven by a power that comes from without and, at the same time, fully autonomous. This autonomy, however, should not be confused with that of individuals who act selfishly, without internalizing any higher goals or meanings. The person is autonomous relative to physical reality and his body; in other words, his acts are not determined by simple material causes. He is capable of moving himself (EF, 271): "the more we are free from the senses, the more we are persons, capable of thinking and acting by means of concepts" (EF, 272). This freedom to think and act, however, does not take place in a void; it is precisely what the person has in common with everyone else in society. The freedom from material determination, from brute causality, along with the concomitant possession of certain inalienable human rights, is what constitutes the larger commonality and is therefore the power that binds everyone together; it is the modern form of mana. "What makes a man a person is that by which he is blended in with [*se confond avec*] the other men, what makes him a man, and not a certain man" (EF, 271). The very thing that eliminates man's individuality, submerging it in the group, is what enables the person to perform independently (for this is what he shares with everyone else), so long, of course, as his actions are in the larger interests of the group. When he is possessed by the group, animated by it, he is living rationally, thinking for himself and carrying out his civic duties in good faith. Through this logical tour de force, Durkheim is able to demonstrate a process of economic exchange through which the person derives from the group a communal energy that is nothing other than a reflection of his own capacity for logical, moral, and autonomous action. The frenzied cultist twisting in an orgiastic dance, who is possessed by mana and has seemingly lost all personhood, is, in his modern, fully self-conscious avatar, the independent thinker who makes rational judgments for the good of society – Durkheim himself, in other words. The cult of the person is inseparable from both responsibility (or subservience) to the community *and* free judgment; it is, in this way, sharply distinguished from crude bourgeois individualism, which poses no higher ideal than the selfish individual, and which leads only to anomie and suicide. In the same way, the modern rational community necessarily recognizes the "sacredness of the human person" (his totemhood for that society, we might say), and his capacity for free judgment; it is the opposite of a despotism that sees only the mass and which finds any given person expendable.

As in the case of the totem, mana, and the soul, sacrifice is of interest to Durkheim because it is a symbolic expression of a universal social logic. In sacrifice, first of all, the give and take between person and community reaches its most developed phase. Following (but attempting to correct) Robertson Smith, Durkheim sees sacrifice as a circle, an exchange in which nothing is lost.[6] People sacrifice, killing what is sacred and eating it, while offering it, or a part of it, to the god. This ritual, which serves on a regular basis to reaffirm and renew the community and its gods, is only a symbolic representation of what takes place in society itself: "If, as we have tried to establish, the sacred principle is nothing other than society hypostatized and transfigured, ritual life must lend itself to interpretation in lay and social terms. And in fact, like the latter, social life moves in a circle. On the one hand, the individual receives from society the best of himself, everything that gives him a physiognomy [*une physionomie*] and a special place among the other beings, his intellectual and moral culture. . . . On the other hand, society exists and lives only in and through individuals" (EF, 347).

But why must this representation of social exchange be ritually repeated? Here again we find the idea of social force, but it is a power that in itself, finally, is only a function of a larger mechanism of representation. Sacrifice as a social ritual is, for Durkheim, a kind of homeostatic device by which society renews itself, checks and renews its internal pressure, so to speak, by renewing the enthusiasm of its members. The rhythm of religious life is an expression of the rhythm of social life itself; but religious life not only represents, it acts on society in order to reinvigorate it continuously. "Society can revive its feeling of itself only by assembling. But it cannot perpetually reaffirm its foundations. The demands of life do not permit it to remain indefinitely in the state of congregation; it therefore disperses in order to reassemble when it feels the need" (EF, 349).

Sacrifice, then, is a representation of social exchange (between person and community) and it is also an active device by means of which society can remain unified. But this action itself is subordinate to a larger economy of rational representation. Durkheim remarks at one point that the sacred beings of sacrificial ritual "while superior to men, can only live in human consciousnesses," since the god "is real only insofar as it has a place in human consciousness, and this place is whatever one we may give it" (EF, 347). In the same way sacrifice itself can live only in the consciousness of the community, where it serves as a force of renewal by periodically reflecting back to the social group its own constitution – which, not surprisingly, is itself a mechanism of reflection, in which the person receives what makes him a person from the group, and then returns what he has received. And the element received, of course, is what is held in common with all members of the group: the ability to represent and judge accurately. The person's reflection, in turn, is of importance, is genuinely human, only if it in some way accurately depicts the life of the group, enabling it to progress ever further toward its goal, the fully human. The holiest totem-animal of primitive sacrifice, torn open by the priest's knife, is, in its modern incarnation, nothing other than each human person himself; he is not of course a mutilated cadaver but is instead all the stronger for having

33

taken part in a ritual, for having represented to himself, and to all the others, his sacredness in their sacredness, and theirs in his.

The circle of sacrificial exchange is thus part of a larger circle – society reflecting itself back to itself – and it itself contains smaller circles, smaller structures of reciprocity-reflection. Here again we think of Durkheim's characterization of the delirium power of ritual as only a "pseudo-delirium" (E F, 228), because behind it, as its ultimate signified, there is always rationality, the process of a society becoming ever more conscious of itself, growing, representing itself to itself ever more accurately. Force is subject to, and recuperated by, a movement of communal awareness in which the person is nothing if not subordinate to the community, at the very moment of his greatest autonomy. As Durkheim states, "Social life, in all its aspects and in all the moments of its history, is only possible thanks to a vast symbolism" (E F, 231).

Durkheim was a professor of education at the Sorbonne. His main interest in ethnography was finding the rational bases of "primitive" religion. If these could be discovered in tribal Australian societies, it stood to reason that the same mechanism could be transposed, in lay terms, onto modern societies. By studying the aborigines and isolating what he took to be the logical kernel of their thought, Durkheim hoped to make it possible for us to catch up with them – to do consciously what they were already doing unconsciously. Reason, omnipresent in the purely technical functions of our society but absent where it was most needed, would therefore be reinserted into the very heart of its moral life. A Durkheimian secular religion is necessarily an unprecedented (and, we might argue, utopian) synthesis of the truth of "primitive" religions and the purely objective, scientific knowledge made possible for the first time in the modern (Western) world.

Durkheim's writings alone could not do this – it was the function of the public school system, and its thousands of teachers on all levels, to carry out this task. Here we see especially clearly Durkheim's role in the never-ending debate in France (familiar in the United States as well) over the role of secular humanism as a replacement for religion in the schools. Durkheim, a good republican, was in favor of supplanting religious studies, and priests, with his own conception of morality (which in its basic premises was meant to be universal) and with his own corps of secular priests – the *corps enseignant*.

The central thesis of *Moral Education*, Durkheim's major work on the subject, is that the teaching of religion cannot simply be excised from the schools. It must be replaced, not with another arbitrary and even irrational religion, but with that which is fundamental to all moral training.[7] Moreover, the child must not only be taught precepts – that in itself cannot replace the powerful hold of religion. The teacher must be able to instill in the student a "religious feeling" which recognizes as sacred certain social realities. The violation of rules or codes of conduct – those that protect human rights, for example – instills in us a much greater horror than does a "scientific heresy."[8] This experience of shock is part of the power associated with moral inhibitions, which, finally, must be taught in the schools. The task of the teacher is not simply that of imparting information or commandments; he or she must act as a kind of energy relay, conveying the force of the values of social life to the student. The secular priest must be possessed by a kind of moral fervor in order to inspire the young. "The feeling he had of speaking in the name of a higher reality raised him above himself, and communicated to him an extra dose [*un surcroît*] of energy" (ME, 11), Durkheim says of the teacher of religious morality, and the same force must now somehow possess the lay teacher.

This secular mana is ultimately derived from society itself, of which God is merely the symbolic expression (ME, 11). The teacher must instill in the child both an "autonomy of will" (ME, chapter 8) and a "scholarly discipline" (ME, chapter 10); the first reveals to the child the necessity of his acting as a member of the community, thinking for himself; the latter will enable him to be responsible, to work hard and sensibly, following the rules of logic. Discipline, in other words, when internalized (after being administered by the teachers) will make it possible for the child to *become* an autonomous person as he matures, taking a universal morality and "adding a few lines to it [himself]" (ME, 14). The adult will then become a conduit for secular morality, either on his own or officially, as a teacher.[9] He will then live up to his own sacredness as a human person.

We see here the same structure of exchange that characterized sacrifice: the teacher is possessed by the force of society but then returns that force to the community, adding a bit to it, and, it is hoped, inspiring the student to add to it as well. The normal growth process of the student, along with this teaching, will enable him to become a member of society in the fullest sense of the term. The teacher is an agent through which the community becomes aware of itself, since he or she works to enable all the "cells" of the larger "organism" to reflect back to society what they receive from it – and more.[10]

The teacher works in concert with the institutions of the larger society, organized through the state; Durkheim at the same time proposes another kind of cleric, this one working *against* the immediate demands of authority. In the essay "Individualism and the Intellectuals," we see how far the autonomy of the thinker can go. In this essay, written at the height of the Dreyfus affair, Durkheim defends the right of the individual to speak out freely against a repressive government. While rightists would argue that the "intellectual" Dreyfusards are mere symptoms of the decay of society, proof of the loss of higher collective values, Durkheim maintains that only one type of individualism is the legitimate target of such a critique. That is the utilitarian doctrine in which each person strives only for what he perceives as his own good and ignores the larger good of the community. Against this anomie, the intellectual, even when acting alone, represents a higher source: "The cult of which he [the intellectual] is at once both object and agent, does not address itself to the particular being which he is and which bears his name, but to the human person wherever it is to be found, and in whatever form it is embodied. Impersonal and anonymous, such an aim, then, soars far above all individual minds and can thus serve them as a rallying point. The fact that it is not alien to us (by the simple fact that it is human) does not prevent it from dominating us."[11]

Even though it might seem at first that the intellectual is much more an active agent than is the schoolteacher, it is nevertheless clear that they both share the same task. The intellectual must operate more independently because he exercises reason *against* a dominant state power that is often fundamentally irrational, that refuses to recognize the rights of the person and hence free inquiry. The teacher, on the other hand, operates in an institution whose organization and operation is guaranteed by a state that fully recognizes, and is dominated by, a larger rationality.

This leads to the question of the state. For Durkheim, the state must be an "organ of reflection." In an important posthumous essay dating from 1905, "The State," he argues that the state itself must be a kind of mind. It represents to itself and to its citizens what they all have in common: their rationality. It is, or should be, an institution by which society comprehends itself, thereby eradicating the chaotic and senseless drives of the crowd. The less-developed state is simply an assemblage of desires, a mass that is "like a permanent crowd, and everyone knows that the conduct of crowds is based on a total lack of reflection: various pressures circulate there, and the most violent is the one that leads to the act, even when it would be the least reasonable."[12]

The primitive state is a heterogeneous collection of unreflected, even unconscious drives. When it is most powerful, under a despotic ruler, it is the arbitrary and unthinking embodiment of one of those drives. Hence it is an "exterior" state, expanding by swallowing its neighbors, its blind movement consisting of nothing more than "violent, aggressive act[s]" (s, 47). The Durkheimian state, on the other hand, is synonymous with political society (s, 45), it is "internal," peaceful, and moral. It acts as a center through which all social acts receive their direction and meaning, all "secondary groups" are oriented, their excesses limited. Through it, the irrationality of some tendencies is revealed – and they are discouraged; other forms of behavior, logically necessary, are fostered. All the activities the state commands only strengthen it, enabling it to become an ever more efficient organ of reflection. As a kind of larger consciousness, it can evaluate the "general necessities of life in common" and make sure they are not subordinated to individual (anomic) goals.

We see here a downplaying of the *force* of social action that is identical to what we found in the cases of the totem, mana, the soul, and sacrifice. Here too the energy of social relations is subordinated, within the functioning of consciousness, to a higher rationality. The state's activities, which are sometimes necessarily violent (as when it is conducting a war, fighting crime, or mandating the imposition of discipline in the schools), derive their larger significance and legitimacy only from (and hence are an integral part of) the state's ability to reflect upon, and grasp logically, its own actions and therefore itself. Yet it itself is subject to a larger community, which is the very society that is subordinated to it: it "also needs to be contained by the ensemble of secondary forces that are under it; without this, like any organ that is not controlled, it develops without moderation [*sans mesure*] and becomes tyrannical and imposes itself" (s, 49). This very highest consciousness, is, when fully accomplished, subject to the very human person whose life it orders and directs and to which it gives meaning: "The stronger and more active the State, the freer the individual. It is the State that liberates him" (s, 50).

Between individual and society, and between society and state (which is also a kind of individual), there exists a system of exchange, of mutual regulation; that exchange, moreover, always involves enthusiasm, force, energy, power, even violence. The individual receives his raison d'être, his moral energy, from the community, and then returns it. Mana, like electric current, flows from the object that represents the collectivity to the person; he in turn, newly possessing this force and now sacred himself, returns it to the collectivity through rituals. In the same way the state derives its power from the larger society – both from persons and from smaller institutions – which it represents; it in turn returns that power to the smaller organisms, which return it in the form of commitment and strength. This process goes on endlessly: it is civilization. But a question nevertheless arises: what are the connections between force and delirium? The force of crowds is a kind of by-product of the larger reason of society, yet that force would seem to be harmful: it is necessary for Durkheim to domesticate it, so to speak, by characterizing it as "pseudo-delirium." So force is somehow both produced and annulled by reason. Is there a "real" delirium? How is it to be distinguished from pseudo-delirium? (The very term seems to imply that there is a real one.) Are the two related? How? Can pseudo-delirium be maintained at that state, without turning into something else?[13] If so, where does the force for the maintenance of pseudo-delirium come from? How can reason, and its process of reflection, which are essentially static (society progresses only as it changes less – i.e., as it accedes to ever-higher levels of self-awareness, self-adequation), somehow both generate and recover violence? What is the nature of society's complicity with violence when it (in the form of enthusiasm, energy, delirium) is the very glue that appears to hold the reflecting sides of consciousness (the person and the community, the state and smaller institutions, etc.) together? Above all, what is the importance of the totem's role in the active generation of this social cohesion?

II

Force, it would seem, can be generated only out of society's self-consciousness. But early on in his discussion of the totem, Durkheim recognizes that if the force of the totem (mana) is a product of society's self-reflection (if it serves to symbolize society), at the same time society is a product of the imposition of the totem, in its broadest sense. Durkheim introduces his brief remarks on this theme in a curious way. He writes: "That an emblem is, for any kind of group, a useful [*utile*] rallying point – that's what is useless [*inutile*] to demonstrate" (EF, 329). The proof of the utility of the emblem is useless. We will have cause to return to the reason for this strange way of presenting – and at the same time retracting – the affirmation of the active nature of the totem's role in the founding of the social group.

The totem "is not only a convenient procedure which makes clearer the feeling society has for itself: it serves to make this feeling [*il sert à faire ce sentiment*]: it is itself a constitutive element." It is when all the signs that manifest a "particular sentiment" (of a person) merge together in a "single, unique result" that the persons of the group become aware "that they are in unison and [this] enables them to become conscious of their moral unity" (EF, 230). They are unified, in other words, by "shouting the same cry, pronouncing the same word, performing the same movement" (EF, 230). Such cries, words, acts, and movements are the totems which serve to unify the group, homogenizing it by delineating it – causing it to be aware both of what it is and what it is not (and causing it to be aware of what it is by being aware – i.e., excluding – what it is not).[14] Durkheim goes on to state: "Once this homogeneity [of the movements of the members of the group] is established, once these movements have taken form and have become stereotyped, they serve to symbolize corresponding [collective] representations [i. e., the group's awareness of, and feeling for, itself]. But they symbolize them only because they have led to their formation. Moreover, without symbols social feelings could only have a precarious existence" (EF, 231).

Totem emblems – such as homogeneous physical movements in ritual – therefore serve to symbolize a group's consciousness of itself, the ability of persons to "meet and communicate" through "collective representations." A group's self-awareness, which is itself a kind of representation (or self-representation), is both symbolized by the emblem *and is the result of its imposition*:

38

"[emblems], necessary for enabling society to become aware of itself, [are] no less indispensable for the continuity of this consciousness. . . . Social life, in all its aspects and in all the moments of its history, is only possible thanks to a vast symbolism" (EF, 231).

Words, gestures, emblems, shouts, all symbolize because they have always already instituted. The formation of any social grouping, of any moral authority, is the result of a certain act, the imposition of a signifying emblem of whatever type. The force of this imposition is prior to the possibility of social grouping itself. "A clan is essentially a reunion of individuals who have the same name and who rally around the same sign. Take away the name and the sign that materializes it, and the clan is no longer even representable" (EF, 233). Without the sign the clan itself can no longer exist.

The existence of the clan – the collective representation of the clan members when they are together – is a function of the arbitrary imposition of the emblem, and that emblem represents mana. The totem, in order to be a totem, in order to found or reinstitute the clan, must be possessed by, and must impose on, other things (most notably on the clan itself) the force of the sacred. The enthusiasm of the clan members for each other and for the clan – the manifestation of the imposition of the totem – is nothing other than this force. But what is mana? Recall that, earlier, Durkheim defined it as being without qualities, completely impersonal: "It [mana] is not a defined and definable power, the power to do this or that; it is, in an absolute manner, Power, without any epithet or any determination of any kind" (EF, 193). Mana by itself, or power, or force, thus cannot be characterized, "means" nothing, refers to no originary signified; yet, when it inhabits the totem (its presence makes the totem a totem) it institutes both the society (a certain collection of individuals) and the individual (as a member of society). The community and the person can be nothing more than an aftereffect of the arbitrary imposition of this force (arbitrary because mana "is not fixed on a determined object; it can be conveyed on [amené sur] any kind of thing" [EF, 194]), a power which symbolizes in turn only what it has already instituted.

It is no wonder that Durkheim is quick to declare as useless the demonstration of the usefulness of the emblem as a rallying point. Everywhere else in *The Elementary Forms*, and throughout his work, Durkheim presupposes the priority of the social grouping, its static self-representation/self-consciousness and reason, over force, power, delirium, and violence. Here, however, at least if his remarks on the priority of the emblem and its instituting power are to be taken seriously, that order would have to be reversed. It would indeed be useless to attempt to found a rational, humanistic sociology on mana, a force that is wholly impersonal, that refers to nothing in particular, and that cannot be characterized in any way. And so it is useless for Durkheim to investigate this problem any further. In effect, he uses the force of his authority as an expert on mana to cut off any further consideration of the nature of the force of mana. He can silence a consideration of mana only through a certain application of mana in his text. But what kind of mana is he applying? We, as Durkheim's readers, having focused on this problem, cannot dismiss it so lightly: we lack his authority, the particular force of his mana.

How could sociology or anthropology take into account the positing violence of the totem, its very peculiar kind of mana? Claude Lévi-Strauss, in his introduction to a collection of the works of Durkheim's collaborator (and nephew) Marcel Mauss, *Sociologie et anthropologie*, notes first the close ties between Mauss's conception of mana in *Outline of a General Theory of Magic* and Durkheim's in *The Elementary Forms* (Mauss's book preceded Durkheim's by ten years).[15] For Lévi-Strauss, "mana," since it refers to nothing and plays the role of a kind of algebraic symbol, is "itself empty of meaning and thus open to the reception of any meaning" (1, xliv). "Mana" is a term situated in the gap resulting from the "overabundance of the signifier" over the signified (1, xlix). It has a "zero symbolic value," it is a "symbol in the pure state," marking "the necessity of a symbolic content supplementary to the one already overloading [*qui charge déjà*] the signified" (1, l).[16] In this way it is able to coordinate and reconcile glaring conceptual (and social) contradictions, such as "force and action," "abstract and concrete," and so on (1, l). Mana is susceptible to any definition, depending on its immediate context or usage, and its "unique function is to fill a space between signifier and signified, or, more exactly, to indicate the fact that in a given circumstance, on a given occasion, or in one of their manifestations, a relation of inadequation is established between signifier and signified" (1, xliv). In this way it epitomizes the operation of all codes, which convey meaning through the juxtaposition of arbitrarily imposed signs and which, through certain terms, reflect back on the arbitrariness, the "forced" nature, and the resultant conflict, of their own metaphors. (Lévi-Strauss, moreover, implicitly links the imposition of meaning, and the forcing of metaphors, to the force of mana when he notes on page xliv the etymological links between *machin* – an all-purpose word that, he claims, plays informally [like *truc* or, in English, "thingamabob," "oomph"] the same role that "mana" plays formally – and "machine," a word that itself implies "force" or "power.")

For Lévi-Strauss, the social is nothing more than the functioning of language; if mana is a kind of algebraic term, it is because language, along with all the social codes that are part of language, itself functions with the precision and regularity of a mathematical equation (or, for that matter, a machine). The "precise rules" of the language of social life generate "cycles of reciprocity whose mechanical laws are . . . known" (1, xxxvi). Meaning itself is a function of the differences and frictions between signs rather than of the inherent "meaning" of any given sign. Mana as an empty signifier is a crucial element of the symbolic functioning of society (and thus of society *tout court*), since the logic of social relations, which operate according to rules that are not different in kind from those of any purely formal language, necessitate a term (whose efficacious power can be seen only as magical) situated in the gaps between codes, and between signifiers and signifieds, one that allows the coordination of apparently contradictory terms. (Of course in "modern" society many words – such as *machin*, *truc*, "oomph" – continue to play this role, although they are not explicitly accorded magical and sacred status or power.) The force of mana is intimately tied to the forceful imposition and the forced reconciliation of meanings and can therefore be said to be inseparable from the driving force of language itself. It is odd, however, that for Lévi-Strauss understanding the laws of this universal language in turn leads, on the part of the sociologist or anthropologist, to a comprehension of the "generalized expression of human thought"; ethnology "contributes to the extension of human reason" (I, li). *Pace* Lévi-Strauss, thought, consciousness, intention, would seem to have nothing whatsoever to do with the necessary and purely "mechanical" (and forceful) operation of a symbolic logic or of a language's grammar.

Another way of looking at mana tends to ignore this tactic of seeing human society as wholly dependent on the impersonal rules necessary to the establishment of any code (and, more specifically, to the language's syntax rather than its semantics). Pierre Bourdieu, in his important book *Ce que parler veut dire*, relates the power of the totem to the speech act, as analyzed by J. L. Austin in *How to Do Things with Words*.[17] For Bourdieu, institutions are dependent on rituals that regularly use the speech act (as in ceremony) to stabilize and guarantee an existing system of unequal and exploitative power relations. Austin had isolated in the speech act any number of instances in which language did not have a referential or denotative function (its use was not "constative," to use Austin's term), but, on the contrary, it did something in the world, it performed an act (it was a performative). Declarations, commands, promises, excuses, and many other uses of speech do not represent anything, but they cause something to happen: people are wed, wars are declared, orders are given, and the important thing is that something has been posited, brought into existence apparently out of nothing (in this sense the performative is different from the constative in which what is already there – the signified, the referent – is *re*-presented). Bourdieu maintains that a purely formal study of speech acts, such as Austin's, ignores the political dimension of the performative. Anyone can declare war, but that declaration will be inoperative unless the performer occupies a certain social position, in relation to a specific body of laws and institutions. The analysis of the latter necessarily entails a sociological study: the power of the speech act is subordinate to, and a reflection of, larger social and economic questions (such as the question of why certain individuals, at certain times, are invested with the authority to do things with words). As Bourdieu says, "The study of the purely linguistic principle of the 'illocutionary force' of discourse thus gives way to the purely sociological study of the conditions in which a single agent can find himself, and with himself the word, invested with such a force" (PVD, 73). For Bourdieu, the successful speech act is always both a function of and an imposition of a larger – unjust – set of social hierarchies and institutions. In this sense, the power of the speech act is inseparable from the other attributes or markers of power of a speaker – the influential university professor who has mastered a certain difficult language (even if it is a dead one), or literary style, is a favorite example of Bourdieu: "style is . . . an element of the *apparatus* . . . by which language aims to produce and impose the representation of its own importance, and thus contribute to assure its own credibility" (PVD, 74). Style in this sense is a speech act through which a certain person acquires or reaffirms his authority to produce efficacious speech acts.

Bourdieu's identification of the speech act with social power is an important one, but he runs into the same difficulty that Durkheim faced. If the performative serves constantly to found and refound society, then it is a mistake to presuppose the simple prior existence of society. It is the community itself that is posited by the act: otherwise the act is nothing more than a signifier of the community and is thereby folded back into the constative. The speech act, we would argue against Bourdieu, is something more, or other, than a simple marker of social injustice or division.

Lévi-Strauss's error would seem to be the opposite of Bourdieu's. His performative (although he does not invoke Austin) presupposes the pure, arbitrary positing power of a language, devoid of signification. This view tends to ignore the aftereffect of the "illocutionary act," which is representation. In other words, Lévi-Strauss ignores the fact that language, and hence society, is anything more or other than a formal expression of "difference" and syntactical structures. But when we consider the positions of Bourdieu and Lévi-Strauss together, it begins to seem that their incompatibility is a fundamental one, one that is also deeply inscribed within Durkheim's text itself. Either the arbitrary force of the speech act is subordinated to the already established larger meaning (and even existence) of the group (Bourdieu), or the syntactical mechanism made possible by the arbitrariness of the force of the "zero-degree" sign entirely eliminates representation as an important factor in the functioning of languages and codes (although in Lévi-Strauss this movement itself is unconvincingly presented as nothing more than a representation of "human reason"). It should be stressed that no coordination (in a dialectic, for example) of these two options can be envisaged, because they do not adequately reflect each other, they are not symmetrical. (The force of the illocutionary act, in its incessant repetition, is always *more than* the circular, closed form of meaning exchange.) If they were symmetrical, they would be a function only of a logic of representation and self-reflection: they could be brought together in a "higher synthesis." In that case, the force of the act would ultimately be subordinated to the morality of meaning.

It is Paul de Man, in *Allegories of Reading*, who has most clearly indicated and analyzed the inseparability and the conflict of the performative and constative levels of language. While de Man always seems to give priority to the force of the act, he nevertheless recognizes a crucial paradox: on the one hand, "grammatical logic [i.e., the repetitive mechanism of the illocutionary act] can function only if its referential consequences are disregarded"; but, on the other, "no law is a law [or, we might infer, no linguistic construct is such] unless it also applies to particular individuals. It cannot be left hanging in the air, in the abstraction of its generality" (A R, 269). Repetitious grammar therefore both precludes and mandates the function of representation; de Man himself says as much a little later on the same page: "every text generates a referent that subverts the grammatical principle to which it owed its constitution." And even if grammar always generates an excess (or shortage) of reference, that reference is nevertheless an integral part of grammar's mechanical function (or malfunction): it could not be grammar without it (at no point in *Allegories of Reading* does de Man attempt to argue that grammar, or the performative, can simply be sundered from, or bears no relation whatsoever to, reference). In that way, syntax is not only dependent on semantics, it is in a sense generated by semantics. Reference will always necessitate a grammar, and subvert it. The relation between these two sides – between, finally, the constative and the performative – is symmetrical in its very asymmetry. Their symmetry is founded on the violence of the incongruity of their relation, yet this asymmetrical violence, in the force of the performative, inevitably enters into a symmetrical relation with the form of representation.

I stress all this in order to make a simple point: neither speech act nor the referential function, finally, can gain the upper hand, can be established as definitively prior. De Man defines "text" as the "contradictory interference of the grammatical with the figural field" (A R, 270); in other words, this "double perspective" entails the necessity of both of these systems and at the same time their radical incompatibility (thus the "text" itself, according to de Man, is impossible).[18]

I introduce these three possible versions of the relation between the performative and the constative (Lévi-Strauss's, Bourdieu's, de Man's) in order to reconsider the role of the performative in Durkheim. I will call this performative the totem act, because the instituting acts in Durkheim are not simply elements of speech but can be one of any number of signs, from shouts, words, and gestures, to painted, sculpted, written, or even living emblems, all of which serve as clan markers, or serve to institute the clan. Following de Man, we can note in Durkheim both the necessity and the impossibility of the coexistence of the figurative and the grammatical functions of the totem: if it (through mana) necessarily refers to nothing beyond the force of its own operation, and repetitiously founds the community, at the same time it refers to the very element it institutes. Durkheim's text lacks the mastery that would enable it to confine metalepsis (the reversal of cause and effect) to a single phase of its argument (the point at which the totem no longer represents but institutes): at any given moment, in other words, there may be at work a metaleptic reversal through which cause and effect are substituted. The two functions are thus intimately bound and can never simply be distinguished (is the totem simply repeating its act of foundation? or is it representing?): in our reading we therefore lack the capacity to determine definitively whether metalepsis can be limited to a single instance (which would be the case if the totem *was* an effect of representation-knowledge rather than an imposition of force), or whether it extends throughout and permeates the text. We shuttle between these options, caught in our own never-ending metalepsis. Yet this impasse (if we can call it that) is itself doubled, and destabilized, by another factor: the radical incompatibility between the performative and constative duties of the totem also dictates that any text (such as Durkheim's) that blatantly attempts to privilege reference, cognition, stasis – the rational secular humanism, finally, which depends on the subjugation of violent positing – will bear the traces of another text, its ghostly twin, in which the violence of the force of the act erupts. And since Durkheim's theory seeks to refound political and social institutions, this reemergence of force will inevitably assert itself in the representation of those domains as well. But how can this force be read?

We might start with the problem of the state. Recall that Durkheim's apologia for a strong state was based on the assertion that the state was itself a kind of giant consciousness, the official autoreflection of every person in and through the larger community. But a question immediately arises: how can such a consciousness, which must be fundamentally static (its truth is the adequate reflection of its truth back to itself), *act*? The state is a kind of brain of society; it is the organ of reason of the community. It is therefore more than just another institution: it is the master institution which brings all the others together in their activity, uniting them in and through itself. But how does this consciousness move from a passive representation of the principle of reason itself to the active imposition of laws and judgments?

In his brief essay on the state, Durkheim makes a neat distinction between the earlier, despotic state, and the later, just one. The former is characterized by "violent, aggressive acts"; it is constituted by its spontaneous gestures of appropriation of the territories of other states. The sovereign of such states does not represent the state so much as he incarnates its violence: "A Prince of whatever type is above all the head of the army: the army is, par excellence, the instrument of his activity and the organ of conquest" (s, 47). The state *is* war, *is* aggressive expansion, the arbitrary imposition of its control on other lands or peoples; the army *is* this violence; the sovereign *is* the army. All representation seems to be excluded from this model: the primitive state is, and individuals are neither represented by it, nor do they represent it. "It is not there for the men whose activity it coordinates, it is there for itself. It is not the means by which more happiness or more justice is to be realized; but it appears as the objective of all the individual efforts" (s, 47–48). The primitive state is not a means but an end. It is nothing more than a giant will that imposes itself: that will, that determination, that sign ("the Roman Empire," etc.) is stamped on lands and people alike. In that way the state is continuously founded and refounded, and lands and peoples are incorporated into it – in other words they *become* it (without representing it or being represented by it) at the very moment they are subordinated to it. The state's is a kind of positing or instituting force on an inflated scale, subject to no control, constantly imposing its own gratuitous meaning, and thereby constituting itself. Under such circumstances, such a "will" cannot even be considered anthropomorphic: it is not so much a "person" doing something as it is a repetitious act that produces an effect.

The modern state, on the other hand, is characterized by reflection through mediation. This takes the form of the ever-increasing size of the bureaucracy, which Durkheim sees as a good thing: on one side (that of civilization) there are "deliberating assemblies, multiple ministries, numberless administrations which are subordinated to them"; on the other there is the "rudimentary form of the State in . . . rudimentary societies" (s, 48).[19] In the advanced state, decisions must be made by the state, which is a "sovereign" force "more elevated than all the others" and which is therefore able to "control their excesses" (s, 49). Each institution, each administration representing specific forces, is coordinated by the state. It is an organ of comparison and decision – of thought. "The reasons alleged in favor of their tendencies by parties in conflict must be presented to governmental organs which, alone, have the ability to decide; the different currents that shape society are presented, [opposed] to each other, submitted to comparative appreciation; and then the choice is made [literally the choice makes itself: *le choix se fait*] if one of them seems to be better than the others, or some new solution comes out of these confrontations" (s, 46).

The modern state, then, is "peaceful, moral, scientific" (s, 50). But what is remarkable about the above quote is that in it the state is presented as *deciding* – an activity, finally, that implies the imposition of a determination. The state, of course, does not decide anything – an individual, or a group of individuals, decides, and its decision is implemented through a speech act. "The State finds that . . ." implies an active agency imposing a decision after deliberation. No matter how reasoned, at a certain point the finding is arrived at by an individual or body acting in the name of the state – but for which an individual must bear responsibility. Yet Durkheim's formulation obscures this: it is written with passive constructions, so it does not appear that someone, some "I" or "we" acting in the name of the state, is doing something (with words). Instead, it seems that the decision is being made. By whom? By the state, Durkheim would probably answer – but he does not need to, because this active agent (which is not so much a consciousness as a grammatical element: in the phrase "I decide," "I" is only a shifter, it has no inherent meaning, but it is a necessary term indicating a certain line of force) has been lost in the passive construction (*le choix se fait*). Durkheim therefore avoids having to face the inevitable next question: who or what acts in the name of the state? On what authority are the decisions made? What is the process by which an "I" decides? What is the role of rational deliberation, and what is the role of force or power, in the act of announcing and imposing a finding?

Lost in this passive construction is the possible irrationality or bias of a leader or leaders – the inevitable share of a personal viewpoint, which entails prejudices, a specific class orientation, specific interests in any reasoned judgment. Just as important, however, is the fact that Durkheim is also losing the speech act here: the fundamentally arbitrary imposition of a determination. In this instance, the performative must be the act of an individual, and it can have meaning only if it is backed up by the authority of the state. But that authority itself depends on the "illocutionary force" of the totem act: one could not have a state without the acts that incessantly refound it. Moreover, the judgment is an act whose power is indistinguishable from the force of the acts that gratuitously found the state itself. Indeed the rational judgment of the leader in the modern state must be seen as such an incessantly founding totem act: it is a totem that stands for the very raison d'être of the modern state.

And we can see why the occlusion (through the passive construction) of the active agent (the leader) "responsible for" these acts is important: if judgments are acts, so is the leader. The figure of the leader too is the emblem of the state: it is a totem of even the most civilized state. And as such it does not simply represent the state or even embody it; it is not only the rational principle of evaluation and synthesis of a number of conflicting viewpoints. As the ultimate totem of the human person, as the object of respect that "is" the state, the leader reinstitutes the state every time its "sacred" person manifests itself through an act (or even when it "appears" in its official totemic function).

It is not so much that this act is simply irrational or barbarous – as Durkheim caricatures the "absolutely unreflected" acts of crowds that the state must contain (s, 46). Rather the risk for Durkheim is that the performative, through the totem act, generates the state and its rationality but is not reducible to it. The rational, fully reflective state may very well be dependent in this way on a force that must be assigned to a "primitive" state if the "civilized" state is to constitute itself.

This leads to a problem for Durkheim, one that is directly related to his arbitrary subordination of the totem act in *The Elementary Forms*. His refusal of the activity of institution – the force of mana, or of the illocutionary – is itself the product of an illocutionary act (its subordination through a declaration that it is unnecessary to investigate it fully); it is paralleled by the fact that, if he were to set aside this declaration (based on nothing other than his own authority as one of the founders of modern French sociology), reason itself would force him to recognize that the reason of the state is founded on the violence of the totem. Durkheim the intellectual (and schoolteacher), who, in his theory, most accurately represents the state (in his thought he affirms the very necessity of the state's thinking function), would be forced to recognize the dependence of the ultimate institution (a kind of metainstitution) on the very violence that characterizes the primitive state.

The intellectual, as the "brains" behind the state (which is itself a higher consciousness), is a kind of higher sovereign – he formulates, in his theory (in the article "The State"), the very place that rationality occupies in the constitution of the state. Yet his theory itself bears the traces of an active force – the totem act – which identifies the state with the savagery of primitive empires. The intellectual is thereby identified with the sovereign who does not "represent" his state, or any higher meaning (such as "the community"), but who imposes it through aleatory acts of conquest. Or, put another way, he is identified as well with the individual caught in the grips of anomie, who continuously reposits meanings for his life, none of which can be believed in; such behavior eventually leads to suicide. Both the primitive sovereign and the modern anomic individual, in fact, are closely related: both attempt to exist outside the circle of Durkheimian societal-sacrificial exchange, by assigning gratuitous and inevitably faulty meanings to their own, and others', existences.

Thus the identification of the rationalist intellectual with the "primitive" sovereign does not lead only to the thinker's secret but fundamental complicity with the head of a contemporary evil empire (Durkheim was probably thinking of Imperial Germany when he wrote his essay on the state) or with the

47

arbitrary imposition of various inherently repressive (rather than beneficial) institutions – even, and above all, in a fully rational state.[20] It also involves a kind of suicidal, or self-mutilating, rational (and authoritative) reflection on the constitution of the intellectual's authority. This inwardly directed violence itself, though, may be fundamentally opposed to an unjust and violent state power.

To see how this opposition is possible, one must return to Durkheim's theory of sacrifice. The theory of sacrifice is a circular and closed economy of exchange, as a circle; it is in fact a response to Robertson Smith, who, in his *Religion of the Semites*, posed a problem which he considered a "logical scandal": if sacred beings, gods, always "manifested their power in a perfectly uniform way," why should men think of "offering to them their services" quoted in (EF, 491)?[21] In other words, how can one imagine sacrifice as an *exchange* if one party – the god – has no need to receive? When, in fact, the power of the gods is exercised without need of reciprocation, why should men give, sacrifice, to them? How can an economy be established if one group – divinities – are capable of an infinite expenditure?

Durkheim's theory of sacrifice is intended as a solution to this scandal. For him, sacrifice is a *representation* of what people do when they gather in a ritual; it is an *act* in that it constitutes the very object of that ritual. In sacrifice, the relation of the individual to society – the give and take of life in civilization (the person's existence would only be that of an animal without society; society would be nothing without the contributions of the individual) – is what is *depicted* in a mystified form (the deluded practitioners think they really are "giving to and receiving from the gods"). And sacrifice (as a kind of totem) *acts* to strengthen society (in effect, to reinstitute it) by causing all its members to reassemble periodically at times of ritual effervescence, the very moments at which individuals give their strength to, and in turn receive it from, society.

Despite the fact that representation seems to be subordinated to the act in this model, on a larger scale it is the other way around. By fully demystifying sacrificial practice, Durkheim would have modern society fully and consciously represent itself to itself through rational ritual (of whatever type; but these rituals would certainly include emblems of the state or its morality that would stir the enthusiasm of the people, and for this reason would very likely also involve state institutions – such as schools – as totems, along with the sacred, clerical incarnations of those totems: teachers). Robertson Smith's "scandal" is abolished: the community and its highest institution, the state, needs the representation of ritual to renew itself – and so does each individual in society. By rationalizing the model of sacrifice, and showing what it "really" represents, Durkheim has dispelled the scandal, the break in the closed economy of reflection. The way is open for an implementation of this new rational sacrifice in a secular society.

This model of sacrifice as exchange is identical in its logic to the relation between totem act and representation that I discussed earlier. Just as the scandal of the god who expends force without needing it returned is cleared up by positing sacrifice as exchange, and just as what we might call the scandal of the "delirious" or violent act in sacrifice is subordinated to the larger process of society's and the state's self-reflection, so too the making of society by the totem act is immediately subordinated to the totem's representation of what it has made (see EF, 230–32). In each case the logic is the same: Durkheim either dismisses the possibility of a repetitious founding force (in a mystified form: "the gods") that cannot be subordinated to the economy of representation-exchange, or he presents it while arbitrarily refusing to consider the implications of a totem that itself always already founds society. In the latter case there seems to be a kind of relation of "sacrificial" reciprocity between the totem as act and the totem as representation (the totem founds and represents: it both contributes to, and receives from, society), a relation which itself, by the very fact that it establishes a fully comprehensible equivalence between the two terms, subordinates the blind force of the act to representation-exchange. Once again, finally, it is signs that are exchanged rather than totems that act. And it also seems that any kind of model of exchange in Durkheim can be seen as a "sacrificial" one of an equalized trade between symmetrical terms – even that between performative and constative.

We might consider, however, the implications for the person – or the individual, as Durkheim calls this figure in the section of *The Elementary Forms* on sacrifice – if the logical priority of the totem act to representation cannot simply be contained within a single moment of Durkheim's argument, if the metalepsis cannot be limited. Recall that for Durkheim the "human person" was *the* "sacred" element of rational civilization – the person was the functional equivalent of a god: the full (self-)knowledge of the person was the ultimate totem of modern society, because the possibility of the person as a rational, autonomous entity was the common denominator that linked all members of the secular collectivity. But how can a modern individual know himself by knowing his position in sacrificial exchange (as Durkheim would advocate) if that exchange itself is only an aftereffect of a forceful and arbitrary positing of meaning – and of society itself? If the sacrifice of the god is something other than a simple representation of the person's useful contributions to society, and its donations to the person – if instead it can be associated with the forceful imposition of meaning that in itself refers to nothing, with, in other words, an expenditure without return of force – then the person who knows himself as a god will necessarily know that he himself – his own positing power – is

49

unknowable. And he will recognize, not that he is a term in a homogeneous relation of exchange and meaning, but that he is violently heterogeneous to any formation that promises, in any sense, to represent him. His force will not lend itself to relegation (through an illocutionary act) to a position within any given economy. Moreover, the person will "know" that he himself is not even (or not simply) a "person," since the distinction person/society is itself an arbitrary product of the very imposition of the totem act in which he recognizes himself. His own origin, which he must fully know in order to establish himself as a person, is not a simple origin but an aftereffect of the imposition of a force that is alien to (but which nevertheless institutes) the reflection-constitution of society and person. At the same time, though, that force itself is attained, can be known, only after following through a process of rational investigation – in this way, force as a knowable entity can be said to be the product, the result, of that investigation. To know himself fully, to push reason as far as it will go, the person must experience not the secular equivalent of the "pseudo-delirium" – and even the pseudo-death – of the sacrificial victim (the divinity totem) in Durkheim's model; instead he must somehow undergo a force, a power, a death that cannot be translated into rational terms and inserted within a model of consciousness and reflection. His self-knowledge through sacrifice will be shattered (sacrificed in the scandalous sense, Robertson Smith's sense, of expenditure without return) at the very moment it is consummated. But how?

This is precisely what cannot be known, at least according to the criteria of a rationality within the sphere (or circle) of adequate self-reflection. In this model of the automutilation of self-consciousness, no neat symmetry (and no opposition-reciprocation) between force and representation, performative and constative, violent and peaceful, can be established. Any interpretation of this impossible knowledge will always be a betrayal, a recuperation of force, its retrospective depiction. It will once again save sacrifice by knowing it as an adequate representation of something else; the violence of the act will be easily mastered in a larger economy of social or human representation. And yet no firm ground, no sacred institution, can be established from which the observer can accurately judge when distinguishing reflection from act, accurate representation from force of judgment. There are no logical criteria by means of which the repetitious founding of the totem act can be distinguished from the posterior representation of the totem sign.

Part of the problem is that the force of the act is as dependent on the peace of representation as vice versa; as de Man reminds us, it is figural language that "subverts" the grammatical machine. The apparatus of grammar, the force of the performative, cannot function in a void; it cannot free itself of or abstract itself from the excess signification that it generates, which in turn knows or represents it. In the same way, the delirium of the totem act cannot be conceived apart from societal and personal self-representation. At any given moment, the two sides cannot simply be distinguished from each other. The violence of the act is itself a function of rationality – the act is simply nothing if it is not impossibly inserted into the procedure of self-knowledge. Conceiving a pure experience of sacrifice as power, death, violence, is for this reason out of the question: each side, in its incessant generation of and betrayal of the other (in the saturation of the textual field by an undecidable critical metalepsis), precludes a straightforward interpretation of – and representation of – what such a thoroughly radical, and ahuman, experience could "really be." The disintegration of Durkheim's model of exchange-sacrifice is also the demise not only of his but of *any* grandiose but rigorous utopianism. And yet, at the same time, and for the same reason (the act and reason-reflection cannot simply be distinguished), it is impossible *not* to represent such an experience, *not* to situate it fully within a model of knowledge and representation-prediction.

An indication of the problem can be found in a 1930 essay by perhaps the most astute reader of Durkheim, Georges Bataille. The essay, "Sacrificial Mutilation and the Severed Ear of Vincent Van Gogh" (VE, 61–72), posits a sacrifice in which the full violence of "oblation" is recognized and experienced. For Bataille, the madman who bites off his own finger and the madwoman who tears out her own eye are both sacrificer and sacrificed; in Durkheimian terms, each of these persons is both the individual who gives to and receives from society, *and* the larger community that receives and returns – but this movement does not amount to a self-reflexivity or self-adequation within the person; it is not one of self-consciousness. In sacrificing himself or herself, the victim/god accedes not to knowledge but only to a horrifying "stupor." "Such an act [is] characterized by the fact that it [has] the power to liberate heterogeneous elements and to break the habitual homogeneity of the person" (VE, 70). In addition, such violence is inseparable from humanity itself: Bataille writes of these "gestures that are incontestably linked to madness" as elements that can be "spontaneously designated as the adequate expression of a true social function, of an institution as definite and as generally human as sacrifice" (VE, 67).

We might characterize the position of Bataille's madman in this way: to know himself fully as human, the individual must perform an operation that breaks his humanity, rupturing the "homogeneity of the person." His personal economy will impossibly incorporate the same violence that the larger social economy both depended on and necessarily excluded. He will have to experience the very untamed violence that Durkheim subordinated in order to establish the reciprocity of the sacrificial model and the sacrificer as a person. Inseparable from individual and communal self-incorporation there is a senseless expulsion. But having achieved this, the automutilator will once again be in contact with fundamental "human" urges. Biting off his tongue and spitting it out, he will know himself through unknowing. He will reinstitute his humanity, in other words, by automutilating. He will come to embody and reflect the larger community, just as much as Durkheim's person does when *he* engages in sacrificial ritual.

This is not to say that Bataille's position is "simply" the same as Durkheim's. The Bataillean victim is, in his violence, heterogeneous to Durkheim's. He is the emblem, a totem, that is nothing more than the representation of the self-destructive violence of its own positing. He is the principle of the "individual" that Durkheim first exiled from the social world ("individuation is not the essential characteristic of the person" [E F, 271]), and then inadvertently let back in when he used the word in his discussion of sacrifice, thereby indicating the very hidden seam of violence that Bataille was to read in French sociology.[22] But, at the same time, Bataille betrays the violence of automutilation by characterizing it as "human." Once again it is a question of simply "knowing" an unknowable violence – and not of knowledge somehow losing itself in that violence. In fact, the real automutilation involved in Bataille's text is not so much the sociological or psychological "reality" he depicts as it is the inevitable self-betrayal of a text that can recognize an unrecognizable violence only by . . . recognizing it. This is why any attempt to depict the unrecuperable violence actively ignored by Durkheim inevitably leads to the point where that violence is inscribed in the very text that would describe it – through the very betrayal of violence that that depiction necessarily entails. The text, in other words, automutilates at the point at which it "knows" the force of positing but does not know that what it "knows" is itself only a function of arbitrary positing. Yet a true knowledge of that positing would only be another betrayal, another automutilation. It is at this point that the distinction between cause and effect, violence and representation, force and form, performative and constative, becomes most acute and most necessary but at the same time most ungraspable.

Yet sacrifice "goes on." And even reading sacrifice, depicting it as textuality or a function of a performative rhetoric is a betrayal of it. It is "knowing" it one way, arbitrarily, positing it in a speech act, with the authority of the official commentator, and then presenting that act of determination as if it were a definitive depiction of some state of affairs. (Which, of course, it also necessarily is.) I would like to note at this point the ending of Bataille's essay on sacrificial mutilation. Bataille cites several cases in which automutilators made subversive political gestures. Anaxarchus of Abdera bit off his tongue and spat it in the face of the tyrant Nicocreon; Zeno of Elea spat his in the face of Demylos: both did this after having been subjected to "frightful torture" (V E, 71). The interest in this observation, I think, is that it indicates a certain "truth" concerning textual automutilation. If this violence is a product both of consciousness-reflection and of force-positing, it will in a sense recognize the precariousness of its own violence. It will not confuse itself with the violence of Durkheim's "primitive" state, which regards its own self-positing (and the exclusion of reason or reflection) as an absolute right. Such an attitude, strangely enough, puts the primitive state in complicity with Durkheim's "advanced" state. Both entail a refusal to reflect on their genesis through the "other." The primitive sovereign sees himself as the embodiment of godhood, the "truth of his race," kingship, the principle of war, and so on – in other words, of a homogeneous irrational force, an absolute signified that only in its ideology eliminates the critical labor of reason (it nevertheless depends on it when it establishes bureaucracies, a monetary system, colonial or provincial administrations). Durkheim's modern state, on the other hand, refuses to recognize the aleatory violence of its instituting totems, and posits "reason" as an absolute and static principle.

Bataille's secular priest, therefore, is not a pillar of the state, the lackey of an arbitrarily violent state institution; instead his automutilation, the gesture by which he "knows" himself (not through incorporation-exchange but through expulsion-expenditure), takes the form of the violation of the very community he (as a cleric, the very highest totem, the reason and legitimation behind the sovereign and the sovereign's theory) founds and embodies. In the figure of the intellectual, the individual becomes a sacred object, one that is unrecuperable within the painless autoreflection of person and society; he is the functional equivalent of the spit-out tongue. He is to the community what his bloody tongue – formerly the organ of authoritative speech acts and now, we might say, the organ of a repulsive mute act – is to his own person. By spitting in the face of the sovereign, by betraying the very political order he grounds, the cleric violently exits from the Durkheimian-Maussian circle of sacrifice where, as Bataille says, the "rites of sacrifice stupidly aborted." Automutilation as sacrifice becomes a totem of an impossible collectivity founded on incessant expenditure rather than avaricious exchange. Its highest functionary (the philosopher, the teacher, finally) spits in the face of the reason and law he inevitably incarnates (and which he incarnates even in his gesture of spitting, since that act has a larger moral and political significance). In other words, he spits in his own face, a gesture as impossible as looking in the mirror is possible.

As de Man points out (AR, 299), the grammar of the text generates a surplus of signification; excuse making (a speech act) always produces more guilt than it can excuse – so its task is infinite. In the same way, any text that "recognizes" the violence of the totem act will always spit out a multiplicity of necessary but inadequate depictions of that violence. Bataille's essay on mutilation misreads the recognition of that act as an individual event: various "persons" grasp their personhood in and through that which is most heterogeneous to it – and then spit it out. But the individual is only an aftereffect of the totem act: how can he be the primary locus of its violence? Nor can we assume that the text will replace the person in this instance: how could the text, that unholy amalgam of performative and constative, be the exclusive shrine of automutilation? The text, after all, cannot simply be divorced from the social function (and the "truth") of the intellectual-teacher, no matter how sundered he or she as a figure might be. It cannot be separated, in other words, from the author – Anaxarchus or Zeno, you or me – and from the society the author embodies and violates, represents, and imposes. Nor for this reason can the text be exempted from the kind of sociological and political critique that Bourdieu suggests in *Ce que parler veut dire*.

The representations of the intellectual function of self-constitution, then, will always be generated in a surplus; there will always be more than can adequately "describe" an indescribable situation. They will be in the wrong even in their necessity; and they will be right, for the transcendental position from which they can be proven wrong may itself only be the arbitrary product of the force of positing. There is no master model of expenditure; but even this statement is a betrayal.

"Betrayal," with all its social implications, is an appropriate word here. Much of French literature and theory since the death of Durkheim is a failed effort to situate a radical or uncompromising violence in society and in the movement of human history as well as in an individual (or individual's) language or text. Bataille himself attempted to propose a parodic dialectical model of the modes of expenditure throughout history. Paul Nizan, Pierre Drieu La Rochelle, Jean-Paul Sartre, among many others, attempted to posit a sacrificial experience of a violence (in a progressive history) that could not be reduced to or subjugated by a bourgeois conception of human reason. (Their sacrifice, however, written against Durkheim's main tendency, involved the expulsion of the victim, rather than his incorporation in an exchange, as its subject). Others – Blanchot, Derrida, at times Foucault, de Man – attempt and fail to posit a subjectless textuality that alone would embody (and sometimes defuse) the violence of the totem act, and that turns on itself endlessly in self-betrayal. Both of these tendencies are the necessary and erroneous, and necessarily erroneous, residue of the decomposition of Durkheim. When the violence of the act is inscribed in the circle of exchange between society and person, state and teacher, these two sides come apart; their perfect adequation is supplemented by a radical inequality, in which the society (or society's obsessions within the text) overwhelms the person and his language, or where the sundered individual scribe – his text – in its very violence comes to eclipse the collectivity.

2

Nizan, Drieu, and the
Question of Death

*I've often heard the glib motto "The Pen and the
Sword Join in a Single Path." But in truth they can join only
at the moment of death.* – Yukio Mishima

I

IT MAY BE a mistake, when considering French literary practice of the
1930s and 1940s, to separate politically committed thesis novels from seemingly apolitical or antipolitical avant-garde experimentation. Traditionally, of
course, such a neat distinction is usually made; the rise of socialist realism in
Communist literature – a kind of ossified nineteenth-century naturalism in the
service of Stalinist dogma – has often been seen as a terrible betrayal of the
invigorating formal adventure that dated back at least to Baudelaire. And it
goes without saying that right-wing *romans à thèse* can be seen as equally
reactionary in their form, and at the same time politically reactionary in their
content.

But when we look closer at some of the thesis novels of this period we are a
bit surprised to find their authors grappling with many of the same problems
that avant-garde writing in general (and prose in particular) was coming to
face. After the euphoria of the late teens and early twenties, writers within, and
at the edges of, the surrealist camp were questioning the roles of collective
exaltation, sacrificial violence, and madness in society and politics. It was not
enough to glorify the marquis de Sade or the Papin sisters, and posit a purely
fantasmatic gratuitous act; the order of the day was now to consider violence
and ecstasy *in* society and in political formations. Perhaps André Breton's
Nadja posed this problem already in the twenties, but it was in the thirties that

57

it really came to the fore: one thinks of works like Antonin Artaud's *Hé-liogabale*, L.-F. Céline's *Voyage au bout de la nuit* (*Journey to the End of the Night*), Michel Leiris's *L'Age d'homme* (*Manhood*), Georges Bataille's *Le Bleu du ciel* (*Blue of Noon*), the investigations of the College of Sociology, as well as the strange mixture of naturalism and late surrealism in Sartre's *La Nausée* (*Nausea*). The interest in Freudian psychoanalysis and the exploration of the unconscious gave way, in part, to an interest in French Durkheimian anthropology and sociology. What role did madness or ecstasy play in society? How could ritual murder (sacrifice) be seen as liberating? How could the collective frenzy of crowds – seen first at Fascist rallies – reinvigorate a society that offered nothing but alienation and exploitation? What role did the thinking, critical individual (the intellectual) play in the reform and renewal of society?

Writers of thesis novels faced these same problems, and it would be naive to make a facile distinction between stimulating "writerly" avant-garde texts and "readerly" potboilers that do little but teach a boring, absolutist moral through the use of cardboard villains and heroes.[1] In both "genres" (if we can call them that), I would argue, there are many texts that work less to point a simple moral than to find solutions to ideological problems and conflicts that may be unresolvable. Elsewhere I have analyzed Bataille's *Le Bleu du ciel* (1935), attempting to see in what ways the novel establishes an impossible mediation between useful labor and orgiastic expenditure, between the political commitment and the betrayal of the intellectual.[2] Thesis novels of the period often deal with the same problem, while approaching it, no doubt, from a different angle. How is effervescent collective experience – and violence – to be integrated into a positive revolution? How is the apparently purely negative experience of death to be seen in a positive light? How can a sacrificial death have value in itself but also have a positive social role? How can the individual intellectual abandon his willed or unwilled alienation from society, and actually act to spark a collective upheaval – one in which crowds are moved in ways that are not entirely rational? Like Bataille's *Le Bleu du ciel*, Paul Nizan's *Le Cheval de Troie* (*The Trojan Horse*) (written in the same year, 1935) attempts to resolve (albeit in a very different way) the seemingly unresolvable problems of progressive change and communal exaltation; of the intellectual's resistance and action in the face of an inevitably pointless individual death; of the value of constructive collective activity in the context of a frenzied sacrificial death.

This is not to say, however, that works like *Le Bleu du ciel* or *Héliogabale* performed a task identical to that of *The Trojan Horse*. Bataille and Artaud were valorizing an unrecuperable violence, one defying simple insertion into any larger cultural or social enterprise. In Bataille's avant-garde parodies of thesis novels – such as *L'Abbé C.* – the concern is not so much with the "uses" of violence as it is with the social and textual consequences of the impossibility and necessity of "recognizing" a violence so extreme, so useless, that it defies any kind of comprehension. *The Trojan Horse*, on the other hand, can be seen as at least attempting to posit a sacrificial death that is both fully comprehensible and *useful*: social renewal and the self-consciousness of the group as a powerful force are made possible through the collective representation of death – a representation that passes for the experience of death.

The Trojan Horse tries to present a model of social growth (and revolution) through a positive sacrifice, but it also assigns itself the larger task of confronting and disproving the avant-garde model of sacrifice. This latter model can easily be seen as nihilistic and potentially fascistic: a "useless" violence may present itself as corrosive of all the world's complacencies, while in fact lending itself only to cynical and dangerous manipulation by reactionary forces. Breton imagined, in the *Second Surrealist Manifesto*, the true surrealist act: going into the street and firing blindly into the crowd. Such an act of pure terrorism, while forceful, is easily perceived as either cowardly bluff (the way Sartre presented it in his story "Erostrate," and Bataille in his essay "The Old Mole") or as fascistic nihilism. As a thesis novel, *The Trojan Horse* has a double purpose: to demonstrate the proper relations of the intellectual and the people to violence and death; and to condemn the improper (avant-garde) attitude toward death, an attitude that might present itself as destructive to all established values, but one which, in its nihilism, can easily be put back to work by the bosses or the Fascists. The novel's ostensible purpose is thus both the practical one of eventually provoking revolutionary solidarity through the depiction of a "healthy" kind of sacrificial activity, and the theoretical one of demonstrating to its readers that they should adopt a constructive, Marxist, model of violence rather than a purely destructive, avant-garde, one.

In *The Trojan Horse*, two intellectuals square off in this conflict between the two versions of sacrificial violence: Pierre Bloyé, the Communist, seeks to organize workers around the memory of a dead comrade; Lange, a rootless philosopher, wants to pose a violence even more radical than that of his acquaintance Bloyé. The novel will attempt to demonstrate the fallacy of Lange's position – indeed even its inherent danger – and the necessity of Bloyé's. But, as we will see, the opposition of these two models of violence – and these two models of the intellectual – might not be so easily maintained after all. And if these oppositions cannot be maintained, the easy distinction between a thesis novel that follows certain canons of utility and verisimilitude and an avant-garde project that disrupts those and all other canons will collapse.

With the decline of the Third Republic in the 1930s – with the decline of a centrist consensus and with a concomitant strengthening of the political extremes – the notion of the intellectual as put forward by thinkers such as Durkheim and Julien Benda also suffered. In the 1930s it became difficult for anyone – save perhaps Benda – to believe that the intellectual is above the immediate, intense, conflicts of the day, through reason alone elaborating a morality that scrupulously takes into account, in order to judge them, conflicting positions.[3] Instead – and we see this very clearly in Nizan's 1932 work *Les Chiens de garde* (*The Watch-Dogs*) – younger critics, and especially those who reached their intellectual maturity after World War I, could see this rational detachment only as a bourgeois ideology that was good for nothing but keeping society in its present state. Young people studying philosophy at the Sorbonne or the Ecole Normale, in Nizan's view, were inoculated against doctrines such as Marxism by the application of a rationalist method that encouraged the most radical doubt possible, but which then demonstrated, through the superseding of this purely theoretical doubt, the necessity of the world as it was.[4] Thus the philosophers with their detachment were little more than tools of the bourgeoisie: Nizan was able to turn the tables on Benda, accusing *him* of betrayal, to the extent that a rational, abstract, atemporal philosophy was necessarily a betrayal of the workers and of the historical process itself.[5]

Along with the decline in the faith of rationalism there was an increase in interest in the problem – and the phenomenon – of death. The most radical experience (which cannot be experienced) – the one that establishes a temporality within our lives whether we want it to or not (the feared "day of our death") and before which we experience dread – necessarily reasserts itself with the decline in faith in atemporal reason. The intellectual historian can trace two main influences here: that of an anthropologizing surrealism, with its interest in primitive rites, sacrifice, the occult, and with its reinterpretation (and transmission) of a French literary heritage that includes writers like Sade, Baudelaire, and Lautréamont; and that of Hegel, Kierkegaard, and Heidegger, for whom the experience of dread and the inescapability of death were central concerns.[6] Marxists such as Nizan, while not interested in the alternatives to abstract rationalism that phenomenology seemed to offer (Nizan was engaged in political organizing and writing when his friend Sartre was in Berlin reading Husserl), nevertheless recognized the importance of the problem (and the "experience") of death for a theory of history that posited the necessity of temporal development, and the role of death as an unavoidable component of that development. As Nizan puts it in *The Trojan Horse*, "The idea of death was in the air. . . . The philosophers and poets had been the first to sense it, but it became an essential element of the air, breathed by everybody."[7]

The Trojan Horse presents a kind of cross section of a small industrial town (Villefranche) in south-central France at a very specific time in history: the period in 1934–35 when the depression was intensifying (it only really hit in France in 1931) and the bleak economic conditions were contributing to the radicalization of the workers. In the novel, the small town is convulsed for the first time in many years by workers' strikes and protests; the middle classes respond with counterdemonstrations of Fascist groups. *The Trojan Horse*, then, is really about the very first gestures and acts – and deaths – by which the workers become aware of themselves as an oppositional group (a majority) that not only is acting defensively, fighting the possible rise of a Fascist regime (the Popular Front theme is affirmed in the novel through a depiction of Socialists and Communists working together), but offensively as well, fighting in the final revolution.

The novel presents two ways in which the workers come to be aware of their plight, and come to recognize that their isolation and alienation can give way and be replaced by their fusion into a revolutionary group: they paint revolutionary slogans on walls, and they form a group that confronts the Fascists (and through this confrontation they confront the fact of the murder of one of their comrades). Significantly, both instances involve the leadership of Bloyé, who (like Nizan) is a product of the Ecole Normale Supérieure and is employed in the local lycée. More important than his official teaching duties are his revolutionary activities: he helps the workers produce a newspaper, and he leads a group of men in what might seem to be an act of petty vandalism. Very early in the morning, as the town sleeps, Bloyé and his comrades go from place to place – the memorial to the war dead, police headquarters, the wall of the town's largest factory – painting revolutionary slogans. In this first gesture, the unsullied walls are marked, the false placidity of the town is disrupted, as workers – those painting the slogans and those seeing them – become aware of their own solidarity and power.

This gesture is perhaps the intellectual's dream come true. He is still writing, but now on big, empty walls; and his message is getting through. The gesture of writing is violent, but it is the violence of sexuality, not of combat; moreover, the wall is "as virginal as a strip of paper waiting to be written on" (TH, 138) – it is a virginity that seems somehow to call down on itself the sudden penetration of writing. Out of the violence of this sullying arises the exciting bond between the men, the feeling of being a part of, and contributing to, a group: "He was buoyed up by an unaccustomed exaltation. He was accomplishing something of his own will, together with others. He was not being coerced; it was one of those rare undertakings into which a man may freely enter" (TH, 138).

But this is a clandestine occupation of the city; the men are as surreptitious as those that came out of the Trojan horse. It is a betrayal of the false order that reigned in the town, in the daylight; against that order – and, consequently, against the alienation of the workers – there is the nocturnal writing that unites and defies.

Another, more powerful union comes when the workers, massed in the city center and singing the *Internationale*, confront a group of Fascists who are leaving their own rally. Violence erupts and there is shooting from the Fascist side (triggered by circumstances I will discuss below); one unemployed worker, Paul, a co-conspirator of Bloyé in the wall-painting project, is killed. The really important fusion that takes place within the workers' group is the result not so much of the confrontation with the Fascists as it is a consequence of the recognition and assimilation of Paul's death. And in coming to recognize the importance and value of this death, Bloyé once again plays a key role.

After a long period of illusory peace, the developing class war has claimed its first victim in the town. After going to the morgue and identifying the body, Bloyé and his friends return home and discuss the significance of the death. Paul's death was not in vain. First there is the obvious conclusion that his death will serve as a rallying point for future organization, that it will be a sacrifice in the conventional sense: one man gives up his life so that others can experience his death as an element that unifies their community. The narrator tells us: "One speaks of vengeance, and vengeance is a vindication of life; one speaks of sacrifice, and sacrifice is dignity" (TH, 243).

Paul's death has a unifying power because it gives the men a reason to live and fight. In this sense it grounds their community in a more powerful way than mere blood ties, which are only the result of chance (TH, 243). This death is also an annunciation: it is a precursor of the thousands of deaths that will follow in the class war. In light of this, a second question arises: how does one face one's own possible – or probable – death? It all comes down to finding, or imposing, a meaning on it. Maillard, a comrade, says: "The important thing is to know for what one is dying. . . . It's better to die cleanly than to live as they make us live. I can understand a man being scared of dying like a rat in a corner, an animal – there's no meaning to that – or dying alone. But this other way is different" (TH, 247).

Faced with the choice between living a life of misery and humiliation, and dying to end that misery in the lives of others, one accepts death willingly. The most important thing in accepting one's own death is comprehension. As Philippe, another comrade, says: "It's always hard to die. But there are some deaths that mean nothing, and others that one can understand" (TH, 247).

One can block the dread of death by putting up a smokescreen of words (TH, 249); in this way one forgets death. Or one can die a death that has a meaning, unlike the "animal death" that Maillard refers to, which is senseless. This is the death that, as Philippe puts it, "resembles a sacrifice, or rather an exploit." Sacrifice implies heroism as well as a mythical act that generates community; so does "exploit," although the latter lacks the religious overtones of the former. Philippe admits that he has trouble expressing what is "in his head," and it is up to Bloyé, the intellectual, to step in and, fulfilling his function, express it for him: "Accept death, when it offers the last chance of being a man" (TH, 249).[8] For Bloyé, the secular cult of "man" replaces divinity ("sacrifice") and heroism ("the exploit").

The last chance of being a man, of assigning oneself meaning, is through one's own death. In a life that affords no dignity, the worker accords himself meaning through his definition, and thus through his acceptance of, death. But we can accept only our own deaths; we cannot accept deaths for others (this would seem to be a subtle critique, on Nizan's part, of Stalinism). We can, however, accept the *meaning* of the other's death, and even use it to further our cause. ("The injustice of his death does not affect its meaning for us. He died for a world which we must help to bring to birth.") "Our cause" is the abolition of the kind of death that Pierre suffered, one caused by the injustice of other men, and not by unavoidable causes. As Bloyé puts it, "Men must not eternally betray each other" (TH, 249).

This raises a difficult problem. A man gives his own life meaning – makes himself a man – through his product: death. He does so, however, because his needless death (caused by men) contributes to, and is a necessary part of, the creation of a world in which men will no longer kill men. Death has meaning only if there is group solidarity; without it, unjust death will not be stopped, we will continue to face our death alone. But how will death continue to be acceptable to the one dying – and have meaning for those in solidarity with the dying man – if there is no longer a reason to die, to sacrifice one's life? If *senseless* (cruel, unjust) deaths have been eliminated, meaningful deaths, it would seem, will also disappear. Put another way, a meaningful, human death can take place only if it contributes to the revolution. *After* the revolution – and at the end of history – there can be no more deaths caused by men, or at least individual deaths unjustly caused by men: death will no longer be able to contribute to the group solidarity essential to furthering the revolution. Death will lack meaning not because men are senselessly killed but because there is no more injustice in the world to die fighting against. How will we be able to face death then, after the final battle has been won?

This is the gist of the question put to Bloyé by Berthe, the wife of one of the comrades, after Bloyé's condemnation of deaths caused by other men.[9] "And after that? People will die anyway, they'll always end up in the hole" (TH, 250). Bloyé is quick to contradict this defeatism – and we are meant to take his response as definitive – but his reply is unconvincing. He says that death *not* caused by another person will also have to be given a meaning. He goes on to make an implicit comparison between two different types of solitary death: by torture, and through sickness. These deaths can be given meaning without the aid of group solidarity, if the dying person faces them with courage. But these, we might argue, are entirely different deaths, and a death from cancer after the revolution can hardly be compared to death by torture during it. Bloyé can only say that the ability to face a fatal illness "with honor," like facing the enemy, is a final "victory of consciousness." (Once again "man," this time in the form of his consciousness, is invoked; but this is a man who is necessarily struggling alone.) The insufficiency of this reply is underscored by the fact that Bloyé, Maillard, and Louis all then agree that this problem – how to give meaning to a solitary death outside the struggle – is a difficult one and is better faced later; as Maillard puts it, "Once men have stopped fighting, there will always be time to fight what they call fate."

One of Bloyé's attributes is to know when to stop questioning, or to stop talking. At this point in the story, this is no doubt meant to be seen as a strength; when political action is at stake, there is no time to waste speculating on the future. As an example of what Bloyé would avoid, there is his friend Lange, who in effect questions too far, is *too* critical, with the result that any solidarity with others – or any life, for that matter – becomes impossible.

Like Bloyé, Lange is a product of the Ecole Normale. In fact Lange and Bloyé were friends there, though they have since drifted apart. Lange teaches at the same lycée as Bloyé and is also haunted by death – but his notion of death is very different.

For Lange, death and solitude are inescapable phenomena. The narrator tells us that "He had arrived at that degree of solitude where so many ties have been severed that it is no longer possible to regain a footing among men" (TH, 58). Lange believes that changing the world (Bloyé's goal) is pointless, because only the word "scandal" can be used to define this world, or any imaginable world. No revolution could change that; it is not so much one universe or another that is scandalous but that there are "worlds that exist." Bloyé wants to do away with the scandal of *this* world; for Lange, the scandal is as all-pervasive as Being itself. Man relates not to other men but to Being – in other words, to the scandal of his own individual existence. Lange tells Bloyé: "I don't like Marxists. I don't like psychoanalysts either. . . . Those people who tell you, 'you're not what you seem to be, what you think you are.' The world hasn't a false bottom, nor have men. . . . The only important thing is to define the relation of individual man to Being. . . . It is more radical to negate the whole world, rather than just the bourgeois world" (TH, 59).

Lange contends that there is no hidden explanation for the way things are: each person confronts Being directly, without intermediaries, be they doctrines (Marxism, psychoanalysis) or other men. There are no "false bottoms" under which secret things are stored.

It is obvious that the character Lange is a thinly veiled and particularly nasty portrait of Nizan's friend from the Ecole Normale, Jean-Paul Sartre.[10] We are not concerned here, though, with the faithfulness of Nizan's portrait of his friend but with the implications of Lange for the movement of the novel as a whole.[11] Lange's fantasy, according to the narrator, is to have a kind of X-ray vision; he watches girls walk by from a certain vantage point, and on a sunny summer day their bodies are visible under their clothes. The point is not only the cheap one that Lange is a typically decadent bourgeois voyeur but that he sees too far and that his motives for that vision are silly. He sees through the world – but, because he does not believe in false bottoms, he sees clear through it to the void of the other side. He sees nothing, finally, but his own solitude and the pointlessness of his life.

A little later, Lange talks with the city fathers, who are openly considering the value of fascism as a way of resisting the workers. (Lange, on speaking terms with both Bloyé and the wealthy power brokers of the town, is the living embodiment of the futility of trying to steer a middle path between the two extremes.) Lange is of course apolitical, and he contends that if in fact we are all alone, we can no longer believe in anything but our own death: "While people believed in God, in reason or progress, mankind advanced. But now we believe in only one thing, a thing which excludes politics. Nowadays, we only believe in death" (TH, 118).

Yet Lange still clandestinely believes in the possibility of a new social order, a new civilization. Such an order, unlike capitalism, would keep people from thinking about solitude and about nothingness; it would forcefully impose a new meaning on life. Lange considers two possibilities: the Nazis and the Soviets. He is not fascinated by the Nazi mythology of race, but in the "blood and . . . a certain mystical exaltation" (TH, 118) associated with Nazi ritual. Another possibility for the future might be the Russian model: "There are times when I almost believe that Soviet society is trying to establish a genuine community in which men will for many years believe in something besides death" (TH, 120).

But when questioned by the now somewhat nervous capitalists about the possibility that he will become a Communist, Lange comforts them: "I am a bourgeois. Forever. It seems to me that the transition would be impossible." This leaves fascism as the only alternative, the only social formation through which a meaning can be imposed on life, exaltation can be derived from collective action, and death can be forgotten.

Lange's total skepticism, his X-ray vision, has led to his affirmation of the need for fascism. He has arrived at the same point as the bourgeois of the town who sees fascism protecting his economic interests – but in Lange's case, he arrives at fascism by following to its logical end the impasse of a bourgeois, avant-garde philosophy. At this point in the novel, however, he is still unwilling to admit to himself that in practice fascism is his only option.

Lange never does admit to himself this complicity; he continues to live in a blissful bad faith. He does not have to; he is literally swept along with the Fascists when they are retreating before the onslaught of the workers, during the epic confrontation at the climax of the novel. Lange thought that he was only an innocent and curious bystander, but by being in the wrong place at the wrong time he finds himself suddenly wedged in among a group of fleeing reactionaries. Just as, involuntarily, he finds himself part of a group in dispersion – running desperately – so too he picks up, without thinking, a weapon he finds in the street: a revolver. His soft hands, accustomed only to touching books, now grasp the ultimate tool: "A fascinating object, easily handled, frightening like all such sleek implements which conceal a destructive mechanism, and noticeably associated with weakness and fear" (TH, 205). It is only later, after he has seen a happy young working-class couple, that Lange starts fondling the gun – out of pain, resentment, and humiliation (TH, 209). Without actually aiming at the couple Lange pulls the trigger, and this leads other Fascists to fire at the workers in front of them: in this barrage, Paul is killed. It is only now that we can clearly see what lies behind the surrealist gesture of firing a revolver blindly into a crowd.

Even though he is supposedly above the world, Lange, through his isolation, is led into a series of inadvertent acts that end with a real death. Lange seems to have a political affiliation and commitment that operates on a more profound level than that of his "sophisticated" but deluded consciousness. In the silences of his discussions and in his involuntary acts Lange is fully in complicity with the Fascists. For all the acuity of his intellect, Lange cannot see the false bottom of his own aloofness, nor can he see the sinister political unconscious that lies under his words and deeds.

We can now consider further this question of the unconscious. Lange, in condemning false bottoms, associates Marxism with Freudianism, no doubt because both posit a structure of meanings and motivations that is not consciously known by the subject. Bloyé does not contradict him, and indeed – if we can associate the narrator's and the novel's point of view with Bloyé's (not an unreasonable association, if this is a thesis novel) – we see in the presentation of Lange's later acts the very strong suggestion that he is a closet Fascist: that his personality too has a false bottom, which eventually pops open to reveal that which, consciously, Lange would only scorn.

Reading the novel critically, however, we are forced to conclude that Lange is not the only one who is repressing something: Bloyé too – and thus necessarily the novel itself – would seem to have an unconscious. It is clear at the end of the novel that Bloyé does not *want* to consider a very important problem:

how death will be given a meaning at the end of history. Death, an essentially meaningless phenomenon, has a meaning imposed upon it by those who die well – that is, by those who die for the revolution. But this meaning can be given only by and through the collectivity: both the living and the dying recognize the value of a death in its relation to the larger social group. After the revolution, an individual death will no longer have meaning for society at large: it will have meaning only for the immediate family and the close friends of the deceased.[12] Moreover, not only death is at stake here; as we saw in the death of Paul, the community itself is constituted or reaffirmed through this death-as-sacrifice. If death cannot be given a larger social significance (beyond the vague and ahistorical social value of a demonstrated "courage in the face of death"), it is highly unlikely that there will be the possibility of a cohesive society.

The first, most basic thing repressed by Bloyé – and by the novel – is therefore the awareness of the *impossibility* of giving a meaning to death – and of giving a meaning to the larger community – after the revolution.[13] In fact, the frontier between life and death and that between the pre- and post-revolutionary periods have a lot in common: in both cases there is a radical divide, and there is a meaning that must be given to – or imposed on – the unknowable element on the other side. This is more than an analogy: according to the sacrificial logic elaborated in the novel, without the unifying power of meaningful death, revolutionary practice, and the postrevolutionary era itself, cannot be instituted. This is a terrible thing for a revolutionary to contemplate (especially for an intellectual like Bloyé, who up to now at least has depended on significant death to strengthen the community and who has used death to strengthen his own leadership role within it), and it is not surprising that the question is set aside very quickly.

If Bloyé is engaged in a kind of repression, then we are forced to note his kinship with Lange. In fact there is a perfect symmetry between them. Lange cannot conceive of a community in the present – he is utterly alone – but he imagines a future when there will be a community, if only because a strong state imposes higher values and unifying themes and rituals. Bloyé, on the other hand, conceives a community in the present (which he, an intellectual, animates and directs), but the community of the future, in which sacrificial death no longer serves as the unifying element, is for him unimaginable. These two fiercely opposed intellectuals are negative images of each other. And we can go so far as to state that, for Bloyé, Lange represents the repressed, a hidden set of positions that will be unavoidable for Bloyé if he fully comes to recognize the implications of his own orientation.

Lange is able to think the future because he recognizes the violent, aleatory imposition of meaning and values. He has no illusions about the regime that will be able to create a community. And we have seen in Bloyé's own practice the violence of the imposition of a community-generating meaning; when he painted the slogans on the walls, penetrating and sullying a virginal white surface, his gesture seemed little more than a metaphor for a violent, disruptive sexual act, a rape. But despite Bloyé's enjoyment of this violence, he habitually masks the disruption implied in the act of giving meaning. The workers accept the meaning given to Paul's death (largely by Bloyé, in his discussions with them), and it brings them together. It should be noted, though, that this imposition of meaning seems peaceful and natural; the violence associated with it is directed outward, against the enemy, the Fascists, who act as the sacrificers. Meaning is established through an externally directed violence, which has no place *within* the community of workers. Now what if history has ended? What will then happen to the death associated with meaning giving? Bloyé is able to repress that question because he refuses to think about the postrevolutionary period. But if we consider that epoch, we must conclude that meaning in it will be granted through violence (this novel provides no other model for its establishment): if there is no more enemy and thus no more heroic death outside of the private sphere of the family, then meaning and values will appear only through a harsh state that somehow forces them on the populace. Rather than turning outward, toward an external enemy, the violence will be turned inward (there will be nowhere else for it to go), into and against the community itself.[14]

There is a hidden complicity between Bloyé and Lange. Lange sees the necessity – and inevitability – of some form of fascism or Stalinism in the future (he even considers the possibility of becoming a Communist) that will *impose* an arbitrary meaning on life and death. Bloyé is certainly not susceptible to fascism, but the temptation of Stalinism must be seen as a constituent element in his (political) unconscious. If the only way to give death a larger social meaning *after* the revolution is through violence, then Bloyé's single option will be some form of Stalinism. It goes without saying that the risk of Stalinism is the unthinkable for anyone (like Bloyé) who would maintain the nonviolence, the "naturalness," and even the idealism of the imposition of meaning on death in the course of revolutionary action and after (recall that he speaks of the good death as a "victory of consciousness"). Nevertheless, the affirmation of the very notion of a meaningful death accepted freely is the most efficacious way to absolve oneself of the difficult task of recognizing the necessity of the violence connected with the imposition of meaning in the postrevolutionary future (a violence that is most often mandated in revolutionary societies, it should be noted, by apparently selfless clerics or intellectuals like Bloyé).[15]

If the narrative of Bloyé's exploits has a false bottom, that bottom conceals both Stalinism and another, seemingly contrary element – an element that establishes, in a different way, Bloyé's complicity with Lange, not in the dogmatism of Stalinism, but in the arbitrariness of the labyrinth. If the ultimate values for which men die do not arise naturally out of their struggle for liberation – if all existence is a scandal and we are all essentially alone – then any meaning that can be imposed by force will be a matter of chance. The consequence of this is that Lange goes from one system to another, able to navigate in each one – and able to master each one easily. The narrator tells us: "Systems of thought are like those boxes, those labyrinths, which are used for experiments with rats or guinea-pigs – the rat always ends up finding the center of the labyrinth where the bait is. Lange always ended up by arriving at the center of a system, and he was always cheated, for the bait was worthless. The only thing then was to enter a new system: that was his life" (TH, 193).

Each system is as claustrophobic as a labyrinth, and the movement from system to system can itself be nothing other than wandering in a labyrinth. The ratlike Lange moves mechanically from one method to another; even if he were to accept the truth of a system (which seems likely) – one that, because it is "worthless," would have to be imposed through force – this acceptance would be a bad-faith gesture, since he would know in advance that the values were fraudulent, that they were being accepted out of convenience, in order to escape a solitary death. (In this sense the recognition of arbitrariness, and the frustration associated with that recognition, always precede the imposition of values and meaning.)

The labyrinth is yawning under Lange's feet, but it is yawning under Bloyé's as well. Bloyé starts to think about the problem of death *after* the revolution. But, as in the case of the death of Paul, without a violent struggle (one directed outward) death cannot come to have a larger significance; in the same way, without a meaningful (sacrificial) death, there can be no community. Without death as cause and consequence of a unified community, and without death as the guarantor of social and even philosophical meaning, meaning must be imposed gratuitously through violence. In such a scheme the intellectual is reduced to the status of restless wanderer, moving from system to system, giving orders, no doubt, but finding nothing. The meanings the intellectual imposes through force in the postrevolutionary future will be generated at random out of the labyrinth of the totality of truths.

The senselessness and violence of the imposition of meaning results in the conflict between Lange's labyrinth and Stalin's terror – which are, needless to say, in hostile opposition. If Stalin is the brutal silencing of the labyrinth, however, the labyrinth is always there underneath Stalin and will reappear as soon as he loosens his grip, or suddenly and unpredictably changes his position. The labyrinth/terror combination is the repressed part of Bloyé's (and the novel's) intellectual stance (a combination represented by the hated figure, Lange), and the labyrinth of meaning is, at the same time, the repressed part of Stalinism: the Stalinist can draw any meaning out of the labyrinth of meanings, but in doing so he must always, in bad faith, actively forget the source of the meaning he is imposing. The violence of a Stalin is always a measure of the bewildering arbitrariness of his decisions.

This maze of meaning is therefore the ultimate repressed of the novel, hidden even deeper (if we are still using the false-bottom analogy) than Stalinism. Yet the labyrinth and Stalinism, even when in total opposition, are nevertheless twins, hidden beneath the mediation that the novel seeks to carry out between death and political progress; they are the repressed upon which the novel depends and which is also violently opposed to it: in order for revolutionary activity to have meaning, there must be a postrevolutionary epoch, but such an epoch cannot be conceived without the aleatory and violent imposition of meaning that would have to take place in it.

The labyrinth that threatens to swallow Bloyé is also a coffin: in both the tiny center of the labyrinth where Lange the rat finds his valueless reward of abstract philosophical truth, and in the room that closes in on Catherine, the worker's wife, as she slowly bleeds to death after her abortion (TH, 177–78), we see the claustrophobic space associated with meaningless and asocial death.[16]

And yet that pointless death is already contained within the progressive social message of The Trojan Horse as thesis novel: death can never lose its arbitrary and corrosive action, just as Bloyé can never lose Lange. Here we return to the question of the relation between the thesis novel and the avant-garde: it is perhaps not that the thesis novel is simply identical to an avant-garde practice – clearly The Trojan Horse is an effort to isolate the question of death from the entire avant-garde problematic – but rather that it is never fully able to extirpate the imperative of an untamed or unrecuperable violence, which lies just below the "false bottom" of its own textual practice. Lange's violent analysis is the aesthetic equivalent of Breton's gun fired point-blank into the crowd: it destroys all illusions, but at the same time it is susceptible to dangerous misuse. It can gratuitously generate fascism out of its store of possible interpretations, to be sure, but, perhaps even more dangerous from the perspective of a committed literature, it is capable of turning writing away from activity in the service of any cause: an ungraspable death can be inscribed in the interstices of the text itself. Lange's analysis, in fact, performs a sacrificial function that cannot be limited, and that reveals – and is inseparable from – a never-circumscribed labyrinth of possible meanings and distinctions just underneath Bloyé's, and the novel's, position; in this respect it is the asymmetric opposite of the sacrifice ostensibly put forward by Bloyé, which reveals, by making the revolutionary community (and hence the revolution) possible, a straightforward truth – class struggle, the working class as the embodiment of historical progress – just under the surface of everyday life. Lange's labyrinth of labyrinths, if we can call it that, underlies, generates, but also betrays, both his own protofascism and Bloyé's proto-Stalinism – and the possibility of any simple belief in a novel's political message.

The "unconscious" of an exemplary thesis novel like *The Trojan Horse*, when read critically, reveals a death resistant to all coherent projects, but through which, gratuitously and violently, all such projects find their origin: this negativity, the maze of writing and rewriting, is, when grasped as an untotalizable totality, indistinguishable from the uncommitted, self-reflexive avant-garde works that the thesis novel had to refuse in order to constitute itself. At the heart of an infinite series of labyrinths (labyrinths of labyrinths of labyrinths) one finds not the ecstatic masculine camaraderie of a phallic in-scription, and not the placidity of a postrevolutionary period that has put death to work (as a challenge always again to be successfully conquered), but the "hole" in which, as both Berthe and Catherine indicate, we all end up – a grave, or an empty room the macho revolutionaries have abandoned to a dying woman, and also, perhaps, just another compartment containing just another truth: the truth of truth's own dissemination, the infinity of its violent and senseless applications.[17]

Unfortunately – and this is the problem faced by any interpretation, in-cluding this one – this final truth can never be simply known: what lies beneath the false bottom can never be read; to formulate it is already to reduce it violently, rewriting it in a single, inevitably worthless, interpretation, and thereby betraying the infinite regress of the labyrinth.

II

The Trojan Horse is founded on the mendacious refusal of the necessity of Lange – and that very refusal signals a sundering within an intellectual, Bloyé, who is both the bringer of the gospel and, inevitably (because his double, Lange, cannot be denied), the secret Judas of his own secular religion of revolutionary renewal. In Pierre Drieu La Rochelle's later thesis novels, on the other hand, there is an open recognition of the fragility of the overt political meaning assigned to sacrifice. But how can a thesis novel convey a message if it already recognizes that any politically motivated sacrificial death must be a betrayal – or be betrayed? In fact, as I will argue, the awareness, on the part of the text, of the failure of the projection of a stable and efficacious political meaning onto sacrifice, results in the open resituating of violence within the limits of the text itself; at that point, the avant-garde as repressed comes to light – a light in which nothing is simply *visible* and in which awareness is impossible – and the thesis novel embraces its Other.

Like many French Fascists before and during the second World War II, Pierre Drieu La Rochelle was faced with something of a paradox. On the one hand he derived inspiration from the Fascist movements of Italy, Germany, and Spain, and he hoped for their support in the event of a Fascist uprising in France; on the other hand, he was forced to recognize, especially as the years of the Occupation dragged on, that the Germans, precisely because they were Fascists, had no respect for the national or cultural independence of any other nation.[18] A basic goal, then, of any French Fascist had to be a national independence, not only from the Soviet Union, or from American cultural imperialism, but from the mighty Fascist empires already established. In *Gilles* (1939), "Walter" (a nom de guerre of the eponymous hero) tells two Fascist friends – an Irishman and a Pole – that they must effectively implement fascism in their own countries; if they do not, they will be easy prey for other Fascist nations: "If you do not succeed in making fascism the victor in your own countries, you will bear the burden of the terrible consequences of your weakness, and you will be forced to defend these countries against the Fascist powers, even at the risk of enabling the anti-fascist forces to win."[19]

Fascism is the only bulwark, in other words, against both communism and the fascism of others. We see here a preoccupation with a problem that was to haunt the French throughout the war years, and the postwar years as well: how is a political and national "third force" to be established in France that will be subservient neither to Russia nor to Germany? (In the postwar years the question was, How can we develop a third force that will be neither Russian nor American, neither Stalinist nor capitalist? Sartre, especially, came to be concerned with this question after 1945.) In Drieu's case, and despite his obvious misgivings about other fascisms, the solution after 1940 was to collaborate with the Germans, hoping they would allow the development of a strong, autonomous Fascist state in France. Of course the Nazis had no such intention, and it seems astonishing that Drieu, who had been so wary of them in 1939, could turn around, suspend his suspicion, and attempt to curry favor with them in 1940 and 1941. The sad results are recorded in his *Fragments de mémoires*, a monument to reactionary self-delusion.[20] Perhaps the opportunity of establishing a regime that conformed to his own political desires enabled him to override his suspicions; in any case, it is clear from his memoir that he could not even interest other French Fascists in his plan for a future government.

That plan was itself the result of Drieu's desire for a kind of third force, this time on the level of national politics. Drieu was opposed both to the Left and the Right as they were constituted in France, and Marshal Pétain, who had been installed in Vichy with the blessing of the Germans, was the model of everything that Drieu despised in right-wing politics and political groups. In fact, Drieu had little but contempt for the parties of either Left or Right; both, in his estimation, were "sclerotic," both worked more to crush revolutionary fervor than to unleash it. In a 1934 essay entitled "Les Evènements de Février" (The events of February), Drieu examines the co-optation of spontaneous street violence by the moderates of the parties. Both the left-wing groups (Socialists, Communists, and the Center-leaning "radicaux de gauche") and the right-wing parties, including the Action Française, were eager to compromise after the street fighting of February 1934; the effervescence of the Fascists, rioting on February 6, was soon reined in by established groups, and in the same way the violence of the Communists on February 9 was easily controlled by the PCF (the French Communist party); both Left and Right, in containing the crowd violence, only helped strengthen the center and the bourgeois (democratic) mode of government.[21]

Like many other nonconformists of the 1930s, Drieu hoped for a political renewal through which the endless corruption of parliamentary parties could be replaced by the spontaneous, orgiastic movements of crowds in the street.[22] This was a fundamentally antirationalist vision, and no doubt it seemed more appropriate for Drieu to ally himself with the Fascists than with the Communists (his hero Gilles, however, at the height of the events of 1934, had declared himself willing to go with any group that had the nerve to fight in the street).[23] Drieu was nevertheless against stratified hierarchies in society: against both Hitler and Marx, Drieu put forward Nietzsche, who, at least in writings such as *The Will to Power*, argued for a "permanent revolution," against frozen caste systems and so on.[24]

During the war, disillusionment soon set in. The Germans ignored Drieu's behind-the-scenes efforts to set up a more dynamic government; he instead fell back as the new editor of the *Nouvelle Revue Française*, ignobly refusing to publish Jewish authors. As it became clear that the Germans were going to lose the war, Drieu (unlike Robert Brasillach, for example) was not defiant in his collaboration; instead, he retreated once again to a third (or fourth?) position, attempting to posit an alternative to communism, nazism, and Anglo-Americanism. But by 1943 what other options were there?

This in fact is the terrible dilemma posed by Drieu's last completed novel, *Les Chiens de paille* (Straw dogs) written in 1943 but published only in 1964 (its imminent publication was halted after the liberation of Paris in August 1944). In it we find Constant Trubert, an adventurer who has lived since World War I outside of France, and who returns in 1939. After the defeat (the novel is set in 1942), he accepts a job as a strong-arm man for an apparently apolitical black marketeer, Susini. In some godforsaken marsh in northern France, Susini has a base of operations that includes a large cache of weapons, hidden in a house. Trubert goes out to guard the cache, and in the area he meets a number of shady characters, all of whom are collaborating with a foreign power: Préault with the Anglo-Americans (he is a Gaullist), Bardy with the Nazis, and Salis with the Soviets (he is a Communist). Trubert – who is clearly a spokesman for the narrator, at least at first – observes that all these people think they are patriots, while in fact they are all collaborators with one occupying force or another.[25] Trubert tells Bardy: "You are a patriot against the English, he's one against the Germans. Neither of you are patriots any longer. . . . Bardy prefers that France be German rather than be run by Préault, and Préault prefers that it be English or American rather than in the hands of Bardy."[26]

There is only one true Frenchman in the lot, a young veteran named Cormont, whose face was badly disfigured in the fighting of 1940. Cormont is alone in wanting all the occupiers out and in wanting to establish a strong French regime. He leads a tiny band of partisans in the area.

The plot now becomes a rather crude allegory of the contemporary situation in France: Préault, Bardy, and Salis have all agreed to keep their hands off the sinister Susini's arms cache. Trubert, acting as a simple mercenary without ideology, guards the weapons. Cormont is determined to get hold of them, and in the process he is perfectly willing to risk not only his own destruction but that of Préault, Bardy, and Salis as well (the accidental revelation of the cache will also reveal to the Germans all the clandestine groups that are trying to protect it). As the novel reaches its climax, Cormont has forced his way into the house and is holding Trubert at gunpoint.

Recalling Drieu's "third force" ideology, we would now expect to find Trubert suddenly throwing in his lot with Cormont. This does not happen, however, because, as we can easily imagine, by 1943 Drieu had lost faith not only in the idea of a third force but in any possibility of an independent, powerful role for France in the world. Trubert fully recognizes France's third-rate status, and therefore he also recognizes the futility of any action independent of either first-string foreign powers (Russia, America) or second-string ones (Germany, Japan). "France is a corner of the world that has been forgotten" (CP, 120). In that sense, the idealistic but mutilated young Cormont is nothing more than a historical curiosity.

As a thesis novel, *Les Chiens de paille* could be expected to show how a third force can arise to put an end to the occupation; from the very first, however, it is clear that, within the framework of verisimilitude established by the novel, there is no way of solving this dilemma. No god can come from the sky to save and justify the totally independent Cormont: he is doomed. France will always be occupied. What solution, then, is possible? Trubert, while not politically committed (commitment means only betrayal or impotence), is, in a sense, religiously committed. He is a student of all the religions of the world, and he spends his spare time copying religious texts and annotating them with commentaries ("He returned home and, after having washed, compared a passage from the Zohar with one from the Brihad Aranyaka Upanishad. On beautiful paper, he transcribed the two texts, one facing the other. Beneath, he wrote a brief commentary" [CP, 83]). Perhaps if no political solution is in sight, there is a religious one. Trubert is fascinated with the story of Judas, and he becomes convinced that Judas was not simply a despicable traitor: he was, in fact, a necessary player in the drama of Christ's sacrifice. Christ could not be sacrificed, and society renewed, without the intervention of the agent who carries out that sacrifice.

But what kind of renewal was possible under the conditions that obtained during the Roman occupation? Judas quickly realizes that Jesus cannot be a temporal leader (as Judas had first thought) and lead the people out of their enslavement. Jesus has no intention of revolting against the Romans, and he is too gentle to lead the people away from the established clergy – the main goal of his movement (CP, 136). Judas at this point thinks of betraying Jesus simply because he is fed up with him – at least the clergy "has a feel for the possible. If revolt is impossible, the conservatives are right, they're justified" (CP, 136).

Judas, however, soon realizes that, if a political revolt is impossible, a religious renewal is very much a possibility. Talking with the apostle John, Judas learns that Jesus might be not a temporal king but a celestial one; reading Isaiah and Daniel, they come to the conclusion that Jesus is the Messiah, a disguised heavenly power who nevertheless must suffer (CP, 144–45). Salvation from this perspective is not temporal but spiritual; yet implicit in the idea of the Messiah is the notion of a very real physical death, the sacrifice of the god. Now, suddenly, Judas sees a new role for himself: rather than betraying Jesus out of disgust, he will betray him to usher in the new era of spiritual renewal. "Judas . . . saw in this death not a stopgap solution, but on the contrary the very precondition for the triumph of glory. . . . In this last case, it was still necessary to find the practical way to make Jesus die" (CP, 147). Judas then betrays Jesus, and Jesus' death and rebirth lead to the spiritual salvation of all mankind.

This is all an obvious allegory for the political and spiritual decline (and the possible spiritual renewal) of France. For Drieu the Fascist the "decadence" of the Jews at the time of Christ is the same as the decadence of the French in the 1930s and 1940s. In a familiar strategy (one thinks of Céline) Drieu turns his anti-Semitism against the French themselves. "Judas belonged to a conquered people, a weakened people who had been trampled by twenty invasions, occupied by twenty occupiers" (CP, 149). The result of these occupations was that the Jews became more and more decadent, and they attempted to compensate for their loss of temporal power through the development of a feeling of spiritual and intellectual authority. "The Jews were nothing more than intellectuals and literary men" (CP, 149). The narrator, apparently speaking (in style indirect libre) for Trubert, then goes on to consider the "vile promiscuity of the French" who are becoming "what the Jews became" (CP, 150).

The narrator-Trubert figure, in his attack on the Jews and the French, is echoing, in a Fascist register, Nietzsche's analysis of *ressentiment*: both peoples, impotent and full of hate, create an imaginary superior (intellectual or spiritual) realm into which they project themselves as the true masters. Indeed we learn a little later that Trubert is also a Nietzsche enthusiast, believing that, instead of this decadence, there should be a manifestation of the will to power in the new France. But this poses a familiar problem: if this renewal is to be carried out through a sacrifice, will it be a political or a religious murder? The story of Judas and the valorization of Judas's decision to carry out an essentially religious sacrifice seems to imply that a sacrifice in contemporary France could be effective only if it were carried out as a spiritual undertaking. The death of the victim could not be expected to result in a political renewal, in a new temporal kingdom. At the same time, though, the Nietzschean critique of *ressentiment* implies an all-out assault on decadent cultures, ones that would replace an actual violent physical revolution with imaginary, spiritual refusal and renewal. But the figure Trubert is invoking is not simply Judas but the Jesus/Judas sacrificial dyad – and no figure came in for more criticism from Nietzsche than Christ (or at least the spiritualized Christ created by the Christians). What then of Trubert's Nietzscheanism?

The narrator, again speaking for Trubert, attempts to resolve this contradiction. It seems that Nietzsche himself was not only the exemplary exponent of power; he was also a decadent. "Deep down, he did not want anything all that different from what Jesus wanted" (CP, 152). "Intimately mixed" (CP, 153) are the two sides of Nietzsche's personality, which his followers will be unable to disentangle: the mixture of warrior and decadent, hero and saint (CP, 153–54). Nietzsche was not only the ultimate critic of decadence; he too was "ultra-intellectual . . . frightened, nervous, anguished" (CP, 152). It seems, finally, that both tendencies must always be seen together in the human, and are in fact what distinguishes the human from the animal.

If we can grant all this, what then are we to make of the elaborate political-religious allegory of Judas? How can the sacrifice he carries out be situated both in a social realm (manifesting the implementation of the will to power) and in a spiritual one (resulting in redemption)? It seemed earlier that political power and decadence were firmly separated; the narrator distinguishes the "Hebrews" (a vibrant, conquering nation) from the "Jews" (a decadent, intellectual one), the France of Louis XIV from that of Léon Blum and Marshal Pétain. Now it appears that strength and decay, activism and transcendence, are simply dialectical opposites, resolvable in that higher term, the human. But, in that case, how would sacrifice – as presented in the story of Judas – both represent and implement this double imperative?

For an answer to this question, we should turn to the end of the novel to see how Trubert's sacrificial project finally ends. Trubert has tricked both Cormont and Susini; they are his prisoners in the basement of Susini's house, where the arms cache is stored. Trubert intends to blow the place up, sacrificing both himself and Cormont (Susini's death at first would seem circumstantial, since he is nothing more than a vague anarchist and a black marketeer – later it turns out that he is an "internationalist," favoring both Moscow and Washington, and so his death too seems appropriate). Cormont's sacrificial death is essential: he is the last Frenchman of a truly independent France, just as Jesus was the last Hebrew (CP, 237). He is literally the last possibility of a French messiah. At this point, however, Trubert's motives become rather mystifying. He seems to want to carry out a sacrifice to effect neither political change nor spiritual redemption; instead, he wants to carry it out because it is the basic gesture of all religions; it is somehow life itself. As Trubert prepares to blow everyone up, he gives a lecture: "You understand, little Cormont, that there is only sacrifice, life is a sacrifice. All the ancient religions, which held the secret of man, said it and did it. Life is a sacrifice, a hecatomb, a perpetual slaughterhouse smoking before the gods. . . . The true religion is the Mexican religion: rip open a man and tear out his heart. A beating heart in a man's hand – that's life itself" (CP, 238). In addition, Trubert observes that the sacrificial relation is double: "One must sacrifice the others, and one must sacrifice oneself." The Aztec sacrificer, finally, caught up in the frenzy of his gesture, is unable to keep from disemboweling himself.

We have now passed from redemption to a simple making manifest of what life "is." It "is" sacrifice, and sacrifice must therefore be carried out. This murky thinking is met with derision on the part of Susini, who observes: "It's a drag having to listen to this pedant before dying" (CP, 239). What is remarkable is that the narrator seems to have a certain amount of sympathy for the two men who are about to die, and he turns against Trubert, who is starting to seem more and more like a simple lunatic. At one point the narrator observes that Trubert, as he harangues his victims, is waving his gun histrionically, like a movie hero (CP, 238). Finally, he is raving, announcing that he is Melchisedech, the High Priest: "With my hands I am going to finish off France" (CP, 240). But his two victims ignore him, preoccupied as they are with their own deaths.

The novel ends with a sudden surprise: just as Trubert is about to carry out his sacrificial gesture, a Royal Air Force bomber, flying overhead, accidentally drops a bomb on the house, blowing up everyone. The narrator, referring to Trubert, tells us: "a Frenchman, even insane, was no longer master of his own house" (CP, 240). The ultimate impotence of the Frenchman, then, is that he cannot, for whatever reason, even sacrifice his nation's last independent patriot.

This abrupt end leaves us literally in the air. How are we to interpret Trubert's doctrine of sacrifice? Does it signal a political or spiritual renewal? Or is it simply another sign of decadence? Are we to see sacrifice as a manifestation of a liberating third force, or as just another dead end? If the novel is to play the ordained role of the thesis novel – persuade us of the truth of its version of social conflict, and tell us, through the story, how we should change our lives and those of others – then it would have to posit the sacrificial third force as a positive option. But, having put forward sacrifice as the last option, the novel then seems to take it away.

We should first note that Trubert's sacrificial gesture – as he prepares to blow up Cormont and Susini – adds nothing to life but only represents it. According to Trubert, life "is" sacrifice; but sacrificial ritual, it also seems, is carried out in order to show what life, or Being, "really" is: sacrifice as a public practice doubles existence and serves as a kind of heuristic device. Sacrifice as ritual is therefore pure representation, and it leads to a fundamental knowledge of "life."

On the other hand, sacrifice does not lead out of itself: it is itself, it is life. It is everywhere and everything, yet it is secret (for it is not obvious to everyone that "life is sacrifice"). Silent sacrifice, performed everywhere but never recognized, is therefore not representation but a kind of ever-repeated, omnipresent tautology. As performance, sacrifice is literally senseless violence, the mechanical repetition of "life" (which is also sacrifice: sacrifice is sacrifice). It does not necessarily play the role of causing a political or social renewal: this is underlined by the fact that Trubert is prepared to sacrifice his acquaintances in an unknown cellar. Even if their bodies were to be found, no one would suspect Trubert's real motives behind this hecatomb: the explosion might even be seen as accidental. This of course contrasts with Christ's crucifixion, which was both a public event and the subject of a number of supposedly factual written narratives. The most that Trubert could have, then, would be the necessarily fictional account of his life (it could not be factual, because any person who would know of the real events and the real motives behind them would not live to tell the tale). In the absence of public ritual, then, Trubert would need fiction to propagate his message ("life is sacrifice"). What he would need, on a more basic level, is some form of representation; he would therefore be forced to have recourse to a public variety of sacrifice (sacrifice as representation) in order to convey another, secret one (what I have called "silent sacrifice"). But what strikes us at this point in the novel is that Trubert, even while he prepares to carry out a sacrifice that is inseparable from its function as representation (he even patiently, if deliriously, explains it), refuses that very representation by attempting to carry out the sacrifice not publicly but secretly. There is a reason, however, for this secrecy.

Trubert is far from being his own evangelist, or even his own narrator. He shuns the role of novelist; novel writing is the kind of decadent intellectual activity he associates with the decline of France. Instead, he prefers merely copying religious texts, perhaps writing a brief commentary but refusing to play the role of the aesthete, the propagandist, or the prophet: "I am the most secret of men because I do not write, I don't paint, I have no political opinions. My secret is my religion and my religion is my secret. . . . Under the shadow of a bridge, I write an anonymous sentence that no one will ever read" (CP, 89). Still, we note a certain ambiguity in this passage: first Trubert tells us he does not write, then we learn that he does write, but only secretly. But why write if one's writing will remain secret? Why sacrifice, for that matter? Why, like Drieu (or Drieu's narrator) write about sacrifice and then publish it?

Only the decadent, critical intellect chooses to broadcast his opinions and analyses. In refusing this self-propagandizing Trubert affirms life, silence, and sacrifice (all are necessarily the same); he refuses representation and publication. This last position, however, is the result of a series of critical demystifications: first, as we saw, Judas's role as *political* traitor/savior was refused; then even his role in ushering in an era of spiritual renewal was dismissed. Then the two sides, political and religious, heroic and saintly (or decadent), were synthesized in a higher figure: Nietzsche. Finally, Trubert, at the end of the novel, sees sacrifice not as a regenerative act so much as a manifestation of life itself. It is Trubert who proposes sacrifice's different configurations: all along, however, he has also been devoted to silence, to the refusal of any intervention in the public sphere (as early as page 89, as we have seen, he was refusing writing, or at least writing for a public). And, at the same time, it is the novel itself that carries out these demystifications: it is clearly a meditation on sacrifice, and it puts forth one solution after another. This critical function abruptly becomes clear at the end, when Trubert posits the last solution to the enigma of sacrifice in society (the necessary secret that "life is sacrifice") – a solution radically incompatible with the other solutions, because they entailed the ultimate efficacy of sacrifice, either in the political or the religious realm (or, as in the case of Nietzsche, in an apparent synthesis of the two) – and the novel's narrator, who had spoken from Trubert's point of view, suddenly distances himself. It is then that Trubert is presented as nothing more than just another insane, impotent Frenchman. The narrator, who almost until the end *was* Trubert, is suddenly Other, reflecting on him, just as Trubert has been Other to himself all along, critically reflecting on the various modes of sacrifice, and through that reflection incongruously arriving at a version of sacrifice that would seem to be the refusal of all critical reflection – a version that, as power and silence, he had held from the beginning.

The critical function that Trubert and the novel had seemed to share thus abruptly breaks down, and we realize that they were incompatible all along. If novel writing is decadent, any account or representation of Trubert's life will be a betrayal, and Trubert would necessarily refuse it on principle. The narrator is therefore perhaps the true contemporary figure of Judas in the novel, for he, like Judas, is the ultimate "traître, traditeur, traducteur, transmetteur" (CP, 115). He not only betrays, translates, and transmits Trubert's life, but he is a kind of *traditeur* as well – the ancient Christian who, under torture, gave the pagans sacred books and objects. In other words, the Judas-narrator is the one who writes and transmits the story and thus desecrates that which was meant to be kept apart, in the tabernacle of secrecy: Trubert's (failed) act of sacrifice itself.

We can see that it was wrong for Trubert to attempt to present Nietzsche as a figure who somehow resolved the contradiction between the will to power and decadence. Indeed the impossibility of such a resolution is inseparable from the last (if not final) gesture of sacrifice that the novel can present: its own self-sacrifice. The relation between power and intellectual decline, between Trubert the secret sacrificer and the narrator-novelist-propagator (the narrator plays the role of the evangelists, those "best-selling novelists," as Trubert calls them at one point), between the eternally recurring, tautological will to power of life and its decadent representation, is thus one of betrayal; put another way, at the end of the novel, when we realize the narrator's critical stance, betrayal and sacrifice are situated in the writing of the novel itself, between narrator and hero. When the deus ex machina, the RAF plane, drops the bomb on the house, it is the narrator who has the last laugh and who sacrifices Trubert. Sacrifice is now a textual function, the very tear in the novel's texture. Sacrifice (life itself) is a secret and powerful act, the novel that represents it and its supposed forms from an ironic distance is public and decadent; yet sacrifice is inseparable from its representation, sacrifice *is* representation, and it thus needs the novel if it is to be anything more than mere silence, just as the novel needs sacrifice if it is to have an object worthy of its betrayal. The very critical distance that allows the inventory of the dialectic of the forms, functions, and syntheses of sacrifice throughout the novel (and the arrival at sacrifice's final, impossible form) is a betrayal of sacrifice, because a critique is an essentially negative (constative) representation, while sacrifice, as a performance of the will to power, is active, repetitious (tautological), and nonreflexive. Thus the novel is totally committed to sacrifice and is indeed essential to its elaboration and representation, but at the same time it inevitably and necessarily violates it. That betrayal of sacrifice is, however, the "ultimate" sacrifice – which, as sacrifice, will itself always again be betrayed.

Put another way, the ultimate self-sacrifice in the novel is not that of Trubert – he dies a failure – but that of the novel itself. True, Trubert is both sacrificer and victim, hero and saint, the last in a line of Christ figures (which includes Nietzsche), and in his unresolvable duality he is the double of the narrator, and eventually of the novel itself. But Trubert is not a person; he is only a fictional figure, a principle of sacrifice put forward within a novel. It is the novel alone that (like the Aztec priest to whom Trubert refers), at the end, finally sacrifices itself and is impotent. It originally set out as a thesis novel to put forward an argument for the possibility of the renewal of society through sacrifice alone, all the other forms of social regeneration being only manifestations of collaboration and betrayal; it ends up discovering the inevitability of betrayal *in and as* sacrifice, and performing its own demystification and betrayal of any sacrifice promising renewal in the world, of any secret sacrifice promising nothing, and, finally, of its own gesture of betrayal, which is also necessarily a sacrifice. It betrays its own betrayal, and its own impotence, through the very fact that it continues to transmit and thereby promote a powerful doctrine, no matter how negative, of sacrifice. In this way, the point at which the novel ends is not so much the result of the failure of the gesture of sacrifice at a particular moment in history as it is a consequence of the rigorous following through of the logic of sacrifice itself.

By moving from "actual" human sacrifice in the world to textual self-sacrifice, the novel only certifies its own impotence: *Les Chiens de paille* is remarkable for the self-reflexivity of its critical function, which turns on itself, scrutinizing its own "solutions" (the different modes of sacrifice), until that very examination comes to be nothing other than the sacrifice that the novel had originally meant to use or implement. Rather than being unaware of the futility of its project, this novel is so destructively aware that its awareness finally allows us to recognize the self-sacrifice of the tradition of the thesis novel that valorizes sacrifice as a means to political renewal. (In my recognition and simple formulation of this or any self-sacrifice – in this commentary – I nevertheless betray the duality of the novel's act of betrayal.) In betraying this tradition – while nevertheless *transmitting* it – *Les Chiens de paille* reveals its power, a power as unsuspected as that of the dead god or the automutilating madman.[27]

It can be argued that the thesis novel depended on the conventions of verisimilitude and the thematics of sacrifice: verisimilitude presented reality "as it is" (at least according to bourgeois conventions); the thematics of sacrifice allowed radical change to be inserted in a structure of realism that, on the face of it, was as static and unremarkable as the inglorious rounds of everyday life. The thesis novel not only presented or represented life but showed how it could or must be changed; sacrifice enabled the characters of the novel to come together and perform decisively as active agents, while verisimilitude ensured that that sacrifice would at least seem to be something that could be implemented in real life, unlike the sacrificial mythological fantasms of the surrealists.

Between *The Trojan Horse* and *Les Chiens de paille* we see this model break down. *The Trojan Horse* was still able to argue that sacrifice, betrayal, and doubt could be limited: sacrifice would be useful, would contribute a meaning to the struggle, would in turn receive a positive meaning from that struggle. The fact that the text had an unconscious of unlimited doubt, meaningless death, corrosive analysis, and arbitrarily imposed violence was apparent only after we read the novel against itself, uncovering the points at which it had to be blind if it was to carry out its task of teaching and inspiration. *Les Chiens de paille*, on the other hand, openly posits its own ideology critique, relentlessly exposing every collaboration and then posing, and demystifying, the various avatars of sacrifice. The thesis-novel tradition meets its Other here; verisimilitude, sacrifice, and an unrelenting critique of ideology lead, finally, to what we might call the self-sacrifice, or the automutilation, of the text itself. The external referent, the question of the implementation of sacrifice in society, does not so much drop by the wayside as it becomes caught up in the vicious circle of the novel itself, in the rent of its affirmation and betrayal of sacrifice. The ghost of a politicized sacrifice remains, however, in the text, always seen through (one thinks of Lange's vision), always betrayed, always situated within a dialectic of the forms of sacrifice – but also, as we see in *Les Chiens de paille*, always necessarily *transmitted*, desecrated, given over to the enemy and thus made public. We cannot say, for that reason, that the politics of sacrifice – no matter how odious or inspiring – simply disappear from the text.[28] Indeed, the phantom of a decadent political stance – one dependent on the representation of a position in the public sphere – will always come to haunt, and betray, any writing that too confidently puts forward exclusively the will to power of its own textuality, or that, in order to arrive at an all-powerful textuality, affirms the presupposition that various forms of sacrifice can be situated within, and therefore be comprehended by, a dialectic.[29]

After a reading of *Les Chiens de paille* it becomes difficult simply to distinguish the thesis novel from the avant-garde tradition that projects the violence and death of sacrifice into the writing of the text itself (here one thinks, above all, of Blanchot). This is not to say, though, that through this novel one can imagine a union of thesis novel and avant-garde. The secret and the public, the powerful and the decadent, instead always remain intimately fused in mortal combat: sacrifice becomes secret, finally, not because it is hidden in a basement but because, in its textual manifestation and automutilation, it becomes unreadable; at the same time, sacrifice becomes public not in the text's straightforward valorization of (literary, political, or spiritual) meaning but in its transmission-through-betrayal of that meaning.

3

The Performance of
Nausea

IN THE NEXT three chapters I will analyze three works by Jean-Paul Sartre: *Nausea*, the last fragments of the projected fourth volume of *The Roads of Freedom*, and *The Critique of Dialectical Reason*. What interests me most in Sartre, and what justifies (I hope) my devoting so many pages to him, is the consistency of his effort to derive a model of a human community, based on the interpersonal recognition of the freedom of the Other, from an event – for lack of a better word – that precludes any formulation of consciousness or subjectivity. Sartre's work represents an important variation of the Barthesian "writer's" project: unlike Nizan and Drieu, Sartre is interested not only in the founding of a viable community as an alternative to fascism, repression, or democracy but in the establishment of a dialectic that is politically progressive and that entails the mutual recognition of desire on the part of autonomous subjects.[1] That his model of humanist-aesthetic subjectivity depends on, and falls before, an ever-recurrent and empty act (in different guises: commands, promises, excuses) certainly indicates the greatest difficulty facing a committed intellectual who, in the end, can only *posit* a coherent society of freely and fully communicating consciousnesses. *The Critique of Dialectical Reason,* published in 1960, represents the last major attempt to form rigorously the task of the (Barthesian) "writer." Many others have argued for the committed writer and the need for progressive social change – but Sartre alone relentlessly treated the problem of the formulation of the dialectic and the establishment of a coherent social grouping (with its figure of the intellectual) out of and in relation to it. That no one has returned to this kind of project may signal its impossibility – or only the fact that, for a while at least, critics have chosen to recognize its impossibility, and to use that recognition as a reason for not attempting to follow it through. No doubt the Sartrian effort is no more and no less impossible than any other elaboration of a social or linguistic model containing within itself a role for the intellectual.

Perhaps by the very fact of his repeated efforts, Sartre nevertheless indicates that he "knows" more than he is letting on – to himself or to us. There may be no need for a commentary on the blindness of his text, in that his repetitions entail, if nothing else, at least an awareness of the recurring failure of his project. Or, conversely, in the very attempt to "reveal" some modes of failure in his project I too am playing the Sartrian game, attempting to force a higher knowledge out of a blind repetition.

I

Seeing Roquentin's experience of Nausea in *Nausea* as a rewriting and, at least up to a certain point, an inversion of the Kantian sublime enables one to understand much better how disparate elements of the novel fit together – for example, the apparently surrealistic descriptions of matter in the nature experiences, on the one hand, and the naturalistic descriptions of Bouville and its society of jerks (*salauds*) and humanists, on the other. It not only makes clearer Roquentin's condemnation of adventures and the possibility of having them, but, I will argue, it explains the sudden proposal of a new kind of aesthetic project – and even a new kind of adventure – at the end of the novel. Above all, Kant's sublime provides a model against which, and also through which, the novel operates, proposing as it does new standards of aesthetic judgment and a model of contingency that will serve as the basis for much of the theory elaborated by Sartre in philosophical works written after *Nausea*. As we will see when we consider the role of speech acts (performative rhetoric) at the end of the novel, however, this contingency, derived from a critique of Kantian subjectivity, may entail a model of consciousness so radical – indeed it may even be *impossible* – that it throws into question much of the later, constructive, Sartrian enterprise.

First, without pretending to be exhaustive, we might recall a few of Kant's arguments concerning the sublime in *Critique of Judgment*. Sublime objects in nature for Kant (waterfalls, volcanoes, mountains, etc.) are "boundless" not only because of their grandeur, their great size, but because their "formlessness" affects us in a certain way: we are pleased because "admiration or respect" is inspired in us; the mind is alternately "attracted and repelled" by the object. Above all, the sublime object in nature is a violation of the purposive because of its formlessness ("Any object is monstrous if, by its size, it destroys the purpose which constitutes the concept of it"); and it is in this lack or violation of purpose (which "does violence to the imagination") that we find "a negative pleasure."[2]

We see from the outset that Kant's discussion of the sublime has to do not with objects "out there," in nature, but with "a sublimity which can be found in the mind"; the object itself, in its "chaos or in its wildest and most irregular disorder" is only "horrible" (CJ, 84). The truly sublime object, because it is "absolutely great in every point of view" cannot be compared with anything; there is no standard for comparison outside it; "it is a magnitude which is like itself alone" (CJ, 88). In other words, it is radically heterogeneous. For that reason, the "sublime is not to be sought in the things of nature, but only in our ideas." Kant goes on to define it: "the sublime is that in comparison with which everything else is small." This precludes things of nature: no matter how huge, an object can always be contrasted with an even greater object.

The sublime has now been shifted from objects in nature to a capacity of the mind: because there is "in our imagination a striving toward infinite progress and in our reason a claim for absolute totality," we perceive a limitlessness not in an object but in "the state of mind produced by a certain representation with which the reflective judgment is occupied" (CJ, 89). The sublime, then, is not so much the "infinite progress" toward which the mind strives, as it is the "supersensible faculty" that does the striving. "The sublime is that, the mere ability to think, which shows a faculty of the mind surpassing every standard of sense" (CJ, 89). The mind comes to perceive its own "supersensible faculty" (which alone is capable of thinking the infinite) as that which is truly sublime.

The limitless, the boundless, is now the reason itself, which dwarfs even the "aesthetical estimation of magnitude formed by the imagination"; the latter is still grounded in sense, while the "law of reason," independent of the senses and measurement, is "absolutely great" (CJ, 96). It is the tension, the "want of accordance" between any "sensible standards" and the "ideas of understanding" (that is, the "supersensible destination") that results in both the pleasure and pain of the feeling of the sublime.

In this view, the mind seems to turn toward itself, perceiving its reason, as the sublime; the relation to this limitlessness is characterized as *respect*. This relation, moreover, is both painful – because it indicates the discrepancy between sense perception and the law of reason – and, at the same time, pleasurable – because our "judgment of the inadequacy of our greatest faculty of sense" corresponds with "rational ideas" (CJ, 96).

Sublimity is now the movement of the law of reason in our mind. If anything, the sublime in nature is nothing more than a metaphor, a representation, that reflects back to us the limitlessness of the supersensible. Kant writes: "Sublimity . . . does not reside in anything of nature, but only in our mind, in so far as we can become conscious that we are superior to nature within, and therefore also to nature without us (so far as it influences us). Everything that excites this feeling in us, e.g. the *might* of nature which calls forth our forces, is called then (although improperly) sublime" (CJ, 104).

We erroneously feel pleasure in nature, but what we are really feeling pleasure in is our own capacity for moral ideas. We are, in a sense, misreading the sublime in ourselves by projecting it outward onto nature; we are misleading or deceiving ourselves by confusing what is really sublime – the "absolutely great" law of reason – with what is only apparently great (or formless, monstrous) in a given sense perception. Kant writes: "The feeling of the sublime in nature is respect for our own destination; which, by a certain subreption, we attribute to an object of nature (conversion of respect for the idea of humanity in our own subject into respect for the object)" (CJ, 96). Note that the "supersensible destination" is associated here with the "idea of [and respect for] humanity in our own subject": it is a moral feeling.

This all too hasty summation of a few themes in Kant's exposition of the sublime will enable us to consider Roquentin's Nausea as an *inverted sublime*. The objects of nature in Roquentin's vision are monstrous and formless. Unlike Kant's objects, these "existences," as Roquentin calls them, are small and weak; they pass in and out with great rapidity, feebly "existing" for a moment, only to be arbitrarily replaced with others, identical in their insignificance and weakness. It is a world of microevents: "But why, I thought, why so many existences, since they all look alike? So many existences missed, obstinately begun again and again missed – like the awkward efforts of an insect fallen on its back? (I was one of these efforts.) That abundance did not give the effect of generosity, just the opposite. . . . I began to laugh because I suddenly thought of the formidable springs described in books, full of crackings, burstings, gigantic explosions. There were those idiots who came to tell you about the will to power and struggle for life. Hadn't they ever seen a beast or a tree? . . . Every existing thing is born without reason, prolongs itself out of weakness, and dies by chance."[3]

These subobjects are the absurd parody of the sublime objects of nature (those "formidable springs described in books"); yet they too have a kind of limitlessness. It is not that they seem to go on indefinitely, in their grandeur lacking any limits; instead *within themselves* they are heterogeneous and lack any limitation which might serve to define them and give them consistency or coherence. "Colors, tastes and smells were never real, never themselves and nothing but themselves. The simplest, most indefinable quality had too much content, in relation to itself, in its heart" (N, 130). The radical exteriority of the immense natural object is here internalized *without ceasing to be external,* and becomes the sordidness of the replicable, unstable, and ignoble object. This no doubt explains why the objects, colors, and words in the Nausea always seem to be in excess, always seem to be "overflowing" themselves ("The simplest, most indefinable quality had too much content"; "All these paltry agitations . . . overflowed the leaves and branches everywhere" [N, 130, 132]). The definitive situating of an unrecuperable (unassimilable) exterior *within* the object (or subject) results in a kind of repetitious action of purgation in which the gelatinous insides are somehow, impossibly, always again forced out, made external: it is an eternally recurring, feeble (not mighty and awe-inspiring, like Kant's sublime) catharsis. Because of this weakness, the "contents" of things (and people) do not shoot out forcefully (this is not a Nietzschean vision); they ooze.

Roquentin, unlike the Kantian subject, experiences no terror, pleasure, pain, or reverence before these series of "existences": he only feels disgust and Nausea. And the sublime in nature here is not "the idea of humanity in our own subject" projected, through "subreption," outward; on the contrary, it is an object so exterior that it is untouched by any anthropomorphism: reason, language, necessity, models of causation, all are incapable of incorporating such a heterogeneous thing into a larger "system," narrative, or subjectivity: "Faced with this great wrinkled paw [the tree-root], neither ignorance nor knowledge was important: the world of explanations and reason is not the world of existence. This root . . . existed in such a way that I could not explain it" (N, 129). These are objects beneath explanation and use: "The words had vanished and with them the significance of things, their methods of use, and the feeble points of reference which men have traced on their surface" (N, 127). "I thought without words, *on* things, *with* things" (N, 129).

The fact that Roquentin thinks "*with* things," however, does not mean that things are somehow invested with the "being" of thought; on the contrary, the "objects" Roquentin sees, feels, smells, are not the products of the intervention of consciousness, and they bear no relation to it: "you can never deduce anything from them," he says (N, 129). "All is free"; there is no necessity of any kind; the basic freedom, or rather contingency, of things was plastered over when higher concepts – God, Man, rights – were invented. It is not, as Kant said, that we project the sublimity of our own "law of reason" onto nature; instead, all we project is the useful lie (as Nietzsche would have said) that we ourselves, and consequently the objects "out there" (in their relation to us), are "necessary."[4] All is *superfluous* (N, 131) – both the stable objects we arbitrarily create through the application of deceptive metaphors, as well as our own "subjectivities." If anything, then, it is the radically exterior disgusting objects that project their inner lack of limits *into* us, causing us from the first to come apart or wretchedly overflow.

The discarding of Kantian humanism – with its baggage of rights, reason, necessity, and subjectivity – leaves a nature radically exterior to man. But contingency does not stop there: Roquentin depicts various bourgeois "individuals" – the wealthy town fathers, the hapless Autodidact – as without any fundamental subjectivity as well. The absurdity of nature is now situated *within* man: "no one has any rights; they are entirely free, like other men, they cannot succeed in not feeling superfluous" (N, 131). Sartre inverts the Kantian gesture of demonstrating the priority of subjectivity and moral ideas: now it is the formlessness of nature that has always already invaded subjectivity itself.

Roquentin's sublime – the radical exteriority of objects, the contingency of a nature that completely lacks any common measure with what is normally associated with the integrity and necessity of the human subject – comes to be recognized as prior to, and at the basis of, subjectivity in general. By this I mean that not only is the Kantian, or bourgeois humanist subject, disarticulated but also that the possibility of the subject in humanism as a philosophy, but especially as an ideology, is dismantled. In fact, in two different cases, Roquentin displays the fragmentation of the "subject" both as person and as the embodiment of a doctrine of subjectivity. There are two major representatives, in *Nausea*, of different versions of the quasi-official rationalist and humanist philosophy of the Third Republic: on the one hand, the jerks, whose portraits Roquentin studies in the municipal art museum of Bouville, and, on the other, the Autodidact, a lonely, self-proclaimed humanist who haunts the Bouville public library.[5]

The jerks are the wealthy town fathers; they still cling to the idea of "rights" (as in the "Declaration of the Rights of Man"), but rights for them are always their own rights. They represent the right wing of French republicanism. For these bourgeois, the notion of rights serves as a principle that unifies their being and, in a sense, subjugates, and gives meaning to, all of nature. As Roquentin writes of Jean Parrottin, one of the jerks in the gallery: "This man was one-ideaed. Nothing more was left in him but bones, dead flesh, and Pure Right. . . . Instead of the slight headache I feel coming on each time I visit a museum, he would have felt the painful right of having his temples cared for" (N, 88).

That headache, in fact, is a precursor of the Nausea that Roquentin will later experience. He feels it coming on when he sees beyond, so to speak, the surface of the paintings: in them there is not the moral dignity of the authorities, represented by their medals, mustaches, and powerful gaze. Staring back, defeating that gaze, Roquentin sees not the mastery of the subject or the symbols of that mastery but only formless micro-objects: "blind eyes, the thin mouth of a dead snake, and cheeks"; "vaguely obscene flesh"; "bones, dead flesh, Pure Right" (N, 88). Indeed the ultimate idealized sign of the authority of the subject ("Pure Right") has itself now been materialized, and it is just another contingency, no different, really, from the revolting tree root.

It is important to grasp that the power of the jerks, their conversion of contingency into necessity, and the "subreption" that allows them to misread contingency as necessity, is dependent on mendacious representation. Their subjectivity and its authority is constituted for them and for others through metaphors or objects that stand for their lofty position – such as the portraits themselves. The jerks are nothing but the creation of their portraits; it is the technique of representation that is capable of creating the authority and rights of the jerks by dishonestly eliminating all heterogeneous elements. "Thus, with the help of Renaudas and Bordurin [the two portrait painters responsible for all the images in the gallery] they [the jerks] had enslaved Nature: without themselves and within themselves. What these sombre canvases offered to me *was man rethought by man*, with, as sole adornment, the finest conquest of man: a bouquet of the Rights of Man and Citizen. Without mental reservation, I admired the reign of the human" (N, 90; trans. modified, emphasis added). Art, as a form of static representation, is thus fully in league with a doctrine that authorizes an overweening subject (these men are all "leaders," controllers both of other men and of nature).

If the jerks represent the right wing of Third Republic ideology, the Autodidact represents the left. He too, in his presentation of a lofty, synthetic signified ("Man") ignores the swarming multiplicity of everyday life: he too uses larger, abstract terms to represent that which, strictly speaking, is a fiction. The Autodidact does not use representation to project the grandeur of his own destination onto nature – as Kant would have it; instead, he creates both inner unities (the Self) and outer ones (Youth) and then is able to convince himself that they exist. The Autodidact never really is interested in people as individuals (he has no friends), nor does he really notice them; a young couple in a restaurant are of interest only because they represent "Youth," an old man because he represents the dignity of "Old Age," and so on. Yet when Roquentin asks him about the color of the young man's hair, the humanist must turn around and look: he had not even noticed it. Roquentin tells him: "They're only symbols in your eyes" (N, 120).

Just beneath all these lofty images (and obvious to anyone who has the eyes to look) there is, as in the case of the jerks, only the sublime, only formlessness as a lack of inner limitation or definition. The Autodidact believes in "Equality," but his version of the "education" that was so central to a republican ideal of the propagation of a secular morality is child molestation.[6] He substitutes pederasty for pedagogy, and in doing so he gives the lie to the abstraction of his theory. Now his body too exudes dismembered, repulsive, aroused parts, which he can ignore only by being in bad faith: his finger is a "brown hairy object" with the "grossness of a male sex organ" as he attempts to use it to touch the hand of a young boy in the Bouville library (N, 165).

Roquentin's notion of contingency implies more than a critique of a certain philosophical doctrine: it is also, inevitably, a critique of ideology – neo-Kantian idealism and humanism – as it is unconsciously lived in society as a "big lie" that falsifies the way people see nature, society, and themselves. Humanism especially seems almost impossible to escape, according to Roquentin; there are many varieties of it, Catholic, Communist, anarchist, Manichean. There is even an antihumanist humanism, which absorbs and puts to its own use the positions of its enemies. For this reason, Roquentin is unwilling to declare himself against humanism; he will only say that he is not a humanist – "voilà tout" (N, 118).

While I do not want to confuse Roquentin with Sartre, as so many commentators have done, I will nevertheless note that Roquentin's across-the-board critique of bourgeois idealism, in its theories of perception, subjectivity, and morality, can be directly related to Sartre's critique of the neo-Kantianism in vogue, as the official academic philosophy, in France at least until the 1930s. Sartre always characterized this philosophy, usually associated with its most prominent exponent, Léon Brunschvicg, as an "alimentary" (or "digestive") one.[7] Like the jerks and Autodidacts who constitute their subjectivities through a cloying, inward-turning gaze, this mode of thought manages to transmute exterior, independent objects and individuals into dematerialized contents of the mind. As Sartre says in his 1939 essay "A Fundamental Idea in Husserl's Phenomenology: Intentionality," "We have all read Brunschvicg, Lalande and Meyerson, we have all believed that the Mind-Spider drew things into its web, covered them with white goo and slowly swallowed them, reducing them to its own substance. What is a table, a rock, a house? A certain assemblage of 'contents of consciousness,' an ordering of these contents."[8]

We recognize easily enough in Sartre's caricature the Kantian gesture of dissociating the sublime from exterior nature, and resituating it in the mind. Sartre, following Husserl, hopes to reexternalize these objects, thereby cleaning out the mind. Everything is now external: even our fear of an object is due not to the fact that we ourselves are frightened but to the fact that the object itself is inherently frightening ("It is a property of this Japanese mask to be terrifying . . . and not the sum of our subjective reactions to a piece of sculpted wood"). The idealizing of the object is now reversed: in Sartre's version of Husserl, the object stands before us in all its raw specificity. Consciousness – as opposed to the subjectivity of the Kantians – is now defined as a purifying "great wind," the "outside of itself," and "an absolute flight," a "series of explosions that tear us from ourselves" (1H, 40). Consciousness is now always consciousness *of* something; being is always "being-in": "Understand this 'being-in' in the sense of movement. To be is to burst into the world, it is to start from a nothingness of the world and of consciousness in order suddenly to burst-out-consciousness-into-the-world. If consciousness tries to take itself back, to coincide finally with itself, to be warm, with the windows closed, it comes to nothing. . . . Husserl names [this consciousness] 'intentionality'" (IH, 41).

It is easy to see how this dynamic, explosive, clean consciousness (it is highly reminiscent of the 1920s futurist – and Fascist – aesthetic of cold, phallic, forceful machinery) is an alternative to the static, narcissistic, oppressive, and above all abstract subjectivity that Roquentin encounters everywhere in Bouville, that microcosm of republican secular virtues.[9] But a problem appears, one that has much to do with the difference between Roquentin and Sartre. For Sartre, writing his essay on Husserl, the transition from the digestive philosophy to that of dynamism is easy: we recognize that consciousness is really empty, that objects "out there" really are external, lacking the necessity of the inner objects of the mind, and we are then free to intervene actively in a world of resistant matter and other consciousnesses. But Sartre never mentions what we have called "Roquentin's sublime." That experience seems to call into question all possibility of active consciousness – and not merely the Kantian variety. Nature was so external then that its contingency, its lack of congruence with human expectations and desires, seemed to permeate everything and everyone. The "inside" itself was invaded by the limitlessness of the exterior, but the result was not the clean, hard force of explosions: rather it was weakness and perversity, accompanied by the repetitious vomiting of the very slime the Kantian Mind-Spider had seemed to swallow. At the height of the Nausea, "bursting" into the world seemed out of the question for Roquentin. Instead the contingent world had burst into him. Refusing his own earlier bad faith, he saw that he himself, like everyone and everything else, was secreting a series of poorly cloned fragments. How is it possible to go, then, from that recognition (if we can call it that), and its attendant passivity, to the "great wind," the transparency and vigorous activity of consciousness ("in the dry dust of the world, on the rough earth, among things" [IH, 40]) that Sartre reveals in the Husserl essay? How can Roquentin become Sartre – in other words, how can a new consciousness be salvaged out of the ruins of Roquentin's sublime?

II

Perhaps the Nausea can be seen as more, or other than, a dead end; it may serve a useful purpose after all. It does seem to present a kind of phenomenological reduction: after the zero-point in which all internal limits are expelled – the limits of representation, of the subject, of society, of nature and its objects – a new aesthetic and moral practice can be instituted. It may be that, after crossing the barrier of Roquentin's sublime, and through the apparently radical purgation of the consequences of Kantianism that it effects, a consciousness (apparently similar, if not identical, to the one elaborated by Sartre in "A Fundamental Idea in Husserl's Phenomenology") can be elaborated.

The last few pages of *Nausea* are therefore of crucial importance. Roquentin, after abandoning his biography of M. de Rollebon, determines to return to writing. This time, however, he will write a novel, one that will communicate his own life as directly as the song "Some of these Days" communicates the image of the life of its composer (N, 176). After his experience of the sublime, Roquentin has a new moral foundation for aesthetic judgment, a grounding that allows a "communication" between the artist and his listener or reader (the imagined sweating songwriter in New York communicates with Roquentin through the purity of his song): one that makes possible a community based not on the authority of the jerk or the fantasy of the humanist but on the recognition of the freedom of the Other. In other words, this community is based on the awareness that the Other too is an "empty" consciousness, not a substance but the open clarity of its acts (like songwriting) in the world. Aesthetic judgment is therefore inseparable from the establishment of a new rational morality of freedom (a not entirely un-Kantian gesture).

The creative act posited at the end of the novel follows directly from the Nausea; the latter was a purgation (just as nausea is usually associated with vomiting), and the aesthetic experience that follows it seems to involve not the purification of individual moments – that would result only in a bad-faith attempt to live a "necessary life" *in* the painting or song – but, rather, fully in the midst of all the contingency of the world, living with, or suffering with, the artwork that *is* (that has, in other words, itself attained a clarity through the expulsion of its gelatinous, superfluous substance). One's consciousness can only emulate the artwork, somehow actively engaging in a similar performance: "On the other side of existence, in this world which you can see in the distance, but without ever approaching it, a little melody began to sing and dance: 'You must be like me; you must suffer in rhythm'" (N, 175). And for Roquentin, "suffering in rhythm" with the notes of the song means an aesthetic act, writing purgative fictions that would be "beautiful and hard as steel" (N, 178) – that would be, in other words, like the saxophone notes in the song: immutable, pure, "without complacence, without self-pity, with an arid purity" (N, 174).

It was the ground-zero of the Nausea that allowed Roquentin to take stock of his position, recognizing the extent of contingency, recognizing above all the role of representation in the masking of contingency, in the synthesis of a phony necessity that only conformed to "Man's" needs. Metaphor above all enables us, when we are in bad faith, to lie to ourselves and interpret the incoherent elements of the world as useful and dependable. But through the Nausea, the hold of representation is broken: "Black? I felt the word deflating, emptied of meaning with extraordinary rapidity . . . black, like the circle, did not exist" (N, 130).

Words too lose their inner substance, just like all the pompous people and objects of Bouville. Words too are disarticulated existences. Only after their deflation, their catharsis, after representation has been expelled and Roquentin, without words, can "think *on* things, *with* things" (N, 129), can he think *with* the rhythm of the song, *with* a language that, like notes of music, is purified of its stickiness, and is not figurative. This is the only language – an aesthetic one – that does not simply betray the empty but decisive consciousness put forward at the end of Sartre's short piece on Husserl.

Through this new aesthetic standard – by engaging in the production of a timeless and active work of art – Roquentin can move from the subjectless state of sheer contingency in the Nausea to a dynamic consciousness. This forceful agency, like that of the songwriter who turns out "Some of These Days," would animate his life from now on, and would enable him later to look back on it "without repugnance" (N, 178). In fact, some of the clarity of the new aesthetic object "might fall over my past." His entire life would then be thoroughly cleaned out and redeemed, and he would escape, at least in his own consciousness, from the false totality, and opacity, of the jerks.

When we return and reexamine the experience of the Nausea, however, we realize with perhaps a certain amount of surprise that no reduction can in fact take place, because representational language – the language of metaphor – has never really been escaped.[10] Roquentin has misread the nature of his experience: it is not that words deflate; instead, their dominion becomes absolute. Contingency is structured like a figurative language. Any existent is always so weak that it seeps out of itself into what it resembles, and then into another resemblance. Nothing simply "is"; it is always "like" something else. And every object and concept – there is no clear distinction between them – is nothing more than an image. The sickening, deanthropomorphized proliferation of existences is as dependent on metaphor as are the lofty concepts ("Mind," "Rights," etc.) of the jerks and humanists. "Absurdity was not an idea in my head, or the sound of a voice, only this long serpent dead at my feet, this wooden serpent. Serpent or claw or root or vulture's talon, what difference does it make?" (N, 129). But what difference does this seeming omnipresence of metaphor make?

It is hard to imagine how any person – any subjectivity *or* consciousness – could perceive a reality that is untouched by human intervention or language. How can we ever know that nature, or reality, or whatever one wants to call it, is really superfluous, is really structured, if at all, in a way that has nothing to do with the "mobile army" of lying metaphors and the "abstract inventions" (such as sight) that man puts to work in order to create a useful scientific or philosophical truth?[11] How could we ever intelligibly posit a reduction to such a bedrock state of being, let alone experience it? How can we confidently propose the notion of a contingency that would be adequate to such a hetero-geneous being?

This same problem haunts what Sartre calls the "in-itself" in *Being and Nothingness:* the in-itself "knows no otherness: it never posits itself as *other* than another being. It can support no connection with the other. It is itself indefi-nitely and it exhausts itself in being. . . . It is, and when it gives way, one cannot even say that it no longer is."[12] As Vincent Descombes has remarked, there is in fact nothing one can say about this "being" – and it is therefore not advisable to attempt to incorporate, in a coherent philosophy, such a radically unknowable term.[13] Or one can try to write about it, or describe it, as Roquentin does – but then one is *not* writing about the in-itself.

Contingency, like the in-itself, can only be put forward, or can only put itself forward, within the all-too-human realm of representation. The descrip-tion of the contingent world, no matter how scandalous or disordered it may be (in the very materiality of its signifiers as well as in the things it describes) is possible only because it itself is already permeated by metaphor. If words like "claw," "root," and "talon" did not have a relatively stable meaning, if they did not, like all metaphors, willfully and arbitrarily isolate some similarities and ignore others, the representation-regurgitation Roquentin witnesses could not take place. And this isolating and ignoring of similarities can be the product only of a far from disinterested human intervention (not the interven-tion of Man, however; the concept of Man is itself, as Roquentin would be happy to point out, the product of arbitrary and convenient generalizations that ignore the unknowable or ungraspable specificities of things). Perhaps this is why the park smiles at Roquentin when he is leaving (N, 135): there is a secret complicity between them – both are suffused with the human after all. Roquentin, even in his Nausea, has given nature a human face.

This line of argument would seem to refute the assertion that one can experience, or present, a mode of being that is totally alien to human inten-tions. As soon as one attempts to perceive or represent a fundamental con-tingency, one has only established a new, albeit slovenly, army of metaphors. But if the demystifying Nausea at bottom is simply a function of metaphor, then there is no way easily to distinguish Roquentin from the jerks or human-ists who are, as we have seen, also dependent on figurative language and its ultimately idealizing abstractions. Roquentin is a jerk among jerks, because he too thinks that what he is presenting through an arbitrary human construct (the will to power of meaning) is the way things necessarily are; the only difference is that for Roquentin it is contingency itself (represented by its multiplicity of metaphors) that is necessary. (In other words, it is the antihuman that is now replacing "humanity" – and now one is forced to think of Roquentin's observation that antihumanism is just another variety of humanism.)

In the same way, we can recognize that Roquentin's breakdown of "adventures" is dependent on an adventure. Stories are, according to Roquentin, just another way of feeling the necessity of given moments in one's life: adventures play a central role in the maintenance of the fiction of a subject that can confidently gaze at and grasp itself from a fully detached viewpoint. If we imagine life as a story, with beginning, middle, and end, then even the most trivial detail will be necessary for the ultimate denouement. That is why Roquentin gives up his biography of M. de Rollebon: he realizes that, through it, he is attempting only to give his own life the coherence of the abstract, closed form of a dead and unknowable Other, his subject. If narratives cannot be conceived outside the functioning of metaphor, we can see how the difference between Roquentin's activity of reduction and the kind of intellectual activities performed by the jerks and humanists is thrown into question, not only from within – the "existences" themselves in their mutations are simply metaphors – but from without as well: the revelation of Roquentin's sublime is situated within a perfectly comprehensible and conventional narrative.[14] This recognition is, in fact, the climax of a story that tells of the discovery of contingency that has heretofore been suppressed. Roquentin, by recognizing through the Nausea that "there are no more adventures," lives the ultimate adventure.

Roquentin's failure to "reduce" and then expel representation and adventures may be part of a much larger failure – the failure to purge Kant. Roquentin, after his experience of the sublime, turns that negativity outward; by this I mean that he is able to grasp the fundamental significance of "contingency" and put it to work in the affirmation of a consciousness engaged in aesthetic and, finally, moral, activity. The negative internal limitlessness of Roquentin's sublime is now the *power* of catharsis: when it is perceived (in the course of the reduction) it "cleans out" (by demystifying) the stuffy interior of his "necessary" subjectivity, and this same negativity, now that the subjectivity has been transformed into consciousness, can be turned against objects, cleaning them out in turn by giving them hard, pure forms. After this, presumably, this same force can be directed against other subjectivities, and they, through their experience of the art object, can be cleansed as well. The consciousness must emulate the art object ("You must be like me" the rhythm of the song tells Roquentin), spinning like it, producing more art objects, which themselves cut through the muck of other subjectivities, and no doubt inspire them to create as well – and so on to infinity.

Roquentin's incorporation and redirection of his sublime is functionally identical to the fate of the natural sublime in Kant. There it was reason, and not consciousness, that was able to appropriate the frightening power of the sublime. As Donald Pease puts it in an excellent article, "Instead of locating the source of the sublime in its former locus, i.e., in external nature, the imagination redirects the Reason to another locus, within Reason itself, where Reason can re-cognize astonishment as its own power to negate external nature. Through the detour of the sublime, then, Reason realizes the benefits of the negative, a power of destruction underwritten by the power of the Creator Himself, without having had to undergo any specific negation."[15]

The model of the relation between Roquentin's consciousness and what I have called his "sublime" is no different: through his recognition of the sublime in his own consciousness, he experiences an inner limitlessness. This internal lack of limits is no longer situated in impotent objects, but it is transformed into an infinite, always renewed power in consciousness directed against the dead weight of existence. Nothing could be further, it would seem, from the weak, melting, viscous tree root than the hard, arid force of the performance of "Some of These Days." The crucial difference, of course, is consciousness, which now directs the purgative power of the sublime. The indefinitely proliferating metaphors of contingent existence – replicating themselves through the infinite process of autopurgation – have been tamed and put to work: now metaphor is an employee of consciousness, devoted to the task of novel writing. Amorphous, feeble purgation has itself been purged; consciousness is now a powerful, higher-order force of catharsis.

It might be objected that, unlike Kant, Roquentin posits an "empty" consciousness, devoid of any higher, illusory attributes, such as Kantian reason. This is certainly true, but we might recall that, for Kant, the sublime was always already a function of the imagination (in its relation to reason). It only erroneously assumed the sublime was outside it, an attribute of nature. We can say something along the same lines about Roquentin's sublime for a very simple reason: his consciousness, if not his imagination, must have been there all along, from the start of the novel. Certainly it was not created ex nihilo by his experience of the Nausea. Consciousness was perhaps misinterpreted, but it was nevertheless responsible, on some level, for Roquentin's acts and judgments. It was, at least in his case, from the first a force of refusal, of exclusion: of the local society, of M. de Rollebon, of adventures, even of Anny. The Nausea too was a purgation of illusion, a sacrificial liquidation, but it was not a moment of creation; it was a recognition of the omnipresence and omnipotence of purgation, albeit in the form of a proliferating series of undirected, and therefore weak, micropurgations. In other words, it was a recognition of the universality of the very power that (in another, this time truly significant, form) characterizes Roquentin's consciousness. Creation – at least aesthetic

97

creation – could take place only *after* the moment of total reduction and total realization. For this reason, we would have to see the Nausea as nothing more than a device by which the consciousness comes to reaffirm itself by seeing a representation of its own power in nature, recognizing itself for what it is, thereby acceding to its negative, but also infinitely formative, power. In other words, through Roquentin's version of the sublime, consciousness comes to recognize what it always was (and it recognizes it with a certain amount of delight; Roquentin seems quite enthusiastic about his new aesthetic project at the end of the novel). Contingency may have been radically exterior (in its very interiority), but at the same time its real significance is to be found exclusively in the role it plays in relation to consciousness itself.

Roquentin, then, may be not only a jerk but the final savior of neo-Kantianism. We must consider the possibility that Roquentin is not only Sartre's spokesman and hero, but his nemesis as well. By "Sartre" here I do not mean the historical, biographical figure so much as the name one associates with the narrator of all those philosophical works, including popularized ones such as "A Fundamental Idea in Husserl's Phenomenology." This figure of "Sartre" posited as well a consciousness which would, in Peter Caws's expression, "turn spontaneity into project . . . accept contingency and . . . ride it, as it were, rather as one might ride a wave."[16] But Roquentin's joyride on the wave of contingency may not be the same as Sartre's: Roquentin finally assigns a necessity to the works he will create, even yearns for a new adventure (N, 178), and evidently regresses to a point not far from the one he occupied at the beginning of the novel. This is only one more indication, then, that perhaps Roquentin has only situated himself in yet another version of an all-powerful metaphoricity, of a relentless neo-Kantianism. It is possible that Roquentin represents Sartre's depiction or dramatization of the possible pitfalls of his own method.

In this light perhaps another reading of *Nausea* is possible as well: the surrealist-inspired sadomasochistic images, for example (see N, 157–59), link Roquentin not so much to the clean, empty, "uncompromising" explosion of Sartrean consciousness as with the attempts by writers Sartre opposed, people like Bataille, Artaud, and Breton, to formulate a kind of modern secular sacred experience, founded on sacrifice. But while, for Bataille, the heterogeneous force of disgusting matter is powerful and liberating, for Roquentin it is weakness itself; he explicitly rules out the "will to power" as an attribute of his version of the sublime. Roquentin from this perspective is nothing more than a caricature of a weak-willed neo-surrealist who, even when he imagines his own consciousness to be a forceful one, is only engaging in wish fulfillment (the great story will always be written, the great adventure will always be lived, some of these days).

We cannot say, however, that Sartre is just ironically presenting Roquentin's self-formation in order to demonstrate its error – this is his strategy later, in short stories like "Erostrate" and "Childhood of a Leader," whose main characters are versions of Sartre's perennial bugaboo, the surrealist-homosexual-Fascist. After all, the urtexts of *Nausea* were a number of fragments on contingency that Sartre wrote in the early 1930s, whose implications for his own philosophy he apparently took quite seriously.[17] Where then does Sartre stand in all this? Is Roquentin his spokesman or his victim? Where does his complicity with his character begin and end? And, perhaps most important, can Sartre, unlike Roquentin, propose an alternative to the model of representation (i.e., figurative rhetoric) that seems to put Roquentin in complicity with his enemies? Perhaps there is, inscribed in the text, a model for reading *against* Roquentin which nevertheless retains for Sartre the most important elements of Roquentin's effort – that is, the affirmation, or at least the promise, of aesthetic activity, the possibility of a certain radical reduction, and even an emptying-out of involuted subjectivity.

III

While it is true that the song "Some of These Days" is in a certain sense ideal, not existing because "it has nothing superfluous" and because it cuts through layers of contingency – rising above even the wear and tear on the phonograph record in whose grooves it resides – at the same time it is wholly dependent on what we might call a mechanized base: the phonograph record, the needle, the motor of the phonograph. Roquentin himself recognizes this, when he writes of the spinning "little jeweled pain" – the immaculate, rhythmic suffering of the saxophone notes of the song – as a "scythe . . . cutting through the drab intimacy of the world" (N, 174). The cleanness, the "arid purity" of this suffering might stand as a model for the emptied-out consciousness – removed as it is from the messiness of everyday life and engaged in negating it and transforming it – but, at the same time, the metaphors Roquentin uses to describe this suffering come not from any model of an active consciousness but from the mechanical model of the phonograph. If Roquentin is to transform himself and "be" like the song, "suffering with it in rhythm" as he creates, he will somehow have to conform not so much to great acts of human creation – like the creation of "Some of These Days" by the songwriter in New York – as to the mechanical repetition of a machine.

The song rhythm, slicing cleanly and actively through the muck of daily life, also bears a message, one that would at least at first seem to have little to do with machines: it is a promise. Some of these days, you'll miss me . . . I promise you. These last words, of course, are not contained in the actual lyrics of the song as Roquentin transmits them, but they are nevertheless implied: someday, you'll miss me, and I hope that you will; I am not so much unemotionally predicting it as *promising* it as a future I desperately want, even if you don't. But what I promise is not a substance, not a realization or even something that could be realized; it is only a negative term, the lack of coincidence or completion: you'll miss me. The promise proposes not a definitive state, but a void; it is, therefore, a promise that can never *simply* be fulfilled (though it still is a promise), because what it promises is the very absence of the fulfillment of the promise. Of course "missing" something is a significant theme in the novel: Roquentin will miss his girlfriend, Anny; he might even miss his former life of vicarious adventures. Above all, he will miss the song itself: he will miss its "beauty" after he leaves Bouville, but in another sense he will miss its promise. The little melody tells him "You must be like me" – you must *be* rather than *exist* – but the melody *is* as a promise: the lyrics therefore promise that Roquentin will miss it in trying to be like it. Or, conversely, the only way he can be like it is to miss it, or at least to promise to miss fulfilling the promise. The promise of Roquentin's "being like" the song must incessantly be repeated, and incessantly broken, at the instant of its fulfillment. But how can the song not be missed? Roquentin realizes this himself when, on p. 175, he recognizes that he cannot get "into" the song, he cannot live it as if it were a phantasmic adventure. He can only be like it, in rhythm. He can, in other words, be like it only by promising, which is what he does: he promises to write a novel, not in so many words (for he misses a simple promise), but he promises in the ellipses of a formulation: "Couldn't I try. . . . Naturally, it wouldn't be a question of a tune . . . but couldn't I, in another medium? . . . It would have to be a book: I don't know how to do anything else" (N, 178).

There may be a rationale in this promise; after all, in *this* book, the account of his Nausea, Roquentin has missed his goal: he has not suffered with the song, he has not "been" like it. He can only promise that he will do better next time; in the future his reduction will not be a sham, he really will escape representation, adventures, the neo-Kantianism of his own sublime, and so forth. It seems, however, that Roquentin is caught in a double bind: if he carries out his promise, and "is" like the song, he will only miss it – in other words, he will still be stuck in metaphor (for on the simplest level the song is a promise that cannot be fulfilled: it promises that it will be missed). On the other hand, if he does not attempt to emulate the song, he will certainly be no different from a jerk. How then can he "suffer with" the song and "miss it" at the same time, without simply falling into that which the song is not? . . . Perhaps what is most important here is not *what* Roquentin is promising, but *that* he is promising. The repetitious act of promising alone may somehow remain faithful to (while also "missing") the rhythm of the hard, mechanical tones of the song.

The promise is not a function of a figurative rhetoric; it does not represent, but it performs an act. Paul de Man, in his writing on Rousseau, noted that the performative aspect of rhetoric must be identified not with referential meaning, with figurative rhetoric, but with the mechanical repetitions of a grammar.[18] Grammar operates independently of reference, and in that way it is machinelike. "The system of relationships that generates the text and that functions independently of its referential meaning is its grammar. To the extent that a text is grammatical, it is a logical code or a machine" (AR, 268).

Perhaps the true alternative to the Nausea lies not in the content of what Roquentin proposes, in any given project or genre of writing, but in his act of proposing it: it lies in the rhetoric of the speech act. This mechanical movement cannot be seen, however, as offering an alternative model for consciousness, one that would cleanse it while freeing it from the inert, inward-turning existence that the jerks habitually project onto it. We must recall that intentionality in Husserl, as Sartre presented it, was a function of the activity of consciousness, even if that consciousness was stripped of its ability to "coincide with itself." In the positing of the repetitions of the speech act, on the other hand, consciousness and its activity can have no fundamental role. (Consciousness is only an aftereffect of the act.) For that reason, the phonographic mechanism is a figure not only of the rhythm of an aridly pure suffering (and, it would appear, pleasure), but of the operation of a rhetoric that precludes figuration and renders all consciousness radically contingent. This is a final destruction of the anthropomorphic: we are left not with gluey fragments, nor with a dynamic, explosive, creative force, but with the resonance of air vibrations in and through repeated empty promises. Consciousness has been opened out or emptied, to be sure – but a bit too far this time, all the way to the ahuman. The purgative strength of consciousness has itself been purged by an even stronger force: grammar. Along with an abstracting representational language, then, the very possibility of any purposeful language has been lost. One problem is solved: Roquentin is no longer a jerk – but only at the cost of another one: Roquentin's consciousness "is" no longer.

If it is not a question here of the simple replacement of one kind of adventure with another, or of a model of subjectivity with one of consciousness, it is because the conflict we see between figurative and performative language cannot be resolved within rhetoric itself. At the same time, in *Nausea* these two irreconcilable alternatives are dependent on each other: the significance of Roquentin's adventure in the park (the Nausea) depends on the final promise to give it meaning (it is a necessary stage on the way to the resolution, the promise, to write a novel). His quest, his travail, now has a meaning, even if that meaning is a leap into the unknowable and ungraspable (the performative) as a way of "resolving" his dilemma and dodging the seemingly inescapable figurative language. The novel has a teleology after all: his final promise, or excuse, gives all that comes before it stability and significance. Each event can now rest secure in its value – and the leap into the speech act thereby takes on a meaning as well. But this comfortable mutual dependence is disrupted when we recall that the speech act is the product not of a teleology that is dependent on human intentions and retrospection, but on the machine functioning of the grammatical apparatus. As de Man puts it, "There can be no text without grammar; the logic of grammar generates texts only in the absence of referential meaning, but every text generates a referent that subverts the grammatical principle to which it owed its constitution" (AR, 269). We can easily reverse this formulation; we can also say that texts are dependent on reference but that that reference necessitates a grammar – that is, a mechanical functioning that undermines the principle of representation. Grammar and meaning are therefore "fundamentally incompatible," but at the same time each generates and depends on the other. This is certainly the case at the end of *Nausea;* the leap into the speech act (the absent but necessary "I will write a novel") is dependent on the narrative that precedes it, is the fulfillment of it – and, at the same time, in the leap's mechanical movement, its arbitrary positing, it is the violation of the possibility of any adventure or narrative that fulfills its promise by retroactively giving "meaning" to discrete events. And yet the performative in turn is the promise to generate always more novels, more adventures!

This way of looking at the end of *Nausea* answers the question so often posed: does the "aesthetic project" promise the writing of another novel or refer back to the writing of this one? Textual proof can be adduced for both positions, but our preceding discussion would tend to indicate that, though incompatible, both are necessary.[19] Roquentin escapes the metaphorical systems of the jerks/humanists only to fall into his own. By resolving this vicious circle, represented by the Nausea, the novel, through the posited speech act, validates itself as a completed adventure and thereby makes its own writing possible, indeed mandates it. Here Sartre is clearly following in the wake of Proust, while parodying him (the Nausea is a savage-enough lampoon of the link between sense experience and recollection-representation-totalization).[20] At the same time, the very performative-mechanical aspect of the "resolution" of the dead end represented by the Nausea in the park precludes any retrospective movement, any totalization of narrative through self-reflexivity and closure. Because of this, the "promise" of the aesthetic project always requires the writing of another work. Thus the novel to be written is *Nausea* itself, and it is another; these two alternatives, each necessary and each rendering the other impossible, coexist, as Roquentin would say, like two cats in a leather bag.

Here we might recall the necessary distinction between Roquentin the narrator and Sartre the author. Even if Roquentin falls victim to the illusions of the writing of new "adventures" (which are not different in kind from the earlier ones he condemned), might not Sartre, through the mechanism of the speech act, be able to free aesthetic practice from the grip of a neo-Kantianism? Roquentin, evidently, has reached a higher-level dead end; has Sartre? Perhaps not; it is true that Sartre went on to write other novels, and his later performances are not merely instances of a repetitious grammar. In fact in future works of fiction, contingency comes to be fully politicized: bad faith is associated not only with decaying surrealism but with fascism and betrayal. This is already apparent in "Childhood of a Leader" and becomes even clearer in the last fragments of *The Roads of Freedom* (which are examined in the next chapter). Sartre by the late 1940s was a Marxist (if not a card-carrying Communist), and the project of a dynamic, transparent consciousness, through whose activity the human is constituted (as we learn in the postwar essay "Existentialism Is a Humanism"), cannot be separated from a dialectical interplay of individual judgment and collective action. It is worth noting, though, that these dialectics cannot be derived dialectically from the earlier undecidability of performative and figurative language, of textual repetition and closure, of the repetitious fulfillment and betrayal of the promise, which we see at the end of *Nausea*. The arrival of a progressive, dialectical political movement after *Nausea* can itself be the result only of a speech act, a promise: "I will engage in a dialectical project." The decision itself is the result of a performative, and as such it only mechanically repeats the speech-act "resolution" of the end of *Nausea*. It acts as a closure, a resolution, to the problem of commitment that was already evident in *Nausea;* but as a resolution-promise it is opened out to sheer repetition.

The attempt to replace a naive Roquentin with a more "aware" Sartre who would situate contingency properly after Roquentin's failure to escape metaphors and adventures is doomed to failure.[21] While it is true that the performative is the only radical alternative to representation and the legacy of neo-Kantianism (and in this sense it generates an authorial figure who poses a problem that it "solves"), at the same time the performative precludes an active, responsible writing consciousness that we could associate with the name Sartre. An aware Sartre would be just another jerk.

4

The Impossible
Conclusion of Sartre's
Roads of Freedom

IN THE PREVIOUS chapter, we saw a crucial problem facing Sartre: how does one go about affirming an active consciousness in the world while politicizing contingency? *Nausea* ends with an apparent "aesthetic" solution, which would seem to entail a mutual transparency of communicating subjects, made possible through the creation and experience of the artwork. Yet, as we have seen, the aesthetic "subjectivity" (if we can call it that) affirmed at the end of *Nausea* is highly problematic. One possible road open to Sartre could be found not only in the politicization of contingency (which is notable already in "Childhood of a Leader") but in the restructuring of catharsis. In some of his later writings, which I will examine in this chapter and the next, Sartre attempts to transform the microcatharsis of the Nausea and the catharsis of the aesthetic experience (the purgative effect of listening to music and writing) into a fully sacrificial catharsis that is an indispensable part of radical social change and the constitution of revolutionary groups. In this he follows quite clearly in the thesis-novel tradition that includes, as we have already seen, Nizan and Drieu. But he also effects a major revision of that tradition, in that one of his main goals is to tie the narration to a rigorous, ongoing critique of an established philosophy (Marxism) and its institutional application (the Communist party). Both Nizan (implicitly) and Drieu (explicitly) had questioned the efficacy and co-herence of the sacrificial-narrative model, but neither had really investigated or attempted to alter the ideologemes (in Nizan's case, Marxist-populist, in Drieu's, Fascist) on the basis of which they established their versions of that model. From Sartre's perspective, then, a crucial problem lies in the elaboration of a revision of an established doctrine or party and the coordination of that revision with a sacrifice that contributes to it and results from it.

I

Sartre never completed his proposed series of four novels, *The Roads of Freedom* (*Les Chemins de la liberté*).[1] The original intent of the series was to show the growing, or maturing, political commitment of a number of characters – chief among them being Mathieu Delarue, a French schoolteacher and intellectual – through life in prewar Paris, the fighting of May and June 1940, internment in a prisoner-of-war camp, and finally life in Occupied Paris. The final, never-to-be-completed fourth volume – projected when the third volume, *Death in the Soul* (*La Mort dans l'âme*) was published – was then to have taken the reader up to the Liberation, with the various factions of the Resistance united and in power. Mathieu himself was to have died bravely under torture during the Occupation, but even his death was meant to be a kind of victory, signaling his gesture of "making himself a hero," certainly a big change from the impotent and self-mutilating peacetime bachelor we see in the first volume, *The Age of Reason*.[2] Most important, Mathieu's politics were to be a version of a Popular Front agenda that once again seemed possible during and immediately after the Occupation, when a broad spectrum of groups – from the Communists to the Gaullists – fought together to defeat the Germans.

The Roads of Freedom was to be both a thesis novel and a roman à clef: the leading character, Mathieu, was never meant to be anything other than a thinly veiled portrait of the very public Sartre himself (as he was, and as he hoped to be). Personal development – the evolution of Mathieu during the war years – would exactly parallel political developments in the *postwar* period – the epoch of the novel's publication and consumption; the maturation process of Mathieu in the camp, through which he joined his "bourgeois" (but necessary) individual independence to a strict, selfless political commitment, was to be mirrored after the war by the society at large, which would, in its government, be melding the Socialists, who advocated and respected subjective autonomy, with the Communists, who were the embodiment of the solidarity of the proletariat and who were models of revolutionary discipline. Sartre, in other words, clearly hoped his novel would prefigure as well as make possible the definitive accession to power of a united, libertarian left in the postwar period.

Perhaps part of the problem that Sartre faced was to be found in this effort to bring together thesis novel and roman à clef. The distinction between these two semigenres, in fact, is not so different from the distinction that Sartre was attempting to resolve in his novel: on the one hand, "objective truth" and communism (the thesis novel); on the other, subjective experience and initiative (the roman à clef). True to the traditions of the thesis novel, Sartre wanted to show not only the problems facing his characters but the revolutionary acts and moments of obedience needed for progressive change: his characters thus had to serve as emblems of various larger political positions and social classes.

On the other hand, as a roman à clef, the novels were to maintain a high level of verisimilitude: they were to show specific, autonomous persons, as they really were, with their capacity for free choice but also with their contingent moments of senseless cowardice and bad faith.

At a certain point the two strands, the two genres of novel, were to coincide, and not just in fiction, but, necessarily, in reality: Sartre, like Mathieu, would be a committed but fully independent intellectual, carrying out a vital task in the world, and there would be a context in which his commitment would be meaningful: an influential party would embody the seemingly impossible union of independent responsibility and selfless discipline, of subjectivity and objectivity.

That juncture point, however, proved to be elusive. Sartre was unable to live personally in a postwar world that followed a model, worked out in his thesis novel, based on a romanticization of Resistance politics and action under the Occupation. In fact Sartre abandoned the political party he founded in the late 1940s with, among others, David Rousset, Georges Altmann, and Jean Rous – the RDR, the Revolutionary Democratic Assembly – when, instead of maintaining a "third course" between Russia and the United States, it veered toward the Americans. In the same way, it is possible to argue that Sartre was unable to finish *The Roads of Freedom* because the future was not following a plan mandated by the novels: instead of a union of Socialists and Communists, and the discovery of some middle ground between them, the postwar period saw only the breakup of the pre-Liberation (clandestine) alliance of the Left, and the abandonment of the dream of another Popular Front government (the dream of reenacting the euphoria of June 1936 would continue to be an important one for Sartre, and it goes a long way toward explaining his enthusiasm for the student rebels of May 1968). And, on the subjective level, the difficulties Sartre had with the Communist party in the period from 1946 to 1950 indicated the impossibility of living Mathieu's life, of joining strong commitment and autonomous judgment. (This was about the time a Communist writer dubbed Sartre "a hyena with a typewriter.") The last two installments of the projected fourth volume, provisionally entitled *Drôle d'amitié* (Strange friendship) were published in *Les Temps Modernes* in November and December 1949. After that, Sartre abandoned the project.

Sartre's great novel series, then, became nothing more than an exercise in wish fulfillment. The cold war was intensifying, and it became impossible to imagine a future for a socialist, independent France, in bondage neither to the United States nor to the Soviet Union. In the same way, it was also impossible to imagine an independent, committed French intellectual of the Left steering a path between selfish individualism and Communist orthodoxy and conformity.

The recently published *Oeuvres romanesques* of Sartre, a critical edition that includes many hitherto unpublished fragments and notes, throws new light on *The Roads of Freedom:* in addition to reprinting the fragments of *Drôle d'amitié* from *Les Temps Modernes,* the editors have published for the first time the contents of a notebook misplaced by Sartre and only recently rediscovered, which contains a number of further chapters, all admittedly in a rough state, of this work. They have grouped them under the title *La Dernière Chance* (The last chance), the title Sartre himself most often used when referring to the final volume as a whole.[3]

The problem is this: how do these fragments of the ill-fated fourth volume attempt to resolve the conflict between the individual and discipline, a conflict that is not separable from the much larger, indeed international, conflict between capitalism and communism? Their reading indicates that it is not enough to explain the failure of Sartre's project by simply invoking inauspicious historical circumstances and implying that they "caused" Sartre to relinquish his task. We might say that the external conditions Sartre faced must *necessarily* be cited to explain the failure of his project but that, at the same time, they are not *sufficient* to explain it. For, of course, by 1949 Sartre was no longer attempting to write *with* events but *against* them. The text of the novel thus had to bear the full weight of an ideological mediation that could not (yet) be carried out in practice. If the despair of the late 1940s was the undoing of *The Roads of Freedom,* it was also, at least as far as the last volume was concerned, the condition of its genesis: on a phantasmic level the text was working to resolve the terrible contradiction between not only capitalism and communism but also between subjective volition and objective determinism – the latter a dilemma that, not coincidentally, also haunted Sartre's philosophical writings (such as *Being and Nothingness*).[4]

How then does the work attempt to resolve these contradictions? What are the strategies it uses in its labor of purely imaginary synthesis? It may be through the text itself, then, and through its various gambits, that the failure of Sartre's greatest novelistic project can best be understood; assuming the simple predominance of "external" events, at the expense of the ideological labor of mediation that goes on within the novel, ignores the very impetus behind Sartre's project – the inescapability of an independent affirmation of freedom through fighting or writing in difficult situations.

Sartre's larger goal in the last half of *Death in the Soul,* the third volume of *The Roads of Freedom,* is to show the necessity of an independent, "third" force by depicting the crisis faced by a French Communist leader, Brunet, who is attempting to organize POWs in a German camp (located in France) after the capitulation in 1940. We see Brunet slowly forming a dedicated group of activists out of the undifferentiated mass of prisoners. In this he is aided by another POW, Schneider, who seems to be an intellectual but whose background and motives are not clear (he is not a Communist). As the novel ends, the prisoners are on a train, leading, as some of them think, to an assembly point in France, and freedom; Brunet, however, knows it will lead to a prolonged captivity in Germany. He also knows that organizing the men politically will be possible only when they realize that they are to be prisoners for a long time. As long as they think liberation is at hand, they will be concerned exclusively with their private lives: only when they realize they are to remain POWs, and forced laborers, will they think about larger goals such as collective liberation. As the novel ends, the train has turned in the direction of Germany, and Brunet sees that he will have a job to do after all.

In the opening pages of *Drôle d'amitié,* Brunet, Schneider, and other POWs are in the camp in Germany. Five or six months have passed since the fateful train ride depicted at the end of *Death in the Soul.* Brunet seems to have been fairly successful in his organizing, if only because the men now appear to have a sense of purpose as they carry out their assigned daily tasks. (Their activities have given them a political education, but it is very hard to see how they are leading to the downfall of the Nazis.) Brunet has used the men's nationalism as a basis for organizing them. Sooner or later the Soviet Union will enter the war; every prisoner must consider himself a soldier in the war. Moreover, Pétain had no right to sign the armistice; sovereignty comes from the people alone (OR, 1490).

But since being taken prisoner, Brunet has been out of contact with what remains of the PCF leadership in Paris (the story is set in early 1941, after the fall of France but before the Nazi invasion of the Soviet Union). Suddenly another Communist leader appears, Chalais; he is a former member of parliament who was drafted, and then taken prisoner; he has only just arrived in Germany, so he is aware of the most recent positions of the party, which has gone underground. Brunet is astonished to learn that the party has not sanctioned anti-Fascist activities; on the contrary, the underground Communist newspaper *L'Humanité* has even praised workers who have been friendly to German soldiers. There is talk of legalizing the party and *L'Humanité,* and negotiations are under way. Chalais, who is a party theoretician with no experience in political organizing (unlike Brunet), is horrified to learn that Brunet has been using antifascism as a tool to organize the prisoners. After some consideration, he gives Brunet his orders: Brunet must step down as leader of his group, because his methods and teachings have violated the party line (OR, 1498). The unit he has formed will remain dormant; Chalais will hold regular classes on the history of the party and on Marxist doctrine.

The result of all this is that Brunet's organization collapses. The men are bored by Chalais's teaching, yet Brunet cannot even meet with them to answer their questions. Nor can Brunet disobey Chalais; Chalais's rank in the party is higher than his, and the functioning of the party depends not on one's individual initiative but on the obedience with which orders are carried out. We see here the paradox of Stalinist communism, a paradox that is also to be found in Arthur Koestler's *Darkness at Noon:* often the only way that the Communist can be faithful to the party is by not doing the very work that would be in the interest of the workers. If we are to believe Chalais, Brunet should never have used nationalism and antifascism to organize the prisoners in the first place; but without these tools it is clear that Brunet would never have been able to bring the men together at all (in fact there seem to be very few Communists in the camp; most of the ex-soldiers Brunet organizes lean to the Left, and they respond well to his Popular Front–era rhetoric of antifascism). This becomes clear when Brunet's organization starts to fall apart after Chalais takes over.

Brunet's dilemma is heightened when it turns out that Schneider, his second-in-command, is none other than Vicarios, the editor of a leftist paper in Oran who broke with – and criticized – the PCF after the Hitler-Stalin pact. Chalais immediately recognizes him when the two meet (OR, 1481). Vicarios, after publishing several editorials against the pact, had quit the party and then joined the army.

Brunet immediately drops Vicarios from his clandestine group. The party has declared him a traitor, and put out a *mise-en-garde* against him: he is to be avoided by all party members, literally like the plague. In the party there is solidarity; outside it there can only be an isolation as total as death.

But Brunet comes to recognize that he may be in greater solidarity with Vicarios than with Chalais. The paradox of communism is now situated in the very being of Brunet: he, an extremely capable organizer, can loyally serve communism only by vanishing, or by killing himself (which Chalais subtly suggests). Even if he wants to help Chalais, he has come to represent, for the other prisoners, the deviation of his obsolete, 1930s Popular Front line (the very fact that he worked with radicals and unaffiliated socialists like Schneider indicates the nature of his deviation). Chalais tells him: "You have to understand that you are burned up. If you silence yourself, if you hide, you still retain an unfortunate authority. But if you talk, if you tell them what I've been telling them, they will laugh in your face" (OR, 1512). Even if Brunet attempts to adopt the message of Chalais, the men will not believe him – or, worse yet, they will see that he is only taking orders.

Like Rubashov in *Darkness at Noon,* Brunet realizes that in his being there is a resistant element, a contingency, that refuses the necessity of the abstract doctrine that has been imposed from above and that in practice must be obeyed. His thoughts constantly return: if the party is wrong . . . if the Soviet Union is beaten; these are independent thoughts, thoughts that he himself is coming up with, that are not simply elements of a doctrine that he is implementing.

This is in violent contrast to Brunet's former opinion of the role of his "self." Earlier, in the second part of *Death in the Soul,* he had told Schneider: "I have complete confidence in him [Stalin], yes, and in Molotov and Zhdanov – as much confidence as you have in the solidity of the walls. In other words, I know that history has its laws. . . . I think no more about them than you do about the foundations of your house; my knowledge is the floor under my feet and the roof over my head" (OR, 1423).[5] If one doubts, one asserts one's independence, one's ability to judge apart from the correct, official determinations: one asserts one's *self.* For Communists, however, there is no self: thus when Chalais confronts Brunet with the new party line, and they argue, Chalais makes it clear that their personal opinions and judgments are not at stake: "Don't deceive yourself; we are not in the process of debating our positions. I had contacts when you didn't; I'm informing you, and that's all. Neither your self nor mine [*ni ta personne ni la mienne*] is involved" (OR, 1494).

Brunet, formerly the staunchest supporter of unquestioning political labor, now must confront the possibility that he is a traitor not only because he did not follow the party line (and whether he wanted to or not is irrelevant: it is the effect that counts) but because he doubts, and what he doubts is the wisdom of the party's condemnation of his doubt. Without the party, however, he is completely alone; the very subordination of one's self to the party (which amounts, in fact, to the self's elimination) guarantees a solidarity with it (and in it) that cannot be found anywhere else.

Brunet in a sense projects his fear of his own doubt onto Vicarios when he accepts the party's judgment that Vicarios is a traitor. The difference between an actual traitor who provides information to the enemy and an intellectual traitor who simply doubts the party's wisdom is moot; both *result* in the same thing. Brunet accuses Vicarios of being exactly what, according to Chalais, Brunet himself is: a kind of living sign that is the embodiment of doubt and betrayal. Vicarios's personal beliefs are irrelevant; what counts is that he, through his very presence, is a demoralizing force for the party comrades (OR, 1516–17).

Brunet, however, comes to recognize his solidarity with Vicarios, a solidarity of the damned. Vicarios reminds Brunet that he is not "really" a traitor; he disagreed with party policy, but he did not sell secrets. "It is not the same crime." Suddenly Brunet assents to Vicarios's denial of the charge; in a moment of radical doubt he realizes that Vicarios is innocent or, put another way, that he himself is as innocent or as guilty as Vicarios. He had needed Vicarios to be a traitor, because if Vicarios is not, the party is wrong and solidarity between men is impossible. "*If the party is wrong, all men are alone.* All men are alone, if you are not a traitor. . . . Brunet stares at the pale face of Vicarios; his own face is what he sees. . . . All men are alone, Vicarios and Brunet are alike" (OR, 1517).

Brunet ceases to blame Vicarios for the isolation of men; Vicarios is no longer a scapegoat, and Brunet recognizes himself in Vicarios. At that moment of true solidarity, there is a paradoxical recognition that all men are fundamentally alone, without the authoritarian and dogmatic control of the party. The two men are brothers in their solitude. Once this new solidarity is established, Brunet decides to violate the party directive and try to escape with Vicarios. We now see a community or fusion more profound than any established within a party. This is a community of people who recognize that solidarity has meaning only if acts are engaged in freely, on one's own responsibility. For thinking individuals – for men – like Brunet and Vicarios, blind obedience is impossible.

These two are not just engaged in a common goal: they are doubles, almost two sides of the same sundered self. Vicarios is deviation, Brunet orthodoxy, yet within each of them there is the same tension between orthodoxy and deviation. Their "selves," such as they are, are precisely this tension. And the larger self they discover between them is itself based on a tension between faith and doubt, discipline and rebellion. Vicarios, even though a "traitor," originally fastened himself onto Brunet (when they were still in the first POW camp in France) because he was "tired of being alone" (OR, 1485). But now that kind of solidarity is impossible; the strict party discipline is a thing of the past. The human bond is one of the acceptance of discipline *and* disloyalty, the latter necessitated by the individual responsibility one must inevitably take for one's own actions.

The end of *Drôle d'amitié* is, however, somewhat confusing. Brunet and Vicarios decide to escape, but someone has alerted the Germans; Vicarios is shot and killed, and Brunet is recaptured. It appears that they have been betrayed by Chalais, who was hoping to get rid of the two traitors before they further demoralized the men. Does this mean that Sartre, the author of this thesis novel, was simply rejecting communism and party discipline? It would seem so: within the fiction, neither Vicarios nor Brunet can survive in the party, and the only real community lies outside of it. But to take this position means the total abandonment of the party, and of communism itself, a step that Sartre in 1949 was clearly unwilling to take. (Indeed in the novel the attempt to escape to the outside fails.) It is evident from Brunet's and Vicarios's organizing activity in the POW camp that meaningful acts can take place only when ends justify means, when individual wills are subordinated to larger determinations, and when men can take orders. Where, then, does one draw the line? When does one accept or refuse discipline? Brunet balks at following all the party directives, yet he expects obedience from his men when he assigns them tasks. When should one doubt, and who should doubt? These questions are left unresolved at the end of the last published chapters, and indeed it is hard to see how they could be resolved.

We might see the community between Vicarios and Brunet as one of productive tension, but the refusal of communism raises an unresolved issue: to what extent must one subordinate oneself? This question was not one limited to Sartre's fiction, of course; the years 1948–52 were years in which Sartre changed from a stance highly critical of the party (the play *Dirty Hands,* 1948) to one of solidarity and support (*The Communists and the Peace,* 1952). The new affirmation of the party (Sartre never joined it, however) is registered in the last, aborted fragments of *The Roads of Freedom,* aptly titled *La Dernière Chance.*

It is clear from these last sections, and especially from the long, final one (OR, 1628–54), that Sartre cautiously reevaluated his stance toward the party. Indeed if *Drôle d'amitié* can be seen as a fictionalized depiction of the harshness of the French Communist party in the late 1940s – in essence, the situation of 1949 projected onto that of 1941 – then *La Dernière Chance* can be seen as a novelization of Sartre's new affirmation of the party in the early 1950s: this time 1952 is projected onto 1941. (These fragments, according to the editors of the *Oeuvres romanesques,* may in fact have been written as late as 1952 [OR, 2137].) It turns out that the traitor who spilled the beans to the Germans was not Chalais, the loyal Communist, but the minor character Moûlu, another POW. (Moûlu's sole motivation, it would seem, was that he was offered gold-tipped cigarettes by the Germans [OR, 1648].) Moûlu is summarily strangled and thrown into a toilet.[6] Chalais, vindicated, is also disposed of; while Brunet was recovering from the wounds received in the escape attempt, Chalais, along with some other Communists, was denounced (also by Moûlu) and shipped off. The plot is now free to move into a new phase. Brunet returns to the camp to find the Communists vindicated and Mathieu, the bourgeois intellectual hero, in charge of an escape network in the camp. Mathieu, presumed dead fighting off hordes of Germans at the end of the first part of *Death in the Soul* (OR, 1344), in fact survived this epic battle; he suddenly reappears and is now a changed man, because he has killed. This gesture of killing seems to have almost magically transformed him; no longer is he the impotent philosophy teacher who has a crush on one of his students, chases her all over Paris, and finally stabs himself in the hand (*The Age of Reason*). Now he is a man of action. This Sartrean Mittyesque wish fulfillment (the meek philosophy teacher as hardened non-Communist Resistance fighter) is less interesting than the transformation of the Vicarios/Brunet relation into the Mathieu/Brunet relation. If

Vicarios was unsure of his relation to the party, there is no doubt in Mathieu's mind: *he* is outside the party and its discipline. He helps men escape not for doctrinaire reasons but only as an affirmation of their freedom. He tells Brunet: "We are opportunities, steppingstones, we do not judge, we demand nothing from them in exchange for our services, not even that they be good republicans. We belong to everyone. Isn't that what you always, basically, wanted: to be the opportunity for the freedom of others?" (OR, 1646).

Mathieu, however, recognizes his incompleteness because he is not able – and not willing – to join the party. At the same time, though, he counsels Brunet to remain a member, fighting for change from within. Brunet observes, quite rightly, that this cannot be done: one does not debate within the party. He tells Mathieu: "You take the Communist party to be a Radical-Socialist convention" (OR, 1653). Mathieu can see this impossibility of changing the party from the inside, but he also notes that the party without Brunet will be certain to do what Brunet does not want. Brunet, however, reminds Mathieu that even if he reenters the party, he can no longer "forget himself" (that is, forget his individuality and his doubt); a part of him will always "remain outside." Mathieu responds with this stirring conclusion, which Brunet apparently accepts (and which we, it seems, are meant to accept as well) – and which amounts to nothing less than a redefinition of man: "Outside, outside and inside at the same time. Totally in it [the party] and totally out, wanting the impossible and knowing that you want it and wanting it as if it were within reach: that's what a man is" (OR, 1654).

We have a strange situation here (as well as another strange friendship). Mathieu advises Brunet to do something he himself is incapable of: staying in the party, working to change it from within (which is nevertheless impossible). Mathieu is claiming a peculiar sort of intellectual authority for himself: Brunet should take his advice seriously even though Mathieu is incapable of doing (or unwilling to do) what Brunet has already done (i.e., working as a party militant). We can, however, see why Mathieu is necessary to Sartre at this point. If Sartre is to continue to valorize the party, he will nevertheless have to argue along with it that Vicarios is a traitor: Vicarios has repudiated the party, a step Sartre himself is now unwilling to take. Vicarios is conveniently gotten out of the way, and Mathieu replaces him. Mathieu has never been *in* the party, so he cannot be seen by Sartre or by anyone else as a traitor of the Vicarios type. He remains outside the party: he retains his independence of judgment. Nevertheless, *independently* he arrives at the conclusion that Brunet should continue to submit himself to the party. Sartre has it both ways: in the very act of affirming the party (through Brunet), he still is able to affirm the independence of subjectivity (Mathieu), and vice versa. Together, this two-character dyad forms a new self, a new intellectual, even a new "man." For it is the insuperable tension between party allegiance and individual action – that impossibility – which, according to Mathieu, constitutes the new Man.

At the same time, however, it would seem that we have not really progressed that far beyond the Vicarios/Brunet duality. There too we had an impossible conjunction of independence and submission, of individual doubt (highlighting the self) and impersonal obedience (selflessness). In a sense, we had two narratives, that of Schneider-Vicarios and that of Brunet, and they fed off each other. The experience of Vicarios really was vicarious: in order for him to experience his personal liberation, he needed the much larger story of the liberation of humanity that the Communists provided. He had to work with them, to believe in their myths (which negated his autonomy), while at the same time, through the affirmation of his own self, he refused them. He was a parasite on the grand Communist narrative of human liberation. Brunet in a similar way needed Vicarios. He saw from the first that Schneider-Vicarios was not a Communist, but he identified with him, especially when fully confronted with the inflexible party in the person of Chalais. He then recognized himself in Vicarios, the deviant, the one who willfully and self-destructively imposed the truth of his own identity, his own consciousness; he had to be in solidarity with Vicarios at that point, if his life was to have any meaning at all.

Mathieu replaces Vicarios in the role of excluded (or self-excluding) intellectual. But unlike Vicarios he *affirms* the party. Strangely, in Mathieu's case the dilemma faced by Schneider-Vicarios/Brunet is posed in a positive light, whereas it would seem to warrant presentation as an essentially negative situation. Brunet, after all, faces and even wants what is clearly stated to be the *impossible:* he is both inside the party and outside it, both a selfless Communist (the embodiment of what is supposed to be blind historical necessity, but which often reveals itself in practice to be nothing but the violent imposition of a convenient, if not erroneous, interpretation) and a doubting self (the gratuitously self-imposed, decadent, bourgeois). These two sides are at war, and the novel presents no way in which they can be reconciled; the Communist side will always see the "self" as a meaningless extravagance, as an arbitrary element that is in excess and should be done away with; the "self" will always regard the Communist side as a tyrannical and capricious machine that, while officially "correct," nevertheless is inimical to human freedom, and therefore to human life. And it is the movement toward the *impossibility* of the coordination of these two sides that Mathieu, through metaphorical legerdemain, defines as "man"!

At this point Sartre's narrative seems to be starting to stutter; it repeats the same impossibility, first devalorizing it in the Vicarios/Brunet composite "self," then affirming it in the Mathieu/Brunet "self." Though in the first case there is a refusal of Stalinist communism (they are fleeing not only the camp but Chalais) and in the second an apparent affirmation of it, the problem remains essentially the same. The leftist intellectual self is caught in self-betrayal as it attempts to narrate itself: it is really composed of two narrations, each a parasite on the other. It is not surprising that Sartre's novelistic project grinds to a halt at this point; the very impossibility that Mathieu affirms seems to preclude any further narrative progression.[7]

And yet a nagging question remains: if these two alternatives – party discipline and individual judgment – are simply in opposition, why can't they be resolved in a larger dialectic? (Clearly Sartre himself did not give up on this dialectical resolution to this opposition; he continued it in another genre, abandoning fiction.)[8] The dialectical route is clearly the one Mathieu would like to follow, even though he ends up affirming an "impossible" that seems quite undialectical. Parasitism after all implies mutual dependency, perhaps even complicity and the opportunity for coordinated action. What in all this, then, is really impossible?

In this problematic conflict between wayward revolutionaries and the inexorable force of communism, those in revolt, it seems, are attempting to reaffirm the signification of "man" (and all that it implies: independent judgment, an active consciousness, the sacredness of individual rights and duties) in the face of an impersonal, machinelike communism. There appear at first to be two different dimensions of rhetoric at play here, and much of what seems a political conflict can in fact be analyzed as (if not reduced to) a conflict within language itself. Communism functions as a performative rhetoric: it issues commands, promises, and excuses regardless of what the individual can or will perceive as the true political situation of the moment. (This absolute – but also erroneous – inflexibility is the problem Brunet the Communist faces when Chalais appears in the camp.) Its acts appear *impersonal* and *arbitrary:* we might say, following Paul de Man, that it functions as a grammar, continually positing and repositing meanings which bear no necessary relation to what can be represented as the *truth.*[9] On the other hand, the revolutionaries' activity is, or at least first appears to be, exclusively that of a figurative rhetoric; belatedly, and fully recognizing the "impossibility" of their effort, they attempt to confront communism (remember that Brunet is to remain within the party) and humanize it by making it recognize, in its functioning, the *true* needs, desires, and, especially, interpretations of specific individuals. In other words, they attempt to modify the mechanical repetitions of party discipline by inserting into the inexorable functioning of the dialectic, at specific moments, accurate (truthful) representations of current states of affairs. (Here we think of figures like Hoederer in the play *Dirty Hands,* who attempt to modify party decrees on their own initiative when they can perceive, and formulate, a course of action more likely to prove beneficial.)

This does not mean, however, that a political performative rhetoric is only a deviation from the norm of an absolutely accurate representation of social reality. On the contrary, the self-representation, and representations, of revolutionary activity appear to be only an aftereffect of, and a reaction to, the various performances of the Communist dialectic and are thus not simply opposed to it, since they are already generated out of it. This dialectic is now characterized not by the operations of various mediations and internalizations of signification but instead by a repetitive and aleatory positing of meaning. Party decrees and determinations have no meaning outside of particular revolutionary acts taken on individual initiative, and yet it seems the party will always be implacably opposed to those individual gestures. Now what is striking in all this is that Mathieu himself has recourse to a speech act, an element of performative rhetoric, in positing the very necessity of individual responsibility: it seems that Brunet is persuaded that he must be both inside and outside the party not through rational argumentation – a decision that would be made after a careful weighing of accurate representations of various options – but by a strange kind of promise. Mathieu tells him that being a man consists in "wanting the impossible and knowing that you want it and wanting it as if it were within reach": if Brunet really wants it, really wants to be a man – if he really wants the solidarity of men *outside of* communism, and the necessity of their independent judgments *within* Communism practice (and thus their solidarity within communism) – then (Mathieu promises) it will come to pass. And yet "it" is impossible, and Mathieu says so!

The irony here is that humanist self-engendering ("that's what a man is") can be effected only by having recourse to a speech act, a promise: if you want the impossible, then you get to be a man (the robotlike dogmatic Communist who does not want the impossible is not a man). If you want it, you will be rewarded. Through its very imposition this speech act is, however, in complicity with communism, which also functions through rhetorical performances (commands, declarations, promises, excuses – but above all in its arbitrary production of representations of the truth). The bourgeois revolutionaries are thus far from being simply opposed to the method (if we can call it that) of orthodox communism. Why this complicity? The answer, I think, is quite simple: the Communist dialectic itself is only a mechanically generated series of meanings; therefore, any dialectical "going beyond" of this dialectic, such as that attempted by Brunet and Mathieu, will itself entail a forceful and blind positing of truth. Communism, at least as Sartre presents it, cannot be argued with, one cannot definitively reform it, expecting it to recognize "the ways things really are" and conform to certain standards of rational decision making. All that is impossible (as Mathieu admits, perhaps in spite of himself, when he uses that word). One must stay in the party, working against it, but it can never be changed. The language of the legitimate representation of the truth is therefore always only an aftereffect of a mechanism for the chance imposition or promising of the truth (it is always an aberrant and belated reform effort). It cannot be derived logically from *within* the functioning of that mechanism; it can only be posited *after and against* such a system. Truth, or a dialectic based on, or elaborated through, the representation of truth, can itself only be imposed through a speech act – and the same goes for the solidarity between (or a dialectical resolution of the conflict represented by) comrades in revolt, like Brunet and Mathieu, who necessarily must be true to each other. The speech act as an inevitably social or political act cannot be dominated or domesticated through truthful representation.

And yet we realize that this arbitrary positing of truth can be recognized only through that which it precludes: unconditioned, accurate representation. The word for what Mathieu offers Brunet as a substitute for official Communist solidarity – "the impossible" – is therefore literally true. What both men want is impossible first because a full resolution of the contradiction between independently, rationally, derived truth and mechanically generated political performance (between, in other words, the "inside" and the "outside") can never be achieved. Such a resolution – which itself depends logically on the possibility of certainty and truth – can be a function only of a willful positing, a promise, which will always betray the very resolution it puts forward, and which will always therefore entail a *repositing* of "man" and of a dialectic of truth. The impossible has meaning only if it is wanted, known, and strived toward, but it can literally and in truth be the impossible only when it is inevitably and finally unknowable, the result not of deliberate labor but of a forceful, repetitious and gratuitous reaffirmation. Put another way, one can be a man only through solidarity and meaningful action ("inside and outside" of communism) – these are what makes a man a man – and yet solidarity and action are the *impossible* because they are, in the end, nothing other than the product of a promise (the promise – and the tautology – that one will be a man by, finally, being a man). The vicious circle is complete. It is finally the very union of these poles in a dialectical opposition – the coordination of self-representation (being a man) and performance (the promise that one will be a man) – that is always again impossible. Most interestingly, this impossibility of the committed individual *subject* comes to the fore, is represented in its unreadability, not in Sartre's philosophy or anthropology (such as *The Critique of Dialectical Reason*) but in the incompletion of his fiction. For it is fiction, in the genre of the thesis novel, that sets itself the task of representing a dialectical resolution rather than demonstrating it.[10]

Despite the fact that representing this bond between bourgeois and Communist, free subjectivity and harsh discipline, is literally impossible, we should note that the text nevertheless does advance a second strategy to seal the union of the Vicarios-Mathieu figure with the Brunet figure. Curiously, this gesture is not so much political as it is *sacrificial*. As in so many thesis novels, the fundamental gesture here seems to entail the exile or death of a third, an Other. Such a gesture is necessary to effect the consolidation of the community – in this case a community of two, but two who represent a vast number of individuals opposed along exactly the same lines. In order to constitute themselves as a unity, two individuals turn against a third, who is refused, rejected, or killed: the scapegoat.[11]

Now, what is remarkable in these fragments is the shift in scapegoats that takes place as one unified couple is replaced by another. *Drôle d'amitié* ends with the escape attempt by Brunet and Vicarios, and Vicarios's death. But the sacrificial victim here is less Vicarios than it is Chalais, the Stalinist whose law both men are attempting to flee. Chalais is not put to death – he conveniently disappears, arrested, in the sections that follow – but the recognition of his status as Other, as that which must be refused and escaped, is what draws Vicarios and Brunet together again in a common project. Vicarios's subsequent death can also be seen as sacrificial, but its significance is quite different. Vicarios, rather than dying as an excluded, cursed element, dies as a martyr for a new cause (one to be fought for by Brunet), the one represented by the coming together of Vicarios and Brunet: individuality joined to selfless discipline.

There is, however, a problem in this model. The scapegoat, Chalais, represents at least half of the desired union to be instituted through his rejection. He cannot be fully Other if his two enemies, rejoicing over his demise, simply recognize themselves in him. After all, Stalinism itself is not being overtly rejected (just as Sartre in 1952 did not simply reject it); Brunet, even at the end, still believes in discipline and the objective, immutable direction of history. Because the sacrificers can fully recognize themselves in Chalais, he is not sufficiently Other, and thus not really a suitable victim: a new victim must be found in whom the community (in this case composed of only two) can or will see nothing of itself, who at least appears to be utterly heterogeneous, utterly repulsive.

This is not to say, of course, that the scapegoat cannot resemble the ones who reject him in order to constitute their society; on the contrary, he is their double, but he cannot be rejected unless he is (erroneously) seen by them as the embodiment of that which they are not, of that which is most different from them. Perhaps Sartre himself most clearly worked out the dynamics of this relation in his story "Childhood of a Leader" ("Enfance d'un chef"): Lucien Fleurier is able to disavow the "contingency," the lack of "reality," he finds in himself only by projecting it onto other things or people, and then punishing them.[12] As a child, he beats and breaks a lowly thistle bush; later, older and more sinister, he becomes a member of a Fascist group whose scapegoat is now human: a Jew.

Chalais is unsuitable as a scapegoat because he represents not something that Brunet and Vicarios would reject but, rather, something they would subsume. It is a different matter entirely when, at the end of *La Dernière Chance*, Brunet and Mathieu do away with Moûlu and then plan their escape. Moûlu, as we know from *Death in the Soul*, is a flabby, effeminate, somewhat nauseating character (his name contains the word *mou* – "soft, weak") who refuses to bathe, who is the very embodiment of a kind of inert but fundamentally dangerous human "in-itself." It is this inward turning, gooey softness that Sartre (whose misogyny and homophobia has never been adequately investigated) always associated with the feminine and the homosexual: one thinks of Marcelle and Daniel in *The Age of Reason*, Lucien's homosexual fling in "Childhood of a Leader," the Autodidact in *Nausea*. And it is no coincidence that both Lucien and Daniel identify with the Fascists, as of course does Moûlu: all such figures live in a world of total bad faith, passively gazing inward and masochistically loving to take orders.

For Sartre, the antithesis of this homosexual/feminine/Fascist/surrealist combination was the outward-turning and hard-bitten man of action to the Left.[13] We see quite clearly, however, at the end of *La Dernière Chance*, how these "men of action" – Brunet and Mathieu – are able to constitute their society; Moûlu, after characteristically begging for forgiveness by kissing Brunet's hand (OR, 1640), is killed, and his body goes into the toilet (OR, 1648–49). Mathieu coolly tells Brunet: "It was him or us" – the real man (as Mathieu now is, *because* he has killed) feels no emotion when he does away with an enemy.

It is only at this point that Brunet and Mathieu really decide to act together; as Brunet says, "There's a cadaver between us, you have to admit" (OR, 1651). The narrator assures us that this soft, filthy corpse guarantees that the new "complicity" of the two men is worth more than a "childhood friendship." Now they can plan Brunet's escape – and, more important, carry out their fusion of individualism and the party, subjectivity and objectivity. (We should note that both in the case of Brunet/Vicarios and in that of Brunet/Mathieu an escape attempt consecrates the bond uniting the two men: this signals not a rejection of the lesson in male solidarity learned in the camp but the will to disseminate it in a much wider arena.)

The society of men of action – more a utopia than a collectivity, really – can arise only through the destruction of the Other, which is its double. Moûlu clearly represents an all-male society that the two men must violently refuse in order to constitute their own: the homosocial group must violently repress the homosexual.[14] The homosexual is therefore always implied, always a risk for the homosocial; the homosocial is always already homosexual to the extent that only by excluding the homosexual can it be homosocial; in this way it is fully dependent on that which it finds most odious. Those involved in a nonsexual male bonding (like Brunet and Mathieu) recognize themselves in ambiguous figures like Moûlu; to deny, in bad faith, their kinship – their identity – with such persons, they can only violently refuse them, wounding or killing them. But Moûlu's corpse will always be there, waiting in the toilet, waiting to rise and to be wiped out once again, because the difference between homosexuality and homosociality is utterly ephemeral – as ambiguous as a sexual arousal that is nothing in itself, that consists only of the fundamentally arbitrary interpretations and signs which are imposed upon it.[15] The repressed will always return, the men will always need another victim, another Other, secretly to recognize and then refuse, to unmask and then destroy.

In a single murderous gesture, a human society is constituted, for there is never, in this text, a clear distinction between "man" as "human," irrespective of sex, and "man" as "male." In one stroke a bond of what amounts to fraternal love is established between two men (their dialogue is quite sentimental, even when it is supposed to be "tough") and a profound philosophical and political problem – the liberalization of the Communist party – is resolved.[16] This conjunction makes perfect sense when we recall that, for Brunet, communism was inseparable from community. True solidarity between men was possible only within the party. By flirting first with Vicarios, then with Mathieu, Brunet was, according to party orthodoxy, risking the loss of the community that the party represented. But now, through his bond with Mathieu, Brunet accedes to another, higher, community, one that maintains the Communist community (and its discipline) but also negates it by dialectically raising it to a higher level: it is the community of a larger project that includes spontaneous, independent action along with Communist Truth. And it so happens that that necessary action, in its founding moment, entails the elimination of a heterogeneous figure: a gesture through which Brunet and Mathieu's rending inner interpersonal and ideological conflict is to be projected outward, but also a gesture identical in its function to that used by the proto-Fascist Lucien (in "Childhood of a Leader") in order to reaffirm *his* community.

Sartre – the author and strategist behind this thesis novel – seems caught in a vicious circle, attempting to envisage a strategy for the defeat of the enemy (Fascist brutality and scapegoating), but not recognizing (or recognizing only too well) that that strategy is only a double of the one employed by the enemy.

This may provide another way of reading Mathieu's advocacy of "wanting the impossible": the word "impossible" comes to stand, as a kind of master metaphor, for this entire complex of male bonding and bonding of individuality and discipline. Everything is impossible: the perfect homosocial society of "men"; the utopian joining of bourgeois individualist and Communist; the exorcism of scapegoating through more scapegoating. Yet by pronouncing the word "impossible" Mathieu wants to be able to dissipate this mass of impossibility: "wanting the impossible" is a speech act that, when pronounced, magically should make the impossible possible. By invoking the impossible, Mathieu promises the possible. In this sense the use of this word is analogous to sacrifice: when it is pronounced, as when the victim is killed, the community is hypothetically instituted through the act, the promise, and the shared project is ratified. Nevertheless, in practice (if we can speak of such a thing), "the impossible" is only the metaphor of its own impossible disappearance: the word is fated to be repeated indefinitely.

In fact, if we recall our earlier discussion of Mathieu's speech act ("that's what a man is"), we can see the profound complicity between the sacrificial gesture and the speech act. In sacrifice, as in performative rhetoric, a new "meaning" is generated out of an inherently senseless act: "human" solidarity (i.e., between men) is a function of an expulsion of otherness, a pure positing of violence. This positing is meaningless, or, put another way, it is a tautology: at the moment of sacrifice, the victim is Other (and we are we) because he (or she) is Other and we are we. Sacrifice, like the speech act, has to do here not with mimesis or the closure of signification but with a violent, aleatory, and repetitious imposition of sense, a stuttering of historical options. Any attempt, therefore, to coordinate this violence with a politically progressive dialectic of truth (which "puts negativity to work"), as Sartre seems to have been attempting in these fragments, is doomed to impossibility.

5

Sartre's Critique
of Dialectical Reason:
The Re-counting
of History

WE SAW in the previous chapter the difficulty, on the level of fiction, that Sartre faced in dialectically resolving a subject-object conflict. The dispute between, for example, Brunet and Chalais was in the end nothing more than an allegory for the conflict between the impulse toward a radically free subjectivity and an absolutely determined and frozen objectivity. This distinction, however, could be resolved only by having recourse to a sacrificial model that was inseparable in its functioning not so much from the dialectical resolution of the contradiction between freedom and determination but from the arbitrary and repetitious movement of the imposition of the speech act.

Sartre's *Critique of Dialectical Reason* (1960) can, in fact, be seen as a monumental effort to solve the problem of sacrificial solidarity in the face of a recalcitrant performative language, no longer on the level of fiction, but, as in *Being and Nothingness,* in philosophical prose. No doubt this latter genre gains in theoretical specificity what it lacks in vividness or even concreteness; as we will see, the *Critique* puts forward, through the analysis of an event in the past (the storming of the Bastille in 1789) – rather than in the elaboration of a fictionalized and utopian homosocial bonding – the very sacrificial and politically progressive fusion that Sartre's later fiction was unable to imagine or represent. This fusion entails nothing less than the subordination – and even, perhaps, the liquidation (or fulfillment) – of the recalcitrant speech act, the *impossible* term that so bedeviled Mathieu and Brunet in *The Roads of Freedom*.

The *Critique* has been called "the last great example of French philosophy of the 1930s," and its concerns really are the summation of the set of problems that French Hegelian anthropology set itself after what I have called the "breakup" of Durkheim's larger project.[1] It would require an entire study to chart the connections between Sartre's *Critique* and Alexandre Kojève's *Introduction to the Reading of Hegel;* suffice it to say that for Sartre, as for Kojève, the dialectical progress of history is characterized by a never-ending search for transparency, for full reciprocity between subjects and the mutual recognition of the other's desire, for the renunciation of the exercise of oppressive power by one subject over another (a power that results in the transformation of the victim into a simple object to be manipulated) – a transparency which, ironically, can never be grasped except through the mediation of opaque and obstructing matter (through, in other words, the resistance of objective Being).[2] Unlike Durkheim, Kojève, and after him Sartre, saw the agency of violence and destruction as integral to the movement of history and to the completion of a larger historical reason. If the violence of the Hegelian master/slave dialectic is crucial for Kojève, for Sartre this same violence is just as important when it is part of the praxis by which the social group, in a violent but "fusing" state, acts upon and against the inert force of political reaction that opposes it. Individual against individual, group against group, self against crystallized or even gelatinous matter – praxis, in this tradition, is inseparable from a strategically applied violence that may lack a universal justification, but which, in a given contingent situation, and perhaps only in retrospect, must be indissociable from the movement of history itself.

At the same time, Sartre's *Critique* breaks with Kojève in its very act of transmitting a dialectical and anthropological model of history that is, inevitably, built on the ruins of Durkheim's system. Sartre, attempting to put forward a "totalization without a totalizer," undermines both Durkheim *and* Kojève. First, of course, Durkheim: despite the fact that Sartre clearly continues, as we will see, in the Durkheimian tradition by depicting historical movement as a series of moments of sacrificial unification in which the group constitutes itself through a morally and physically uplifting awareness of itself by acting *against* an Other (and this also necessarily entails a Sartrian theory of the sacred and of the intellectual), he nevertheless wholly rejects the reification of society – its formulation as a fixed organism composed of social cells and with, no doubt, a more or less despotic head – and of the individual as a stable component, and ultimate totem (or fetish), of that grouping. But this destruction of the Durkheimian institutionalized social consciousness results as well in the elimination of the possibility of a Hegelian "end of history," which was virtually an article of faith for Kojève. Kojève, after all, had never been able to think of the Marxist end of history along any lines other than those laid out by Hegel, and that meant a figure like Napoleon, or Stalin, who would inaugurate the final era and embody its reason. Such an "end of history" could serve as a terminal point toward which all things are headed, and from the perspective of which all problems are resolved, with truth definitively recognized and falsehood banished. For Sartre, on the other hand, history was always the dialectical conflict of subject and object, dynamism and sluggish reification, *praxis* and *exis, without* a master subjectivity-objectivity. After the revolution, the progressive spirals of history will doubtless continue to unwind, as the powerful group in fusion is always again institutionalized by the very inertia it sought to combat, by a sovereignty (a head), and a corresponding seriality – which is once again overthrown by another group in fusion. In this way, it is hard to see how any "end of history," with a heroic figure who establishes it and sums it up by a kind of metonymy, can be established within the Sartrian model. The differences between various historical formations – and even prehistorical ones, which follow the same laws of the interaction of subjectivity and matter within the framework of scarcity – can be only ones of degree, not of kind.

These preliminary remarks are necessary, I think, to put in perspective the Sartrian group in fusion, which is understandable only as a necessarily ephemeral dialectical event, in opposition to a static and oppressive antidialectical milieu, seriality. If the movement of history is at every point (and in every point) dialectical – and if no complete and final knowledge of history can be attained – then the dialectical union of subjectivities *in* history is, as Sartre shows, over in an instant. What replaces the ever-vigilant and just state in Durkheim – the ultimate fulfillment of the community *in* the state – is for Sartre an evanescent group transparency that clearly motivates and justifies history's movement, but which is itself attained only in privileged, seemingly spontaneous moments. When sought, this transparency only leads those societies that would attempt to impose it to various forms of justified or unjustified terror.

Since that terror itself is indissociable from seriality, the *Critique* eventually appears as a vast fresco of historical events which chronicle the rise of seriality, its sudden and momentary overcoming in the group in fusion, and then its slow and inevitable decay as that group itself is institutionalized and serialized. The tiny segment of the infinite dialectic of human history highlighted in the *Critique* is nothing more than the recounting of the all-too-brief appearance of a just dialectical relation between men, a relation that is itself inevitably swallowed by a larger, antidialectical movement, but which in turn generates history and provides mankind, even during the most terrible periods of repression, with a legitimate goal. To understand the moment of fusing (the periodical Sartrian culmination of history) we must, then, first understand seriality, and the role played by a differential *ordination* within it: for seriality, as we will see, is nothing more than the social inscription of the injustice of the impersonal, frozen speech act and of a differential, arithmetic system of ordering, separating, and instituting.

I

The most important thing to grasp in any discussion of seriality is that it is inseparable, in its very materiality, from an arithmetic ordering – or, as Sartre calls it at one point, an "ordination."[3] One must see, then, how numbering operates within the series, and what it implies for the serial "gathering" (*rassemblement* – which Sartre is usually careful to distinguish from the "group," a term he reserves for the dialectical opposite of the serial relation, the group in fusion).

The best-known example of seriality in the *Critique* is the gathering of people waiting for the bus in the Place St. Germain, Paris (CDR, 256). Each person is alone; each is a solitary member of a social entity which is constituted only because of a "common interest." (No one talks to or looks at anyone else.) That interest – to find a seat on the bus when it finally comes – ensures that each person, for the Other, is nothing more than an additional Other who also wants a seat. Each person for the Other is only a cipher; each has significance for the Other only to the extent that he represents a possible privation. "The group has its unique-being outside of itself in an object to come [i.e., the bus], and each individual to the extent that he is determined by the common interest is only differentiated from every other one by the simple materiality of the organism" (CDR, 259).[4]

Nothing "interior" to each individual could serve to distinguish him or her from the others; each is constituted as a member of the series only in that he is just another potential bus rider, a physical presence that will occupy a seat. The only "unity" of the members of this gathering is, therefore, the fact that each is an Other to all other members: "since all the lived characteristics which could serve as a determination from inside fall outside this determination, the identity of each with each Other is their unity there [in the gathering] as being-other and it is here, now, their common otherness [*altérité*]" (CDR, 260). Each member is the same as every other member – each member is part of the gathering – only to the extent that he is just an Other to every other member. The very anonymity of each one – his or her inert materiality, waiting, and nothing more – is what constitutes membership in the gathering, and the member's "unity" (as Sartre says in a footnote on p. 263: "Insofar as he is *the same* he is simply and formally *an other*"). This facelessness comes to be internalized by each additional member, and to constitute his or her presence: "Each one is the same as the Others to the extent that he is Other than himself" (CDR, 260). This "identity as otherness," a "scandalous absurdity," is the only unity possible in a social aggregate whose unification is the result of a praxis, a human activity, that immediately leads to the freezing of praxis into an alienating inertia: "The identity [of the gathering] is the practico-inert unity to come in that it is determined in the present moment as *separation stripped of meaning"* (CDR, 260).[5]

This series is determined by the inertia of materiality, in its peculiarly Sartrian sense: materiality is never anything more or other than the resistance of scarcity, and scarcity itself is not an "absolute" lack within nature that exists prior to and apart from man but, instead, the fact that there is always an excess number of Others competing for a limited quantity of goods or places.[6] Rarity, itself based on seriality, breeds only more seriality: "The material object will determine the serial order as the social reason for the separation of individuals. The practico-inert exigency comes here from scarcity: there are *not enough places for everyone"* (CDR, 260). Scarcity defines each person as potentially "in excess," as nothing more than "another one," who can be added or subtracted depending on the number of places available: "The Other will be the Other's rival by the very fact of their identity." This mournful procedure – clearly meant by Sartre to be representative of all processes of selection and group formation in bourgeois society – is summed up, in the bus example, by the necessity of taking a ticket, which indicates one's place in line for a seat. This number, as Sartre notes, is purely arbitrary and has nothing to do with one's inner being or identity: it can reflect the order in which people have arrived at the bus stop, but certain persons are automatically given priority, others arrive late because of accidents, and so on. In addition, it confers "no particular characteristic, but only the power to get on the bus first." This numbering, or "ordination," is only the "negative principle of union and of determining the fate [*sort*] of each as Other *by each Other as Other"* (CDR, 261).

Ordination, then, is an arbitrary, mechanical way of uniting people by distinguishing between them; through numbering, otherness "is manifested in the concept as common to all and designates each as a molecule identical to all the others; but it becomes, in the series, a rule of differentiation" (CDR, 263). Each is defined, and posited, only as an Other – in other words, as Other to itself. Its identity in otherness (and not in itself) can be expressed as an arithmetical relation: "All whole numbers . . . present the same characteristics: in particular, [they] can be represented by the symbol $n + 1$ (supposing that $n = 0$ when it is a question of the number one). But *precisely for that reason,* the arithmetical series of whole numbers, in that they are all constituted by the addition of a unity to the preceding numbers, is a practical and material reality, constituted by an infinite series of non-comparable entities, and the originality of each one comes from what it is, from the one that precedes it in the series, which is what the latter is to the one that preceded it" (CDR, 262).

For Sartre, this "inert" series is matter itself "in that it is non-adaptability." As the practico-inert, it absorbs the energy, the free praxis, of each of its members, and returns that energy to each member as power coming from another, as the praxis of a thing that itself alienates the subject from himself – that, in other words (and to use a Lukácsian term that Sartre himself often uses in this context) "reifies" it. Through the alienated series, in its inorganic materiality, the subject itself is reified and transformed into a quantified digit, or "molecule."

This series, though it "symbolizes" nothing and is only an inert materiality (CDR, 264) is, in itself, a kind of language, a series of oppositional or diacritical marks. (Sartre often writes of serialized matter as something that has received a differentiating "seal" or an "impression.")[7] It is circular and repetitious, rather than dialectical and progressive; the "meaning" of each unit is nothing more than its difference from each other one, determined by addition or subtraction. There is, for this reason, no "concept" in which "each is the same as the Others in that he is himself [*en tant qu'il est soi*]" (CDR, 262). On the contrary, each is "defined," if we can use that term, only as a differential marker (it is the same as the Other in that it is Other than itself) in a larger, open-ended, recurring aggregate.

It is interesting to note here that Sartre uses the term "ordination" to describe this repetitious/differential system, which entails "neither the simple relation to a common unity, nor the encircling movement of organisms" (CDR, 261). For ordination, in French as in English, more often refers to the "ceremony during which a person is admitted to the ministry of a church" or "the admission itself."[8] This is significant, I think, not so much because of the resonance between an established or institutionalized religion or sacred and the differential ordering of the series – this comes later, when Sartre writes of the pledge (see pp. 417–27) – but instead because the action of this numbering, like the formula used to "admit" priests, is a kind of speech act or totem act (as I called it in my discussion of Durkheim) by which the "autonomous" subject is instituted and is also invested with a certain status – or in this case, a lack of status, a powerlessness – within serialized society. The mechanical function of serialization – the assignment of everyone's numbered place – is accomplished through a designating act, or an "inscription," that either accords one a certain numerically defined position, or refuses it. One thinks of the people waiting for the bus: the lucky ones have a low number; for no apparent reason they have been invested with the privilege of getting on first. The others get to wait in the cold for the next bus. Now it is clear that, for Sartre, the series entails, most fundamentally, a performative, an act in which the subject is invested not with a presence or substance but with a lack. The lucky ones who "succeed," who manage to get on the bus or accomplish anything else in bourgeois society, are merely the exceptions that prove the rule: the exclusion of the "self" in general, not only from conventional material success or comfort (for these things are only the outer markers of a serialized society) but *from the unity of authentic selfhood*, is the fundamental characteristic of the larger series. The act, which is intended, or imagined, to enable the subject to "do something," is only the repetitious performance of a nonperformance, in which selfhood – subjectivity as plenitude, "in that he is himself" – is *subtracted*. And, most important, this disinvestment entails not only the serialization of society through a kind of arithmetic language or inscription but the subtraction of the power of the intellectual function within that arbitrary and empty system, by means of that system. What remains is not only an emptied-out, repetitious subjectivity – the sameness of the potentially infinite series of selves as Other – but the palpable void remaining after the disappearance of the authoritative intellectual.

We see more clearly how a certain materiality breeds seriality in the case of the "otherness" of radio listeners (CDR, 270–76). Here Sartre discusses a facticity in the form of a machine that, through a mechanically repeated act – a fully political speech act – generates a serial ordering that is the very negation of the intellectual function.

The radio – the "singular voice of a certain person" – addresses me specifically ("no doubt the voice addresses me – to me and to Others, it says, 'dear listeners'"); it is an address that (as a speech act) would ordinarily presuppose the possibility of response, applause, or objection on my part. At the same time, though, this act is the impossibility of the fulfillment of the speech act of address as it is conventionally conceived, because the listener is addressed not as a possible respondent or interlocutor, but only as an inert thing: "I am, as an inert object, subjected, as inorganic materiality, to the human labor of the voice" (CDR, 272).[9] This "human labor" as mechanical reproduction is itself materiality, solidified and inert praxis, even in the apparent volatility of the radio waves.

The series determined by the "object" is the group of listeners who are "ordained" by the act – they are identified (to themselves) as listeners called, but also frustrated because they cannot respond to the voice ("above all when it is a question of political broadcasts"). The listener is utterly powerless; he or she cannot argue with the voice, and, worse still, cannot address other listeners to convince them that the voice is wrong. Nor does turning off the radio help: "For this purely individual activity changes absolutely nothing in the real labor of this voice." Even when the listener silences the voice in this way, it continues to act, because this gesture has only caused the listener to "throw himself into the useless and abstract solitude of private life." In other words, the voice can be refused only through the antisocial act of negating the larger "gathering," – the last thing the listener wants to do, if the goal is to refute the voice.

Sartre's ideal listener (the narrator, in fact, who refers to himself as "I") would like to combat the voice. He knows that he cannot be swayed by its lies – but will the others resist? "The voice is intolerable to me *in that* it is listened to by the others." These Others are (as in the case of the bus riders) both the same and Other: their identity, their gathering together, lie only in their distance from, and their otherness to, each other. The mechanized speech act short-circuits the possibility of intellectual resistance: the "I" of the narrator, who is necessarily a thinker (he is, after all, narrating the *Critique*) is as powerless in his ability to address the Others as the radio voice is all-powerful. "It seems to me I could combat the arguments it puts forward before the Others, even if they do not think like I do: but what I experience in fact is *absence* as my mode of connection with the Others" (CDR, 272). His inability to convince the other listeners "one on one" of the correctness of his doctrine only increases his feeling of "scandalous impotence." He listens not "on his own account," but "from the point of view of the Others" in growing anxiety: he is united with them, not by successfully addressing them (i.e., convincing them that his positions are the right ones), but because he is unable to influence them against the voice, an incapacity that also characterizes each one of the Others. His identity in Otherness – is marked by the powerlessness of the intellectual function as a successful completion of the speech act (the address that elicits the correct response – one that indicates approval and understanding). The narrator's "I," in its "lateral" membership in the series, is identical to all the other Others in that they are all, in relation to each other and to the mechanized voice, impotent intellectuals: none can reach any of the Others, in order to address and convince. They can only passively allow themselves to be moved, as Others. And the "I," even if it refuses the perceived "viewpoint," of the Others, must necessarily listen to the voice with their attitude in order to refute it: in this way it undergoes the temptation of this noxious ideology, and as Other (as it can only imagine the Other, impotent and thus swayed by the voice) is itself convinced, if only for a moment. "What counts above all is that my inability [or impotence: *impuissance*] to act on the Others (who can allow themselves to be convinced) comes back to me in order to turn these Others into my destiny" (CDR, 274). The narrator's "I" is now only another inert cipher within a differential and repetitive series: the necessary incompletion of his speech act returns to constitute him as a member of the gathering in his very Otherness, in his self as its own subtraction from itself.

By the very nature of the group, no speech act can be successfully carried out in this version of seriality. No one can, in other words, do anything with words. If the radio listeners are united only in their impotence, then the radio voice is just as powerless. It cannot sway them with its arguments, or form them into a unified group, any more than can the narrating, intellectual "I" of the *Critique;* the voice of ideology – at its worst, we might suppose, a Fascist harangue – leads, apparently, only to aimless serial violence.[10] Sartre writes that the "glue" (*mastic*) of seriality is impotence, but that this powerlessness in the gathering can become "unorganized violence": "to the exact degree that I am impotent through the Other, it is the Other himself who becomes active power in me" (CDR, 277).[11] The "indignation" of the Other is internalized and "I act under his control." But this action apparently does not involve simple obedience. My otherness to myself – and thus the otherness of all Others to themselves – as impotence becomes an inward-turning violence; this aimless and unfocused power – the power of powerlessness, and vice versa – in turn is the "glue" in which the gathering is stuck, the principle of its false cohesion. The noncompletion of the mechanized and indefinitely reproducible speech act, we can say, results in a differential and incoherent series of molecules; each of these is a micropower whose energy is turned against itself as well as against all the others in the gathering, and which thereby itself only generates more inevitably aborted performatives. The power of the voice's act (the voice as act) seems absolute, but really it is a negative quantity, one of dispersion, subtraction, and the creation of a field in which the force of the performative can be only failure. Conversely, the impotence of each member of the series in his address to the Others is the aimless expenditure of power: it is escape, leakage. "In the connection of otherness, the whole is the totalization of escape [or leakage: *totalisation de fuite*]; Being as material reality is the totalized series of *not being* [*n'être pas*], that is what each one makes the other become" (CDR, 267).[12]

It should not be assumed, however, that for Sartre all language results only in a series whose "rule of differentiation" is but the purely impersonal addition or subtraction of quantifiable terms, and whose completion is effected only through an unsuccessful and interminable performative. Sartre instead presents a group that will be the dialectical overcoming of the "series [that] reveals itself to each one, in effect, in the moment when he grasps in himself and in the others their common inability to suppress their material differences" (CDR, 277). In fact, there will be a way to suppress this difference, and the group (now used in its technical sense, as the "group in fusion") will "negate this inability, in other words, seriality." This negation will entail a radically different conception of social grouping, but also of difference and identity within language, and of the power of the speech act.

II

Seriality is dialectically overcome in the group in fusion.[13] But how? In effect, Sartre faces the same "vicious circle" that we found to be implicit in Durkheim, when he posed the totem act: which comes first, the act which institutes the community, or the already existing and integrated community that assigns itself the totem, and subsequently reaffirms it through various acts? Sartre would resolve this problem, but he cannot do so while maintaining the primacy of the performative. He therefore shifts away from totems, symbols, and speech acts – the region that, as we saw, proved so difficult for Durkheim – to "needs," "common danger," and the "common objective." Sartre states: "We arrive at a vicious circle: the group is constituted on the basis of a need or a common danger, and is defined by the common objective which determines its common *praxis;* but neither the common need nor common *praxis* nor the common objective can define the community if the latter does not make itself a community by experiencing [*ressentant*] as common the individual need and by projecting itself into the internal unification of a common integration toward objectives that it produces as common" (CDR, 350).

We need an outside threat to define our group – but the danger or need cannot determine the group's praxis if the group has not already defined itself in relation to "common objectives." Why, given this "vicious circle," do individuals not fight among themselves instead, as dogs do over a scrap of food? Which is prior: unifying threat or unified group?

There is no question here in the *Critique* of determining the place or role of the totem or totem act – or speech act – in relation to communal activity. Instead, one must examine the role of subjects and their interaction during moments of crisis. The community, as we learn from the outset, defines itself in relation to needs: the problem, then, will reside in determining how subjects interact in such a way that seriality gives way to a real group, which alone can resist an external threat. Only then can we know how the vicious circle will be overcome. In this instance, the need felt by all is the removal of an external danger. Sartre reveals that this new mode of interaction between subjects must be, for the first time (following the morass of the serial relation), dialectical.

The series is transformed into a group by the action of another "order"; Sartre uses as an example the famous uprising in 1789 that led to the storming of the Bastille. Here it is the "negative order of massacre" that causes the group to find its inner coherence. Each resident of the St. Antoine quarter feels threatened by the potential violence of the king's troops, aimed at *any* person in the neighborhood, whether he or she is directly involved in the early stages of the revolt or not. It's now or never – one *must* see the threat to the Other as a threat against oneself and struggle with that Other to protect one's life and livelihood. One cannot remain "neutral," just another Other on the fringes of a historical drama. The threat of destruction, experienced by everyone in the neighborhood (which hitherto was a mere serial collective), causes each subject to recognize simultaneously the group of which he is a member, and its goal. "Each one continues to see himself in the Other, but he sees himself there *as himself,* in other words here as totalization in himself of the population of

Paris, through the saber-blow or gunshot that will wipe him out . . . each one sees in the Other his own future, and discovers on its basis his present act in the act of the Other: *imitating* through these still inert movements is to discover oneself at the same time" (CDR, 354). The Other is no longer the otherness of oneself in oneself, to oneself; rather than insufficiency or void, the subjectivity now reveals itself to itself ("discovers itself") through the Other *as* itself (rather than as the Other). Thus full subjectivity is possible not in isolation but only as a member of a group solidarity.

Sartre presents this change as a dialectical transformation of the "third" (*le tiers*). In seriality each person is a third in relation to each Other and to all: "The third is absorbed in the seriality because it is structured *a priori* as the Other, thus as Other than each one and all" (CDR, 366). In this model, the violence of otherness is inscribed in the third; it is thus turned against itself as well as against all Others. That is its only identity with them. In the group in fusion, on the other hand, inertia and violence are external; the third is now dialectically integrated into the group through its solidarity with the group against an alien force: "But when the practical unity of the surrounding materiality constitutes, from outside and negatively, the multiplicity in totality, the objective for the third is produced for him as a *common* objective and the plurality of epicenters is revealed to him [*se découvre à lui*] as unified by a *common* exigency (or a *common praxis*) because it deciphers [*déchiffre*] the serial multiplicity on the basis of a *community already inscribed in things,* in the manner of a passive idea or a totalizing destiny" (CDR, 367).

We see here the return, in a refined form, of the sacrificial model at work in Nizan's, and later Sartre's, thesis novels. Each member of the serial "gathering" was a "third" in that he was excluded, or that he excluded the Other and the larger collection of Others (and only in that way was he a member of the collective). He was Other to himself in that he was excluded in and through his very membership. In the dialectical model, on the other hand, the third is unified with (he sees himself in) each Other and in all Others (in the group); together they must and will fight an "external" materiality, in this case the soldiers of the king, who would "pacify" the neighborhood by killing *any* of its inhabitants, irrespective of his or her political orientation. There is no alternative; one either unites with the others or one dies, and dialectical unification takes place because everyone recognizes this. The group itself, unlike the serial assemblage, is therefore not constituted as material inertia, or in otherness to itself. Instead, the materiality that "constituted" seriality (the inert collection of potential victims) now is externalized in and as the bearer of negativity (the forces of repression). The group is united against it. Goal and group are formed simultaneously and instantaneously, in response to the external, and potentially serializing, danger. Only in this way, through the dialectical-sacrificial model of group formation, can the vicious circle, the vexed question of the priority of group and goal, be overcome.

The problem of unification through outward-directed violence – through expulsion and catharsis – therefore still remains in Sartre's last major work of philosophy. Group solidarity, and the full presence of the self to itself through its status as group member, can be purchased only at the cost of violence. Conflict is certainly not done away with, but instead it is more intensely focused; it disappears to the extent that it is no longer internal to the makeup of each group member but is directed out of the group, against an Other with whom, temporarily, at least, each member has nothing in common.

This violence is, however, recovered, in that it makes the dialectic of the group (group synthesis through the "third") possible. And through the group, the larger, progressive dialectic of history becomes possible. Now if violence is externalized, this means that the inequality that characterized the hierarchies of the former society will be banished as well. The empty reverberation of the arbitrary and mechanized command – the oppressive speech act, the address, order, or promise which can never reach a unified Other and be fulfilled – will be replaced, in the group in fusion, by a unity in which the order and the carrying out of the order cannot be separated, and in which the author of the order and the one who successfully carried it out are inseparable. There can be no vicious circle, no question as to the priority of the command, watchword (*mot d'ordre*) or rallying cry over the formation of the group, or vice versa, because the unanimous production/reception of the command *is* the fusing of the group in response to the murderous threat of an enemy. Imitation of the Other and self-discovery as a member of the group are simultaneous and inseparable.

We must nevertheless recognize that this dialectical synthesis can be carried out only when the performative – in this case the command and watchword that make possible group resistance and totalization – is itself fully subordinated to the solidarity of the group. In fact it is this very subordination that makes that solidarity possible, for the Sartrian speech act is nothing if it is not entirely subsumed by the group's fusion. Sartre in this way eludes rather than resolves the Durkheimian vicious circle because in the end he favors the community over the imposition of performatives. Within the Sartrian model the command is successfully carried out only because it is *already* grasped and carried out; its "reception" from another person, and thus the submission to the will of another, a "leader," and to a command coming from the frozen past, proves to be unnecessary. If self-discovery and imitation of the Other are simultaneous, then the speech act, which is meant to cause something to be done, and must therefore serve as a link between two different time periods ("before" and "after"), cancels itself before the instantaneous praxis of real subjects. The dialectical overcoming or subtraction of the speech act, in other words, is the condition for the formation of the group.

Like the speech act, the function of the intellectual – the theorist, the "head" – is also gone beyond in the group in fusion. "Mediated reciprocity" (as Sartre calls it [CDR, 374]) is possible only when the objectivity of the series ("There is thus something like an object that flees on its hundred pair of legs" [CDR, 372]) becomes a multiple subjectivity: "To the extent that I discover [it] through *our* flight, it is necessary that my synthesis return onto me and integrate me fully into it [the group] as its part" (CDR, 372–73). This integration is possible only because the intellectual function – which we saw as *absence* in seriality – becomes omnipresent in the group. But omnipresence here means only another kind of absence: in the group, everyone will be an intellectual, an orator, a leader, but only for an instant, and he or she will formulate only what everyone has already realized, and give commands that everyone has already started to carry out. Power is "shared" not as in a conventional democracy – Sartre characterizes "free" elections as just another manifestation of seriality – but in a moment in which each person has power, each gives the order and carries it out simultaneously: "A little while ago, he fled because everyone was fleeing; now he shouts 'Let's stop!' because he stops and it is one and the same thing to stop and to give the order to stop" (CDR, 371). In this utopia, a group is founded at the moment in which language – the speech act – no longer serves as a barrier between the positing of an action and its completion. My stopping and the order to stop are simultaneous: moreover, the function of the "regulating third" – the third who at any given moment "totalizes" the situation, and who projects into the future a "regulating and totalizing praxis" – freely circulates between all members of the group. Each, through the order, becomes the "instrument of his own *praxis*"; watchwords "circulate," but no one is the authority, no one is imposing an inert or reified will. On the contrary, "Everyone . . . follows the regulating third, surrounds him, goes beyond him, the group reabsorbs him [*le reprend*] as soon as another third by an 'order' or an act visible to all constitutes himself for an instant as the regulator. But the watchword is not *obeyed*. Who would obey? Who would be obeyed? It is nothing other than common *praxis* becoming a third, the regulator of itself, in me and in all the other thirds in the movement of a totalization that totalizes me with all" (CDR, 379–80). Finally the appearance-disappearance of regulating thirds takes place with such fluency – orders are given and carried out with such rapidity – that the "authors" of the speech acts, the potentially tyrannical directors and thinkers, disappear entirely: "At the limit [*A la limite*], the regulating third does not even appear: watchwords circulate" (CDR, 380).

We can say that this circulation of orders serves as a mechanism by which a full subjectivity-in-praxis is constituted through the reflection of the subject to itself in each Other member of the group (each totalizing third) and in the group in fusion itself, "on the basis of the common future sketched out by the common movement" – in other words, on the basis of the speech act and its instantaneous realization and hence its immediate withering away in praxis. The order of the third reflects back to the subject only what was there already: "But this operation does not transform me into a thing because the totalization by the third only reveals [*ne fait que découvrir*] a free praxis as common unity which is already there and already characterizes him" (CDR, 379). The performative disappears as soon as it appears; the order is already its fulfillment in the fusing multiplicity of free praxes: "I carry out the command, I am the 'watchword.'" The speech act, in other words, does what it promises to do. The self is separated from itself in the issuing, reception, and carrying out of the order so that it can return to itself and be realized as a common self, a third dialectically synthesized with the Other and with the larger group. The otherness of the speech act, the alienation of the self in seriality that is inseparable from the obfuscations and inertia of language, is always immediately and dialectically overcome in the totalization of the group (the group *as* successful completion of the act) and of the "common self" in the group. "The phrase without an author, and echoed by a hundred mouths (including mine) does not appear as the product of the group . . . but, in the act which comprehends it by actualizing its meaning, I grasp it as pure totalizing and regulating presence of the third (as *the same as me*)" (CDR, 380–81).

Sartre is quick to distinguish the order from another kind of sign that also travels from "hand to hand": a coin. Like money, the speech act of the group in fusion is also "material," but it is radically different in that it "does not circulate." A coin is struck only once; the watchword, on the other hand, "even if it 'comes from afar' [is] produced here as if new, in that, near or far, each place is, in the group, the same *here*" (CDR, 380). The word's incessant re-production, even when it is rigorously identical in each case, means that it is not inert, like a coin whose meaning is dead and fixed – subject to constant, alienated, and alienating misinterpretation, in other words, and nothing more than a number in a series. Even when the phrase is exactly the same, each time it is "new" – absolutely free of embedding in the material substratum – because it is appropriate; for each person, united with the others, the "object," the goal, is exactly the same: "This object, known, grasped, reproduced in the immediate overtaking [*dépassement*] of *praxis,* is only totalization itself in each person, to the extent that it must be carried out through a sign [*s'effectuer par un signe*]. I read [or decipher: *je déchiffre*] this sign through my act, by conforming to the maxim produced, and the absence of the first signifier (of the third who first shouted out the phrase) alters nothing in the structure of my *praxis*" (CDR,

380). This is a difficult passage, but one well worth deciphering. Rather than coming from an Other and alienating each from himself and from each Other, the performative here ("the sign") unites each one before a common task (each "place" – each person's object or goal – is the same "here") in praxis, and thus it unites each one with himself as an active and free subject (the object or purpose, carried out or "read" in the act through the sign, is only "totalization itself in each person").

Not an orthodox speech act as conceived by Austin, perhaps, but it is clear that for Sartre the "order" or "sign" does not refer to a given state of affairs, it is not in a relation of reference. The "reproduction" of the word in a command is inseparable from a praxis, which is an immediate "going beyond," a *dépassement,* of the command and of the situation that command is responding to. There is no delay between the giving of the command and its carrying out, since it is produced "here" as new, by the very subject who acts. The deciphering of the word is the act, the totalization of praxis rather than a fixed sign, written down, broadcast on the radio, or stamped on a coin.

We see in this moment of fusion the immanence of language, society, and history: nothing separates the order from the will of the subject; nothing separates the order from its fulfillment by a subject who is by his own act united with the group and united with himself in the fullness of socialized subjectivity. Everyone is a leader, everyone a follower of himself as leader; the group has many leaders and none, because even the "absence of the first signifier" – the first one who shouts the order – changes nothing in the way the "authorless phrase" is repeated by a "hundred mouths."

This grand process of totalization, however, is made possible only by a subtraction. It is difficult to see, on the simplest level, why this process of group formation is any less "arithmetic" than seriality. In the series there was "always one more" to be added; here there is always one more to be subtracted. It is the absence of the dead hand of the first author or leader that guarantees the power of the momentary one – and who is himself always subtracted as soon as he is added. Only if the phrase is authorless can it be *my* phrase; only in this way can I be the author, if only *now*. Put another way, only if the author removes himself as soon as he shouts the phrase can I share his status fully. There is no originary "I" behind each phrase (the "I" is thus purely grammatical); in the same way, each phrase is exclusively valid here, in this place, now, for me: "each phrase [or place: *lieu*] is, in the group, the same *here*." It does not matter if the order comes from far away, from another here; at once its place is here, and only here – but, at the same time, everywhere is "here" (and nowhere is). The phrase is literally a commonplace. (Indeed the French word *lieu* can stand for "commonplace," hence "phrase," as well as "place.") It is applicable equally well there and here; each time it is repeated it is appropriate, fully adequate to the place and the situation. It is, without any delay, "deciphered" in the act; act and phrase are identical. It perfectly designates the situation and the act to be carried out in the situation. Just as it lacks an author, then, we can say that the phrase lacks a larger, fixed meaning outside its immediate application, and its immediate application is evanescent, disappearing as soon as it arises. A word like "here" – or an order like "Right! Left! To the Bastille!" (given by the narrator on p. 379) – has no meaning at all except when applied in a specific situation. The phrase does not carry with it a baggage of reified, alienating meaning. Its meaning is *here,* and here only. Like the word "I," "here," or "now," it is a shifter; its actual meaning is evidently only its immediate use.[14]

The speech act is now identified with an empty shifter: "here." It is no longer a question of "doing something" with a command – for, Sartre tells us, any command is superfluous. (The command is nothing more than its accomplishment in the action.) The command and the authority of the commander's "I" – thus his "I" *tout court* – have been subtracted: what we are left with can therefore only be an empty "here" which is true everywhere to the extent that it is connected to an empty subject (an "I") and an empty moment ("now"). By voiding the speech act and the authoritative (commanding) subjectivity, Sartre's revolutionaries are inevitably left with nothing other than a statement – "I am here now" – that is both tautologically true and simply false.[15] But by linking the authorless speech act to the empty shifter – in fact by identifying the two – Sartre manages to eliminate any possibility that that speech act, or shifter, can be dialectically overcome at the instant of the group in fusion.

If I discover a piece of paper with the message "I am here now" written on it, I will find it to be false.[16] The phrase might have been absolutely true for the one who wrote it, when he or she wrote it (even if it was only a moment ago), but it is not now (as soon as I read it, the "I," the "now," the "here" – all are different). Or, put another way, it can be true only by being untrue, by referring to a "now" that escapes it, that is different from the "now" to which it first, impossibly, referred (the act of designation inevitably entails a temporal gap between the "now" indicated and the "now" of designation). It is an authorless watchword for a community that is unified only when each author-member is, as an author, absent in his very presence as a member. The "I" clearly does not refer to me, and wherever this "I" is, he or she is not "here" "now" (nor am "I" as "you" read this). This "I" can be nothing more than a grammatical subject, a marker in a syntactic unit. But the statement "I am here now" is also absolutely, tautologically true: I am, in fact, here now, as I write this, and read this. And I always will be, as I reread this – and as you will be, as you read this. (But the statement will *also* be false as I reread it, since my "I" at the time of writing will not be the same as my "I" at the time of reading.)

Shifters are "gone beyond," *dépassé,* then, not so much through the dialectical movement of praxis, as Sartre would have it, but through the process of their repetition. The Sartrian shifter grants an absolute truth (of the "here" and "now), but it also immediately subtracts that truth, in the same way that it grants and subtracts the possibility of an author (its author is only the circulating and empty "I"). The immediacy of its truth can be obtained only at the cost of the subtraction of a larger validity: the two are inseparable. The "I" in its *general* meaning or use is a void, a negative totem, the empty and mechanical repetition of a differentiating term. And yet it is absolutely full and true, but only *for the moment* – a "moment," a "now" which itself (as a shifter) is a void, a negative totem, and so on. The affirmation of this "I," in other words, is inseparable from its negation. The placement of such a stage of truth, of the immediate certainty of the "here" and "now," and its dependence on the shifter, might be appropriate early on in the development of a dialectic, suitable for *dépassement* at a higher stage (as it is in Hegel's *Phenomenology,* in the "Sense Certainty" section). This is not the case for Sartre, however; the group in fusion, with the "immediacy" of the empty command, plays the role, in the *Critique,* of a kind of point of absolute political truth, toward which any dialectic must strive, as its impossible final moment, and away from which it inevitably falls.

The speech act of the group in fusion cannot be inserted into any positive temporalization. It is only the immediate repetition of a shifter. It acts, then, exclusively through its own incessant subtractions: the validity of a determinate meaning carrying over through time, authorship as an originary and full subjectivity, are taken from it not dialectically, but arithmetically. The shifter is the empty term that remains after the simple removal of any positive content. In this way, it is related to the "zero symbolic value" noted by Lévi-Strauss; it too is "opposed to the absence of meaning without carrying in itself any particular meaning."[17]

Sartre, through the notion of the group in fusion, is grasping at a utopia of language, a moment of radical reduction (or, as Paulhan would call it, Terror), in which the inertia of a fixed language or a tyrannical intellectual (imposing his will through dead signs in writing) no longer stands in the way of direct communication, interpersonal union, and efficacious action. He opts for the speech act as shifter, and he thereby makes a pact with the devil; he avoids the inevitable "reification" or "sclerosis" of the revolutionary watchword, its "inscription" in thickened matter – its Stalinization, in other words – only by posing an empty term. It is no longer the "n + 1" of seriality, but "n − 1." The term, after the subtraction from it of the speech act and the author, can enter into a linguistic relation with nothing that adds to or qualifies its sheer immediacy. Yet that subtraction of meaning (the subtraction of the "I" itself) is itself already a differential operation, one that places the now purely formal term in a differential relation with other terms. It cannot help but be a term in a larger political equation – not later, when the revolutionary act is, as Sartre would freely admit, inevitably co-opted by a Stalin, but "here" and "now," in the operation that guarantees the word its immediate meaning and the act its validity in relation to subjectivity and the group. The Sartrian group in fusion, which can come together only through the anonymity of the self-subtracting speech act/shifter, the repetitive absence of the author, is in this way fully in complicity with the differential series that would seem to be opposed to it. It is not a question here of a dialectical opposition, because the group in fusion is not only a moment of dialectical synthesis; it is also a simple repetition of the earlier seriality. Nor does it conserve seriality while negating it, by raising it to a higher level: it only repeats it, differing from it only arithmetically. The relation between seriality and the group is itself only differential, and not dialectical.

This is not to say that Sartre's version of the group in fusion is necessarily false, or even that, in 1789, it did not happen that way. Maybe it did. But we have no way of knowing; as soon as the argument is based on the reliability of the shifter "here," or of any shifter, we can say absolutely anything about it "now," and it will be true – or false.

Only if the revolutionary moment, the "here" and "now," is fixed can we discuss it. And there is a way of fixing Sartre's revolutionary "I," of providing it with a stable meaning that is nevertheless faithful to its evanescence, its subtraction; there is a way of writing an "I" that is both absent in its authority, its domination, and, at the same time, omnipresent. This is the written statement "I am here now," which, as we have seen, is both the total subtraction of all "I"s, and yet is the affirmation of a kind of vast, collective but empty "I." A piece of paper with "I am here now" need not be the only available example of the group in fusion's subject-less subjectivity available. Any shifter written down in isolation, finally, will do. "I," "we," "here," "now," "there" – it amounts to the same thing. Sartre himself gives us a good example of such shifters, but they are inseparable from the book itself, the *Critique*, whose pages we turn and whose shifters we read, in phrases such as: "each phrase [place] is, in the group, the same *here*." This guarantee of the immediacy and the sense of the shifters cannot be distinguished from their inscription, or printing, on the page. The only real and immediate example that can be given of the workings of the group in fusion (its "commands"), and of the imposition of its meaning is the page of the *Critique* on which its "commands" are printed.[18] And these shifters become, once written and arbitrarily fixed, differential terms in a larger equation, a larger written project.[19]

Beyond the evident link between the group's shifters and the arithmetic relation of the series, we should note the complicity between the sinister radio broadcaster who generates seriality on a mass scale – who could be said to be the embodiment of seriality – and the narrator of the *Critique* himself. If the *Critique* – the artifact whose pages we turn – is the only real example of the fusing (through *mots d'ordre*) of the group, in other words if Sartre's book, sitting there open on my desk, is the only thing (what else can we call it?) in collective life that escapes from seriality, it is also the foremost example of the serial relation and its concomitant alienating meaning. *As* the prime example of the politically efficacious shifter, the narrator's "I" is both radically present (it, as the spokesperson for the revolutionaries, is necessarily always "here" "now") and, at the same time, it is absent, dead, fixed on the page forever in its abstract sense, and locked in a differential relation with other signs. I cannot respond to this "I," I cannot reason with it or refute it; like the radio personality, it issues vacant commands and statements and I, alone, am united with all other readers only in my isolation, my inability to confront the "I" and argue with it (and perhaps convince it). Of course I can get together with other readers in a study group, but that will have no influence on the "I" – it will only lead to more disputes, serialized conflicts with other readers over differences in interpretation. Any number of arbitrarily determined meanings can and will be imposed. The narrator, like the radio voice, is absent in its presence, the "origin" of empty or botched speech acts whose only function, it seems, is to institute an Other in each Other, to constitute "me" (as reader) as an empty "I," present only in my absence, my inability to combat the absent/present (written) voice. The latter's deadness, which is also its life, is for that reason inscribed in me, in my inability to oppose it and in an "inward" turning violence that "it" lets loose in me. That violence is also the doubled violence of the shifter, both "I" and "not-I."

If we can state at this point that the dialectic, at the moment of its most complete *dépassement* of the series, is indistinguishable from the series – in its completion – we are both undermining Sartre's dialectical project and confirming it. If seriality is always already implied in the moment of dialectical synthesis, the dialectic itself, as Sartre makes clear, itself always issues from the series, and the group in fusion can be preserved from total disintegration only through its reserialization. Sartre foresees the decline of the group, and the necessity of instituting a "terror" in which members will be lynched as punishment for their betrayal (CDR, 455–56). In the absence of the fervor of the group at the moment of its revolutionary act, a pledge – another speech act –

must be instituted in a last-ditch effort to maintain group cohesion. The one who pledges his loyalty to the group is willing to accept capital punishment as the penalty for his perfidy. Although necessary, the pledge, like all examples of the sacred for Sartre (CDR, 457), makes the continued existence of the group possible only at the cost of its dependence on the inertia of materiality. For the pledge, like a formulaic prayer to a common divinity, is only a sclerotic residue of a once dynamic praxis: "The Sacred constitutes the fundamental structure of the Terror as juridical power. The Sacred is manifested through things; it is liberty producing itself through worked matter, both as absolute sovereignty and as thing. Or, put another way, it is liberty coming back to man as petrified and superhuman power" (CDR, 457). A definition worthy of a warped Durkheim. My pledge of loyalty to a group, whether openly recognized as such, or camouflaged as worship of a deity or leader, inevitably entails a brutal curtailment of my spontaneous freedom – the Terror – as the only way of ensuring group loyalty and coherence. Revolutionary dynamism can be maintained only through its dialectical opposite, the literally serial killing of the Stalinist purges.[20]

I am not interested here in issuing a condemnation of Sartre for his not-so-implicit affirmation of the necessity of Stalinism – after all, even the nicest dialectics seem to have to pass through a moment of Terror, and it is by no means certain that one can simply "go beyond" a dialectic, naively attempting to negate it in order to affirm a presumably liberating differential model, a "dissemination."[21] After all, that move beyond, that *dépassement* itself would be fully dialectical. Even Sartre himself is able to incorporate the Lévi-Straussian algebraic kinship model into his dialectic, presenting it as a practico-inert "skeleton" that, when internalized, gives a society its strength (CDR, 486–95), and that is the "necessity of liberty" (CDR, 494). His dialectic, in other words, is supple enough literally to incorporate even what would seem to be the most recalcitrant seriality. The problem instead lies in the *limits* of the dialectic. Could the moment of synthesis – the group in fusion at the moment of its sheer praxis – somehow incorporate and dialectically transform the mathematical seriality on which it is founded? "Sartre," the narrator of the *Critique,* clearly does not think so, but it is hard to see, in principle at least, why the infinitely resilient dialectic could not, even at the moment of its "totalization," recognize itself in its dialectical Other.[22] It is impossible to say, however – and this is the crux of the problem – whether such a moment of recognition itself would be dialectical, or instead the loss of the dialectic in seriality, in the differential relation and open-ended repetition. For if seriality can enter into a dialectical game with the dialectic, seriality is also the death of the dialectic, the very principle of functioning that is asymmetrical in its opposition to the movement of dialectical opposition. The dialectic cannot function as seriality does; it is defined as the *exclusion,* the subtraction, of the serial relation. The problem is, finally, how to conceive of the moment of periodical dialectical fulfillment in the group as a totalization that undecidably dialectically incorporates seriality in its operation and, at the same time, repels it in order to constitute itself. The real risk to the dialectic, as Sartre must have been aware when he set aside the possibility of the serial relation *in* the group in fusion, is not the simple elimination of seriality, which means nothing more than the reaffirmation of seriality over the dialectic *at a later stage of the dialectic,* but a doubleness in which the dialectic enters, so to speak, a differential relation with itself, as both seriality and dialectic. The elimination of seriality, after all, only mandates its dialectical opposite, the simple replacement of the dialectic by a serial relation, a replacement that apparently, and deceptively, takes place at the margins of, or outside of, the dialectical relation. The moment of periodical completion of the dialectic *as* the serial relation of seriality and dialectic – what we have seen when the group in fusion is "recognized" as an arithmetical relation – is, however, the only moment of defeat that can problematically be inscribed within the dialectic, as the undecidability of the dialectic's triumph and defeat. And it is the moment at which the intellectual sees himself, impossibly, as both the powerful self-annihilation of his own power through his dispersal in a series *and* as the ultimate intellectual power, through his subtraction within the group in fusion, where "everyone" is a leader, a theorist, a "head," but no one can simply incarnate that function in his own reified figure. He is, in other words, the serial link between the intellectual as impotent in his power (in seriality), and the nonintellectual as powerful in the universality of the intellectual function (the group in fusion). But, since the conjunction of the serial and the dialectical can never simply be arrested in seriality either, it is also the inevitably dialectical conjunction of dialectic and seriality in the person of Sartre, the theorist of Terror – or, put another way, it is the fealty of the intellectual to Terror through the massive pledge that is *The Critique of Dialectical Reason.*

2

6

Paulhan and Blanchot:
On Rhetoric, Terror, and
the Gaze of Orpheus

UNDERLYING much of the current debate about rhetoric among American literary critics there is an earlier "controversy," which has as its reference point not so much contemporary German phenomenology (although that too is at least implied – especially in the French rewriting of the Heideggerian herme-neutic circle as a vicious circle) as the problem of the intellectual (the lay cleric) in a newly secularized France.[1] As we have seen, about the turn of the century Emile Durkheim was working to reorient religious impulses and institutions, thereby creating a rigorously rational secular religion that nevertheless would recognize, and utilize, the force of the "moral enthusiasm" that made seem-ingly irrational religious ceremonies – some of which, at least in "primitive" societies, were openly orgiastic or mystical – possible. And the autonomous intellectual, the figure who based his defense of Dreyfus on reason alone, was to be the high priest of this new cult.

After Durkheim's death in 1917 official French anthropology and sociol-ogy seemed to abandon the idea of reviving a religious experience through education in the public schools (Durkheim's avowed intention), but the tradi-tion of a "scientific" revival of the question of sacrifice and the sacred found a new home in the postsurrealist avant-garde. Here one thinks in particular of Georges Bataille in the late 1930s, who, through his efforts in the College of Sociology, hoped to spark a kind of atheistic religious revival by studying (and eventually reimplementing) sacred rites – a "left-handed sacred" that entailed not the conservation and reaffirmation of authority but its radical destruction. Where Durkheim posited "the sacredness of the human person," Bataille put forward man's death in an orgiastic frenzy; where Durkheim affirmed an au-thority of the intellectual that transcended, at times, even the influence of the state, Bataille argued for the self-mutilation of the shaman (himself, in other words). Sacrifice was secularized by Bataille in a completely new way: it was the object of a fully rational analysis, to be sure, but that analysis itself led not to a reasonable sacred, as in the case of Durkheim, but to a fully irrational one: the senseless imposition of the sheer force of mana, through the agency not of the state but of a secret society (most notably the Acéphale group).

One cannot help but think that much of this change in emphasis – the death of humanism arising literally out of the apotheosis of man – was intimately related, paradoxically enough, to Julien Benda's thinking about the intellectual. Especially in *La Trahison des clercs*, Benda argued for the necessity of a "cleric" who was quite different from Durkheim's intellectual: while devoted to reason, Benda's modern-day monk was devoted to it *alone*. Durkheim's larger concerns – especially the human person and indeed the whole problematic of the manifestation of the energy of the sacred in the collectivity – was allowed to fall by the wayside. Eventually (as in Benda's *Exercice d'un enterré vif* [1946]), all concerns beyond the cult of pure rationality are abandoned; the writer, as the sole incarnation of atemporal reason in a seemingly insane world, allows himself to become fully asocial: "How many times, returning to my little room after a bad meal, [Benda, a Jew, was in 'internal exile' under the Vichy regime], have I felt myself to be privileged in this world, by thinking that I was about to spend a number of hours with myself, with me alone, doing nothing other than elucidating my ideas. . . . I have never understood so well that the intellectual is a monster, and must never forget it."[2] Benda quite clearly indicates here that the monstrousness of the clerk – his own monstrousness – is not a function of the particular injustices that he suffers under a barbarous regime but, instead, a general condition, the result of his devotion to a heterogeneous order that in many ways bears no relation whatsoever to the everyday concerns of life in society.

It is not that far, then, from Benda's absolute – and absolutely monstrous – alienated abstract rationality to Bataille's irrationality, derived as well from the act of "pushing reason as far as it will go." Bataille, however, after Benda's despair, attempts to reinsert the "monstrous rational" back into the functioning of society itself.

It is against this background that Jean Paulhan's *Les Fleurs de Tarbes* (1936, 1941) must be read. For Paulhan's apparently strictly apolitical attempt to rehabilitate rhetoric is nothing other than a late attempt at reconciling abstract reason and sacred violence, language and that which exceeds it, in a new version of the intellectual, the Rhetorician. And the various twists and turns of the mediation Paulhan is attempting anticipate – and, through their revision by one of Paulhan's most astute readers, Maurice Blanchot, mandate – many of the problems that continue to haunt literary and cultural theory today.

I

From the outset one is struck by a basic similarity of approach in Paulhan and Benda. For the latter, the ultimate "betrayal" is carried out by the intellectual who is a traitor to his own clerical function: instead of devoting himself to an abstract, rational, and disinterested search for the truth, he genuflects before an earthly power. The "truth" that Benda excoriates is a relative one, and it is dependent upon a contingency: it is the sole property of a certain social class at a certain moment of history, a certain race, a certain nation or political entity. Truth is no longer universal, and the intellectual who subordinates it to purely pragmatic concerns – of the Left or the Right – is responsible for the downfall of the lay cult of reason. In *Les Fleurs de Tarbes*, Paulhan carries this debate into the realm of language. For him, the traitor (although he does not use such a harsh term) is now the writer who would deny language itself in order to reach beyond it and present a truth or state of reality that is apparently more genuine, more profound, than mere "word play" or "formal rules."[3] Like Benda's traitor, Paulhan's terrorist refuses his time-honored clerical task (which is dependent on well-established, logical rules and procedures) in order to grasp at what he takes to be a more profound level of reality – but which is really only a will-o'-the-wisp. The social-realist novel, the right-wing thesis novel of the "earth" or the "locale" (Maurice Barrès), literary "engagement," surrealist automatic writing, Bergsonian philosophy grounded in the instant (all of these Benda's targets too, by the way) – all would deny the very writing that makes them possible in order to posit, and somehow transmit, a more profound "beyond" or "inside." Paulhan diverges most profoundly from Benda, however, when he eventually comes to consider the complicity between Terror and Rhetoric – a complicity whose consequences he debated for more than forty years, and whose implications he was never fully able to grasp (indeed they may very well be ungraspable) – and when he tries to subordinate Terror to Rhetoric by incorporating it *within* rhetoric.

The Terrorist, according to Paulhan in *Les Fleurs de Tarbes*, has a fundamental objection to Rhetoric: it manipulates people through words, in two distinct but complementary ways. Either "words act directly on the mind, carrying it along, disturbing it without permitting it to see clearly," or "on the contrary, it is the mind which, by a cold deliberate calculation, subordinates the freshness of its inspiration to language, rules and clichés."[4] In the first case, "big words" ("revolution," "class struggle," "God," "tradition") manipulate people, causing them to act without thinking: they are slaves to empty phrases (one thinks here of the argument in George Orwell's essay "Politics and the English Language"). On the other hand, we have language as used by the Sophist (indeed, Plato, according to Paulhan, was the first Terrorist): a cold and usually disingenuous combination of words, cynically arranged following a virtually me-

chanical system or set of rules. Paulhan sums up the Terrorist's double position: "But whether or not it is spontaneous, habitual, or naive, the power of
words reveals in all cases a gap [*décalage*], a break in the relations at work
within language between word and meaning, between sign and idea. One of
the two elements, whose joining makes for normal speech, is amplified to the
extreme and hypostatized, while the other is reduced and brutalized. And
there simply are men who cede, more easily and more joyously than others, to
brutality and slavery" (FT, 63).

Clearly, though, the proper "joining" of "word and meaning, sign and
idea" in each case takes place for the Terrorist at the expense of word and sign
("the Terror admits freely that the idea is *worth more* than the word, the mind
more than matter" [FT, 64]). The Terrorist wants to see a full awareness of
meaning – a complete "thought" – rather than the rhetorical and linguistic
mechanisms that (according to the Rhetorician, at least) make this thought
possible. He thinks the mind is either oppressed by words, or that it cynically
uses them: in either case, the word does not perfectly coincide with meaning.
The mind does not constitute itself, it is not present to itself as an idea, or
thought, in the "letter." Instead, it either brutalizes or is brutalized through
language; the sheer authoritarian force of word, sign, grammatical, or rhetorical rule sees to that, by drowning out everything else.

Paulhan's response to this is double: the Rhetorician is, in and through his
very Rhetoric, capable of attaining meaning or thought; the Terrorist, in spite
of his arguments, is inevitably caught up in formulating another (idiosyn-
cratic) Rhetoric, another system of tropes and commonplaces, whether he
recognizes it or not. Paulhan notes, first, that no one has ever actually experienced first-hand being "oppressed" by words, nor has anyone, through the
misuse of language, ever been aware of oppressing others. When one uses a
commonplace (a *lieu commun*), or when he reads or hears it without noticing
that it is a commonplace, one does not notice it: it is simply a meaning, or an
idea. It is only when we listen to or read someone else with whom we disagree,
or when we read what we wrote when we were young, that the commonplace,
the cliché hits us. The manipulative "big words" are always somebody else's.
For the democrat, "religion" is a cliché; for the reactionary, "democracy" is.
What each takes to be a cliché in the other's language is for him a truth, a
thought; in the same way the young writer experiences the clichés he writes as
burning truths – and in the same way too the Rhetorician uses his various
devices (tropes, the three unities, etc.) without thinking about them (they are
his "language," which comes naturally and without which he could not express
himself). If one is not initiated into the "society" of these commonplaces (or
words), they are empty, oppressive; within that society, they are meaning,
thought, even life itself. "All families, all clans, all schools form their 'words,'

their familiar locutions, which they invest with meaning, and which is secret to the foreigner. . . . Such words are far from giving us, when we use them (even if it so happens that they give our neighbors), the least impression of wordiness [*verbalisme*]. Never, in fact, does our thought seem to us to be more free of language than at the moment in which we use [words]" (FT, 89).

It is not only the naive who take their clichés to be "ideas" or "thoughts"; anyone (including the Terrorist) does so when he uses a commonplace or a word. It is only when one is aware of the word rather than the idea that it seems that the author is "wordy" or "trite." The Rhetorician, by formulating rules and tropes, and using them, enables the reader and writer to accede directly to the idea, without being preoccupied by the word. The result of his labor, then, is an awareness of a meaning that is *not* contaminated by the recognition of the commonplace or the abstract rule. In this sense, the Rhetorician's "end product" is closer to what the Terrorist is seeking than the Terrorist's own enterprise, because in the Rhetorician's writing, if he does his job well, and learns the rules well, one is aware only of thoughts and not words. One thinks, has ideas; one does not decipher.

Conversely – and this is Paulhan's second major response to the problem of Rhetoric and Terror – the Terrorist is himself the ultimate Rhetorician because, instead of somehow miraculously acceding to the realm of ideas or experience without the intercession of words or abstract rules, he must pay attention *to* words, in order to avoid using the clichés that he accuses everyone else of using. The Terrorist falls into the trap of "verbalism": "The Terror depends first of all on language in this general sense: the writer finds himself condemned to say only what a certain *state* of the word allows him to express: he is restricted to the space of the feeling or thought where language has not yet been used" (FT, 135). In effect, each Terrorist must invent his own Rhetoric – rules that have never been used before, it is true (and thus not clichés in the usual sense of the term), but rules that are even more constraining than the "other" rules of Rhetoric, because they make communication with the reader so much more difficult. Each avant-garde project entails its own Rhetoric, which the reader must learn, with great difficulty; thus the Terrorist may find more "fanatical" readers, but far fewer of them, than does the "Maintainer" (the Rhetorician) (FT, 159).

One is never able simply to avoid language, or write one's way out of writing: "It is through *other words* that one establishes that he has escaped from words" (FT, 136). And once one has mastered the "new" rules of the Terrorist's rhetoric, his writing becomes just as much a cliché as that of the most conservative hack: "a surrealist poem is more easily imitated than a sonnet" (FT, 136). The Terrorist, however, refuses to recognize this fundamental identity between his own practice and that of the Rhetorician: from this springs a bad faith, a "fear of being a dupe" (FT, 147), and the dishonesty of his own writing: "it cheats, and does not admit that it is language" (FT, 158). Moreover, the undesirability of clichés is not the result of any of their inherent qualities; instead, Paulhan argues, it is only "because [Terrorism] proscribes them that they become hateful" (FT, 162). The very act of ostracizing or purging rhetoric makes it odious. When one analyzes Terrorism one finds a peculiar form of bad-faith Rhetoric; in the same way, through the investigation of the criteria used by Terrorism to determine unacceptable words or figures of speech one recognizes that such determinations are themselves, like the rules of Rhetoric, the result only of fundamentally arbitrary linguistic decisions. Even though he might like to, the Terrorist can never escape a Rhetorical strategy, even at the moment he would purge any given strategy, or even all of them. He is caught in a vicious circle. "[It is] as if there is no pure observation of language, but rather that a play of reflections and mirrors constantly shows us in this language (and in Letters) the very reflection of the movement by which we approach it" (FT, 162). And that approach, of course, is through language.

Yet if the Terrorist is only a Rhetorician in bad faith, at the same time the Rhetorician is a kind of higher-order Terrorist. Behind Paulhan's famous statement "We have pushed Terrorism as far as it will go, and have discovered Rhetoric" (FT, 151) is this simple discovery: the pure idea, or thought, or emotion that is vainly sought by the Terrorist is achieved every time a person uses a cliché without being aware of it. Any commonplace, if understood, is an "infinitely transparent expression to the mind" (FT, 143). By seeking an "innocent and direct language," by following the Terrorist and seeking a language which escapes itself *as* language, we are led to figures of speech, rhetorical devices – all the old tricks, in other words, of Rhetoric, which are meant to efface themselves when we read a work of literature (whether good or bad, at this point it hardly matters) and grasp an idea, experience, or emotion. The successful use of rhetorical devices leads to the utopia envisaged by the Terrorist, but now conceived within the framework of the peaceful and harmonious republic of letters, the social sphere or public park (*jardin public*) into which one *must* bring the flowers of Rhetoric, the "flowers of Tarbes" ("It is forbidden to enter the public park without flowers in your hand," Paulhan writes, thereby parodying a park sign in Tarbes which, the story goes, would exclude flowers that have been brought in from the outside, and which are therefore liable to be confused with ones illegally picked within the park). The use of Rhetoric is the only way to accomplish the Terrorist's dream; indeed it is the Rhetorician in the end who takes that dream seriously, and who "pushes it as far as it will go."

Paulhan's design for Rhetoric that would go beyond Terrorism – while taking into account its most fundamental desire – is thus necessarily social and even political. Any given cliché is such only because of a basic social disagreement: some people see it as natural and as the conveyor of a straightforward meaning; others as duplicitous, trivial, or (having been used so often) meaningless. This is why Paulhan characterizes commonplaces as being "oscillating and diverse expressions, lending themselves to double or even quadruple meanings, [monsters] of language and reflection" (FT, 139). Paulhan's plan, a utopian one to be sure, is to regularize clichés, giving them a standard meaning through a universally accepted Rhetoric: "Clichés can once again be established in [*retourner droit de cité dans*] Letters, once they have finally been stripped of their ambiguity, of their confusion. Now it should suffice, since the confusion comes from doubt as to their nature, simply *to agree*, once and for all, that they will be taken as clichés. It suffices, simply, *to make common* commonplaces – and with them these larger devices: rules, laws, figures, unities, which share their fortunes and which are governed by the same laws" (FT, 139).

Clichés, in other words, only work to the extent that all readers and writers agree on not only their meaning but their significance; only if all people are members of the same community can the commonplace simply *mean* in an honest and even transparent way. In Paulhan's view, it is evidently not so much the agreement on the uses of clichés that generates the community but, instead, the "simple decision" of the community, acting with "good will" (FT, 139). But once these things are agreed upon, by a return action they will serve to guarantee the cohesion of the society, which is divided when language "gets between" people (as it does when each person, each Terrorist, is creating his own Rhetoric). If the rules of Paulhan's rhetoric can be agreed upon in good faith (which replaces the Terrorist's bad faith), then this "preventive method" (FT, 140) will accomplish the very immediacy in relations between people that the Terrorist could only dream of: "Who would refuse [this 'simple decision' to agree on the uses of Rhetoric and the meanings of expressions], if he wants to remain faithful to the same concern for understanding and communion that secretly animated the Terrorist – and which is pursued here in broad daylight?" (FT, 139–40).

The purgative violence of the Terrorist is directed against linguistic "victims" whose cursed status is nothing other than the representation of the senseless violence of the Terrorist's own act of expulsion. The Terrorist is now replaced by the rational "Maintainer," who acts in the clear light of day. It seems we have returned to a certain version of Benda: once again we have the critique of a traitorous tendency, on the part of the cleric, to embrace the relative, particularized, or instantaneous truths or languages that elude the serene mastery of a reasoned and authoritative procedure. And just as Benda is, in his own person, the incarnation of the true intellectual, who would reform the world in his own image (at least when he does not see his own person as simply "monstrous"), so too Paulhan is the ultimate Rhetorician, positing with his own authority the possibility of a universal community (or *République des lettres*) of Rhetoricians who would agree on a limited system of rules, tropes, and commonplaces which would, through its very limpidity, guarantee the peace and stability (and thus the very existence) of the community of all writers and readers, all speakers and listeners.

Of course Paulhan differs from Benda in that he recognizes the fact that language is not simply a vessel that can efface itself when communicating pure ideas. Yet the paradox is that, through Rhetoric, language can be made to do just that; by recognizing that language cannot simply be done away with, the Rhetorician guarantees, in effect, that it does do away with itself in the very act of conveying "thoughts" and "ideas." And – again going against the individualistic Benda – this power of Rhetoric as presented by Paulhan is itself dependent not on abstract and impersonal truth but on the accord of a specific collectivity at a given time (whose decision is no doubt the result of the common recognition of the truth of the writing of the master Rhetorician; the truth, in other words, of *Les Fleurs de Tarbes* itself).

Although Paulhan's stated desire to "regularize" the use of clichés (in and through the regularization, and rationalization, of the community) might at first seem not only utopian but far-fetched, it should be noted that he took his critique of Terrorism seriously enough to propose what amounts to a direct projection of the arguments of *Les Fleurs de Tarbes* onto the political situation in France in the immediate postwar period. The basic assumption behind his political pamphlet, *Lettre aux directeurs de la Résistance* (1951) is closely linked to the one that underlies his essay on Rhetoric and Terror: that a divided community *can* confront and overcome a violent tendency to purge by peacefully and unanimously recognizing the authoritative status and the proper place of a coherent, reasoned body of (legal) rules and the "spirit" of their nonpartisan application.[5] Once again that Rhetorician-jurist the Sophist, the apparently cynical manipulator of rules and laws, will turn out to be the real hero.

Paulhan's argument in this pamphlet is clear: he states that, after the war, various "collaborators" – some innocent, some guilty – were judged, most often in courts whose juries were made up exclusively of Communists, to be "traitors." This accusation was a very specific one; Article 75 of the French penal code states that the punishment for treason is death, and thousands of people (no one is sure of the exact number) were in fact executed because they collaborated with the Germans, most often by serving Marshal Pétain's government faithfully. Paulhan's point is that these judgments were fundamentally unjust because they ignored the "grammar" of the criminal code – in other words, the Rhetoric of justice: Article 75 declares treason to be "the giving over to the enemy" of "stores, arsenals, munitions, buildings, materiel, cities, fortresses" and so on (LD, 14). Now, Paulhan goes on to argue, because the government of France – a "legal" one, if not a "legitimate" one – was at Vichy, and was recognized as such by foreign powers (the United States, the Soviet Union, the Vatican), any person following its orders, even if he or she is morally repulsive, certainly cannot be accused of treason, in the legal sense of the term. The "France" specified by the code is the legal government of the time, and is not some mystical state having to do with the physical properties of the land, or with such laudable notions as reason or the rights of man; Vichy was the official government resulting from the armistice of 1940, and it was the successor to the government of the Third Republic (LD, 20). Indeed, it is those who refused to obey the dictates of this government who are technically traitors (Paulhan does not make this point, but it is the only conclusion one can draw from his argument).

Paulhan, however, is not attempting to defend collaborators by arguing that they were "in the right" when they committed atrocities. On the contrary, he maintains that the purge carried out by Communists after the war is identical to the injustices of the period of the Occupation. The only antidote to such potentially endless reciprocal purgation is the "grammar" of the legal code, and it so happens that unless one hypocritically rewrites that code in order to find people guilty of not foreseeing in 1940 that, in 1944, they would be found to have been "traitors" for having obeyed the then legal government (LD, 24) – what he calls the *prévision du passé* – one must find the garden-variety supporters of Pétain "innocent" of treason. Perhaps they are guilty of something else, but they should not be accused of treason in its literal sense. In any case, all persons should be tried fairly, through the rigorous application and interpretation of the code, by impartial jurors.

This latter point, one senses, is really the most important one for Paulhan, eclipsing even the question of the actual punishments meted out to specific individuals. When the grammar or system of the code is ignored, there is only Terror: first there was the collaboration with the Germans, and all it entailed, then there is the perfectly symmetrical collaboration with the Soviets (on the part of the Communists who judge). The methods of these latter-day collaborators are exactly the same as those employed by the others: "betrayal, corruption, torture, the daily executions, the concentration camps and forced labor." (LD, 32). Paulhan can himself now (informally) judge as traitors the very judges who would condemn others as traitors. The problem, of course, is that without a legal code on which to rely, everyone judges everyone else, and in the very act of judging each person is guilty of the same crime he accuses the others of. Paulhan adds that it is often the people who collaborated with the Germans, who later collaborated with the Russians, first writing for *Je Suis Partout* or *Combat* (the 1937–39 version), then *Les Lettres Françaises* or *La Nouvelle Critique*.

It becomes evident that his *Lettre aux directeurs* contains in turn a rewriting of the thesis of *Les Fleurs de Tarbes*, this time used in a political analysis. Terror is still the main problem – "Terror, with all that it supposes of fear, but also of fascination; of cruelty, but also of attraction" (LD, 32). The Terrorist here too would ignore the official rules of procedure to arrive at some immediate "truth"; and here as well a purgation is involved, a radical expulsion that ratifies the Terrorist's conduct. But now not only are the rules of Rhetoric (along with the larger, coherent community that they imply) being expelled, but so too are specific individuals, victims. This sacrificial and expiatory logic, moreover, is clearly a vicious circle; it turns against itself, because one collaborator always seems to generate another, one community that purges another is itself persecuted by its former victims. There is no larger and objective grammar that can dominate the procedure and control the violence; there is no independent perspective from which the Terror can be rationally studied, and thus mastered.

An added twist also corresponds to *Les Fleurs de Tarbes*: here too the Terrorists, while attempting to attain a kind of immediate, nondeliberated justice, are inevitably caught up in a kind of grammar or rhetoric of their own. Just as the literary Terrorist ended up more immersed in (his own, perverse) Rhetoric than did the Rhetorician, so too the collaborating Terrorist is more caught up in purely technical questions than is the nonspecialist jury member who would follow the rules of the law and give the accused a fair hearing. The vengeful Communists are "experts" in collaboration, and their expertise in the matter, while being perhaps analogous to that of an expert in forensic medicine, nevertheless is not suitable for the impartial activity of judgment. This immersion in the "grammar" of collaboration, in other words, only gets in the way of the impersonal and logical Rhetoric of judgment, and it is necessarily denied in bad faith by the Terrorist. His grammar is one of rancor and *ressentiment* – the Terrorist knows his enemy, his double, his former persecutor so well that he cannot help but be swayed in his judgment by motives of revenge and competition (the Communist, in effect, wants to be a *better* collaborator than the Fascist – he wants to serve his masters more effectively than his rivals did theirs). The result is that grammar and idea, the technical expertise of collaborating Terror and the specific instance of the verdict of impartial judgment, are confused: "Everything happened as if letter and spirit, under the circumstances, were one; the form was rendered spiritual and the spirit literal" (LD, 109).

The problem, then, as it was in *Les Fleurs de Tarbes,* lies in disentangling the two: the proper and universal status of a (legal) grammar, the "letter," must be arrived at so that the "spirit" – an unprejudiced verdict – can be communicated. Such verdicts, like the thoughts or ideas of the Maintainers, will seem self-evident because they are unmediated; that is, they are not the product of the imposition of any particular viewpoint, specialization, or prejudice. Everyone accepts the validity of the grammar; its recognition is a function – and a cause – of the coherence of the community, and its application is perfectly obvious, even unperceived, to the extent that it is universal. At the moment of judgment, the intricate grammar of the legal code effaces itself before the plenitude of meaning of the just verdict. Rhetoric, pushed as far as it will go, ends in Terror – or at least, in this case, to the just verdict's transparency, of which the Terrorists could only dream.

From this perspective, *Les Fleurs de Tarbes* must also be seen as necessarily complementing the *Lettre aux directeurs* in that it proposes a reinscription of Terror *exclusively within the functioning of language itself:* the *Lettre* proposes the critique of a Terror that is nothing other than a sacrificial-cathartic violence; *Les Fleurs de Tarbes* shows more precisely how the Terror, when situated on a purely linguistic level, is itself a part – but only a part – of a larger Rhetoric. The demand for pure meaning (the "idea" – or the "judgment"), to the exclusion of the mechanisms of language, leads in the end only to the rules of Rhetoric, which assure the "thought" through the inevitable self-effacement of a properly functioning grammar. The cathartic religious drive, when located in language, is no longer the fundamentally irrational element that promises only a prolonged sacrificial crisis, the vicious circle of an endless civil war: now the Terror is an integral part of an eminently reasonable Rhetoric (indeed, it is Rhetoric's goal), which, when agreed upon, promises perpetual peace. One is reminded of Durkheim, who also hoped to transmute sacred enthusiasm – and irrational violence – into a rational religion of civic morality.

This subordination and containment of the Terror is possible only if a clear hierarchy can be established between Terror and Rhetoric; if, in other words, Rhetoric is seen as the logical and peaceful fulfillment of the Terror. But Paulhan himself realizes that it is not so easy to bring this off: indeed he planned for many years, but (significantly enough) never completed, a second volume of *Les Fleurs de Tarbes* (provisionally entitled, at one point, *Le Don des langues*) that would adequately deal with the problem of the insubordination of the Terror. He did, however, publish, in the *Nouvelle Revue Française* in 1936, an early version of this projected volume (it is reprinted in an appendix to the 1973 edition of *Les Fleurs de Tarbes* on pp. 231–48). In it, we can see a problem that was never confronted in the "first" volume of *Les Fleurs de Tarbes.*

The problem is this: for the Terrorist, the meaning of the word, the "thought," exists at the expense of the materiality of language; for the Rhetorician, the word, with its "noise, sound, [or] written sign," exists at the expense of the meaning. Put another way, the reader is necessarily a Terrorist – he perceives the meaning and not the word or its grammatical apparatus, and the writer is necessarily a Rhetorician – he is aware of the rules, tropes, and unities necessary for the communication of meaning. These two functions – reader and writer – must coexist simultaneously when the author reads his own work: there are "two men" which the author allows to speak and to decide (FT, 237) – and, it seems, they are in violent conflict. Two aspects of language are involved here, then, both of which are necessary and both of which are at work in the deployment of any given commonplace, but which at the same time are radically incompatible. In other words, they are mutually exclusive and indistinguishable at the moment in which writing-reading occurs. One is a "word that flees the idea," the other "an idea that escapes words" (FT, 239).

The easy subordination of Terror to Rhetoric in Letters is inevitably challenged not only by the Terrorist, but by the Rhetorician (Paulhan) himself: the simple fact that Rhetoric at its most successful can perfectly transmit an "idea" demonstrates the (impossible) elimination of Rhetoric at the moment of its fulfillment. Rhetoric itself provides no way to see conjoined, in a kind of mutual transparency, Terror and Rhetoric: "Far from their coinciding, I do not even see, in any way, what could be the passage or bridge [between them], if there is nothing of the word – noise, sound, written sign – that does not fall under the sway of the senses, but nothing of the meaning that does not escape them" (FT, 239). And it goes without saying that the Terror proposes no "bridge" either.

In fact Paulhan comes to recognize that Rhetoric itself is a kind of Terror, since its logic entails an expulsion or purgation (of the "thought") that is as absolute as that of the Terror: "We thought we were discovering a Rhetoric of pure thought – and it so happened that we discovered *at the same time* a Rhetoric of language and conventions; a Terror of liberation, which was *no less* a Terror of submission and slavery" (FT, 241). In other words, Paulhan has discovered a law of language – but it is just as much a kind of "law of stalemate [*une sorte de loi d'échec*]."

An odd thing has happened. The vicious circle of Terror confronting Terror, with each Terror purging the other, and at the same time "knowing" the other not objectively but only through its own "grammar" of collaboration and betrayal – the situation analyzed in the *Lettre aux directeurs* – had, it seemed, been replaced in *Les Fleurs de Tarbes* by the successful coordination of Rhetoric and Terror, the subordination and fulfillment of Terror by Rhetoric. But in the fragments of the projected second volume of *Les Fleurs de Tarbes*, written, it should be stressed, very early on, it appears that the vicious circle returns but now on a higher level: we learn that even the relation between Rhetoric and Terror breaks down, that the two cannot simply be coordinated from a kind of transcendent, scientific viewpoint. Indeed we are informed that a Cartesian analysis of language is impossible: the very "facts" Paulhan is studying cannot be distinguished from the medium – language – in which they are being posed. Language and thought are themselves "our own product," and for that reason we are not so much "extracting them by artifice from a chaos" as we are "manufacturing" them (FT, 243). Put another way, thought and word, Terror and Rhetoric, rather than being real "*elements* of our object," are only "particular deformations which we impose in order to conceive it [*pour parvenir à le penser*]" (FT, 243).

This Paulhanian version of the hermeneutic circle is straightforward enough: since "idea" and "grammar" are radically discontinuous, and are at the same time indissociable, we can only "know" one through the other, and yet that knowledge, because it is radically different from, while integral to, its object, will necessarily be a deformation of it. Only through words can we know thought – only through thought can we know words. And yet each realm, while posing, indeed alone making possible access to the other, is radically incompatible with it, and excludes it. It is, as Paulhan says, impossible to "look" at the cliché (FT, 245); like the gaze of Orpheus (as Paulhan points out in another essay, "La Demoiselle aux miroirs"), our glance banishes it, sends it away from us by presenting it "either" as one thing "or" another.[6] Yet it is both and neither, and it – language – is our very gaze itself, at which we cannot, but must, stare.

We have the distinct impression that the Terror is getting its revenge. We realize that Paulhan's entire enterprise is guilty of the same fault that, as he argued, characterized the Terror: its "object" is not "out there" in the world but is instead a function of its own positing, distorting, and banishing act. And the vicious circle of the conflict of political Terrors – or collaborations – is now inscribed in the very movement of a rhetorical examination of (and attempted apology for) Rhetoric. *In other words, the sacrificial violence of the mutual political purges of collaborators is also the linguistic violence of the conflict between syntax and meaning.*

We have reached the point at which the repetitious violence of the Terror and the founding violence of Rhetoric are impossible to distinguish, yet they are also fundamentally incompatible: the idea Terror itself can be approached, and known, only through the words that mutilate it, while the Rhetorician's efforts to dominate Terror by understanding it are themselves Terrorist.

These two sides are in fact metaphors for each other, disfigurations of a larger metaphor, an "idea," that is unknowable and that is outside their violence but which comprehends them and generates them: "Malebranche says that it suffices, in order to reach the truth, to pay attention to the clear ideas that each of us discovers in himself; instead, it is necessary to make ourselves attentive, in order to understand these clear ideas, to the ungraspable, dark, but radiant idea from which they are detached, and from which comes to them their share of meaning and clarity" (FT, 244).

If Terror and Rhetoric can be clearly separated and delineated (as they are in *Les Fleurs de Tarbes*), it is, then, only because there is a kind of generating matrix, a master cliché which is unknowable, but which somehow makes all other terms in opposition stable and knowable. It in fact generates their opposition, the duality by which they can be classified. Paulhan thus salvages his enterprise by having recourse to the metaphor of the sun: immediately after the above quote, he states, "The mystics put it this way in an image: even though we cannot look at the sun, by its light the objects of the world appear to us" (FT, 244–45). The heterogeneity of the object, its inability (like Eurydice) to be looked at and grasped, is projected onto a master commonplace, which withdraws from the world of language and at the same time anchors the interaction and mutual reflection of all the "objects" – words and meanings, writers and readers, Rhetoricians and Terrorists – that reflect it, or represent it. These latter elements in turn are clear, and can be gazed upon.

In this way, Paulhan would save the argument of *Les Fleurs de Tarbes* from the dilemma that he himself poses. Once again – as at the end of the "first volume" of *Les Fleurs de Tarbes* – Terror is subordinated to Rhetoric. The havoc it wreaks in the stable operation of the linguistic "machine" is exiled: now too it serves as a guarantee of Paulhan's project, which is nothing other than a stable knowledge of Letters. Everything, in the end, refers to this master idea, or meaning, but the latter's heterogeneity does not count when it comes to posing the everyday relations of Terror and Rhetoric.

And yet nothing has been solved: the violent purgative tendency of Terror has itself only been purged; it has been assigned to a safe place in radical heterogeneity, the metaphor of metaphor, the cliché of all clichés. For this reason it cannot be said that the two sides of language are now simply "visible": their visibility, as Paulhan himself implicitly admits when he uses the metaphor of the sun, is dependent on a larger blindness. While it appears that Eurydice's face can no longer resist capture by the gaze – Terror and Rhetoric alike stand out in their difference, in the light of day – the origin of this visibility, the mystical union out of which this opposition is generated, is itself shrouded in darkness at the very height of its brilliance. By its nature it is always already excluded. To gaze at it is once again to purge it, or, as in the case of Paulhan's own recognition of his *échec*, to expel the very possibility of the analytic rigor of his own method. Yet what Paulhan sees in the sun can only be himself, as a monster: the blinding sun, the blind sun, can only be the impossibility (which he has already recognized) of his own gaze at the moment of identity and self-constitution, the excessive and arbitrary radiation of authority at the moment in which his authority is extinguished.[7] The gaze, seeking the external and knowable object, sees only itself as its own "ungraspable, dark, but radiant idea." The flowers of Tarbes turn not toward a warming and happy sun but toward a black hole; the comfort promised by the harmonious public space illuminated by that sun is inseparable from a self-rending violence. The social peace represented by the *jardin public* of Tarbes – the Paulhanian republic of letters – is always on the point of becoming the ahumanistic, arbitrarily ostracizing space of that other famous *jardin public* of twentieth-century French letters, that of Sartre's Bouville.

The force of arbitrary expulsion generates the possibility of conceiving the Terror rationally, in opposition to Rhetoric. This force is thus always prior to the appropriation of the Terror, which is possible only when it is opposed to Rhetoric. The stable and symmetrical system of oppositions is dependent on a heterogeneous term, the sun (i.e., Paulhan the Rhetorician), which is asymmetrical to the new-found (or newly reestablished) reciprocity of the terms.

This perhaps explains why the status of expulsive force *in society* is never fully resolved in Paulhan. The inevitability of the return of purgative violence is as evident (but also as blinding) as the sun itself. If that force cannot be simply controlled by limiting it to a benign Terror, Rhetoric, or the sun – if it incessantly alternates between these terms, identifying now one, now the other, now all of them in the identity of their difference – then the force of sacrificial violence (in effect, scapegoating) will not be contained in the simple notion of Terror, which by itself can be easily controlled ("We have pushed Terror as far as it will go, and we have arrived at Rhetoric"). Nor, for this reason, will the primary strategy of *Les Fleurs de Tarbes* succeed: expulsion will continue to erupt in social relations, in spite of the efforts on the part of the "Maintainer" – the rational intellectual, finally – to found simultaneously a coherent, universal rhetoric and a peaceful, nonsacrificial society. The Rhetorician himself is not simply at the "heart" of the problem: as the sun, he *is* the problem, the incoherence (which he has already admitted) and violence at the origin of the rational project.

Thus Paulhan's efforts to imagine a new "secret society" of Rhetoricians comes up against exactly the same *échec* as the one that made Rhetoric and Terror, word and thought, both indistinguishable and radically incompatible. Indeed there are *two* secret societies in Paulhan, which are both necessary but which cannot be grasped together, from an objective viewpoint, and seen as forming an opposition-in-unity.

There is, first, a sacred society which, like Terrorist "thought," is transparent and immanent; each time we use a grammatical construction, a metaphor, a commonplace – any word, in fact – we are members of a society of Rhetoricians so secret that we don't even know we belong to it. In the essay "Le Don des langues" (which, despite its title, is *not* the second volume of *Les Fleurs de Tarbes*) we learn of a kind of mystic power by which the profane law of noncontradiction – the basic postulate of Western philosophy, which has it that "A cannot equal not-A" – is violated every time we use language: "*A thing is only a word, the form of this work is not distinct from its content, there is no word that is not a thought* . . . these are common statements in literary criticism. In short, A is not-A."[8] This is the secret power we have as language speakers and writers, which is also a kind of secret science of language: we have the ability to unify, without consciously doing so, in the linguistic act, syntax and meaning, word and thought (or, again, Rhetoric and Terror). "Without our ever having learned to form it, without its ever being possible to distinguish its successive moments, this science is given to us all, outside of which, no doubt, no discussion and no reflection would be possible. Everything happens as if men formed a secret society. . . . all languages, all fragments of languages, all phrases and words, serve to evoke the secret and, if not to evoke it, then to provoke it and start its operation" (DL, 398). This society is a secret even to its members because one cannot "look language in the face": as soon as we start to examine what we are doing when we use words, we are no longer using them – and they, like Eurydice, are exiled from us. The mystical fusion of contrary elements takes place only when we act without reflection: "It sufficed not to pay attention in order for the word to become an idea, the idea a thing and the thing a word" (DL, 421).[9]

This omnipresent secret society is mirrored by another in Paulhan, its double: this one is frankly elitist. In an article published in (of all places) *Les Temps Modernes* in 1946, under the title "La Rhétorique était une société secrète," and later republished as "La Rhétorique avait son mot de passe," Paulhan maintains that the strength of Rhetoric comes from the fact that it is *not* available to everyone, that it is, in fact, a kind of secret and sacred power: "Magic appears still more clearly in the atmosphere with which the world of initiates is shrouded. The *rasa*, or rhetorical joy, seems so mysterious in India, deprived to such an extent of natural causes – being neither object, feeling, nor concept – that merits acquired in another existence alone seem able to explain it."[10] Rhetoric manifests all the signs of the sacred, as analyzed by Durkheim and his followers: it is ambiguous, capable of doing harm as well as good, and it is a "perfectly foreign and baroque faith" that hides its motives from us. It must be perceived "in the same way [as] sociologists see the totem or mana, or even the superstitions or rites of some secret society" (RSM, 116).

Rhetoricians are not to be confused with the man in the street: their procedure is actually the opposite of the everyday relation with words. They undergo an "initiation," which enables them to do things, and create things, with words: "If the common man cries, it is because he feels bad, because he is afraid, because he wants to call someone. He feels passion *and then* he declares his passion. . . . In short, he thinks, he is moved, he hopes, and the words translate his emotion or his ideas. . . . But for the Rhetorician, it is the opposite. What he knows – better yet, what he does – is that love can follow the proposal, fear the cry, desire the demand. Thus he starts by reversing the normal order of expression, if he makes a means what to us is an end; but an end what to us is a means: if passion becomes for him a sign of metaphor, he is far from thinking that a metaphor is the sign of passion" (RSM, 133). The power of the Rhetorician becomes unlimited, because he reaches a "new dimension of the world, where the reason behind things is given to us"; he has attained a grasp of the truth that generates all things: "he finds in language and its laws the very cause of all the ideas that we form of things" (RSM, 134). The Rhetorician's effort, finally, is the most efficacious imaginable; its goal is nothing less than "going beyond the human condition as it is presented to us."

We have here two incompatible versions of the secrecy and the sacredness of the cult of Rhetoric. It would be naive, I think, to explain it away merely by noting that one version – the one published in *Les Temps Modernes* – predates the other by nearly twenty years. The fact is that Paulhan continued to work on the earlier version, and by no means intended to discard it. The two versions must be seen as equally necessary; both are derived from the ambiguity of the distinction between Rhetoric and Terror itself, and the impossibility of maintaining that distinction rigorously. On the one hand, we have a secret society that is immanent, that is the furthest thing imaginable from an elitist and exclusionary confraternity of clerks. Everyone in this society is a secret user of grammar, everyone is able to bring about mystical unifications between thinking, meaning and being, subject and object ("in order to know them, it is necessary, if only for an instant, *to be* the fog or the tree" [DL, 422]). Here of course we think of the Terror, the desire to have pure being, pure knowledge, at the expense of the intricacies of language. The common man is like the Terrorist in that he uses language without being aware of it – or he does not *want* to be aware of it (he only "thinks things," etc.). The elitist Rhetorician, on the other hand, can be nothing other than the Rhetorician posited in *Les Fleurs de Tarbes* – he or she is fully aware of the mechanisms employed and is also aware that meaning, and what is indissociable from it (thoughts, ideas, emotions) are a function of figures of speech, commonplaces, and grammar. Now what is extraordinary is this: it seems, in these two versions of a secret society, that Paulhan has reversed the values of the terms posed in *Les Fleurs de Tarbes*. There, it was the Terrorist speaker or writer who was the elitist; he wanted, or thought he achieved, an immediate union with meaning, and he would exclude everyone from his (unavowed) private rhetoric, except those, of course, who were willing to listen to him or read him exclusively on his own terms and who were willing to learn his "language." In "La Rhétorique avait son mot de passe," on the other hand, it is the Rhetorician who is the elitist and who poses an awareness of the functioning of the mechanisms of language that is the *opposite* of those held by the common man; for the Rhetorician, in effect, the signifier always precedes the signified, the language-act precedes the thought. Conversely, in *Les Fleurs de Tarbes* it was the Rhetorician who fought exclusion and elitism by advocating open communication through the *self-conscious* and formalized uses of tropes, commonplaces, and clichés, whereas in "Le Don des langues" it is "everyman" (a complete Rhetorician only because he is ignorant of what he is), with his intuitive and immediate grasp of meaning at the expense of the mechanisms of language, who is both the embodiment of the goals of the Terror, and the living refutation of the exclusionary logic that Paulhan comes to associate with it.[11]

It is not that the elite Rhetoricians are now Terrorists, or that the common man is a Rhetorician in his very (Terrorist) ignorance of Rhetoric, but that the sacrificial or sacred act of purgation, which Paulhan associated both in the *Lettre aux directeurs* and in *Les Fleurs de Tarbes* with Terror, is clearly an unstable term that shifts between the "elite group" and the "common people," between Rhetoric and Terror. The sacred is ambiguous, but not in the simple sense that it works to help or harm society; rather its ambiguity acts to undermine the stable distinction between Terror and Rhetoric first, as we have already seen (in the fragments of the "second volume" of *Les Fleurs de Tarbes*), in language itself, and now in the distinction between social groups or societies. The ambiguity of the sacred is nothing less than the ambiguity of the opposition between "word" and "thought," syntax and meaning – a radical, unmastered ambiguity, because it is composed of two elements that are heterogeneous, that cannot be coordinated symmetrically in a model of representation, knowledge, or mastery. We might go even further and state that the eruption of this ambiguity in society is the result of a failure to master it and restrict it to the level of language alone. The Rhetorician, the intellectual, finally – Paulhan himself – cannot simply subordinate the purgative Terror to a reasoned Rhetoric: there is no simple opposition/subordination between the two terms. The violence of the act of purgation itself (as if such a term were imaginable), which is not simply reducible to the Terror (a term that only enables a version of purgation to be put in relation to, and subordinated to, another term), cannot be purged from society and located exclusively within a safe master metaphor of Rhetoric itself (such as the "sun"): it always overflows again, into society and its rituals.

The utopian and unsolvable problem of Rhetoric and Terror in society must always be posed again, and always again the two terms will be unstable in their opposition. And just as, in language, one can purge the mutual purgation of the two terms only by projecting it onto a third, master, term (the sun) – which serves to ground the opposition of the terms in blindness and violence – so too the stable duality of Rhetoric and Terror (which guarantees the mutual comprehensibility of the two sides) *in society* can be accomplished only by positing a master Rhetorician who takes on the brilliance and darkness of the two terms' ungraspable relation. The purgative *act* of the Rhetorician alone guarantees the distinction between the terms, and, as in the "first volume" of *Les Fleurs de Tarbes*, guarantees one's subordination by the other: but the Rhetorician's act itself, his assumption of power, is an arbitrary exuding of force. The Rhetorician can guarantee the containment of the vicious circle of violent purgation only by himself arbitrarily acting to contain violence in language. This can be done only by establishing a homogeneous society of Rhetoricians – which can, in turn, be accomplished by nothing less, it seems, than the imposition of the force of the authority of the Rhetorician's writing. Paulhan takes this to be self-evident; it is not surprising, for example, that in the debate that followed the publication of the *Lettre aux directeurs*, one of the objections to Paulhan's position was that he lacked the authority to hold forth on questions of justice and purgation.[12] His answer is significant; he is "only" a grammarian – but clearly he held that that in itself was perfectly sufficient. Out of the arbitrary act of seizing power, then, the Rhetorician would (as in *Les Fleurs de Tarbes*) generate first a language, and then a society, in which the clear opposition between Terror and Rhetoric (and Terror's subordination) was evident, and in which a free consensus about meanings and rules was achieved (or at least the imposition of such a consensus was posited). Ultimately it is the Rhetorician who dictates that the vicious circle of purgation be purged, that clear communication and judgment based on a grammar be restored – and his power is based on nothing more and nothing less than his blinding authority as a grammarian (i.e., as the purger of purgation). Here we are caught in a circle every bit as vicious as the one that both ties together and sets in violent conflict the identical but radically opposed "collaborators."

The Rhetorician could respond here that his domination of the Terror is "reasonable," that it is based on rational arguments – but, as Paulhan himself points out in the last two sections of the 1936 version of *Les Fleurs de Tarbes*, the Rhetorician himself lacks the transcendent, "scientific" viewpoint from which to judge the distinction between Terror and Rhetoric, and from which he could subordinate one to the other. If he himself is the sun, which on its own authority throws out the light by which the opposition can be established, there is no way he can grasp his own activity in order to guarantee its reason. He will be a blinding Eurydice to his own Orpheus, and he will be blind to the force he emits, the force that established the very distinctions he "knows."

We must return, then, to the problem we posed at the outset: the Rhetorician, the intellectual, finally, as monster. But Paulhan is not the same sort of monster as Benda. The intellectual function for Paulhan is now a kind of master metaphor, a cliché/matrix that would generate and stabilize the opposition between other metaphors – such as Terror and Rhetoric – and thereby make a master Rhetoric possible. It would guarantee, in other words, the subordination of Terror to Rhetoric, along with the concomitant subordination of the social problem to the linguistic one (it is clear from *Lettre aux directeurs* that for Paulhan the *social* problem of the Terror after the Occupation could be solved only by a return to grammar). But the intellectual cannot play that stabilizing role, because he *is* the sun, the monstrosity that is the impossible joining through force of syntax and meaning, elitism and immanence, arbitrary power and reason. To know himself in and through Rhetoric, he must "see" himself in blindness, he must purge himself – he must, in other words, be the lawless enemy of the same lawful community that he founds and incarnates.

II

Much of Maurice Blanchot's project must be seen as an attempt at rewriting Paulhan, and in effect correcting one of his presuppositions. For Blanchot, the distinction between "thought" and "word" that Paulhan sees as being as central as (and not fundamentally different from) the Terror/Rhetoric distinction is in need of revision: and, as we will see, out of this revision comes Blanchot's focus on the problem of the gaze of Orpheus (a problem that, as we know, was crucial for Paulhan as well). In Blanchot's case, however, Orpheus's gaze can never be subordinated to, or reappropriated by, a sun whose light provides a reassuring illumination for the understanding and expression of the world.

In his 1942 article on Paulhan, "Comment la littérature est-elle possible?" Blanchot seeks to read Paulhan's book against itself; he would like to find a "secret book" hidden in *Les Fleurs de Tarbes*.[13] Blanchot's argument rests on the observation that Paulhan's distinction between thought and language should not be confused with the traditional one, which can be collapsed into the spirit/matter, content/form distinction. For Blanchot, thought is already composed of words, clichés; but they are a "disorder of isolated words, fragments of phrases, a first, chance [*fortuite*] expression" (CLP, 100). Language, on the other hand, is "a regulated expression, the ordered system of conventions and commonplaces." We see quickly where Blanchot's approach is headed; referring to Paulhan's essay "La Demoiselle aux miroirs," Blanchot points out that Paulhan is concerned with the most accurate *translation* of "immediate thought." Paraphrasing Paulhan, Blanchot states: "The translator dissociates the stereotypes of the text, interprets them as expressive metaphors and, in order not to replace them with simple abstract words (which would be another deformation), translates them as concrete and colorful images. This is also how all reflection misrepresents the ungraspable original thought" (CLP, 101). Consciousness, in attempting to grasp "immediate thought," has only deformed it, stripping it of its "stereotypes, commonplaces, and cadence"; what consciousness sees is only its own distorting gaze. It is, finally, only through the use of rhetorical devices that this double deformation (overabstraction, overconcreteness) can be avoided: "if we submit it [i.e., immediate thought] to the rules of rhetoric, if we astonish the attention [*si nous étonnons l'attention*] with rhythm, rhyme and numerical ordering, we can hope to see the spirit [*esprit*] returned to its stereotypes and commonplaces, unified once again with the soul from which it has been separated. Thought will once again be pure, virgin and innocent contact, not at all separated from words but in the intimacy of the word" (CLP, 101). Clichés alone are able to deliver thought from the "anamorphoses of reflection."

Blanchot is attempting to resolve a problem that Paulhan approached from a different angle. Recall that for Paulhan, in the last sections of the 1936 version of *Les Fleurs de Tarbes*, the problem in distinguishing thought from word was that, as soon as one examined these elements, one saw only a "reflection" of one's own thought. And he made the same observation in the essay to which Blanchot refers here, "La Demoiselle aux miroirs": the object, like Eurydice, fled, as soon as one gazed upon it; the word fled the thought, the thought fled the word. This problem is solved, at least for Blanchot, by redefining "thought" as a "disorder of words"; writing then becomes, not the transmission of some ineffable experience of consciousness through the use of abstract rules, but the faithful translation of linguistic force and disorder. We are now in the realm of paradox, which is Blanchot's version of the story of the gaze of Orpheus. Writing is language on language, the necessary and impossible, accurate and totally inaccurate translation of nonknowing by knowledge, of a first "chance expression" by careful artifice. Blanchot ends his essay on Paulhan with these rather cryptic words: "One can dream of this thought which reveals itself in conventions and saves itself through constraint. But that is the secret of language, as it is that of Jean Paulhan. It is enough to understand that the true commonplaces are words torn apart by lightning, and that the rigors of laws found the absolute world of expression, outside of which chance is only sleep." In the end, the ordered commonplaces of the Rhetorician take on the disorder of the thoughts they "translate": they are "torn apart by lightning." Paulhan's solar certainty, in Blanchot, becomes a violent electrical rending. On the other hand, they translate accurately – they are the ordered communication – of the very disorder the surrealists failed to register through fundamentally utilitarian devices such as dream records and automatic writing. Only through the rigorous procedure of writing can the disorder of thought be transmitted – and, no doubt, betrayed. Moreover, there can be no distinction between the originary violence of thought and its "translation."

Blanchot perhaps assumes too much when he presents Paulhan as overtly holding to the traditional and hackneyed distinction between thought and language, and only secretly subverting it.[14] (Paulhan's text may well be beyond any need of correction by Blanchot – but then again Blanchot may well be beyond any straightforward knowledge that could mandate correction.) Blanchot is nevertheless able to collapse the two realms together, thereby avoiding the conflict, the *échec*, that we saw in Paulhan. The two sides are in fact indistinguishable: the perfectly faithful rhetoric, and its conscious manipulations, is *also* the disorder and violence of the thought at the moment of its birth.[15] All this does not mean, however, that Blanchot is able to affirm the clarity and order that Paulhan finally finds in Rhetoric – at the end of the 1936 version of *Les Fleurs de Tarbes*, for example. On the contrary, rather than fleeing from the vision of Eurydice (and attempting to establish a perfectly reliable light of day), he establishes it at the very center of his most important work of criticism, *L'Espace littéraire*. Blanchot recognizes and embraces the very violence and duality that Paulhan would do away with.

Blanchot's version of the gaze of Orpheus is a revision and critique of Paulhan's in that, for Blanchot, the "object" ("Eurydice") is not ungraspable because she is a mere reflection of the writer's own consciousness, but because writing itself is unable to grasp itself in its origin and end. The "self" (which can be distinguished from "others"), is set aside by Blanchot as is the traditional series of distinctions between "thought" and "word," content and form – distinctions, in other words, that are susceptible to resolution or ordering through a dialectic. The oppositions thought/word, Terror/Rhetoric, are rewritten as the movement of writing *on* writing. It is not, however, a question of one style of writing that will be opposed to another: instead, "thought" for Blanchot is the originary division and disorder of words, the moment of their generation, which Rhetoric – the ordering of language – must impossibly translate. The two sides of this movement are indistinguishable and incompatible. Comprehensible language finds its origin and end in the adequate translation of an untranslatable and (by the standards of diurnal logic) incomprehensible text. In this way, literature will always be at war with itself, betray itself, because, as Blanchot points out in "Comment la littérature est-elle possible?" the "soul" of literature is Terror – "the conception that we have come to know under the name of Terror is not just a given aesthetic and critical conception; it covers almost the entire spectrum of letters; it is literature" (CLP, 97) – but, at the same time, no writer can simply do without the "form of [his] art." Litera-

ture is the *only* conjunction of "thought" and "language," originary formlessness and belated reordering: "It is a fact, literature exists. It continues to be, in
spite of the inner absurdity which inhabits it, divides it, and renders it truly
inconceivable" (CLP, 97). Literature is the only movement that is fully dedicated to the necessary but never attained translation of "thought" (or sheer
Terror). Its true "subject" is for that reason the very Terror it always but never
conveys.[16]

We can see here a very different version of the project we found in Paulhan – namely, the resituating of the Terror fully within the (literary) text,
accompanied by the inevitable control of its power and expiatory violence. To
see how and why Blanchot attempts to carry out this transformation of social
and political Terror into textual Terror, we must turn to the crucial essay "Le
Regard d'Orphée," translated as "The Gaze of Orpheus."

If Blanchot appropriates the Greek myth of Orpheus, it is not to valorize a
heroic poetic subjectivity. Instead, from the first, Orpheus for Blanchot is the
double demand of the work (l'*oeuvre*); the work is the necessity, the law, of the
poetic sublimation of a radical force, the "depths" [*la profondeur*], and at the
same time it is the naked confrontation with that force, which violates the law
of the work and is therefore never anything more (by the standards of conventional logic, at least) than abject failure. As Blanchot writes, "The depths
cannot be directly freed, they are only revealed through their dissimulation in
the work. . . . But the myth shows no less that the destiny of Orpheus is also
not to submit to this final law" (GO, 99–100). Orpheus betrays the exigency
of the work, which is the submission of the depths to the ordered form of art.
But not to confront, impulsively and directly, the depths would also be a
betrayal: "Not to turn toward Eurydice would be no less a betrayal of, and
infidelity to, the measureless and imprudent force of his impulse, which wants
Eurydice not in her diurnal truth and her everyday charm, but in her nocturnal
darkness." The paradox lies in the fact that both measure – the subordination
of the unmediated force of the depths – and direct confrontation with the
depths are necessary: "[Orpheus] loses Eurydice, because he desires her beyond the measured limits of the song, and he loses himself, but this desire, and
Eurydice lost, and Orpheus scattered, are necessary to the song, as the ordeal
of eternal worklessness [or idleness – *le désoeuvrement*] is necessary to the work
[*l'oeuvre*]" (GO, 101). Only by breaking the law of the work, and forgetting it,
destroying it, can Orpheus reunite the work with its origin: "only in [Or-
pheus's] gaze can [the work] go beyond itself, be united with its origin and
consecrate itself within the impossible [*se consacrer dans l'impossibilité*]" (GO,
102). The gaze is the refusal of the work, its sacrifice, which is nothing less
than the work's completion and sacralization through the scattering of its
origin.

Paulhan and Blanchot

This double movement of the gaze – the simultaneous destruction and reorigination of the work – must be identified with the movement of literature that Blanchot presented in his 1942 essay on Paulhan. There too the work could be completed only through the patient and impulsive transmission of that which defies all transmission. After all, there is no difference between a fully ordered movement that translates the originary radical disorder of words ("thought") and the impetuous, impatient movement (impatience, according to Blanchot, "must be the heart of profound patience" [GO, 104]) that attains the origin of the work through the violation of its law.

The figure of Orpheus himself is of less importance than is this radical version of the hermeneutic circle, a movement which Blanchot summarizes at the end of "Le Regard d'Orphée." Orpheus can only "write" – "attain the origin, consecrate the song," by writing. "One only writes if one attains the instant toward which one can only progress in the space opened by the movement of writing. In order to write, it is necessary already to write. The essence of writing is also situated in this vexation [*contrariété*]" (GO, 104). Rather than trying to see his way out of the vicious circle, then, as Paulhan did, and rather than seeing it as an effect of the self or consciousness, Blanchot presents it as the movement of writing itself. The violence of the origin can be reached only by that which betrays it: the origin, writing itself, is attained only by already writing – and yet if one already writes, writing cannot simply be the point of origin . . . or be at a simple point of origin.

This impossible duality of the origin, in which writing finds its not-knowing and nontruth, precludes any easy distinction between form and content, thought and language, Terror and Rhetoric. In this way Blanchot is able to carry out the gesture that seemed so difficult for Paulhan; he can subordinate a sacrificial, purgative Terror to the movement of writing (Blanchotian Rhetoric) itself, thereby defusing its violence. In the penultimate section of "The Gaze of Orpheus," entitled "Gift and Sacrifice," Blanchot makes it clear that the "sacrifice" of the work that he has been describing cannot be situated within traditional (and metaphysical) oppositions such as the sacred and the profane, transgression and interdiction. The work may be sacrificed, but it is "an unceremonious sacrifice in which the unconcerned gaze which is not even a sacrilege, which has none of the heaviness or gravity of an act of profanation, returned the sacred itself – night in its unapproachable depths – to the inessential, which is not the profane but rather does not fall within these categories [or which falls short of – *en deçà de* – these categories]" (GO, 103).

In this very affirmation of the sacred and sacrifice, the logic of purgative violence in society is elided. The subject, the community itself (for that is what Orpheus and Eurydice, together, are), and finally the defining and excluding acts of a community, are done away with; Blanchotian sacrifice, *within* the

168

literary text, is on "this side" of the traditional (anthropological) categories of religious life. Gift giving in society, so trenchantly analyzed by Mauss, and so flamboyantly championed by Bataille, is now fully situated within the work: the gaze of Orpheus "unties" the bonds that held back Eurydice and the sacredness of the night, bonds that were associable with "order, rectitude, law, the way of the Tao and the axis of the Dharma." In other words, the gaze "liberates the sacred contained in the work," and "*gives* the sacred to itself, to the liberty of its essence" (G O, 104).

In a sense, Blanchot "recognizes" all the elements in Paulhan's text to which the latter, apparently at least, is blind, and he "solves" Paulhan's greatest problem. (But his "solution," if we can call it that, is a higher-level blindness, or secrecy. It cannot pretend to be only a higher knowledge.) Paulhan, despite his efforts, was unable to maintain the coherent distinction between thought and Rhetoric; because of this, he was, as we saw, unable safely to guarantee a position for the Terror exclusively within Rhetoric. Blanchot's strategy is different; instead of trying to explain away the *échec* of the gaze of Orpheus, or trying to contain its impossibility within the falsely reassuring figure of the sun (and of himself), Blanchot embraces it. No doubt using a Heideggerian strategy, he posits for it a more radical and authentic status than that held by the people and events of everyday life; he is thus able to bracket everything (metaphysics, the world, the conventional community and its rituals) that is diurnal, quotidian. The gaze, and the object of the gaze, is the privileged space of writing – of literature – because literature alone is both the Terrorist disorder of originary thought and the ordered and formal translation of that thought, the simultaneous violation and fulfillment of the work, along with the violation and fulfillment of the disorder itself. Thus Blanchot is able to resituate sacrificial violence in a space without mastery, without a homogeneity based on the trivial forgetting or re-membering of the hermeneutic (vicious) circle of knowledge (the sacred is "given to itself"). This new version of the sacred and gift giving cannot be seen as social in the conventional sense, nor does it respect the conventional categories which make a purgative Terror possible (it is on "this side" of those categories), such as self and other, sacred and profane, guilty and innocent. Yet it arrogates to itself the force of the sacred, denying to traditional sacred forms ("order, rectitude, law"), and to their explicitly or implicitly violent authority, any legitimacy whatsoever.

It goes without saying that this "space," lacking the mastery of Orpheus, is also a locus of the absence of the intellectual (Orpheus is "scattered"). Orpheus, if anything, is the ghost of the writer, the impossibility of his authority and autonomy. He "is" the movement of the work – of writing – and nothing more. But a problem immediately appears: if the ghost is *not* a writer, is instead the exclusion of the former conception of the writer, then Blanchot, in positing this figure (Orpheus), is running the risk of simply reestablishing a new authority – of the intellectual (himself), and his writing – based as before on the logic of opposition and purgation. Vincent Kaufmann has noted this problem in his book *Le Livre et ses adresses: Mallarmé, Ponge, Valéry, Blanchot.* For Kaufmann, Blanchot from the first practices a rigorous and conventional exclusion – of figuration itself. Blanchot, in *Le Livre à venir*, positing the "symbolic" realm in opposition to the communication of meaning, clearly identifies it with what he called the "work," or "writing," in "Le Regard d'Orphée." As Blanchot, quoted by Kaufmann, states: "The symbol signifies nothing, expresses nothing. It only makes present – by making present to us – a reality which escapes any other grasp and seems to come forward, there, prodigiously close and prodigiously distant, like a foreign presence [*comme une présence étrangère*]."[17] Clearly we are back in the realm of Orpheus and Eurydice here, but what is important for Kaufmann is that the "symbolic" (which is not symbolic at all in the usual sense of the term) tends to elide any possible transmission of sense; in the process, the position of the reader, be it stable or (as Kaufmann shows in the case of Mallarmé) contested, is done away with as well. Blanchot's writing refuses metaphor, figuration, in a (doomed but seductive) attempt to efface the mediating role of language between reader and writer, in order to affirm a more immediate contact – but all that results is, in Kaufmann's words, an "impersonal intimacy, always at a distance from itself, which becomes hypnotized [*se fascine*] in the speaking of its own void" (LA, 195). In effect, Kaufmann, consciously or unconsciously following in the footsteps of Paulhan, is accusing Blanchot of literary terrorism.

This "writing," which always "says" the same thing – in its inability to say anything – acts only to "expel words from discourse" (LA, 194), but the only way such an expulsion can be carried out is through the intervention of a mastery: Blanchot's own. "If writing has no authority because it declines all figuration, its lack of legitimacy can be defined as a legitimation founded on the rhetoric of the unrepresentable [*l'infigurable*], of the incommensurate" (LA, 195). It is now literary practice itself that, through a certain rhetoric, is invested with a mastery, and all the more so in that it, on the surface at least, refuses all mastery; at least if, as Kaufmann says, "all mastery passes through the concealment [*dissimulation*] of what authorizes it." In other words, it is the very effacement of mastery, on the part of a Blanchotian writing, that confirms mastery's presence – and, by extension, that confirms Blanchot's own mastery: "in condemning literature to the unrepresentable, Blanchot assigns himself, in a certain way, his own place on the side of mastery." In the same way, of course, the refusal of language as communication – the "emptying out" of language – only leads to more language, and to a more authoritative language.

Paulhan and Blanchot

This is the most fundamental critique of Blanchot that can be established; Blanchot, in elaborating a radical separation between "master" and "student" (as in the quote from *L'Espace littéraire* that Kaufmann discusses in LA, 197), certainly seems to be reinstituting a break that would be responsible for such classical (and oppressive) oppositions as mastery and servitude. Through this separation, and this purgation of representation, in Kaufmann's words, "the other occupies the place of a quasi-absolute unknown, and reading is condemned to *ignorance*" (LA, 197).

The stakes here are high indeed, because the logic of mastery and exclusion is exactly what founds the very kind of community that Blanchot would condemn. It is, once again, the logic of the Terror and expiatory violence. Blanchot in fact makes clear, for example in his recent book *La Communauté inavouable*, that such a monolithic community, established and reestablished through purgation, is not to be confused with the "textual" community – which is the absence of community – in and for which Blanchot himself writes. Writing approvingly of Bataille's prewar Acéphale group, Blanchot states: "The cutting off of the Head [Bataille's image, at the time, of social liberation] did not only exclude the primacy of what the head symbolized, leadership, reasonable reason, calculation, moderation, and power, including the power of the symbolic, but exclusion itself, understood as a deliberate and sovereign act, which would have restored its primacy in the form of degradation [*déchéance*]."[18]

One sees here how difficult it is to accuse Blanchot of the reestablishment of mastery through the gesture of exclusion. He himself, in the above quote, uses the word in two ways; first, a "good" exclusion (the exclusion of the Head, reason, etc.), and then a "bad" exclusion (the very same exclusion, in fact, which, excluding sovereignty, itself becomes sovereign in its very degradation), and then another "good" exclusion (the exclusion of "exclusion itself"), and here we are in a labyrinth of terms "emptied out," made ghostlike, and turned against themselves. A familiar enough strategy, after Heidegger and Derrida, if not Blanchot, and one that anticipates the very kind of critique that Kaufmann directs against it, but which does not at all deny – or exclude – the possibility of such a critique. The full ambiguity, or trickiness, of Blanchot's stance can be seen in a passage that Kaufmann quotes (in order to bolster his own position) from *Le Livre à venir*. The last sentence reads: "It [writing] is not rhetoric, or it is a rhetoric of a particular kind, destined to make us understand that we have entered into that closed space, separated and secret, that is literary space [*l'espace littéraire*]."[19]

If ever it seems that we have caught Blanchot red-handed, this is it: a naive notion of the sacred, tied to an elite, reserved space, no doubt emptied through a cruel purgation – and sanctified in a temple – is identified with the title of another of Blanchot's books! And yet when we return to *Le Livre à venir* and read the full passage from which Kaufmann has quoted, we realize that Blanchot has the last laugh: he is writing, in fact, of a certain notion of writing put forward in Barthes's *Le Degré zéro de l'écriture* – one that Blanchot himself is *not* valorizing. Blanchot, in the essay from which Kaufmann takes his quote, "Où va la littérature?" concludes that the basic strategy of contemporary writing lies really in "wanting to destroy the temple, rather than to raise it"; it is "finally to refuse to cross the threshold [of the temple], it is to refuse to 'write'" (*Le Livre à venir*, 303). In fact, this writing of the disruption of the sacred space can be identified with the Terroristic writing that Blanchot saw as the "soul of literature" in his 1942 essay on Paulhan, "Comment la littérature est-elle possible," which should not be confused with a simple version of exclusionary, violent Terrorism.

If Kaufmann is totally misrepresenting Blanchot in this quote, in another sense he is presenting him accurately. After all, Blanchot has used the very term – *l'espace littéraire* – that most readers associate with his own conception of the "work." This underscores the paradox that Kaufmann seems to be unaware of but which Blanchot himself fully recognizes, even (and especially) when he loses sight of it: sacrificial exclusion and the exclusion effected by the Blanchotian "work" – the movement that separates Eurydice from Orpheus – cannot simply be separated. There is no neat logic of exclusion that can establish a stable distinction, and hierarchy, between them. The two exclusions – and the two literary spaces – are doubles, and one space can never be kept from intersecting with the other. And yet, at the same time, Blanchot always necessarily continues to exclude purgative exclusion.

At this point we can rejoin Kaufmann's critique, but with certain qualifications. The problem is not so much that Blanchot posits a crude and barely repressed mastery but – another version, perhaps, of the same thing – that he definitively excludes the founding of a certain type of community when, on the basis of his own position on exclusion, he must envisage and even affirm it. If his "exclusion" is double, and if its two senses cannot be rigorously distinguished (Blanchot's plays on the term itself, and on *l'espace littéraire*, indicate this), then Blanchot's derealized community of readers, of the kind he describes in *La Communauté inavouable* ("a small number of friends, each singular, and without any obligatory relation with the others, makes up [the community] secretly through the silent reading that they share, by becoming conscious of the exceptional event with which they are confronted, or to which they are devoted" [CI, 39]), can never be rigorously distinguished from a more conventional community, one perhaps without a head, a master, but one that nevertheless has its own inevitably cruel and carnal exclusionary rites, its own particular (or peculiar, or piacular) conception of the sacred, its own version of legitimated violence, and so on.

This second community is the one that, on the basis of his own logic, Blanchot is prevented from simply excluding (although this gesture is also necessary). And suddenly, after a long detour, we are back at the problem we saw facing Paulhan. Terror as sacrificial violence cannot be maintained exclusively in language or writing; it always threatens to spill over, to contaminate a ("textual") community that has been established against it. And always again the figure of the intellectual, in his "monstrous" split, comes to represent this duality (even and especially when he is engaged in the act of obscuring it). If Blanchot, in his "unavowable community," is only the work itself, in the other community (which cannot be definitively distinguished from the first), he runs the risk of being a leader, even (and above all) at the moment when he cannot avow it, when he authoritatively *disavows* (or unavows) it. It should come as no surprise that, shortly after publishing *La Communauté inavouable*, Blanchot in 1984 came out with an article, "Les Intellectuels en question," which presents a much more conventional version of the social and political responsibilities of the intellectual.[20] This article, a kind of autocritique that never acknowledges itself as such, is no doubt a recognition of the importance of the fact that its author did indeed write Fascist, anti-Semitic propaganda before the war.[21] It is, in other words, a belated recognition that there is another community beyond the textual one and that those fully immersed in the latter must nevertheless recognize the importance of their acts – and the consequences of their theory – in the *other* community, the one of flesh and blood, of murderous violence and purgation. Far from being confined, then, to sheer, ethereal textuality, Terrorism, and its monstrous intellectual, are torn between, on the one hand, the necessity of the "work" and, on the other, the possibility of an inevitably cruel, exclusionary society – secret or otherwise.

We come to recognize that much of the current critical concern, in the United States at least, with rhetoric can be traced back to a debate that always places the conflict within rhetoric (between meaning and grammar, for example) in a larger context – one of political terror, sacrificial violence, sacred and secret societies, and the problem of the committed intellectual. "Anthropological" problems, perhaps, but ones belonging to an anthropology that never loses sight, in the end, of the necessity and difficulty of all attempts to situate (and safely confine) violence within a textual community that bears as its totem the "death of man." We face yet another monstrosity, then – the anthropology of the death of man.

7

Foucault and
the Intellectual
Subject

IT IS OFTEN argued that Michel Foucault's work entails a radical critique, even a total elimination, of the subject, and thus of the humanism that (as we have seen, for example, in Durkheim's models of education and the state) both depends on and makes possible the production and reproduction of the entity "man." Thus Luc Ferry and Alain Renaut, in their recent book *La Pensée 68*, insist that Foucault's work all along has consisted of a somewhat dangerous repudiation of a subject that can serve as a "figure of the universal" and as a "pole of intersubjectivity": it favors instead a kind of wild individuality that precludes a common moral base, adequate communication, respect for the rights of the Other (*les droits de l'homme*, in effect), and so on.[1] Ferry and Renaut's argument is that even Foucault's last work – volumes 2 and 3 of *The History of Sexuality* (1984) – still maintains the same valorization of a mad, anarchistic – and potentially very dangerous – "individuality" (as opposed to subjectivity) that was put forward in Foucault's early works, such as *Madness and Civilization* (1961).

In this chapter I will turn to a number of Foucault's writings, both before and after the so-called "turn" from archaeology and genealogy to see in what ways Foucault, while explicitly affirming the Nietzschean "death of man," must, in order to establish his new position, depend on the very strategies he characterizes as integral to the aborted production of "man" – strategies that can be associated most notably with the name "Hegel."[2] Along the way, it will become quite clear, I think, how Foucauldian moves closely tied to the elimination of "man" are inseparable from a conception of language and textuality which itself issues from a tradition – that of Durkheim, Paulhan, and Blanchot – that links the sacrificial radicality of experience to a terroristic elimina-

174

tion of one function of language (stable representation, the possibility of reference, "thought," as Paulhan called it) and the affirmation of another (the repetitious or serial mechanism by which meaning is produced – grammar, in short). But such a tradition, as we have seen and will continue to see, is in no way "separable" from a tradition of stable reference, cognition, and the imputing of meaning to an overarching, responsible subjectivity. Therein lies the problem – for Foucault's detractors as well as for his partisans.

I

One of the most striking things about Foucault's essay on Bataille, "A Preface to Transgression" (1963), is not so much that it quotes sparingly from Bataille, or that it concerns itself so little with a close examination of his writings, but that it is so clearly indebted to Heidegger, without ever explicitly recognizing that debt.[3] One could speculate about Foucault's motives for passing over in silence his ties to Heidegger – as is the case with Derrida, he usually only explicitly mentions Heidegger to note a failing in the master's work, to mark out his difference from him. Perhaps Foucault's silence on this topic can be traced to the fact that in his early writings (such as the piece on Bataille) Foucault is resituating Heidegger in a French context: Heidegger, as rewritten by the younger thinker, is no longer the champion of authenticity, Being, and dwelling in the Black Forest (i.e., the fundamentally positive situation of Dasein in the hermeneutic circle) – nor is he a critic of Nietzsche as the last, and culminating, metaphysician.[4] Instead, the unnamed Heidegger is now explicitly in alliance with a French Nietzsche, the hero of Gilles Deleuze and Pierre Klossowski: his strategies are now associated with sexuality, death, and (as in the climactic episode of Bataille's *Blue of Noon*) with an infinite fall into a starry grave. The reactionary Heidegger, always suspected of collaborating with the Nazis, has now been translated into an aggressively literary (and usually left-wing) avant-garde tradition – a tradition which, moreover, cannot be separated from a larger French anthropology, which the avant-garde both fiercely opposes and doubles. In passing over Heidegger's name in silence, then, Foucault is able to pass over the difficulties of this translation, from hermeneutic to vicious circle, from one culture to another, from one political and social wing to another.[5]

The problem, as Heidegger himself recognized, goes back at least to Kant; if man is finite, limited, how can man also be a plenitude, infinite, unlimited? How can he hope to take the place of God?[6] Man is in fact defined by the very limits that mark the borderline separating that which he is from that which he is not. His limits, in other words, are integral to his constitution as a finite being; the line between that which "is" man and that which must be excluded from him (or that which must be, in any case, external to him) is situated not at the periphery of man's being but at its "center" and at its "origin."[7] The limit is transgressed when it is situated at the empty core of man's being, and at the same time that being, which usually passes as the subject, is itself transgressed, because the limit is situated "in" it. As Foucault states, "The limit opens violently onto the limitless, finds itself suddenly carried away by the content it had rejected and fulfilled by this alien plenitude which invades it to the core of its being. Transgression carries the limit right to the limit of its being; transgression forces the limit to face the fact of its imminent disappearance, to find itself in what it excludes (perhaps, to be more exact, to recognize itself for the first time)" (PT, 34).

The limit is itself defined only by what it excludes, and so it is dependent on it; that "accursed share" (as Bataille called it) is, however, situated *in* the defining limit, constituting it while transgressing it – just as the limit is situated at the core of "man," constituting him while transgressing him. The limit itself is transgressed by a limit at its center ("transgression carries the limit right to the limit of its being"), and so on to infinity. In addition, this movement entails a recognition: the limit – "man" himself finally, repetitively – represents to himself this infinite process. But what is "man" if not an instance, indefinitely repeated, of the limit that both generates its representation and transgresses itself through that representation, that recognition? Foucault would then discard the notion of "man," or the "subject," altogether, and stress simply the infinite regress of language itself, representing, and thus transgressing, the constituting transgression at its center. Foucault links a Bataillean transgression to Blanchot's "principle of contestation": "Contestation does not imply a generalized negation, but an affirmation that affirms nothing, a radical break of transitivity. Rather than being a process of thought for denying existences or values, contestation is the act which carries them all to their limits and, from there, to the Limit where an ontological decision achieves its end; to contest is to proceed until one reaches the empty core where being achieves its limit and where the limit defines being" (PT, 36). No doubt Foucault is playing here (as Derrida does later) with the double sense of "end": the "end" of being, as a goal determined from the beginning, is the "limit," the "empty core" which is the definition of being (or Being).[8] At the same time, however, that limit, which is nothing other than the origin, as Foucault constantly reminds us, is also the definitive "end": death, blindness, terminal transgression, and the night.

The infinite "murmuring" of language is the process of repeating the limit, attempting to reflect on its origin by reproducing it, in order to stave off death. But its origin is itself the movement of transgression, the fatal doubling and "self" violation of a limit that can "live" only by embracing, repeating, and betraying its own "end," its own death. This mechanical process can "take place" only in language; it has no status whatsoever outside of language (indeed it is absurd to talk of anything "outside" language, because language's outer limit, and what it would expel, is always already situated at its divided core).[9] As Foucault states in another essay from the same period, "Language to Infinity" (1963): "Language, on the line of death, reflects itself; there it meets something like a mirror; and to stop this death which would stop it, it possesses but a single power: that of giving birth in itself to its own image in a play of mirrors that has no limits."[10] It is, in fact, the "breakdown of philosophical subjectivity and its dispersion in language" (PT, 42) that is "one of the fundamental structures of contemporary thought." But Foucault's Heideggerianism is closely linked to a vocabulary inherited from the tradition of Durkheim, via Bataille. He states, for example, that transgression, "from this limit marked by the sacred . . . opens the space where the divine functions" (PT, 37). The transgressive sacred, in other words, is a marker of the limit, but also a marker for the translation into French terms of the larger Heideggerian enterprise.

Language, transgression, and the sacred for Foucault are thus intimately linked. It is at this point that Foucault, via Blanchot, rewrites Sartre: if Sartre, in *The Critique of Dialectical Reason*, values a collective subjectivity through an affirmation of a shared shifter/speech act – one which transcends language itself and overcomes seriality through the fusion of the group – Foucault affirms a seriality of language, operating in the absence of any possibility of reference (to an external object) or communication between speaking subjects.[11] The speech act, freed from its job as a mechanism guaranteeing the human group's coherence, floats free in indefinite and inhuman repetition. Foucault, at the beginning of his essay on Blanchot, "La Pensée du dehors," focuses on the paradoxical status of an expression that is both a pure speech act and a shifter: "I speak."[12] Like the "commands" given in Sartre's group in fusion ("turn left," "advance"), it is a statement that apparently does not so much communicate as refer to the moment of its own enunciation, conferring a status, a legitimacy, on that enunciation, and the subject "behind" it. All the bywords of Sartre's crowd could be summed up in a single phrase: "I am here now." The expression grants itself a status as a kind of doubled consecration and representation – or totem – of the group and its collective subjectivity at the moment of a specific and necessary application. Foucault, however, goes in the opposite direction: for him, "I speak" obviously cannot serve as a sacred marker, a totem for a group in fusion, but it cannot guarantee the subject that speaks or the object that is referred to (that same speaking subject) either. The speaker and his speech are inseparable, yet that speech itself, at the moment of the enunciation of "I speak," is destroyed as communication, as stable and adequate reference to outside or inside, and thus to a continuity between objectivity and subjectivity, *and* it is destroyed as well as a totem that would found or guarantee a continuity between subjectivities. If "I speak" refers to speech, it is a strange speech, and there is a strange subject behind it: "'I speak' in fact refers to a speech [*discours*] which, by offering it an object, would serve as its support. But this support is lacking; the 'I speak' lodges its sovereignty only in the absence of all other language; the speech of which I speak does not exist before the nudity spoken at the moment in which I say 'I speak'; and it disappears in the very instant in which I stop speaking. Any possibility of language is here dried out by the transitivity in which it takes place. The desert surrounds it" (PD, 523–24).

Language's only "support" at this moment is the speech act "I speak," which itself is not part of a larger continuity of language but which occurs only in a "stripped" "point," as a certainty that is possible only at the moment in which it is isolated from all other language. But that isolation, which is the guarantee of the truth of the object and the self-certainty of the subject, is only the total isolation of the speaking subject, in the shifter and in the speech act; language is now nothing more than a stuttering series of these "I"s (at the repetitious moment of the enumeration of an infinite number of examples of the phrase "I speak"), all referring to themselves with utter certainty, yet through their discontinuity, their seriality, at the same time incapable of constituting themselves as stable, originary selves within a temporal continuity. "It [language] is no longer speech and the communication of meaning, but the display [*étalement*] of language in its raw being [*son être brut*], its pure opened-out exteriority; and the speaking subject is not so much the element responsible for speech . . . as it is the inexistence in the void of which is ceaselessly carried out the indefinite outpouring of language" (PD, 524).

This language is not, Foucault is at pains to stress, one of self-reflexivity or self-adequation in which language – or the literary work that represents it – grasps itself within clearly defined borders, borders which act as stable limits and rigorously exclude the "external." Rather it is the indefinitely proliferating series of speech acts/shifters that is a movement to the outside: "Language escapes from the mode of being of speech – in other words from the dynasty of representation" (PD, 524); it is the automatic repetition of the movement of force that always again crosses, or transgresses, the limit that divides, and thus institutes, inside and outside.[13] The totem act, in effect, is exercised in a void.

The maintenance of that limit, the traditional specular and speculative moment, which is also a sacrificial moment, always entails a unification-through-expulsion. But the transgressing of the boundaries erected against the untouchable, external element – the thought of the outside – necessarily entails a different notion of the sacred from that affirmed by an exclusionary (philosophical) model of sacrifice.[14] It is not that sacrifice itself is to be expelled, then, but only that one sacrifice – we might call it a Hegelian Durkheimian one – is to be replaced by another: the Bataillean Durkheimian version. As we have seen, for the Hegelian Durkheim, representation (through the constructive effects of sacrifice) entailed the guarantee of the state, and the place of the subject within it; the state was not only a kind of master totem but – since the "person" was for Durkheim the totem of the larger, progressive, society – a guarantee of the subjectivity of the intellectual within it, the intellectual who himself both guaranteed the state and its operations and who was in turn dependent on them. (The problem of subjectivity in Foucault, as in Durkheim, can never be grasped if one ignores the fact that consciousness is always intellectual consciousness *and* the consciousness of the intellectual.) Foucault, opposing this Hegelian strain in Durkheim, instead reads the Durkheimian tradition against itself, as did Bataille, and stresses the violence of the speech act/shifter over the adequacy of official intellectual self-representation. Sacrifice for Foucault is now inclusionary rather than exclusionary, and it is in the figure of the writer himself, and his text, that the violence of the discontinuous "I speak" comes to reside. The totem act now guarantees or represents nothing, and it "founds" only the repetition of the violence of the act of writing: "Writing is now linked to sacrifice and to the sacrifice of life itself; it is a voluntary obliteration of the self that does not require representation in books because it takes place in the everyday existence of the writer. Where a work had the duty of creating immortality, it now attains the right to kill, to become the murderer of its author."[15]

Contestable as this notion of the "everyday existence of the writer" might be, it is clear that the unmoored speech or totem act of the affirmation of subjectivity in language is now linked to the sacrifice of that subjectivity. The intellectual, the writer, as consciousness can be produced only through that very language: "Perhaps there exists in speech an essential affinity between death, striving, and the self-representation of language" (LI, 55). Other than this "self-representation," reference and self-reflexivity have no place in a "work of language" which is "a body of language crossed by death in order to open this infinite space where doubles reverberate" (LI, 59). Language comes to subsume sexuality, indeed "life" itself (PT, 50).

The transgression that Foucault finds in Bataille is an escape from, even a repudiation of, Hegel. Foucault insists on nothing less than the "absence of the sovereign subject"; in the "nondialectical form of philosophical language" (PT, 48), the "universal nature of transgression" is revealed. The era of transgression, of the Bataillean Durkheim, will simply replace the Hegelian era of state, subjectivity in the community, and wholesome moral enthusiasm; Sadian sexuality (which is always *linguistic*) will replace the sober civic virtues of an earlier French tradition: Sexuality is "tied to the still silent and groping apparition of a form of thought in which the interrogation of the limit replaces the search for totality and the act of transgression replaces the movement of contradictions" (PT, 50).

Language, the speech act, can no longer be subordinated to a higher social or subjective realm; it has broken free, it has "replaced" the former order, and it exists, we might say, at the expense of that other order. The elimination of a sacrificial-philosophical limitation-expulsion movement has resulted in a moment in which the earlier epoch is, quite simply, done away with. The logic of language for Foucault is not one of coherent temporal development, of moments of history that are dialectically negated and gone beyond. It is, instead, one of a relentless seriality, of an "exponential series of endless episodes"; it is, moreover, not one of Hegelian conservation. Writing in a Bataillean mode, Foucault states: "The language of terror is dedicated to an endless expenditure" (LI, 65).

Foucault's use of the word "terror" here is most interesting – for he is referring in his article to Gothic horror novels, but the resonance with Paulhan's discussion of literary terrorism cannot be ignored. The language of terror is one of expenditure, to be sure, but its terror is also the thoroughgoing replacement of one kind of language – of one model of representation and historical development – with another, and this second language is the refusal of any representation beyond the infinite mirroring of the impossibility of representation, and of any historical synthesis or fusion. It is, in other words, the refusal of "thought" or reference (along with the neat oppositions between signifier and referent, subjective and objective, inside and outside) and its replacement by an infinitely repetitive and mirroring mechanism of speech acts (such as "I speak"). In arguing for this kind of terrorism, however, Foucault avoids perhaps the most difficult problem: how can the movement of transgression, of the infinite self-transgression of language, which is a *refusal* of the exclusionary logic of a speculative sacrifice, nevertheless exclude what it would replace? And how can an affirmation of a seriality of "endless episodes" be presented as a historical break with a philosophy of historical movements and breaks? (Bataillean transgression is to the twentieth century what dialectical negation was to the nineteenth, etc.) Most important, what is the status of the knowledge of Foucault's own text – the one that would proclaim the necessity of a new mode (transgression instead of dialectical negation) – a knowledge based on a recognition of the definitive preeminence of a language that precludes all knowledge, that is itself nothing other than an infinite murmuring or stuttering?

Derrida, in his article on Bataille, "From Restricted to General Economy: A Hegelianism without Reserve," attempts to avoid the trap into which Foucault apparently falls.[16] After all, it is clear from Foucault's article that something is missing: arguing that Hegel is replaced by Nietzsche in Bataille ignores the fact that Bataille himself, throughout his writings and to the very end, considered himself a Kojèvian-Hegelian. Derrida from the outset argues that Bataillean "sovereignty" must be seen neither as Hegelian "lordship" nor as an experience of death that simply *escapes* the dialectic. The latter is only an "absolute loss of meaning" that Hegel called "abstract negativity" (RGE, 260). Instead, sovereignty is identified by Derrida with "play," a movement that "mimes" the labor of negativity and the "absolute risk of death"; it is neither reducible to dialectical negation, nor is it, as we have just seen, in Foucault, simply separable from it. Indeed, as laughter, as play, sovereignty, rather than being subordinated to the serious Hegelian labor of the negative (and of the slave), is logically if not temporally anterior to it: labor is itself inscribed within play. "In interpreting negativity as labor, in betting for discourse, meaning, history, etc., Hegel has bet against play, against chance. He has blinded himself to the possibility of his own bet, to the fact that the conscientious suspension of play . . . was itself a phase of play" (RGE, 260).

This familiar Heideggerian gesture (we learn that the "*techne* as the unfolding of truth" [RGE, 262] is itself generated out of a difference, a duality, a miming or play, which the *techne* can only cover over) leads to a problem: to what extent is the recognition of sovereignty – of laughter, eroticism, and miming – just another higher knowledge, one fully assimilable to the Hegelian project simply because it is, perhaps, the *final* knowledge? Derrida's gesture is ingenious: he states that Hegel "saw" the radicality of the negative (sovereignty) "without seeing it, showed it while concealing it" (RGE, 260) – a formulation that itself could easily be interpreted along Hegelian lines: Hegel's philosophy, like all others, has a false bottom, a region of negativity that need only be recognized in order to accede to a higher, definitive, knowledge, and no doubt to a higher subjectivity as well. Derrida, however, avoids this move by arguing that one, instead of correcting Hegel, "follows him to the end, to the point of agreeing with him against himself." Just as conscientious labor is generated out of play, and hence is "inscribed in" it, out of and in miming and the simulacrum, so too interpretation is not the product of the application of logic, but vice versa (RGE, 260). Interpretation is itself always reinterpretation, and logic is situated in it. Thus "Hegel's own interpretation can be reinterpreted – against him. This is what Bataille does. Reinterpretation is a simulated repetition of Hegelian discourse." Rather than seeing sovereignty as a higher knowledge "beyond" and distinct from Hegelian absolute knowledge – a necessary step, and a fully Hegelian one, if one argues that sovereignty, or transgression, escapes from the dialectic in a new and definitive historical era – Derrida presents it as a "play," a miming: the "recognition," if it can even be called that, of sovereignty as play, and the inscription of truth and its *techne* within that play, is only an effect of more miming: "reinterpretation is a simulated repetition."

I have stressed Derrida's version of sovereignty in order to point out one possible, and seemingly quite effective, way of confronting a problem that Foucault himself apparently does not recognize: positing transgression as separate from the Hegelian dialectic, in a new philosophical and historical era that replaces the earlier Hegelian one, will tend only to reaffirm one's own Hegelianism. As Derrida recognizes more fully than anyone else, "replacing" Hegel, "going beyond" the dialectic, is an eminently Hegelian gesture (and perhaps an inescapable one).[17] There will be a new knowledge, and, necessarily, a new subjectivity, a new "man," that will reflect back on history, that will "know" – and that subjectivity will be none other than Foucault himself, the post-Hegelian intellectual, the author of *The Order of Things*.[18]

One could argue, on the simplest level, and following Derrida's reasoning, that to demonstrate that the humanist subject never "really" existed, that it was always already a fiction that had to be refused – like God for an atheist – is simply to posit a kind of purely negative subject: as with Hegel's "abstract negativity," the straightforward refusal of a subject only reaffirms a dialectic in which the final stage – an absolute knowledge – entails a self-reflexive knowledge of the absence of "man," at the final stage of its history, in *The Order of Things* as recounted by Foucault himself, the exemplary non-knowing subject or nonintellectual. But this culminating movement could then be said to be the truth of "man" (his nonexistence), and therefore the self-certainty of his existence through the knowledge of his nonexistence. In effect, a symmetrical structure is thereby created through the dialectic, by means of which man's absence and presence are functionally equivalent.

Is it as simple as this? The tendency on the part of commentators – such as Ferry and Renaut – to assume that Foucault simply denies the possibility of "the subject" considerably oversimplifies things. In fact, apparently unrecognized on the part of Foucault himself, there is a necessary subjectivity embedded in the infinitely "murmuring" and proliferating series of representations/speech acts (speech acts that are only representations of other speech acts) that make up the movement of the version of the avant-garde text, the "language to infinity," that he affirms. At the same time, however, Foucault's affirmation of the subject is not as simple as we might be led to believe if we assume that he simply negates it (and thus affirms it). His gesture, in fact, is much more complex. Perhaps it is time to reinterpret Foucault's own reinterpretation of Hegelianism – against him, but also with him – to see how a Foucauldian subject can be situated in a larger contestation (and affirmation) of the intellectual subject.

First we might consider the opposition between the "classical" episteme and the "modern" one as sketched out in the penultimate chapter ("Man and His Doubles") of *The Order of Things*. In the "classical era" (the Port-Royal *Logic*, Condillac, Turgot, Adam Smith, etc.), "negative forms" and the "limited knowledge it is possible to have of them" are situated in "the space of representation"; this space itself was part and parcel of a "metaphysics of the infinite" which was "not only possible but necessary: it was necessary, in fact, that they should be the manifest forms of human finitude, and yet that they should be able to have their locus and their truth within representation; the idea of infinity, and the idea of its determination, in finitude, made one another possible" (OT, 317).

Finitude, in other words, is necessary, but only in that it is located in a space of representation dependent on, but inevitably cut off from, "the idea of infinity." The contents of this space are limited by the inadequacy of man's understanding, but this limit was itself circumscribed by a "negative relation to infinity" (the creation, the Fall, or the conjunction of body and soul), "posited as anterior to man's empiricity and to the knowledge he may gain of it" (OT, 316). The space of empiricity is limited in this classical model, but its limits are outside it, anterior to it; its truth is grounded in a metaphysics of the infinite, and the space of representation, we might say, is guaranteed its integrity by the always-anterior break that cuts it off from, but guarantees its relation to, the infinite. The infinite may be unattainable – "the existence of bodies, needs, and words" cannot be subjugated within an absolute knowledge – but the empirical nevertheless finds a stable "foundation" in the "idea of infinity" that is always beyond its grasp.

In this fundamentally religious model, we can see that the finite itself is circumscribed within the closed space of representation: the finite is not logically prior to a metaphysics of the "idea of infinity." Infinity, then, still grounds the limited and circumscribed world; "man" is not needed to furnish a somehow infinite metaphysical basis for it. Nor is the limitation of this world, this space, internal; rather, contingent internal limitations are only an aftereffect of an always-prior ("anterior to man's empiricity") "negative relation to infinity" – a Fall in the religious sense. After this Fall, man cannot locate the finite in the empirical space he occupies through an infinite "absolute knowledge" of it; a higher metaphysical knowledge cannot be determined (as in Hegel, for example) out of man's fallen position. The empirical world is limited, in other words, separated from the infinite, established in the closed space of representation – but that limitation is not *in* the empirical world, the world of representation, insofar as the logical certainty of the knowledge of the limit cannot be derived from the study and analysis of limited things.

The fragmentary, purely empirical "man" of the classical episteme becomes the modern humanist subject, according to Foucault, when the earlier model breaks down. The limit is now situated *in* man: as Foucault puts it, "the entire field of Western thought was inverted" in the nineteenth century (OT, 317). With the demise of the "metaphysics of the infinite," modern culture was forced to "conceive of the finite on the basis of itself." By this, Foucault means that rather than seeing the limitation of man and the empirical realm securely separate from the realm of the transcendental, where metaphysical knowledge can be established (or revealed), "modern" thinkers are forced to elaborate a fully knowing subject on the basis of the inevitably limited and fragmentary data available. "Man appears in his ambiguous position as an object of knowledge and as a subject who knows: enslaved sovereign, observed spectator" (OT, 312). Man is finite – the defining limit is now *in* him – he is limited by his coming into a language, a history and a culture that always precedes him; he is limited as well by the inevitably finite nature of his observations. At the same time, however, according to "modern" thought, "man" is capable of an infinite reflection on those limitations: "Modern thought has been unable to avoid . . . searching for the locus of a discourse . . . that would make it possible to analyze man as a subject, that is, as a locus of knowledge which has been empirically acquired but referred back as closely as possible to what makes it possible, and as a pure form immediately present to those contents" (OT, 320-21).

The subject here is what Foucault calls the "empirico-transcendental doublet," the impossible conjunction of "the truth of discourse defined on the basis of the truth of the object" (i.e., positivism), and of "objective truth proceeding from man's discourse" (eschatology). Man is the intersection point between these two sides, the space where, for example, an "objective form of thought" analyzes empirical data in order to arrive at a transcendent self-knowledge. "Man is a mode of being which accommodates that dimension . . . which extends from a part of himself not reflected in a cogito to the act of thought by which he apprehends that part; and which, in the inverse direction, extends from that pure apprehension to the empirical clutter . . . , the empirical accumulation of contents . . . of non-thought" (OT, 322–23). Of interest to us here is the fact that while, in the classical model, necessarily fragmentary representations were circumscribed by a limit which effectively separated the finite, empirical sphere from the "idea of the infinite," now, in the "modern" period, there is an attempt to found a *"metaphysics* of life, labor and language," a transcendental, infinite, eschatological subjectivity, on the basis of an *"analytics* of finitude and human existence" (OT, 317). In other words, the limit of finitude no longer circumscribes the universe of representations resulting in a neat "correlation" between the realms of the finite and the infinite; instead, the infinite now finds its origin and end *in* the finite. The limit of the finite is inscribed in the heart of the infinite. We are back once again at the model we saw at play in Foucault's "literary" writings (as in the article on Bataille), where the limit was always internal to the origin of the writing, and where the limit itself always found a limit at *its* origin.

The "analytics of finitude" entails not only the endless project of the establishment of the known out of the unknown when the unknown lies outside "man" (as in the physical sciences); Foucault is interested above all in the infinite process whereby the knowing subject comes to know what is unknown *within* "man" himself. Man's finitude in this case is not constituted by the fact that there is inevitably much in the outside world he does not know, and probably can never know, but instead by his own limitation in relation to what he can know about himself. "How can man think what he does not think, inhabit as though by a mute occupation something that eludes him, animate with a kind of frozen movement that figure of himself that takes the form of a stubborn exteriority? . . . How can he be the subject of a language that for thousands of years has been formed without him, a language whose organization escapes him . . . and within which he is obliged, from the very outset, to lodge his speech and his thought?" (OT, 322).

"Man" is invented as the grounding that unites in itself the fragments left over from the breakdown of the classical model – the known and the unknown, the conscious and the unconscious, the integrated and the alienated – and that indeed discovers in itself the exterior which it goes on to incorporate. "A form of reflection is established . . . that involves, for the first time, man's being in that dimension where thought addresses the unthought and articulates itself upon it" (OT, 325). Hegel, Marx, Husserl, Schopenhauer, Freud, all attempt to think the "inexhaustible double that presents itself to reflected knowledge [*au savoir réfléchi*] as the blurred projection of what man is in his truth, but that also plays the role of a preliminary ground upon which man must collect himself and recall himself in order to attain his truth" (OT, 327).

Foucault views this movement through which "thought, both for itself and in the density of its workings [is] both knowledge and a modification of what it knows" (OT, 327) as *the* characteristic of the "modern" subjectivity. "Man" is established "within knowledge," he *is* the double movement by which knowledge is affirmed through its modification by that which it is not. The texts of the major thinkers Foucault mentions, then, with Hegel, Marx, and Freud as the main targets, are the locus of a blind affirmation of "man" through the movement of a knowledge – and yet, it seems, they are unaware of the fact that this conception of "man" is untenable and unrealizable, that it is, finally, nothing more than a shoddy and awkward fiction. They do not know it, or realize it; otherwise they would not posit an absolute knowledge, a classless society, or a psychoanalytic cure in which "man" is fully constituted through the definitive reconciliation of his knowledge (or the labor of his knowledge) to itself, of his subjectivity or personhood to its (alienated) self. What is the status of these thinkers' lack of knowledge concerning their own knowledge?

This difficulty comes up at the end of the section "The Cogito and the Unthought." Foucault argues that "the modern experience," finally, involves not so much a morality or an ethics as a "perilous act"; the movement of the dialectic, in other words, in any of its guises, entails an operation, a "certain mode of action" rather than a "law of order" or a "code of wisdom." In the transformation of the Cogito through the reappropriation of the unthought, thought is always a "knowledge and a modification of what it knows": "As soon as it functions it offends or reconciles, attracts or repels, breaks, dissociates, unites or reunites; it cannot help but liberate or enslave" (OT, 328). Therefore it is wrong to assign this movement an inherent morality – a meaning, in other words. It is pure performance.

And, in a way, through this movement it is a performance that "knows not what it does." Its significance can be grasped only from the outside, from a perspective that has moved beyond it. As a performance it entails the circular temporal movement whereby the origin recedes, but through which it can be reattained. This movement can be found in theories of history or of the self – the structure is always essentially the same. Hegel, Marx, and Spengler – Freud has dropped out of the picture, for the moment at least, but he could clearly be cited in this context as well – posit a thought that "curves over upon itself, illuminates it own plenitude, brings its circle to completion, recognizes itself in all the strange figures of its odyssey" (OT, 334), one that is, in other words, fully dialectical. On the other hand, Hölderlin, Nietzsche, and Heidegger – the latter makes a surprise appearance here, in one of the very few instances in which Foucault cites his name in a positive context – affirm a movement that is *not* circular, one in which "the return is posited only in the extreme recession of the origin . . . so that what we are concerned with here is neither a completion nor a curve, but rather that ceaseless rending open which frees the origin in exactly that degree to which it recedes; the extreme is therefore what is nearest" (OT, 334). Foucault is careful to note here that there is an effort on the part of "modern thought" (the thinkers associated with Hegel) to return to the origin and to "invent man," whether the promise is one of a reattainment of "fulfillment and perfect plenitude" or one of "the void of the origin." Thought, in other words, in its Hegelian mode, always attempts to "return man in his identity, in that plenitude or in that nothing which he is himself." Thought is prescribed as "something like the 'Same.'" Yet, ironically, it is "modern" thought that attempts to carry out a blind performance – the "solar decline," the movement by which it "curves over upon itself"; "contemporary" thought, on the other hand, exemplified by Nietzsche and, clearly, Foucault himself, knows better. This knowledge is of the impossibility of completion, of the "ceaseless rending open," which is a return but not a turn. We thus face the possibility of a kind of reversal, in which modern knowledge is reduced to the status of an unknowing performance, whereas the "return" that is linked exclusively to "the extreme recession of the origin" – that seemingly is linked only to dispersion, the night, a violent death – is inseparable from a definitive knowledge.

The problem, in other words, is that the knowledge of transgression, of the movement *out* of the dialectic, and out of the sheer performance of "modern" thought, is itself a fully dialectical move. Foucault, for example, uses the verb "to think" at least four times in describing the future task in a Nietzschean world: "It is no longer possible to think in our day other than in the void left by man's disappearance" (OT, 342). This thought will be directed against "Anthropology," against the humanism that is "forgetful of the opening" and that is "standing obstinately in the way of an immanent new form of thought."

Here, just after an invocation of Nietzsche, we are actually closest to Heidegger: in the new epoch, which we might call contemporary, because it comes after the very different nineteenth-century modernism of Hegel or Marx, we remember the forgetting of the forgetting of the "opening."[19] We *remember*, in other words, the transgressive radicality of the "limitation" on which "man" has been established: that remembrance, that moment of higher consciousness, is the only real difference between the "modern" and the "contemporary" epistemes, between Hegel and Nietzsche. That difference, in other words, and the goal of Foucault's entire project in *The Order of Things*, can be guaranteed only through a more advanced knowledge. Both of these configurations, the modern and the contemporary, after all, are grounded in finitude; it is just that the latter is able to recognize fully the implications of the inner, constituting limitation; the other, the modern, cannot, and so it dreams of plenitude and of an adequate self-knowledge. It should be stressed that this remembering or recognition, irrespective of a context that simultaneously invokes and forgets Heidegger (that forgetting is accomplished through the counterinvocation of Nietzsche) is through and through Hegelian, as Derrida would remind us: the opposition to the dialectic, to the "illumination of its own plenitude," can be carried out only through an uncovering that is no different from the uncovering effected by Hegel, Marx, or Freud, who discover the hidden Other, who attempt to open the false bottom, *in* "man" himself.[20] A hidden double is reunited with a version of man in order to constitute it. (We might call it not-man, the certainty of man's absence or death which is, from the historical perspective of the figure of the writing Foucault at the end of *The Order of Things*, simply the next, dialectically higher stage of man.) The death of Anthropology, of man, can be carried out only through a profoundly anthropological gesture. We are, it seems, therefore fully within the nineteenth-century modern, within the space in which man can be constituted (in Foucault's words) "in that plenitude or in that nothing which [man] is himself": how, then, can man "die" if his death is remembered, or returned to in a neat circular movement, through a strategy inseparable from that of a modernism whose essential characteristic is the fabrication of man, a strategy which creates man in his plenitude or in his void (the two opposing terms are equivalent) by remembering or uncovering his Other, his invisible double that is always already "in" him? The unconscious, alienated labor, the *an sich*, or – why not? – Nietzschean power: these terms are the negative doubles that "modern" dialectical thought must recognize as hidden in man in order to constitute him, following the logic of the analytic of finitude.[21] This recognition, remembering, or uncovering is the most fundamental gesture of the internal dialectical constitution of man. The limit and its transgression, identified with power, therefore merely join the series of Others that Foucault has already named and fully identified with "Anthropology." Foucault's somewhat surreptitious melding of Nietzsche and Heidegger (OT, 334) is particularly revealing in this case because, without fully acknowledging his debt to Heidegger, he affirms Nietzsche as the main figure to be invoked when writing of a "thought" or "philosophy" that will remember the forgetting carried out by "Anthropology." In his *Nietzsche*, Heidegger characterized this philosopher, through his affirmation of the will to power, as the culmination of Western metaphysics and as the last metaphysician – not as one who breaks with that tradition.[22] Clearly Foucault is leaving something out – not so much his debt to and his rewriting of Heidegger, but rather (from a Heideggerian point of view) the problematic position of Nietzsche as humanist, and of Foucault *as* Nietzsche the humanist, Foucault as the anthropologist of the death of man, who can only proclaim that death through a fully anthropological gesture, the discovery of a hidden or forgotten definitive truth having to do with "man" (his existence, his absence, or his death – the difference in this case is irrelevant). Foucault must forget, among other things, Heidegger's critique of Nietzsche because Foucault would argue, implicitly against Heidegger, that Nietzsche is something more, or other, than a metaphysician and a humanist, that he was a Heideggerian *avant la lettre*. But he never explicitly puts forward this argument, because, I would argue, he cannot; he cannot definitively state that Nietzsche's project, or his own, is different in kind from an affirmation of "man" through the revelation of a hidden truth.

Foucault has opened a "false bottom," and he has discovered an Other, a hidden, invisible truth, knowledge, or reflexivity to which Hegel and Marx, among others, were blind. It is called, among other things, transgression. He, through Nietzsche and perhaps Heidegger, knows more than do the early "moderns." What he has discovered is radically different from the series of repetitious interpretations analyzed in essays such as "Language to Infinity." It is the knowledge that makes the recognition of those series possible in the first place. But, at the same time, what Foucault recognizes is the impossibility of this knowledge, the unrecuperability of the unthought and of the Other, in other words of the very elements whose recuperation is essential to the movement of his argument: "The Other . . . is not only a brother but a twin, born not of man, nor in man, but beside him and at the same time, in an identical newness, in an unavoidable duality" (OT, 326).[23] For this reason it is misguided to argue that Foucault is only calling for or announcing the "death of man," or that he is revealing – uncovering – the fact that man never existed in the first place. His very revelation of that "fact" is, in effect, a reaffirmation of "man." The moment of the dialectic is an integral part of the affirmation of transgression or "rending open" (*déchirure*); transgression can be recognized only through a dialectical turn. But there is an infinite stuttering, a "murmuring," in Foucault's uncovering of Nietzsche's uncovering: if Foucault himself is unaware of the dialectical grounding of transgression (and thus its inevitable humanism), his reader, on the other hand, is quite aware of it. We inevitably recognize the "false bottom" of Foucault's project, we reveal beneath it the Other of his text: the fact that he too is a humanist in his very uncovering of the "death of man" lurking beneath the mystification of modernist projects. This process is infinite: another reader will uncover *our* humanism in our gesture of uncovering the implications of Foucault's uncovering, and so on. The dialectic in each case continues to function, another humanism is always revealed, another false bottom is sprung open, but the dialectic is merely repeating itself. Much like the limit situated at the heart of the origin, in this case the dialectical sublation in its functioning discovers at its heart nothing more than a mechanized speech act: each uncovering is now only an automatic repetition of the previous one. From this point on, the uncovering process is always already carried out an infinite number of times. This series is mandated from the moment in which an "uncovering" of Foucault's uncovering recognizes that it too will be uncovered. This discovery bears within it, then, the infinite, inexorable series of acts that, as we have already seen, Foucault recognized in "contemporary" thought, an awareness of which he attributed to Nietzsche, Artaud, and Bataille. But it is also indissociable from the performance that Foucault himself linked to the circular movement of modern thought, and the "play" that Derrida affirmed at the heart of Hegelian seriousness. The sheer act, the limit of dialectical knowledge, is the origin and end of that knowledge; it is always "in" it. That knowledge – in other words, Hegel, to use a metonym – can constitute itself only through the "recession of its origin" and end, the movement by which the knowledge of man, and hence of his death, is dispersed. Knowledge, then, can only be a knowledge of a limit, the void of the act of the repetition of knowledges, which casts its shadow across all the figures of the "modern" from Hegel to Foucault and his readers (and his readers' readers' readers – to infinity).

We are perhaps not so far from Foucault's position in "A Preface to Transgression" after all. It was never a question there of simply eliminating knowledge, or the origin, but of seeing how the limit was situated "in" it and in the very process of its self-reflection and representation. Similarly, Foucault's "humanism," his uncovering of the unthought, is a gesture that puts him in complicity with "modern" thought, most notably with Hegel and Marx. As we have seen, "man" is not banished from the historical or posthistorical scene by Foucault; on the contrary, he inhabits Foucault's own method. But "man" is also and inevitably an integral part of a "murmuring" series of uncoverings that itself, like the language of sexuality as presented in the essay on Bataille, or the infinitely repeated literary text in "Language to Infinity," is a lateral series of speech acts, indefinitely repeating only the limit, reflecting on the silence at the always-receding origin and end. In our model of Foucault's project, the "knowledge" – always a knowledge of this silence, this death, but, more important, our own knowledge of Foucault's lack of knowledge, and the knowledge of our own lack on the part of an endless series of other readers, other uncoverers, other humanists, each one in turn uncovered by the next – results not in a positive revealing, "totality attained," the "illumination" of a "plenitude," but only of always another humanism, another "man," who appears as soon as the preceding one is revealed and shown to be only an illusion. Foucault's unawareness of his own Anthropology makes possible the series that is the scattering of that last, and incessantly repeated, instance of man. "Man" and the series of empty and demystifying speech acts or knowledge acts are radically incompatible, yet they are both necessary, and they are fully dependent on, and inscribed within, each other. "Man" may be dead, but he is always again alive at the instant of the uncovering of the necessity of his death.

II

Up to this point we have been discussing works by Foucault written prior to 1970; the reader might object that, after all, there may very well be a return to a subjectivity inscribed in the earlier writings, necessary but invisible (and always again unearthed) but that the later writings – above all, *Discipline and Punish* and *The History of Sexuality* – are a different case entirely. As I noted in the last section, it is John Rajchman, in his book *Michel Foucault and the Freedom of Philosophy*, who makes the strongest case for a radical break in Foucault's project. Not only does Foucault, up to and including *The Archaeology of Knowledge*, and still very much operating in the Blanchotian-Bataillean tradition, apparently privilege language above all else, seeing everything – madness, sexuality, the various natural and human sciences – as nothing more than language (or "discourse"), but, worse yet, he puts forward an "absolute knowledge," if we can call it that, in *The Order of Things*, which entails the completion of the project, the consciousness that looks back over the story of its own genesis as it recapitulates it in the act of fulfilling it. This is nothing other than avant-garde writing itself, the "modern sublime" of formalist writing about writing.[24] Rajchman, with an almost audible sigh of relief, informs us that the "later" Foucault turns away from this navel-gazing privileging of language; clearly, there is a turn to the "out there," the realm of "practices" – or, as others call it, the "nondiscursive" realm.[25] With this turn the position of the writer changes as well: previously a heroic artist who stands up to society (Sade, Artaud, Bataille, etc.), the writer is now a "specific intellectual," engaged in local struggles as a specialist but necessarily incapable of fulfilling the higher priestly or clerical role of spokesperson for, or representative (or representation) of, a people – and incapable as well of being the incarnation of a fully constituted morality. The whipping boy in the following statement by Rajchman, as in so much Foucault criticism, is "literary theory" – in other words, Derrida, Lacan, and American "deconstruction": "[Foucault's] turn to the critic or writer as 'specific' intellectual is his move away from a century-long obsession with language. That is what dies in the swan-song of literary theory. Foucault preserves one idea: that the subject is constituted. But he rejects the Lacanian thesis that the subject is constituted *in language*. . . . The 'author-function' belongs to a larger constellation of individualizing practice; the literary challenges to it belong to a larger politics of subjectivity."[26]

Rajchman is certainly correct in arguing that subjectivity – its "constitution" by various mechanisms of power and its deconstitution by Foucault himself – continues to be an overriding concern in the later writings. But his larger argument is much more questionable: that the early writings only reconstituted a heroic author-subject by privileging literary language, and that the later ones, by focusing on the "practices" that constitute the subject, effectively work to "problematize" it (thereby fulfilling the promise of the early writings). This position, which Foucault himself no doubt promoted, brings us back to the comfortable dichotomies of 1947, and *What Is Literature?* The Sartrian opposition between outward turning "commitment" and involuted subjectivism-aestheticism finds an inadvertent supporter in the very critic who did the most to challenge the validity of that distinction in the 1960s, or who at least worked hardest against Sartre's valorization of an ethical or political subjectivity that was inseparable from that distinction.

Foucault's early work holds that "everything is language" and sees subjectivity and its relation to the "unthought" as essentially a problem (and illusion) within language, while the later recognizes the "nondiscursive" realm, examines the specific political and social production of the fiction of subjectivity-objectivity, and is somehow "liberating."[27] If we look beyond the obvious thematic differences, however, there is a remarkable similarity between the two phases. Both see an element of discontinuity, limitation, finitude, or violence as constitutive of a field that can maintain a supposed (but illusory) exclusionary closure only through a transgressive opening or rupture; both, I would argue, through the necessary awareness or certainty of that opening, that inner negativity, are forced to posit a subjectivity in a space that had seemed to be the locus of the death of the subject. Both, in other words, are incapable of mastering, through a straightforward knowledge and practice, the death of the intellectual subject – even though they try: it is in their effort that they both attain a mastery but, through that very attainment, they miss it. Indeed it is only in this failure of mastery – the same in both of Foucault's "periods" – that the death of the subject is approached.

The earlier model, as we have seen, is based on a transgression at the heart of the law, of the limit lodged in the origin and in the space of the reflexive, but necessarily repetitious, language. In the later work the Nietzschean terms "knowledge" and "power," tend to replace a vocabulary of finitude and the infinite – although, as we have seen, the problem of power was already important in *The Order of Things*. But in the later work "power" becomes central: it is now the finitude of power, its discontinuity, that both generates and precludes the movement of knowledge. Any reflection on or opposition to naked and brutal power in society must be itself a function of power, just as, earlier, any representation of or reflection on transgression was itself, in that very reflection, a transgressive movement. Foucault derives his later approach much more directly from the Nietzsche of *The Genealogy of Morals*, who attempted to rethink history from the perspective of power effects and drives rather than through the dialectical and moral movement of reason. In an important transitional article dating from 1971 that in effect establishes the theoretical grounding for all his later work, "Nietzsche, Genealogy, and History," Foucault makes it clear that the knowledge of history, its truth, is a heterogeneous product of the various impositions of power that occur in any given period.[28] Knowledge, in other words, is an aftereffect of the expenditure of power in discontinuous bursts: knowledge *is* the exercise of power. Traditional "history" has only attempted, finally without success, to put a unifying mask over the heterogeneous assemblages of "truths" that constitute it. Foucault's new Nietzschean history ("genealogy"), on the other hand, will assert itself only in its specificity (its tactical application) and contingency. Just as there is a "will to power," then, there is also a "will to truth" and a "will to knowledge"; knowledge can know itself only as a blind effect of power, in other words as a not-knowing. A full self-reflexivity by which knowledge and the subject are unified and constituted results in the knowledge of the truth of knowledge as power, and hence of the extinguishing – the sacrifice – of the self-certainty, the full subjectivity, of the subject (and, as we will see, the elimination of the authority of the traditional intellectual). Foucault writes: "The historical analysis of [the] rancorous will to knowledge reveals that all knowledge rests upon injustice (that there is no right, not even in the act of knowing, to truth as a foundation of truth) and that the instinct for knowledge is malicious (something murderous, opposed to the happiness of mankind). Even in the greatly expanded form it assumes today, the will to knowledge does not achieve a universal truth; man is not given an exact and serene mastery of nature. . . . Where religions once demanded the sacrifice of bodies, knowledge now calls for experimentation on ourselves, calls us to the sacrifice of the subject of knowledge" (NGH, 163).

Two things should be noted in this argument, whose rhetoric still resonates with the sound and fury of the French avant-garde of the 1930s ("something murderous, opposed to the happiness of mankind") rather than with the idyllic "freedom" Rajchman espouses. First, the problem of the "will to knowledge" (self-reflexivity as a power effect) is identical to the problem of the limit and transgression that we have seen in Foucault's "earlier" period. Here it is power that limits knowledge while generating it: it is the discontinuous origin and end at the heart of a human knowledge that can know itself – and thus know power – only by transgressing or mutilating itself. This leads to a second factor: this self-transgressive knowledge movement can be presented only through a vocabulary of the sacred and sacrifice. Once again, as at so many other points in the story of the intellectual subject, we see the fragments remaining after the destruction of Durkheim's system recomposing to present a figure who is neither the incarnation of reason nor a representative (or representation) of the social totality, but who instead, as knowledge, as truth, is a limited and limiting burst of self-betraying power. "It is no longer a question of judging the past in the name of a truth that only we can possess in the present; but one of risking the destruction of the subject who seeks knowledge in the endless deployment of the will to knowledge" (NGH, 164).

This subject who, in Foucault's rather sinister formulation, experiments on himself, is nothing other than his own sacrificial victim. Where Durkheim and Mauss presented a sacred violence that led from the act of the priest (as representative) to the well-being and reinvigoration of the community, Foucault posits a knowledge-power that short-circuits, that tears the priestly (sacrificial) subject first from any possibility of a unified community and its history (instituted under the sign of a pure Truth), and then from himself, from the very inevitability of his own coherency and integrity.

Perhaps all this seems a bit excessive: after all, Foucault, in his later statements on the intellectual did not dwell so much on this "sacrifice" of a sorcerer's apprentice, so reminiscent of Bataille; instead, he stressed the kind of activities the "specific" intellectual was to engage in – activities that were, in fact, to be local and practical rather than grandiose, mythical, or heroic. We hear little about sacrifice in these later statements.[29] As we will see, however, the dilemma of the knowing and authoritative subject that emerges from two of Foucault's most influential interviews (from 1972 and 1977) bears much in common with the affirmation, at the outset of the genealogical project, of the violence inflicted on the subject of knowledge through the "desire for truth."

Foucault states the problem of the intellectual most succinctly: in the conversation with Gilles Deleuze, "Intellectuals and Power," a fundamental distinction is made between "universal intellectuals" and "specific" ones. The universal thinker represents, or speaks for, a constituency, be it a class or, more typically, mankind itself. In "Intellectuals and Power" Foucault seems willing to grant the "universal" type a certain validity, but only in the past: in periods of crisis, and above all repression (1848, the Commune, 1940), "The intellectual spoke the truth to those who were forbidden to speak the truth: he was conscience, consciousness and eloquence" (IP, 207).

In another interview, "Truth and Power," the universal intellectual does not come across quite so well: he is linked not only to consciousness but to the historical privileging of writing in French culture. Foucault, in rejecting this figure of the secular cleric, is able to cast off not only universalization through representation in the function of the intellectual but also the later Telquelian and Derridean posture that, in Foucault's eyes at least, privileges writing over political practice. At the same time, Foucault is able very trenchantly to criticize his own earlier position that valued avant-garde writing: "The whole relentless theorization of writing which we saw in the 1960s was doubtless only a swan song. Through it, the writer was fighting for the preservation of his political privilege" (TP, 127). Sartre could not have said it better. The "universal intellectual," and the exalted position of the writer – official or avant-garde, it makes no difference – are indissolubly bound to political reaction and a metaphysics of reflection: "The 'universal' intellectual derives from the jurist and the notable, and finds his fullest manifestation in the writer, the bearer of values and significations in which all can recognize themselves" (TP, 128). Writing is his "sacralizing mask" (TP, 127).

We see, then, the sacred or mythical function of the writer, which Foucault is now *rejecting*, clearly linked with the politically progressive humanism of Sartre: if there is an indefatigable writer who attempted to "represent" or "speak for" the oppressed or forgotten, it was surely the author of *The Critique of Dialectical Reason*. Foucault's adroit linking of the avant-garde writing Sartre condemned with classical political "engagement" neatly covers both sides of the role of the intellectual as perceived at least from the 1890s, and no doubt before (Foucault himself mentions Voltaire [TP, 128]), up to the 1960s, thereby cleverly linking Derrida with Sartre and co-opting while dismissing Sartre's distinction between the purely aesthetic writer on the one hand and the "committed" one on the other.

Whether the "universal" intellectual is a cynical charlatan or a valued but anachronistic martyr, the important thing is that he or she is to be replaced by the "specific" intellectual. The spokesman-aesthete is no longer necessary: "the intellectual discovered that the masses no longer need him to gain knowledge . . . : they know far better than he and they are certainly capable of expressing themselves" (IP, 207). Against a larger, universal theory of liberation, such as the Marxist one, Foucault is putting forward a decentered, serial movement of power and a localized knowledge that fully "recognizes" its own implication *in* power. "[The] idea of [the universal intellectuals'] responsibility for 'consciousness' and discourse forms part of the system" (IP, 207). The specific intellectual does not attempt to put forward or embody a historical or social truth; rather his efforts, based on circumscribed knowledge or skills, work to "sap power" and to "take power." His effort is "conducted alongside those who struggle for power," it is not "their illumination from a safe distance" (IP, 208); it is, finally, the finitude at the heart of a would-be universal system. Foucault is thinking in particular of figures like J. Robert Oppenheimer, who, as a nuclear scientist, and on the basis of what he knew as a scientist, was able to oppose official American nuclear weapons policy. (Foucault does not stress, however, that it was Oppenheimer himself who was largely responsible for the development of the atom bomb in the first place.) The specific intellectual's intervention is not meant to be made from the exalted position of the "bearer of universal values" but, rather, from that of a technician whose knowledge and acts can play a part in the "battle about the status of truth and the economic and political role it plays" (TP, 132). "It is because he had a direct and localized relation to scientific knowledge and institutions that the atomic scientist would make his intervention. . . . Under the rubric of protest, which concerned the entire world, the atomic expert brought into play his specific position in the order of knowledge" (TP, 128).

The intellectual now has another function as well, and it is this one that I find of greatest interest: he or she engages not only in local struggles but in a larger struggle against his or her own earlier role as a universal intellectual: "The intellectual's role is no longer to place himself 'somewhat ahead and to the side' in order to express the stifled truth of the collectivity; rather, it is to struggle against the forms of power that transform him into its object and instrument in the sphere of 'knowledge,' 'truth,' 'consciousness,' and 'discourse'" (IP, 207–8). One can take this passage to mean that the "specific" intellectual must struggle against narrow, purely technical duties, which only reaffirm a certain power configuration; at that point Foucault's analysis would have certain affinities with Sartre's, in *Plaidoyer pour les intellectuels*.[30] But if the intellectual is the "object" of forms of power – their instrument – then he is their object in the sphere of "consciousness"; clearly the objectivity of the intellectual cannot be conceived outside his subjectivity, just as the prisoner's objectified existence in the panopticon (as analyzed in *Discipline and Punish*) cannot be produced outside his subjectification, the movement through which he analyzes his conscience, confesses his sins, etc. In the same way the universal intellectual, the unwitting object of certain forms of power – this is about as close as Foucault ever comes to a critique of ideology – is objectivized in his very incarnation of consciousness. In the act of "fighting for his political privilege" he is both the instrument of a certain power configuration *and* a would-be embodiment of its self-awareness. (It makes little difference whether that configuration, and the liberation it promises, is of the Left or the Right, Stalinism, fascism, or the equally dreaded "bourgeois capitalism.")

This is the point at which Foucault's notion of the specific intellectual becomes most problematic. The universal intellectual who would make generally valid statements about the role of the intellectual only in relation to power, doctrines, and the masses is to be replaced by a specific one who eschews larger moral truths and who restrains his activities to situations directly involving his particular competence. But that is not all: the specific intellectual must also struggle against the universal. We should note, however, that the problem lies in the fact that when the universal intellectual is explicitly struggled against, this struggle cannot be carried out from the vantage point of the specific intellectual. Foucault, when he argues against the universal intellectual, is not doing so from the position of the specific; on the contrary, he is making a statement that is meant to be valid about the function of the intellectual *in general*. A true specific intellectual could never make such a large statement. In other words, Foucault is acting in this interview as a representative or spokesman for an emergent group: specific intellectuals. The moment at which the philosopher – the universal intellectual – necessarily turns against his objectification and writes or intervenes as a specific intellectual is *also* the moment at which he necessarily intervenes as a universal one. His critique of his own position as universal intellectual is the only one he can engage in if he adheres to the plan of action of the specific intellectual, who limits his gestures to ones having strictly to do with his own competence. Foucault is, finally, a professor of "systems of thought" at the Collège de France; following a venerable tradition, he writes on larger political and social problems for magazines and newspapers while publishing best-selling works with Gallimard: he is, in other words, not a specific intellectual, a criminologist or penologist, say (let alone a prisoner or a guard), but a universal intellectual.[31] He is a theorist, not a technician, and not even a technician of knowledge. His archival work is exclusively a support of his activity as a general thinker, whose conclusions are meant to have a larger validity. Thus the universal intellectual turned specific intellectual (Foucault) can only analyze the position of the specific intellectual on general grounds. Put another way, he can be a specific intellectual only in relation to his own role, that of the universal intellectual (and not in relation to a purely technical discipline); and he can be a universal intellectual only in his struggle for the specific intellectual. He struggles against his own function: he denounces, in terms that he necessarily means to be universally valid, his own role, the role of the universal intellectual. That is, indeed, the only way he can do what a specific intellectual does. If he did not do this, he would just be another universal intellectual. But even if he does do it, he is still writing (and resisting) not as a technician in any given field, but as a generalist (a universal intellectual) whose positions are meant to apply to *all* specific intellectuals. He can represent these specific intellectuals, then, only by betraying his own position as universal; conversely, his betrayal, which necessarily depends upon his status as a universal intellectual, is his only way of being the kind of specific intellectual that he has mandated. It is his "local struggle" – against himself. This is a different kind of betrayal from the one found in Marxism, where the bourgeois intellectual (Marx himself) betrays his class by joining with the proletariat in their struggle. There, the conflict will be resolved with the triumph of the proletariat and the establishment of a classless society: in the case of Foucault, there can be no end of history, no resolution, because the only way he can ever affirm the necessity of the specific thinker is in a generally valid proposition – which will necessarily betray the very thing he is putting forward. Appropriately enough, his self-betrayal is not dialectically resolved but is a function of the eternal return: it is a vicious circle.

We have returned to the problem of knowledge and sacrifice that we saw in "Nietzsche, Genealogy, and History." There it was knowledge itself that could "know" its origin only through a not-knowing, a discontinuous or internally limited power that precluded any notion of a universal truth: knowledge could know itself only through its own transgression, through a recognition of the violence of the will to truth, of its "empirical roots." In the same way, the universal intellectual can establish or reestablish himself – as Foucault does – only by recognizing the exclusive necessity of the specific intellectual. Foucault's knowledge of himself as an authoritative intellectual subject, whose words are meant to have a wider validity, can be constituted only through the recognition of its origin in the specific intellectual that is its end (in both senses of the word).[32] This is the moment of the "unavoidable sacrifice of the subject of knowledge" (NGH, 164) in the later Foucault. At the same time, though, the specificity of the intellectual is fully dependent on the (self-)knowledge of the universal intellectual.

Just as we note the identity of the problem of knowledge and power in the later Foucault with that of the limit and transgression in the earlier, so too we must recognize the identity of the problem of the subject's *knowledge* of the intellectual's bind with that of the infinite regress of the subject of knowledge in relation to transgressive language. As was the case with transgression, which could only be established through dialectical knowledge, the specific intellectual can find his or her status – or have it guaranteed – only through the knowledge of the universal intellectual (else why would Foucault bother to write?). The specific intellectual – like the transgressive limit or Other – can only be such as an effect of the universal: in other words, it is the subject's knowledge that guarantees a function that is the death of such knowledge. The process will be repeated infinitely: Foucault himself, writing as a general authority, has uncovered a hidden truth or necessity of which no one before was aware, or from which all were alienated: that there is no hidden truth to be uncovered, no alienation to be remedied by the universal intellectual; that role was a mistake, and it is now extinct (indeed, Foucault declares it extinct, through a kind of speech act, in his discussion with Deleuze) – I in turn can uncover what Foucault has forgotten or repressed: the fact that his "uncovering," along with its larger validity, is itself the very thing he proclaims to be dead. My reader will uncover the fact that I am playing the same game of uncovering, the game of the Cogito and the unthought, and so on to infinity. Each higher level of truth will be a dialectical advance over the earlier, and each will reveal the impossibility of the earlier stage, denouncing it as nothing more than a higher dialectical and synthetic stage of knowledge. Each new stage, then, will be an advance of knowledge, but it will also be a sheer repetition of the earlier one. The universal intellectual, knowledge, and his writing – avant-garde or social realist, inward or outward turning, at this point it hardly matters – will always return; moreover, since each knowledge is identical to the earlier one, the process *from the first* degenerates into the automatic repetition of a series of identical higher knowledges, each one declaring in an epoch-making speech act the death of the former. Empty absolute knowledge resonates to infinity: at each "successive" moment the same war of the universal, homogeneous, and infinite (knowledge) with discontinuous, finite power (the act) is staged. Hegel and Nietzsche, the intellectual and his death in another intellectual, representation and a purely technical instance or application of force, are locked together in the orbit of the repeating instant.

8

Derrida
and the Critical
Question

MUCH HAS BEEN written recently on the links between the approaches of
Martin Heidegger and Jacques Derrida, and this work goes a long way toward
clarifying and systematically setting out the strategies and implications of Derrida's project.[1] What is often overlooked in this discussion, however, is that
Derrida's writing cannot be seen solely in the context of the German tradition
running (especially) from Nietzsche and Husserl to Heidegger. Indeed, perhaps surprisingly, one notes in Derrida a series of concerns that are most
directly derived from the French anthropological tradition that we have examined, starting at least with Durkheim. This is not to say, however, that Derrida
opposes a latter-day version of Durkheim to Heidegger; to the contrary, I will
argue (some might say perversely) that Derrida is able to use the remnants of
the French tradition – themselves reread, and their humanistic and sacrificial
system disarticulated, through a Heideggerian critique – as a means of reading
Heidegger against himself, thereby stripping away what remains in Heidegger
of a metaphysics of interiority, self-reflexivity, and presence. In other words, it
is through the opening made possible by a Heideggerian disarticulation of the
French anthropological tradition that Derrida is able to return to analyze the
implicit humanist anthropology of Heidegger himself. The stakes in this
game, one discovers, are very high; for while Derrida's Heideggerian critique
of Heidegger, in 1968, limits itself to the question of the complicity of Heidegger with the very humanism he is deconstructing, by 1987 there is a recognition that Heidegger's inability to read the rigor of his own method opens the
way for his controversial affirmation of national socialism. And, as we will see,
Derrida's rewriting of French anthropology has important implications for his
later interpretation of Heidegger's politics: the very strengths of Derrida's

method are its weaknesses, and his fundamental inability to carry out a critique of Heidegger's politics is a function of the strength, indeed the irrefutability, of his own critique of sacrificial violence.

I

One cannot examine Derrida's "Plato's Pharmacy" without first considering briefly the significance of the *pharmakon* in Marcel Mauss's *Essai sur le don*. Derrida in fact explicitly situates his discussion of this "ambivalent" term in the context of Mauss's theory of "primitive" exchange and gift giving: he quotes Mauss at some length in a footnote in his important section on the *pharmakos*, and it is worth considering the important way in which Mauss's emphasis on the double meaning of certain words, such as the Germanic *Gift* (both poison and gift) and the Greek *pharmakon* (poison and cure), differs from Derrida's.[2]

The sacred is ambiguous for Mauss because it is inseparable from a double, contradictory interpretation – a duality which is evident in the "power in the thing."[3] In primitive, gift-giving economies, the object's power is associated with the fact that, when it is given (and sometimes it is "given" to the other through its ritual destruction), the honor (or honorific force) of both donor and receiver, their "mana" as Mauss calls it, is put in question. The gift-giving ritual is structured as a defiance, a series of challenges, in which both sides risk the loss of everything: the donor risks his standing and authority if he is humiliated by having his gift paid back more than in full (and above all if he is then unable to respond with a counter-gift); the receiver in turn runs the risk of losing his position if he cannot return the other's gift with interest.

It is no surprise, then, that the object thrown down as a challenge is both a wager and a pledge (*un gage*); its designation is an act by which both participants enter into a kind of sacrificial-destructive combat that will eventually determine their social status. The object becomes untouchable, a symbolic element charged with the magic power of attraction (the seemingly universal aspiration to social superiority) and repulsion (the fear of one's own ignominy). It is this seductive-dangerous characteristic of the ritual wealth marker (the fact that it escapes from the normal channels of purely utilitarian exchange and profit making) that enables Mauss to explain the ambivalence implied in terms like *Gift*, *pharmakon*, or the Latin *venenum*: their double meaning conveys both the charm of a sudden success as well as the terror associated with a literally poisonous failure.

What is surprising in Mauss is that, once this "ambivalence" of the powerful or sacred object is posited, it is retracted. In effect, when extrapolating from primitive cultures to modern ones, Mauss can affirm gift-giving rituals only by seeing them as exclusively beneficial for society. This is his larger moral purpose behind the *Essai sur le don*: to demonstrate that modern, industrial economies need to embrace the practice of an exchange that is based on something other than "the fruits of speculation and usury" (EG, 67). Mauss mentions the "joy of giving in public" and of the altruistic British "Friendly Societies" (EG, 67); finally, he writes of the "liberal professions": "For honor, disinterestedness, and corporate solidarity are not vain words, nor do they deny the necessity of work. We should humanize the other liberal professions, and make all of them more perfect. That would be a great deed, and one which Durkheim already had in view" (EG, 67). In this view, one can imagine, there is very little room left for the poisonous "gift."

Capitalist societies will be humanized by the introduction of an equivalent of the gift giving practiced among the Tlingit, the Haida, or the Melanesians. It seems, however, that one can affirm the *value* of exchange rituals only by eliminating the very ambivalence of the sacred that was indissociable from the power of objects of exchange or ritual destruction. It appears that one must always go in one direction or the other; either the gift object is "joyful" or even "friendly," or, as it often is in the writings of Mauss's follower Georges Bataille, "cursed" and "revolting."[4] The sacred can be put forward as an inevitably useful value only by reducing its duality, and thereby eliminating what Mauss identified as the very locus of the origin of its power.

Turning to "Plato's Pharmacy" in this context, one realizes that Derrida's analysis of the *pharmakon* avoids valorizing one "side" of this term against the other; writing – the *pharmakon* of Plato's *Phaedrus* – is not just a "poison" as such, and for that reason cannot simply be affirmed in the face of the phonocentric and logocentric "truth." Instead, it is the stability or the coherence of the very borderline between writing as poison and writing as cure that is thrown into question when the self-representation of living memory is seen as possible only through the intervention of the dead, external supplementarity of writing.

Derrida notes throughout the writings of Plato the privileging of the living memory trace – fully present and transparent to itself, capable of responding to itself without the interference and misinterpretation of the outside – over the mute, lifeless, and enigmatic "monumental" trace of writing. True memory (*mnèmè*) as it appears in and through the Socratic dialectic, is the legitimate child of truth, faithfully referring back to the paternal instance of knowing; it is equivalent to the living philosopher himself, who is present at the enunciation of his own words, and who can vouch for them, properly explicate them, and authorize them. Derrida writes: "Memory and truth cannot be separated. The movement of *aletheia* is a deployment of *mnèmè* through and through. A deployment of living memory, of memory as psychic life in its self-presentation to itself" (PP, 105). This self-presence must be contrasted with the movement of writing and all the "monuments" (*hypomnèmata*) it implies: "inventories, archives, citations, copies, accounts, lists, notes, duplicates" (PP, 107). This is writing that opens out to a "not-knowing," to the movement of a forgetting: writing is external to living memory, it is absent in its very presence, silent, and it cannot explain itself or correct others when they misinterpret it (as can the philosopher in his living presence to himself). It is both dead and promiscuous, lending itself to virtually all interpretations and contradicting none. For this reason one cannot attribute to it any "essence," even that of death or "not-truth." "For writing has no essence or proper value, whether positive or negative. It plays [*se joue*] within the simulacrum. It is in its type the mime of memory, of knowledge, of truth, etc." (PP, 105).

Already we can see that a stable opposition, an ambivalence, between a "good" and "bad" writing *within* writing is out of the question, because the "bad" writing "itself" is not a stable term but only a deceptive and self-forgetting play of simulacra, an outer limit "within" the field of writing, from whose opening-out the metaphysical distinction between good and evil is generated. And the positive term – writing enabling the constitution of living memory as self-presence – is equally illusory: *mnèmè* too needs repeatable (dead) external signifiers in order to present itself to itself, to constitute itself as an interiority: "The outside is already *within* the labor of memory. The evil [*le mal*] slips in within the relation of memory to itself, in the general organization of mnesic activity. Memory is finite by nature. Plato recognizes this in attributing life to it. As in the case of all living organisms, he assigns it, as we have seen, certain limits. A limitless memory would in any event be not memory but infinite self-presence. Memory always therefore already needs signs in order to recall the non-present, with which it is necessarily in relation. . . . Memory is thus contaminated by its first outside, by its first substitute: *hypomnésis*" (PP, 109).

"Bad" writing – the *pharmakon* as poison – therefore cannot be isolated as a unitary or oppositional term (nor can it be one stable "side" in an ambivalent term); and, at the same time, "good" writing – the living memory trace, the *pharmakon* as cure – in its very self-organization and self-reflection is opened out to, and impossibly incorporates, that to which it is opposed, its "outside." Derrida stresses that the *pharmakon* – and writing – is not simply subordinate to and dependent on oppositions such as good and bad, inside and outside, poison and cure; instead in its doubleness it "opens up their very possibility without allowing itself to be comprehended by them"; it is only "out of something like writing – or the *pharmakon* – that the strange difference between inside and outside can spring"; writing "leaves only its ghost to a logic that can only seek to govern it insofar as logic arises from it" (PP, 103).

The force of the *pharmakon* for Derrida lies not so much in an "ambivalence" that effaces itself before a unitary and deciding reading (as in Mauss), but in a kind of originary, generating duality (what he elsewhere calls *dif-*

ferance): its movement, always turning against itself in itself, defeating itself by constituting itself in its other, enables the "announcement" of the indefinitely reproduced and reproducible distinctions and representations from which metaphysics proceeds.[5] So it is not only a question of avoiding the privileging of one term – the cure, life, knowledge – over another – poison, death, not-knowing (or vice versa); rather, by affirming (momentarily, at least, in the essay "Plato's Pharmacy") the *pharmakon*, Derrida problematizes the very possibility of a unique and self-sufficient origin, fully present to itself (and returning to itself) in its own truth and properness: "Differance, the disappearance of any originary appearance, is *at once* the condition of possibility and the condition of impossibility of truth. At once. 'At once' means that the being-present [*étant-présent*] (on) in its truth, in the presence of its identity and in the identity of its presence, *is doubled* as soon as it appears, as soon as it presents itself. *It appears, in its essence, as* the possibility of its own duplication" (PP, 168).

At this point the Heideggerian echo is most clearly heard: Derrida uses the French term for "being" in Heidegger (as opposed to Being), *étant*, to indicate the oppositional terms of metaphysics – terms that can be "identical and identical to [themselves], unique" only by "*add [ing] to* [themselves] the possibility of being *repeated* as such" (PP, 168). But Derrida does not oppose an apparently stable and easily identified "Being" to this reproducible "being-present." Instead there is an open-ended series of terms – writing, the *pharmakon*, the *pharmakeus*, the *pharmakos*, the god Toth, and so on, not one of which can be held up as a definitive or original term against a tradition inaugurated (as we learn within the history of philosophy) by Plato himself. Such an opposition would only naively repeat the oppositions that constitute that tradition. We have only a *fantôme*, a ghost, a trace – writing, or any other term of the series – that perversely allows itself to be situated *in* an opposition, without at the same time ever being fully comprehended by it.

The never explicitly named Heidegger himself, then, passes as just such a ghost at the end of "Plato's Pharmacy." He is not "really" there, he is not a spuriously unitary and stable *étant* being opposed to another *étant*, be it "Plato" or "metaphysics." His ghost is traversing these oppositions, and their impossibility, but, interestingly enough, the "language" Derrida is writing in is not so much that of Heidegger himself as it is that of French anthropology. Put another way, Heidegger in Derrida, at least in this instance, is "undoing" certain oppositions, and certain closures, that make possible the coherence of French anthropology. Heidegger (or Derrida's repetition of Heidegger) in that sense is only the rupture that is necessary to, but at the same time precludes, the coherency of anthropology.

Consider, for example, the problem of sacrifice and sacrificial expulsion. It is clear from the first that there is a certain complicity between Derrida's *criticism* and the figure of the *pharmakos* – the Greek term for the scapegoat, the sacrificial victim – that Derrida in turn associates with the *pharmakon*. How in fact can one justify writing of the *pharmakos* in the context of Plato, who never uses the word? Derrida argues that "like any text, the text of 'Plato' cannot not be in relation, in at least a virtual, dynamic, lateral manner, with all the words making up the system of the Greek language" (PP, 129). In other words, the very possibility of "Plato's text," firmly established with a rigorous border between interior and exterior, presence and absence, property and nonproperty, is itself a function of a certain reading of Plato's text; when this interpretation is itself read critically, the easy distinction or boundary between the text and its other, its proper and its improper reading, will be undermined.[6] The term arrived at in this way, *pharmakos*, is nothing other than the doubled victim who is both criminal and god, "sacred and accursed" (PP, 133), inside and outside the community.[7] "The city's body *proper* thus reconstitutes its unity, closes around the security of its inner courts, gives itself the word which ties itself to itself within the limits of the agora, by violently excluding from its territory the representative of an external threat or aggression. That representative no doubt represents the alterity of the evil that comes to affect and infect the inside, by unpredictably breaking into it. Yet the representative of the outside is nonetheless *constituted*, regularly granted its place by the community, chosen, if you can put it that way, in its heart, maintained, nourished by it, etc." (PP, 133).

We see, then, the implicit identification on Derrida's part between his own critical method, which inhabits and undoes the internalized boundary between the inside and outside of languages and texts, and the scapegoat, who is the impossible "embodiment" of a passage between an inviolable interiority and the exteriority that that interiority must establish *within* itself in order to be an interiority. The coincidence of opposites is incessantly undone by this passage, this "crisis" (PP, 133), and it is clear that the scapegoat's movement is inseparable from the "critical instance." Implicit here is the Greek root of the words "crisis," "critic," "critical," *krinein* (to separate, to split); in the act of reading there is already the movement of separation, of decision or distinction, which means not the stable coexistence of two separated entities, the *coincidentia oppositorum*, as Derrida calls it (PP, 133), but instead the very displacement that is also the generation of this separation.[8] And, a little further on, we see that this border-dwelling scapegoat-critic is associated by Derrida with another figure familiar to us from the tradition of French anthropology, the intellectual; at one point, Derrida identifies Plato's negative evaluation of writing in the *Phaedrus* with his condemnation of democracy in the *Republic*. Like writing, the democrat is so perverse that "he is not even perverse in a regular way" (PP, 145); he gives himself over to all pleasures, "eventually even to politics and philosophy": "Swept off by every stream, he belongs to the masses; he has no essence, no truth, no patronym, no constitution of his own" (PP, 145). He is, in other words, no different from the intellectual who is traditionally accused of speaking out of turn, holding forth on problems beyond his competence, and so on.[9]

The critic, that is, the intellectual, the sacrificial victim, thus undoes a sacrificial logic that would establish and reaffirm a kind of integrity, interiority, and property by symbolically and physically excluding a "third." This sacrificial-dialectic logic is not short-circuited, in Derrida's text, by simply resituating the sacred force of the ambivalent object (the *Gift*, the *pharmakon*) in writing itself – a risky gesture we saw set in motion, for example, by Paulhan. Instead, in Derrida the critical force of writing, of the *pharmakon*, but also necessarily of an open-ended series of other terms, is situated in a space (for want of a better term) out of which the very ambivalence, or indefinitely reproduced duality, of the sacred (of terms such as the *pharmakon*) is generated. Only through the ghost (*le fantôme*) it leaves behind can the *pharmakon*, or writing, be situated within the opposition that proceeds from it (PP, 103). We are therefore not justified in saying that there is simply a "good" or "bad" writing, a poisonous or beneficial criticism (or crisis). Those stable alternatives are in complicity with the logic of a sacrificial gesture that would strengthen or regenerate an essential interiority by rejecting an inessential and wholly foreign element. This clear distinction (of the type we saw in Mauss, where the ambivalence of the *pharmakon* was only a function of the symmetrical chances of winning and losing in the sacrificial ritual of exchange – and where one side would either inevitably "win out" or lose and be forgotten) and the exteriority/interiority it presupposes, is undone at the very site in which that opposition "appears" in its originary duplication. Divisive sacred violence is displaced by the critic who, through his critical gesture, situates himself at an impossible "origin" point of all separation, in the in-folded exterior and the out-folded interior, and who recognizes that while he cannot separate himself from the easy oppositions of sacred violence – to do so would only be to situate himself on one side of *another* stable opposition – at the same time he cannot be "comprehended" by them, either.

We can see in Derrida a gesture clearly related to those of a number of other authors – such as Paulhan, Sartre, or Bataille – who, in different ways, would use sacrifice against itself, or who (put another way) would deflect sacrifice from its exclusionary, speculative, and foundational role; for if Derrida presents the *pharmakos*, the *pharmakon* – and the critic – as inhabiting an impossible space between and against the exclusionary limits of the sacrificial relation, he also recognizes that the violence of writing that he affirms is not simply separable from a sacrificial violence. In order to situate his project against sacrifice, he is forced to recognize sacrifice, or a version of it, at the very inauguration of the closed, exclusionary community of the tradition of metaphysics, which is nothing if not a maintenance of rigorous oppositions and ostracisms. (After all, as soon as one posits the scapegoat, no matter how his function is seen, one is affirming the importance, if not the efficacy or integrity, of sacrifice.) Derrida nevertheless affirms that his critique cannot *simply* be subordinated to the sacrificial oppositions that are "philosophy." Insubordination – which is also a kind of freedom from the tyranny of catharsis through an affirmation of its doubled origin – is possible only by reading "the play of citation," the echoes, communications, and correspondences between terms that are seemingly in straightforward opposition. Reading a kind of "deep" ambivalence within or across terms – within, for example, the *pharmakon*, or between the *pharmakos* and the *pharmakon* – is inseparable from an analysis of how oppositional terms are always already contained "within" one another, how they hold one another in a "pocket," a movement that a straightforward sacrificial logic is incapable of noting or analyzing. Translators may, and probably will, miss this citational play, translating one instance of a word with one term, and another with another term that is simply "opposed" to it. But this kind of reading, which imposes neat oppositions where they are not to be found, is itself a kind of crude "Platonism" – not the Platonism of the play of signifiers in Plato's text but, rather, the simplistic interpretation which itself has resulted from a tradition of translation that does away with the duality and duplicity of terms. As Derrida states, "It could no doubt be shown, and we will try to do so when the time comes, that this blockage of the passage among opposing values is itself already an effect of 'Platonism,' the consequence of something already at work in the translated text, in the relation between 'Plato' and 'his language'" (PP, 98).

It is the bad translation – one which is nevertheless unavoidable – that *decides* between "opposing" terms. By making arbitrary distinctions, the translation, the reading, is inevitably in complicity both with a philosophical tradition that has for centuries attempted to decide between apparently incompatible terms (idealism and materialism, interiority and exteriority, etc.), and with a sacrificial logic that has attempted arbitrarily to impose a culture of political interiority and integrity through the act of violent exclusion. Sacrifice and philosophy in this sense have always been in profound collusion. Derrida's most fundamental gesture is thus to bracket series of neat oppositions or dialectical contradictions whose maintenance as such is inseparable from a "Platonic" misreading or mistranslating. To take these oppositions at face value is to misread the very movement by which they are generated. This of course does not mean that one can escape such distinctions, but it is clear that if the movement of *différance* is inescapable, the various mythemes and philosophemes – or ideologemes – in themselves, through Derrida's reading, lose the force of their content. If Derrida, in his writing, inevitably takes sides (for one cannot straightforwardly escape metaphysical distinctions), "he," on one side or the other, will only leave a ghost, the hollow marker of a position, the always anterior repetition of a term in quotation. The remaining philosophemes are still oppositional terms, to be sure, and for this reason they maintain a diacritical force; but "in themselves," as markers of abstract concepts, truths, or social entities, they have no more meaning. Their opposition is, in a sense, empty. (I use this term "empty" without wishing to imply that a term or an opposition necessarily has an inside or an outside, or that it could be "full.") They are as devoid of inherent significance as is the promiscuous phoneme whose momentary value is derived only from the opposition into which it can enter. In this sense, not just the *pharmakon*, entering into opposition with other terms, is a "ghost"; *all* philosophemes are ghostlike. Their interest for Derrida lies in the complicity of terms in their very opposition, not in any "truth value" that one term might represent or convey, or in the falsity of its neighbor. Derrida does not read Plato – or any other philosophical text – and judge the truth of propositions. (And if he "opposes" a philosophy or its argumentation, it is only *as* a ghost.) We could even say that the refusal to do so is his most basic gesture, the one that has remained "consistent" in his project, from the very "beginning," from the first published writings on Husserl. And it is this gesture that most concerns us here.

The most important difference between Mauss and Derrida, one could argue, lies in their approach to the *pharmakon*. Mauss's goal is largely one of semantic determination; through the ambiguity of the term, Mauss hopes to see a larger, finally nonambiguous referent. He manages to do this, twice: first he sees a troubling psychological state – the mixture of fear and ecstatic excitement on the part of the subject as he enters the sacrificial-exchange ritual; then, later, Mauss posits a happy ending to gift giving, the "friendly" incorporation of "primitive" practices in developed capitalist economies, a kind of end of history that the correct interpretation of the "gift," its truth, will make possible. In this second case, the ambivalence is forgotten, but not the need to find a referent, which this time is a fortunate social outcome rather than a psychological, and even pathological, state. The modern recognition of the gift, for Mauss, is not an act that causes the desired future society to come into being; instead, the gift is a term that, when correctly interpreted, reveals the truth of a society that can be instituted through the exercise of reason. That institution itself will no doubt be founded and maintained through a speech or totem act (gift giving in its contemporary form), but the act itself will be dependent on and posterior to a correct interpretation and determination. Derrida's concerns go in a very different direction; it is clear from the first that for him the *pharmakon* is inseparable from an activity; it does not so much refer to a stable signified or referent as it acts as a differentiating term, one that is, moreover, always differentiated in itself. The *pharmakon*, the *pharmakos*, the critic, each performs an act, each is a kind of act that both enables and undoes: the *pharmakon*, as writing, poisons and cures; the scapegoat enables sacrifice to take place and defeats it by inhabiting the internalized border or limit separating the city and its other; the critic carrying out a reading looks not for the truth value of the text but instead reads the *différance* at the "origin" of that reproduced and reproducible truth. Mauss had already recognized the gift as a kind of sacred marker, a pledge (*un gage*), that did not so much refer to an abstract quantity of wealth as enable an act of differentiation – of exchange, defiance, power – to take place. Derrida, rather than tending to ignore this performative function, in fact affirms it over Mauss's constative.

This is another way of saying that Derrida's affirmed version of the *pharmakon* is grammatical rather than dialectical. It can "play" either side of an opposition, but it itself, as a differential act, is empty; only its ghost is in play when, for example, its movement is situated *against* interiority, self-reflexivity, and so on. There are two consequences that follow from this: first, as I have already indicated, an open critique of sacrificial violence, done in the name of writing or any other term, is of no importance in itself. The defusing of that violence may be an aftereffect of Derrida's reading, but it cannot be the goal, because the movement of grammar is indifferent to the specificity of the terms in opposition. In "Plato's Pharmacy" a philosophical language that entails an anthropological vocabulary is reread; French anthropology, via Plato, is opened out, doubled, "mimed." Its mythemes and anthropologemes are set in motion. The affirmation or negation of its truth-value, however, is never in question: from the Derridean perspective, all oppositional terms are always already "ghosts." The second consequence is that, if rigorous distinctions (and "meanings") can no longer simply be maintained within philosophy or anthropology, they cannot be within rhetoric either. As Derrida notes, "If truth is the presence of the *eidos*, it must always, on pain of mortal blinding by the sun's fires, come to terms [*composer*], with relation, with non-presence, and thus nontruth. It then follows that the absolute precondition for a rigorous difference between grammar and dialectics (or ontology) cannot in principle be fulfilled" (PP, 166). Grammar itself is not simply distinguishable from a dialectic that proceeds through determinations of truth and falsity.

Oppositions always play a structural role, but these are only positional; each term's semantic weight – even in the case of the grammar/reference distinction itself – is set aside. Any given term is always part of a differential series that is so rigorously grammatical that it precludes the maintenance of the

distinction between grammar and the dialectic. It is also, therefore, in a series
that is not isolated from (nor is it identifiable with) the dialectic.

It should be stressed that this contamination (if we can use the word) of
grammar by reference is itself strictly the aftereffect of the forceful operation of
grammar, not of the mediations and representations of the dialectic. The ghost
of reference reenters by the back door; it inhabits oppositions only to the
extent that a positional vocabulary is indissociable from the movement of the
differential system, the "infrastructure."[10] If there is a defusing of ritual violence in Derrida, then, it is not a "goal" (as it was for Mauss, who attempted to
see the constructive aspects of modern giftgiving) but only the inadvertent
result of a Heideggerian displacement of the scene of the referential content of
violence, a movement that necessarily must be indifferent to "meanings" that
are incessantly generated, reduplicated, and reopposed. The language system
continues to function, we might say, but its reference is emptied out – like the
term whose value remains unknown and fundamentally unknowable in a
mathematical equation.[11] There is, however, a price to pay – to use an economic metaphor – for this emptying-out. It becomes noticeable only when
there is an attempt to engage openly in a critique of exclusionary violence and
sacrificial logic – as, for example, in Derrida's readings of Heidegger.

II

Derrida begins his essay "The Ends of Man" with a critique of France. The
France, that is, of the tradition of humanism and the engaged intellectual. The
"dominant motif" of the postwar period is an anthropological humanism
derived from misreadings of Hegel, Husserl, and Heidegger.[12] Of course Derrida could go much further back than this. Sartre is the only author Derrida
singles out: he serves as the metonym for an entire period, a generation, a
nation. It was "France" that was responsible for the "monstrous translation,"
by Henry Corbin, of Dasein as "human reality" (*réalité humaine*). Sartre might
very well have criticized, through the affirmation of a human reality, the earlier
"intellectualist or spiritualist" humanism of a Bergson or a Brunschvicg – and
here Derrida, in a footnote, cites approvingly Roquentin's portrayal of the
Autodidact's humanism in *Nausea* (EM, 115) – nevertheless, the post-Hus-
serlian Sartre never questioned the "unity of man." "Not only is existentialism
a humanism, but the ground and horizon of what Sartre then called his 'phenomenological ontology' (the subtitle of *Being and Nothingness*) remains the
unity of human-reality. Insofar as it describes the structures of human-reality,
phenomenological ontology is a philosophical anthropology" (EM, 115–16).

At no point does Derrida read the text of Sartre. The ideologeme "France-
humanism" is determined through a remarkably naive thematic presentation
of difficult, even enigmatic, literary and philosophical texts. Sartre had the

effrontery to invoke Husserl and Heidegger; from the position of a Heideggerian critique, Sartre's approach simply avoids the most difficult questions. Of course Heidegger had already made this point in the *Letter on Humanism*; it is an easy point to make, especially since Sartre himself wrote the essay flatly stating that "existentialism is a humanism." Sartre – or France – was guilty of an inattentive, even sloppy, reading or translation of Husserl or Heidegger. Moreover, that tradition of humanism, despite the authors it invoked in the postwar period, is associated by Derrida with an earlier tradition of republicanism, Eurocentric rationalism, and imperialism. Sartre is nothing other than a Third Republic ideology – a rereading of Brunschvicg – masquerading as Heidegger; and just beyond lies the most recent incarnation of the Third Republic – its successor in Vietnam, in fact: American imperialism. Derrida establishes these links quite clearly in the introduction to this article, which, as he points out, was completed in May 1968, as a contribution to an American conference in New York, to be devoted to philosophy and anthropology (there is a certain need on Derrida's part, it seems, to justify his decision to enter the belly of the imperialist beast to read a paper; see EM, 112–13): both the Vietnam War and the official reaction to the student protests of May 1968 in Paris ("for the first time at the demand of a rector, the universities of Paris were invaded by the forces of social order" [EM, 114]) are invoked as elements linked to humanist discourse, to the theme of "anthropos" (EM, 113).[13] The "Occident" – America, France, Sartre, the refusal of social or cultural difference – nevertheless recognizes that there is a difference – non-Occidental, non-anthropological – pressing in at the frontiers, and that is why it organizes so many conferences: "This is done no doubt to interiorize the difference, to master it, if we may put it thus, by affecting itself with it. The interest in the universality of the anthropos is doubtless a sign of this effort" (EM, 113).

We have here, then, at a relatively early stage of his project, a more or less explicit elaboration of a set of associations that orient much, if not all, of Derrida's work. No doubt these links are more polemical early on – in *Of Grammatology* and in the essay "Différance" – than they are later. On the one hand, the Occident, anthropology, the metaphysics of presence, interiority, selfhood, *le propre*, humanism, imperialism; on the other, *différance*. I am stating this very crudely, in a way that is in fact itself questioned at the *end* of "The Ends of Man," when we realize that the "frontier" between, say, the "West" and its other is always already internal to the West: "Its margin was marked in its own [*propre*] body" (EM, 133–34). In fact, much of the reading of Heidegger in "The Ends of Man" explicitly questions an easy opposition between, say, Heidegger and Sartre. It is almost as if France, or the "French" misreading of Heidegger, is already a constituent element of Heidegger himself.

Why then is Sartre – "France" – characterized in such a peremptory manner by Derrida? Why is his text not read with the same patience as Heidegger's? I raise this question not to defend Sartre – I have no interest in whether Derrida or anyone else "reads" or does not read Sartre – but only to point out a problem that is already apparent, in 1968, in Derrida's approach: focusing on the problem of *différance* in all its avatars precludes in a certain way the examination of the specificities of the philosopheme or ideologeme being analyzed. This is not to say that Derrida does not analyze philosophical texts with great rigor and precision, but that differences *within* the "borders" of the "West" become virtually irrelevant from the perspective of his reading. France is Sartre is humanism is the American presence in Vietnam is French republicanism – the list could go on indefinitely, and we will see even more astonishing conjunctions later, in *De l'esprit*. Not the least of our problems here will be understanding the logic, the necessity, and the impossibility of this kind of linkage.

Sartre criticizes humanism only in an aberration: *Nausea* (EM, 115, n. 4). Derrida does not clearly distinguish, however, between a Sartrian caricature of humanism (in the figure of the Autodidact) and one by Roquentin ("It is in the discussion with the Autodidact that Roquentin levels the worst charges against humanism"). Are Roquentin and Sartre the same? Does *Nausea* present this caricature of humanism in a straightforward way, as the definitive version of things – as would, say, within the supposed conventions of the genre, a philosophical text with a "reliable narrator"? Is the narrator of Sartre's philosophical works any more or less reliable? Derrida seems to assume that he is both as reliable – and the same as – the extremely problematic Sartre/ Roquentin "narrator" of *Nausea*. This is a particularly interesting question because Derrida maintains that Sartre upholds a unity of subjectivity – of responsible authorship or narration, one would have to conclude – through a lack:[14] "This synthetic unity is determined as *lack*: lack of totality of being [*étant*; being with a small *b*] lack *of* God that is soon transformed into lack *in* God. Human reality is a *failed* God. . . . The concept of *lack*, linked to the nonself identity of the subject (as consciousness), and to the desire and the insistence of the Other in the master-slave dialectic, was then beginning to dominate the French ideological scene" (EM 116, n. 5). The lack, in other words, is always recuperated in and through a dialectical movement; consciousness is reaffirmed through its objectifications ("In this sense," writes Derrida, "what is true of *Being and Nothingness* is even more true of *The Critique of Dialectical Reason*"). Derrida can level the worst charges against (*faire le procès de*) Sartre's work, then, only by imputing to Sartre the very kind of unitary and originary consciousness that he accuses Sartre of upholding; by presupposing, in other words, the kind of subjectivity that he maintains Sartre presupposes. Sartre himself, after an initial strong moment (the caricature of humanism in *Nausea*), becomes, as a unitary writing consciousness, a kind of lack or deficiency that characterizes the unity of a (bad) contemporary French philosophy (or "ideology"), and that must itself be overcome by another (Derridean) reading, which lacks Sartre's lack.

According to Derrida, this very presence-to-itself of consciousness, through the lack, separates Sartre (or "France") from Heidegger. And yet from the first, in *Sein und Zeit* (section 2) it is a proximity that characterizes the relation of the being (*étant*) to himself, through the questioning of Being (*l'être*). Derrida writes: "It is the proximity to itself of the questioning being which leads it to be chosen as the privileged interrogated being. The proximity to itself of the inquirer authorizes the identity of the inquirer and the interrogated. We, who are close to ourselves, *we* interrogate *ourselves* [nous nous *interrogeons*] about the meaning of Being" (EM, 126). Derrida is quick to point out that this proximity or presence to oneself of the "being that we are," of the "questioner and the interrogated," is not the same as a subjective consciousness, because "this proximity is still prior to what the metaphysical predicate 'human' might name" (EM, 126). Nevertheless, Heidegger's approach, for this reason and because the entire project of the questioning of Being becomes a questioning of the meaning of Being (it is a "hermeneutic of unveiling," a "becoming conscious"), seems to be, in a certain way, in complicity with the very metaphysics it would deconstruct. The "complete ontology of the Dasein" is seen by Heidegger as a preliminary condition for the elaboration of an "anthropological philosophy." The proximity of the being to itself (or himself) in questioning, while "demanded by Being" and therefore prior, once again, to the series of metaphysical oppositions (such as being and nonbeing) that are inseparable from the forgetting of Being, is also anterior to, and necessary to, a "higher" elaboration of man. Derrida writes: "We can see then that Dasein, though *not* man, is nevertheless *nothing other* than man. It is, as we shall see, a repetition of the essence of man permitting a return to what is before the metaphysical concepts of the *humanitas*. The subtlety and the equivocality of this gesture, then, are what have obviously authorized all of the anthropologistic deformations in the reading of *Sein und Zeit*, notably in France" (EM, 127).

What at first appeared to be a simple "defense" of Heidegger in the face of all the French distortions is really something much more complex. Heidegger's text itself is not simple, it is divided against itself. The very fact that it lends itself to a misreading by the "French" indicates that it is already "French," that "France" is the limit lodged within it. But its humanism, which is not *exactly* humanism, precedes and even generates the oppositions of metaphysics, most notably the couple human/not-human. Heidegger is "guided by the motif of Being as presence – understood in a more originary sense than it is in the metaphysical and ontic determinations of presence or of presence as the present" (EM, 128). *Before* metaphysics there is humanism: "The thinking of Being . . . remains a thinking *of* man. Man and the name of man are not displaced in the question of Being such as it is put to metaphysics. Even less do they disappear. On the contrary, at issue is a kind of reevaluation or revalorization of the essence and dignity of man" (EM, 128). Metaphysics, it seems, is "de-limited" by a pre-originary humanism. And along with it goes the entire panoply of philosophemes that we have already seen invoked in Derrida's reading of Plato: a "metaphorics of proximity, of simple and immediate presence, associating the proximity of Being with the values of neighboring, shelter, house, service, guard, voice and listening" (EM, 130). We can also associate this logocentric, phonocentric "side" of Heidegger – although Derrida avoids doing so himself, while nevertheless implying it – with the "Black Forest" ideology of peasant labor, the rural locale, and all the sinister complicities to which such an ideology lent itself in the 1930s. The "house," the "shelter," are terms that connote, to say the least, a philosophy of exclusion: one is either in the house or one is an outsider, in a certain language (German, i.e., the language of thought) or outside it; one is in the forest or in the city, in Germany or in France. We are back once again at the problem of the *pharmakos*, of the sacrificial logic of exclusion through expulsion that is inseparable in its functioning from the distinctions and demarcations of metaphysics. Heidegger, however, at least in Derrida's reading, is on the side of the expeller and not that of the expelled; he affirms the violence of the agora and not the *différance* of the scapegoat.

Derrida recognizes a fundamental problem, one that haunts Heidegger and any deconstructive reading of a text: "It remains that Being, which is nothing, which is not a being, cannot be said, cannot say itself except in the ontic metaphor. And the choice of one or another group of metaphors is necessarily significant" (EM, 131). Being can be expressed only in a "thought" that metaphorizes "by means of a profound necessity from which one cannot simply decide to escape, the language that it deconstructs" (EM, 131). But what language will be deconstructed? The French or the German? Is there a difference between languages? How does one *decide* which language is to be deconstructed? Isn't this decision itself, the question it raises, fully inscribed in metaphysics? Is there a way to avoid in some way a metaphysics of personhood, humanization, property, and propriety in the act of displacing the very metaphysics with which those terms are in solidarity? But doesn't such an avoidance itself depend on a decision as to which languages, which positions, are to be deconstructed? The expression "the end of man" sums up the problem: "end" (like *fin* in French) is both the death of man and his telos (EM, 134). In Hegel already this double end was evident; but there man's death implied a sublation, an ascension to a higher level. And in Heidegger? Derrida, in attempting to follow to its logical "end" the Heideggerian critique of humanism (as in Heidegger's response to Sartre, "The Letter on Humanism") faces the problem of an end of man *not* organized by a dialectic, *not* a "first person plural theology." But how can the two ends be separated, if the end (as death) can be expressed only in the metaphorics of the end (as goal)? If metaphorics will always be "ontic," how can we distinguish between metaphoric systems? If, as in the kind of reading presented by Derrida, all philosophemes are emptied out, if their only value is as markers in a larger syntax, how then can we distinguish between metaphoric systems?

Derrida recognizes that the task of "breaking out" of the humanistic enclosure – Heidegger's house – is a difficult one. Transgressions are liable to turn into "false exits" (*fausses sorties*) (EM, 135). From *within* the system, Derrida says – and can we ever simply leave it? – there are two choices: the first, Heideggerian, is to stay within the house, "attempt an exit and a deconstruction without changing terrain . . . using against the edifice the instruments or stones available in the house, that is, equally, in language" (EM, 135). The risk of this approach is that one will only strengthen the house one is trying to break out of. The second option, Derrida implies, is the one that "dominates France today." Here it is "absolute rupture" and "difference" that are affirmed – a total breakout from the house, in other words, which will inevitably be resituated, through the "simple practice of language," on the "oldest ground" (EM, 135). This strategy, no doubt to be associated with Deleuze and Foucault (though Derrida, as is often the case, does not explicitly name the targets of his critique), seems to lead to more or less the same result, then, as the hoariest, most exclusive and exclusionary – and most politically suspect – Heideggerian sylvan housing project.[15] The breakout from the house, and the sacrificial logic it implies, is the functional equivalent to barricading oneself inside; put another way, attempting to change to another system of metaphors, one that would simply escape the vocabulary of self-presence, anthropologism, and France, somehow leads one back again to France, or to the France of Heidegger (or, in other words, to France as Heideggerian Germany, with all its hominess and political compromises). One cannot simply strip the word "end" of one of its meanings ("goal") while retaining the other ("death"). Nor can one attempt to replace a suspect system of metaphors with another one that would be innocent and respectable. If one tries, one is trapped once again in France, one is not Sartre, perhaps, but a shadow-philosopher, one who would only become more Sartrian in his attempt to escape Sartre.

The end of Derrida's essay is far from conclusive: he now presents a third rubric, "The difference between the superior man and the superman" (EM, 135). This strangely synthetic position is, it seems, a "plural" one: in the paragraph before rubric 3, Derrida notes that "a new writing must weave and interlace these two motifs [the 'Heideggerian' and the 'French'] of deconstruction." One must "speak a number of languages" and "produce a number of texts" at once. It follows that this "plurality" is nothing other than a Nietzschean "active forgetting of Being" that "would not have had the metaphysical form imputed to it by Heidegger" (EM, 136); this move, this "change of 'style,'" entails a "dance outside the house" – neither a dwelling in it, nor its outright destruction.

It is not at all clear how this last possibility is different from the naive French "escape" from humanism that Derrida mentions earlier, nor how the Nietzschean *Übermensch* will play a role in it. What is of more interest, I think, is the difficulty Derrida faces at this point, one not unrelated, as we will see, to the problems of some of his very recent writing on Heidegger. Indeed whether one escapes the Heideggerian house or stays in it, or whether one affirms Nietzsche in the face of Heidegger by continuing to haunt the house's boundaries, it seems that the oppositions that keep that house standing – such as humanism versus antihumanism, rationalism versus antirationalism – are of no consequence other than *as* oppositions. The *specificity* of the oppositions, in other words, is of no importance to Derrida: if Heidegger's "shelter" is seen as opposed to Sartrian humanism, or if the latter is presented as having been established against an earlier French rationalist tradition, these differences are important only insofar as they are characteristic of all pairs in the "Western" philosophical tradition, and in that sense they are all in profound complicity. The difference in these empty, oppositional dyads is only part of a larger unity; their identity can be perceived only from the perspective of the closure of metaphysics itself. Their unity-in-opposition is a function of a mutual dependence of terms; in other words, their difference is only a syntactic differentiation which makes the larger coherence of philosophy possible. I would argue that the ways of perceiving the unity of a movement – humanism, rationalism – and the unity of a subjectivity – Sartre's narrative persona as presented at the beginning of "The Ends of Man" – are closely linked. In both cases complexities and tensions within a text – of one "author" or of one "philosophical tradition" – are emptied so that a larger characterization of a self-deluded unity can take place.

Is there an exit to Heidegger's house after all? Whether this third possibility can be opposed to the house – if the superman's dance in the yard really is an escape – or whether it is only a "forgetting," a radical change of style, comes to seem virtually irrelevant when we consider the consequences.[16] If, for example, options one (staying in the house: Heidegger) and two (tearing it down: post-Sartrian French critics) are opposed from the perspective of the one who vacates but does not abandon the house of Being, then the specificity of their distinction will be irrelevant, apart from a purely formal demarcation. "Active forgetting" in this sense is itself a kind of opposition. Being and its French displacement are, as differential terms, negated in order to affirm (if only through forgetting) what amounts to a higher synthesis (the third option, which incorporates both previous ones in its "plurality"). Both sides – both philosophemes – are needed if only to be transcended at the third stage. Reading the first two options as simple opposed philosophical terms (the Heideggerian dwelling in complicity with Sartrian humanism versus the naive French [Foucauldian-Deleuzian] "escape" from that closed space) that are void of content – in other words, as terms fully inscribed in "Western metaphysics" – leads to a third position which is nothing if not a dialectical higher stage.

But if "France" is left behind, Heidegger is purged of his French contamination – which is not only the result of the misreadings carried out by the French – and we are left, after this operation of catharsis, not, say, with Hegel, or with the heroic incarnation of Hegelian knowledge (Napoleon, or, for Kojève, Stalin), but with Nietzsche's Zarathustra. The violence of this movement, then, cannot be *exclusively* Hegelian: if we read the third stage as an active forgetting *not* in opposition to the first two, that is, as a Nietzschean movement that cannot be identified once and for all with a dialectical movement, then the specificity of the pairing of the first and second options (the "content" of the philosophemes) will also be jettisoned; plurality will be affirmed, and difference, if not opposition. There will be a play of signifiers and styles. In those styles there will be a diacritical opposition, if not a dialectical one; the third stage will then still be the resolution of the crisis represented by the doubling of the first two. But like the *pharmakon*, it will leave "only" its ghost in opposition: in that sense it will be the "end" – in both senses – of the dialectic. It will not be subsumable in the dialectic as just another "full" term. Instead it may well open the possibility of the very oppositions it is vacantly reenacting.

This may be only a mock-Hegelian synthesis but it is one indebted to Hegel to the extent that the significance of the two earlier terms – the goal perhaps espoused by Heidegger, and the death affirmed by the post-Sartrian French – is clearly resolved by the positing of, in Derrida's words, what we "perhaps need" (EM, 135). This indicates a strange return, on Derrida's part, to a vocabulary of necessity and utility; one inevitably thinks of Sartre's emphasis on the "lack." What do we *need*? Nothing other than the ghostly resolution that is not a resolution of a contradiction that was not primarily a contradiction. A resolution that is free to forget not the difference it is not resolving but the "content" of the two positions that are paired. But can the resolution (the "end" as, inevitably, "goal" as well as "death") forget the *need for* the forgetting? What if the "contents" of the two positions are *themselves* spirits that, in their very plenitude, come back to haunt a third option that leaves only its phantom in opposition? What, in other words, if the inevitable morality of the two earlier positions – philosophemes seemingly emptied and forgotten in the gesture of affirming difference – returns as a version of guilt, tied to Derrida's evident inability to forget the ethics (expressed through the emphasis placed on "need") of active forgetting? In this case, it may be harder than ever to escape the haunted house of Being.

III

Why use the term *esprit* – mind, spirit – in French, in the title and throughout the text, of an essay on Heidegger's use of the word *Geist*? The connotations of *esprit* are many, and Derrida himself reminds us of a few: *De l'esprit*, by Helvetius – the same title that Derrida uses – was burned by act of Parliament in 1759;[17] there indeed seems to be a strange affinity between fire, spirit, and breath. But beyond this, *esprit* – with or without quotation marks – seems to conjure up, as Derrida notes, a very Latinate tradition: the "Latin compositions in a Ciceronian style," "French materialism of the eighteenth century or French spiritualism of the following centuries that founded . . . the most beautiful canons of our academic rhetoric" (E, 15). What has this to do with Heidegger, who did his best to tear philosophy away from the romance languages, proclaiming that only German – after Greek – was a language in which one could "think"?

We realize from the first that things will be more complicated here than in "The Ends of Man"; it is not simply a question of easily categorizing "France" or the "French tradition," as Derrida did, at least at the beginning of "The Ends of Man" (the end of that essay, as we have seen, already posed the problem of the humanism – the Latinity – of Heidegger himself). In Derrida's *De l'esprit*, there is, from the beginning, an affirmation that a Latin problematic is inseparable from a German one: each is implicated in the other, and one cannot escape certain problems by leaving one or another language, or tradition, behind. "*De l'esprit* is a very French title, much too French to enable one to understand the *geistige* or *geistliche* of *Geist*. But, precisely, one would perhaps understand it better in German. Perhaps in any case we will be precisely more sensitive to its Germanness [*germanité*] if we allow it to resonate in a foreign language, to put it to the test of translation, or rather if we put to the test its resistance to translation. And if we put our own language to the same test" (E, 16–17). "French" – or "Latin" – is now a kind of oppositional term to Heidegger's notoriously privileged German – not so much "in itself," but in the space of translation that it opens up, in the displacement it effects between one language (German) and another (French).

Geist – or *esprit* – is not only fully implicated in the political in both its French *and* German avatars (it is not only the French who associate *esprit* with political reform or reaction); it is "regularly inscribed in high-toned political contexts, in the moments when thought allows itself more than ever to be preoccupied with what is called history, the language, the nation, the *Geschlecht*, the Greek or the German" (E, 18). In addition, *Geist* is not only a recurring term in these discourses, but it "determines perhaps the very meaning of politics as such. In any case, it would situate the locus [*le lieu*] of such a determination, if it were possible" (E, 19). *Geist* in this way opens the possibility of a certain politics, and for this reason it is of crucial importance for the discussions that circulate around the name Heidegger – discussions, Derrida makes clear (by referring to Philippe Lacoue-Labarthe's recent work) that have to do with Heidegger's controversial membership in the Nazi party, his *Rektoratsrede*, his refusal ever to consider seriously the significance of the overwhelming crimes committed during the war – Auschwitz, or the Shoah, above all – and the importance of the part he played in legitimizing Hitler's rule.[18]

We have, then, a more developed version here of a problem that was already evident in "The Ends of Man." There too it was a question of considering "France" in Heidegger (France, moreover, specifically in quotes; see EM, 134), the ways in which traditional ("French") metaphysical problems – such as the proper, self-presence or self-reflexivity, consciousness, subjectivity, humanism – were linked to, and in some sense were indissociable from, even inscribed in, Heidegger's more radical project. In *De l'esprit* there is the clear recognition that the problem is both French and German, that it is situated in the impossible space between languages, and that it is therefore fundamentally tied to the necessity of translation; in addition, there is a more explicit recognition in the later work of the political implications of the *esprit-Geist* combination, which, as Derrida puts it, "determines the meaning of politics." *Esprit*, *Geist*, politics, meaning, translation – all are inseparable from any reading of Heidegger and by extension Derrida, whose work so clearly is a rigorous rereading and rewriting (and, as we have seen, stripping) of Heidegger. We are now in a better position, it seems, to see the links between different national traditions of misreading, and the very meaning (or direction: *le sens*) of politics that these misreadings "determine."

De l'esprit presents a kind of temporal progression through which *Geist*, a seemingly minor word in Heidegger's vocabulary, moves, from *Sein und Zeit* to the *Rektoratsrede* of 1933.[19] Heidegger's first gesture, at the beginning of *Sein und Zeit*, in fact, recalls Derrida's blunt problematizing of "humanism" in the opening pages of "The Ends of Man": Heidegger excludes *Geist* as an oppositional term to "thing," because the simple opposition of "mind" to "thing" – as in Lukács's critique of "reification" – without a questioning of the nature of Being leads only to the embrace of a "problematic or dogmatic" concept (E, 35). In fact the very thing that constitutes the "exemplarity" of Dasein is the "experience of the question," its possibility and its structure (E, 36). Heidegger refuses the term *Geist*, or *esprit* (whether in its Cartesian or Husserlian version), along with "consciousness," "the ego," "reason," "the subject," and "the unconscious." Such terms preclude, bar the way, to any "interrogation of the Being of Dasein" (E, 38). The "force of the question" is met only with indifference when the word *esprit* is used, and its use makes impossible any questioning of the "being that we are" through the question of Being in general (E, 38). This indifference to the question is clearly the unfortunate heritage of Descartes (the French tradition, in other words). The naive conception of the *esprit* is tied to a "substantial subjectivity" and to the necessity of that subject subsisting in time – hence to a "vulgar concept of time" (E, 40). Any rethinking of the "us" as Dasein, then, and of "our" exemplarity as questioners (E, 36), implies a radical revision of our relation to time and of the notion of a time into which the spirit has "fallen."

The second Heideggerian version of *Geist*, according to Derrida, appears toward the end of *Sein und Zeit* (sections 70 and 82); now, rather than avoiding the word altogether, Heidegger uses it, but only in quotes. It is a strategy that recalls one we have already seen in Derrida's own work; the *pharmakon*, in Derrida's reading, came to be the very term that opened the possibility of metaphysical oppositions, but which allowed only its ghost, its *fantôme*, to be situated within them, on one side or another (PP, 103). In the same way, the word *Geist*, in quotes, is not something that "falls" into time, but rather it "is" temporalization (E, 50), the forming of the "transcendental horizon . . . of the question of the meaning of Being" (E, 49). It can thus be interpreted as being prior to the "fall" of the spirit into space and time, and hence as prior to, while generating, oppositions such as space/time, spirit/matter, and so on. This priority is inseparable from another fall: if there is a fall, it is the inevitable but provisional, ghostly, one of this more radical time into the other, "Cartesian-Hegelian" time, of one *esprit* into the other – into, in other words, the one that Heidegger had earlier set aside (E, 50). *Esprit* – in quotes – is a ghost. Derrida states:

> The word "spirit" [*esprit*] comes back, it is no longer rejected, avoided, but used in its deconstructed sense to designate something other that resembles it, and of which it is like the metaphysical ghost [*dont il est comme le fantôme métaphysique*], the spirit of another spirit. Through the quotation marks, across their bars [*à travers leur grille*], one sees announced [*on voit s'annoncer*] a double of spirit. . . . Through the metaphysical Cartesian word, or the word of subjective grafting [*la greffe*

subjective], by traversing it like an index finger that points beyond itself, Heidegger will name in quotes, in other words, *write* – negatively, indirectly, silently – something that is certainly not what the former language called "spirit," but which, *in any case, above all, is not* what would have been considered *the opposite of spirit*: the spatial object, the outside, the body, the inanimate, etc. (E, 45)

"Spirit" (in quotes) is the "metaphysical ghost" or something that "resembles it"; it is a ghost in metaphysics, not the opposite of spirit, certainly, but inevitably situated within philosophical oppositions if only because it leaves its ghost there. The "fall" into a metaphysical dyad cannot simply be avoided, it will always come back to haunt the "spirit" safely held off – in quotes – and, in turn, the spirit *in* metaphysics is a ghost that haunts what it doubles, what it resembles – that haunts, in other words, the "something that is certainly not what the former language called 'spirit,'" but which is not the opposite of it, either.

Like the *pharmakon* or the *Gift*, "spirit" (in quotes) is both a term anterior to metaphysical oppositions – it is the one that "opens the possibility" of their distinction – *and* it is a ghost that haunts them, a spirit that returns to inhabit them without ever being reducible to them. But there is a certain ambiguity in Derrida's formulation that will become more important as he goes on: does the "ghost" in the above quote – the *Geist* – haunt metaphysics, or does it haunt the very (non) "thing" – the "spirit" – that it "resembles"? Does the ghost that never can be opposed to or incorporated in metaphysics, the word "spirit" used in its "deconstructed sense," haunt the "something" that it "names," through writing? Or is it the "deconstructed sense" that is haunted? Already we see a certain distance, perhaps ironic, in Derrida's attitude toward this ghost – a distance that was lacking in the exuberant affirmation of the ghostly *pharmakon* and the dancing Zarathustra in the earlier essays. Perhaps the ghost haunts the very unnameable "something" it was meant to name. On the previous page, in fact, Derrida notes that through Heidegger's new strategy – keeping spirit in quotes – "something of the spirit . . . allows itself to elude [*se laisse soustraire*] the Cartesian-Hegelian metaphysics of subiectity [*subjectité*]" (E, 44). The expression *se laisse soustraire* has a negative connotation, one of shirking or escaping duty. It seems that some element of the spirit *without* quotes is able to "save itself" (*se sauver*) when the quotation marks are applied; this element comes back to haunt Heidegger's affirmation of a *Gemüt*, of a mind that would *not* be mind in the Latin or French sense of the word. As Derrida writes, "Spirit comes back. The word spirit starts to become acceptable again." The quotation marks that permit the recycling of spirit, we are told, are a "catharsis" ("The catharsis of quotation marks liberates it from its vulgar – *uneigentlich* – in a word Latino-Cartesian, marks" [E, 44]) – and suddenly, with the use of this word, Derrida takes us back to the problem of sacrificial logic that the *pharmakon*, through the *pharmakos*, had deconstructed. "Spirit" is able to distance itself from metaphysics – while nevertheless necessarily inhabiting it – only by means of an expulsion, a catharsis, whose logic is inseparable from that of metaphysics itself. The ghost of *Geist* is now not an emptied marker doubling – parodying, miming – a metaphysical term; on the contrary, it is the return of a metaphysical term that haunts the very emptied term that was itself to be a ghost, an element in a larger deconstructive strategy. Through the catharsis (the liberation from the Latino-Cartesian), a "slow labor of reappropriation" gives the word "spirit," now freed from clutches of the French, to the Germans: it is a process of "re-Germanization" (E, 44). The exclusion, in other words, that was meant to "free" the word "spirit" – or *esprit*, or *Geist* – from one tradition only subjects it to, and within, another. The two traditions, the French and the German, are identical to the extent that they are in apparent opposition and are dependent on a mutual catharsis (an affirmation of the proper, of property and propriety, through expulsion) that is in turn inseparable in its functioning from the logic of metaphysics as a whole. The more "spirit" becomes "German," the more it excludes the "French," the more "French" it becomes, insofar as French philosophy is identified with this very process of exclusion: all the metaphysical terms (subjectivity, the human, the rational) make no sense outside of a philosophical demarcation/opposition/expulsion.

Derrida had already suggested this problem in his discussion of the early sections of *Sein und Zeit*, where Heidegger refuses to use the word *Geist*, but where he nevertheless must attempt to make a rigorous distinction between the possibility of questioning on the part of Dasein and the inability to question on the part of the "animal" (E, 27–29, 41). This same privileging of an exclusive and excluding movement can be seen in Heidegger's strategy in his "third phase" of "spirit" – this time, according to Derrida, the curtain is raised, the quotation marks are lifted (E, 53), and the word is used *without* them. This occurs, not coincidentally, in Heidegger's *Rektoratsrede*, the speech that signaled the beginning of Heidegger's brief active involvement in the Nazi party. The obvious question will be: what is the connection between Heidegger's new use of the word *Geist* – without quotes – and his own peculiar brand of nazism?[20] It is clear that from the first Derrida sees the Heideggerian affirmation of nazism in a direct line with the suspect *propreté* that he analyzed in "The Ends of Man": in the *Rektoratsrede*, according to Derrida's interpretation, "spirit can only affirm itself," through the *German* university, "in the movement of an authentification or identification that wills itself as properly German [*qui se veulent proprement allemandes*]" (E, 56).[21] "Self-affirmation," "spirit," and Germanness in the constitution of the university are thus funda-mental. In addition, the spirit is the link between a number of terms: "the world, history, the people, the will to essence, to knowledge, the essence of Dasein in the experience of the question" (E, 63). Spirit, in other words, serves as the glue that holds Heidegger's version of a "world" together – a world that, from the perspective of 1987 reflecting back on 1933, must seem quite sinister in its vaunting of an exclusive and elite "people." Derrida quotes from the *Rektoratsrede* (E, 60–61): "And the *spiritual world* [*geistige Welt*] of a people is not the superstructure of a culture, no more than it is an armory stuffed with useful facts and values; it is the power that most deeply preserves the people's strengths, which are tied to earth and blood; and as such it is the power that most deeply moves [*Macht der innersten Erregung*], and most pro-foundly shakes its being [*Dasein*]. Only a spiritual world gives the people the assurance of greatness."[22]

The spiritual world, the site of a "people's grandeur," through its power thus makes possible the exclusion and demarcation of that domain which is *not* grandeur. This negative, outside space that Heidegger would refuse is, accord-ing to Derrida, the very Nazi ideology of "biologism" that has, ever since 1933, haunted Heidegger's thought. Derrida is therefore not among those who simply and naively accuse Heidegger of anti-Semitism; on the contrary, for him Heidegger's emphasis on the spirit or the spiritual world (in both instances without quotes) is an attempt to oppose the Nazi doctrine that a "people's grandeur" was tied to the distinction of its "race."[23] Or at least, in Derrida's words, the *Rektoratsrede* "seems" not to belong to an "ideological camp" that appeals to biological forces rather than to spiritual ones (E, 64–65).

This "seems," is, however, an important qualification, because this very type of opposition is, in Derrida's eyes, suspect. Heidegger would oppose biologism with spiritualism, but the latter, by the very fact of its opposition, is reinscribed in a metaphysics that, for Derrida at least, cannot effectively demar-cate itself from the biologism it would subsume. By opposing the Nazi posi-tion one grants it a status in an opposition, and by this very fact one incorpo-rates it in metaphysics, in the tradition of philosophy. The Nazi doctrine becomes just another "philosopheme," and in this way the very terms that would oppose it (such as Heideggerian spiritualism) – and the entire opposi-tional structure in and through which they function – enter into complicity with it.

We see here the same critique of a metaphysics based on a series of sym-metrical oppositions that was integral to the argument of "Plato's Pharmacy." One can "oppose" racism only by returning to spiritualism, a "unilaterality" of the subject; as long as one embraces spirit, one can do it only in the name of freedom of the spirit, democracy, and "the rights of man." One is led, in other words, back to a "metaphysics of the subject" if one straightforwardly attempts to oppose a racist, totalitarian determinism with a democratic humanism – and these two options, for Derrida, *are in fundamental complicity*: "All the traps of the demarcating strategy belong to this same program [opposing determinism with spiritualism], whatever place one occupies. One only has the choice between the terrifying contaminations that it assigns. Even if all the complicities are not equivalent, they are *irreducible*. The question of knowing which is the least grave of these complicities always arises [*se pose toujours*], one cannot exaggerate its urgency and seriousness, but it will never do away with the irreducibility of this fact" (E, 65–66). This irreducibility of complicity in turn calls for "absolutely new" (*absolument inédits*) "responsibilities of 'thought' and 'action'" – Derrida is careful to mark these latter two terms with quotation marks; they are evidently not to be taken in the classic Sartrean sense of a "responsibility" that would merely insert them in a dialectic of lack, consciousness, and labor. But, from what we have seen so far, can we assume that quotation marks do such a good job of protecting the terms they set apart?

The irony in all this is that Heidegger, in Derrida's reading, becomes most politically suspect when he embraces a position that would oppose a deterministic, totalitarian, and racist nazism with the weapons that, most often at least, have been used to combat it: those of humanism, the rights of free subjectivity, and so on. These philosophemes and ideologemes are (according to Derrida) in an irreducible complicity with nazism, however, precisely in their opposition to it. *De l'esprit*, then, is a work that attempts to envisage the consequences, in political terms, of the very metaphysical complicities that Derrida deconstructs in other works (such as "Plato's Pharmacy"). Just as those oppositions were seen to be in complicity all along (mere components in a larger philosophical syntax), so here as well a libertarian social philosophy and a crude racism are locked in a "terrifying" mutual contamination. Derrida's choice of Heidegger in 1933 is particularly brilliant, because it is in the *Rektoratsrede* and perhaps only there, that one can point to an example of an affirmation of spirit – an affirmation of subjectivity and the freedom of consciousness – that is so closely tied, in a diabolic compromise, with the crudest and most brutal kind of determinism.[24] The fact that virtually all commentators have taken the *Rektoratsrede* as an affirmation on Heidegger's part of biologism only proves Derrida's point: the speech is precisely the *opposite* of that (it is, ironically, an attempt to oppose racism from within the Nazi party), but in its very opposition, it is also in complicity with the most vicious racism. The most naive accusers of Heidegger were not so far from the real problem, then, at the very moment they accused Heidegger of being guilty of the main thing he was opposing.

This last remark might seem exaggerated, but one has only to read Derrida's next paragraph to see that it is his main point. The "diabolic" nature of Heidegger's program in 1933 is due to the fact that he "amasses [*capitalise*] the worst; in other words the two evils [*les deux maux*] at the same time: the guarantee [*la caution*] of nazism, and the still metaphysical gesture" (E, 66). It is not simply that the two opposing terms are not different in kind; beyond this, it seems that metaphysics itself is an "evil" that is somehow comparable to nazism. For this reason, Derrida can go on to write of a "ghost" that really does haunt metaphysics; "the *Geist* is always haunted by its *Geist*: put another way, a spirit, in French as in German, a ghost, always surprises by returning to speak through the other [*un fantôme surprend toujours à revenir ventriloquer l'autre*]" (E, 66). The ghost we saw in "Plato's Pharmacy" as a remainder to be affirmed, the *pharmakon* left behind as a kind of ventriloquist's dummy in a metaphysical opposition, or earlier in *De l'esprit* (when Heidegger puts quotes around *Geist*) as an ambiguous figure, is now clearly threatening: *Geist* is always already haunted by a *Geist* that *must* be in complicity by virtue of its demarcation from what is *not Geist*. This *Geist*, this "spirit," is not a haunting of metaphysics, in metaphysics, by that which exceeds it or displaces it, while not escaping it; rather it is the haunting of that displacement by the terror of metaphysics (the "terrifying contaminations") itself. It is spirit that "always comes back," that is a *revenant* – a word that means "ghost" in French but that also implies a "returning." The "*Geist* is the most fatal figure of this returning [*revenance*]," Derrida states (E, 66). Heidegger can never avoid this doubling of spirit, its return to haunt itself as a double: "Spirit is its double" (E, 67). Spirit as a necessary brutal return of "nonspirit" is always already contained in the demarcation of spirit itself. Spirit and nonspirit are doubles, and nonspirit itself is the always-returning spirit – the ghost of spirit, in other words, or spirit's spirit.

This is a different kind of "haunting" from that seen in "Plato's Pharmacy." But what is notable here above all is the extent to which *De l'esprit* haunts "Plato's Pharmacy." Derrida's position in the earlier essay was not notably different from the presentation of Heidegger's "spirit" (in quotes) on pages 44 and 45 of *De l'esprit* – there, the ghost of spirit, like the earlier ghost of the *pharmakon*, "named" something from within metaphysics that could not be reducible to it. We might say that a fragment of the argument of the "Pharmacy" is in *De l'esprit*, but it is "gone beyond" – or revised – by the affirmation (E, 66–67) that, if there is a haunting, a *revenant*, it is the return of metaphysics to haunt a deconstruction that naively and blithely tries, through the "ruse" of quotation marks (E, 66) – and through their "catharsis" (E, 44) – to leave metaphysics behind. Or to leave only a ghost behind, in the clutches of metaphysics. In short, the fact that a deconstructive reading cannot simply "escape" metaphysical oppositions – any more than Heidegger could ever leave his house, or his Germanic version of "France" – means that the complicities of those oppositions, and their most terrifying contaminations, will return to haunt not just Heidegger's project, but Derrida's as well.

Is it Derrida's own earlier position, then – from "Plato's Pharmacy" – that is haunted by the later text? Or is it the earlier strategy that haunts Derrida's later attempt to distance himself from Heidegger? Clearly Derrida cannot merely *oppose* his earlier position, which itself was the championing not of opposition but of leaving behind a harmless spirit, or ghost, an emptied-out metaphysical term (one contained, for example, in quotation marks). But Derrida at the same time implies that this sort of position itself must always be situated in a temporal development: keeping a word like *Geist* in quotation marks through a "catharsis" (to make sure that it is only a ghost) inevitably seems to lead to the *removal* of the quotes. As soon as spirit has entered the scene, albeit in quotes, it "starts to become acceptable again," it is "re-Germanized." And at that moment of the *propre*, it becomes an exclusive term that opposes another in a philosophical standoff. But how could Derrida *oppose* this kind of movement, either in Heidegger, or in his own text? He cannot choose between terms to be deconstructed, to be set off in quotes; nor can he simply oppose one to the other, in order to determine which one's ghost is the least harmful. (To do so would be to fall into the same trap as Heidegger, who thinks he has found an acceptable term which, safely deconstructed, can still be used to oppose others.) Rather it is the ghost – the spirit – of metaphysics itself that does the haunting, and in that sense "spirit" – and hence spirit – will always return in Derrida's argument. Quotes will always be used as an alternative to opposition, but that alternative *as* alternative will inevitably play an oppositional role. Through a kind of metonymy, the spirit-ghost in its very emptiness, or in its position within quotation marks, will always come to stand for a much larger – perhaps infinite – series of terms (the self, spirit, consciousness) and those that oppose them (the body, the inanimate, the biological). The ghost of *Geist* will not be separable from that series, any more than spirit can be straightforwardly demarcated from the body, or "Germany" can be isolated from "France." Its dance will be a death dance for the possibilities of a Nietzschean dance that is neither inside nor outside the sinister house of Being.

Derrida's later position as well is haunted by Heidegger's. It is not just that he is unable to oppose a correct word to the incorrect one (spirit). Rather, Derrida's entire strategy, meant as an analysis of Heidegger's bind when he takes the quotation marks off *Geist*, enters into complicity with Heidegger's fundamentally complicitous strategy. Heidegger's opposition to racism, such as it is, is inseparable from – it haunts and is haunted by – a larger movement, which is precisely *not* identifiable with an opposition to various terms, within dyads. Derrida himself recognizes this when he links Heidegger's use of quotation marks around the word *Geist* with their subsequent removal: the two gestures are tied, they are both separated and joined through a temporal movement. They cannot simply be distinguished or demarcated: they haunt each other. One of the problems with Heidegger, then, is that an "emptied" term cannot straightforwardly oppose another; "spirit" cannot effectively counter spirit – or matter, for that matter. Now, *pace* Derrida, it can be argued that the larger weakness of Heidegger's strategy is that he precisely cannot oppose, say, American capitalism to Soviet communism, or (after the war, at least) mechanized agriculture to the production-line death of the Nazi camps. Because oppositions within metaphysics – such as those between the different forms and strategies of technological development within advanced Western societies – can be conceived only within the framework of a "forgetting of the question of Being," the reassumption of the question of Being entails the general devalorization of the necessity of choosing between subordinate oppositional terms. We have seen this same gesture in Derrida ("Plato's Pharmacy") as well: it was never a question there of opting for one philosopheme or set of philosophemes over another. Oppositions within philosophy certainly cannot be done away with – any more than metaphysics can be "escaped" or left behind – but the necessity of "choosing sides" becomes largely irrelevant. It is not the right question. When the same logic of nonopposition is applied, on Heidegger's part, to questions concerning technology and the political formations that are identified with it, the resulting argument can become quite sinister. It is in fact this inability to oppose various political and cultural formations that various commentators have identified as the blind spot that made possible Heidegger's affirmation of nazism. It was easy, in the 1930s, to refuse a "facile" distinction between American and Soviet technoculture: rejecting them both, seeing their demarcation as a mere detail within the now closed circle of metaphysics, Heidegger could go on to embrace a "third" option which was not simply to be set in opposition to the other two: nazism, or at least Heidegger's version of it, which, as Derrida has shown, itself attempted to oppose Nazi biologism with a new version of spiritualism.[25] After the war, nothing changed; now the Nazis too, who had ignored Heidegger's positions on technology, were themselves associated with the Soviets and the Americans. Some measure of the problem can be seen in a passage from a 1949 lecture that has been quoted, in different contexts, by both Richard Wolin and Philippe Lacoue-Labarthe: "Agriculture is now a motorized food producing industry, in its essence the same thing as the fabrication of cadavers in the gas chambers and the extermination camps, the same thing as the blockade and the reduction of countries to famine, the same thing as the fabrication of hydrogen bombs."[26]

Lacoue-Labarthe notes that this statement is "scandalously insufficient," and he is no doubt correct. The problem, however, lies not so much in Heidegger's personal insensitivity – that he could confuse agro-business with Auschwitz – as in his method, which allows this kind of confusion to take place. If various instances of technology are not to be opposed – such a gesture itself partakes of the very logic that is essential to the full flowering of technology – then this kind of statement, one can argue, is inevitable. And it can no doubt be argued that this inability to make necessary critical distinctions and oppositions is fundamental to Heidegger's flirtation and compromise with the Nazis:[27] it made it impossible for him to see the specificity of the threat posed by racism; it also precluded any analysis that would have enabled him to determine "lesser evils" – to opt, for example, for agro-business over genocide; and it certainly enabled him to avoid the vexed question of the responsibility of the German people and their political and intellectual leaders (nazism is simply another manifestation of industrialization and thus lacks the specificity that would make possible the calling to account of its authors).

I certainly do not mean to imply here that Derrida, by displacing oppositions within philosophy, and by refusing to grant them a larger importance, is in any way in sympathy with Heidegger's version of nazism. Indeed *De l'esprit*, as we have already seen, is written as an effort to uncover, and analyze, the bases of Heidegger's complicity. But the odd thing is that the only method that Derrida has at his disposal to analyze Heidegger's complicity is a Heideggerian one that prevents him from recognizing the importance of crucial oppositions; it is, in other words, identical in that respect to the approach that prevents Heidegger from noting the pertinence "within metaphysics" of differences between various philosophemes.[28] (As he puts it in the *Rektoratsrede*, "For 'spirit' is neither empty cleverness, nor the noncommittal play of wit, *nor the endless drift of rational distinctions*, and especially not world reason.")[29] There are astonishing and provocative statements in *De l'esprit* – such as the assertion that the recourse to spirit and nazism are to be put on the same plane, that Heidegger embraces the "two evils at the same time: the guarantee of nazism and the still metaphysical gesture" (E, 66). Nowhere in *De l'esprit* is there a serious recognition that the humanism so closely identified with the spirit, subjectivity, the "sacredness of the human person" may be in any way preferable to nazism; the closest Derrida comes is a grudging recognition that "the question of knowing which is the least grave of these complicities always asserts itself [*se pose*]" (E, 66), but this problem – even posed in such a strangely negative way ("the least grave"), and with a passive construction that effectively omits the act of the questioner (it literally "poses itself," *se pose*) – is never returned to again.[30]

The problem lies in the fact that Derrida attempts to analyze Heidegger's complicity with the Nazis by using an approach that, if anything, led Heidegger to that complicity in the first place. (Derrida, in effect, can still only affirm the "ghost" – in quotes – haunting metaphysics which, as he himself has shown, is itself haunted by the ghost of metaphysical complicity-through-opposition.) Along the way, for both Heidegger and Derrida, crucial oppositions and specificities are lost: we have the strange collapsing, in Derrida's analysis, of nazism and the secular humanism of French republicanism (the "rights of man"). Everything is put in quotes, emptied out – and then opposed. But this kind of conflation, as we have already seen, marked Derrida's project as early as 1968, at the beginning of "The Ends of Man," when Sartrian Marxist existentialism was more or less explicitly tied to French republicanism and American imperialism.

At this point we might return to the problem of sacrifice that haunts so many discussions of nazism and Nazi crimes. In Derrida's analyses the walls of the Heideggerian house are "invaginated," the proper, the exclusionary, interior can be constituted only through the prior incorporation of a radical exterior, margin, or limit. Derrida, in other words, by questioning the logic of philosophical oppositions, undermines the powerful sacrifice-effect with which the naive rigor of those oppositions can be associated. His writing, neither inside nor outside the "house" of metaphysics, *or* the "house" of Being, its ghost always inside it at the moment of exteriority, is the *pharmakos*, the victim rather than the sacrificer, the one who transgresses the institution of philosophical sacrifice itself, but *as* a victim (and therefore as one who nevertheless reaffirms the very institution he transgresses, at the moment of transgression). On the other hand its seems that, by reaffirming the viability or even the necessity of philosophical oppositions (such as spirituality vs. biological determination), we run the risk of simply reentering the house and closing the door: we will be posing "the question" in such a way that it presupposes an answer inseparable from a self-proximity, a self-presence of truth.

But where is the sacrifice? The mechanism of sacrifice has a strange way of replicating itself; this problem is indicated at the end of *De l'esprit*, when Derrida poses the problem of how the Heideggerian project is to be rigorously distinguished from a Christian one (E, 179–83). Christian time, based on sacrifice, loss, and redemption, indeed always seems to haunt the Heideggerian project, and – as Derrida shows in an imaginary dialogue between Heidegger and a theologian – the more Heidegger displaces theology, thinking an "other" anterior to the origin (E, 184), the easier it is for the religious philosopher to incorporate those very displacements in his own approach.

One can see a similar repetition of sacrifice in Heidegger's gesture of uniting disparate elements through their expulsion: especially in the case of "technology," disparate terms (American, Soviet, and finally Nazi ideologies) are arbitrarily linked, their specificity is lost, and the highly questionable amalgam that comes to serve as a scapegoat is held responsible for the crisis of the twentieth century.

Derrida's gesture, by repeating Heidegger's – demarcating both members of the oppositional dyad, in effect putting them in quotes, conflating them, and then sending them packing – partakes of the same sacrificial logic. Derrida can write of the "terrifying contaminations" implied in Heidegger's "opposition" to Nazi racism, of the "diabolical" nature of his "program" (E, 66). It is almost as if we have now returned to religious ritual as analyzed by Durkheim, with its emphases on sacred contamination, the diabolical and terrifying energy of mana, and so forth. Derrida would, of course, refuse any links between his project and a sacrificial gesture of expulsion, but how can one prevent the contamination of one's own writing by a refusal that must be so complete it borders on the gesture of expulsion itself? Complicity is hard to control. Derrida can either refuse the complicities of metaphysics – the linkage of the elevated (spiritual) and base (material) sacred, we might say – thereby falling into a sacrificial gesture of exclusion, and in that way too allying himself with the very totalizing oppositions he would refuse; or he can openly recognize his complicity with those oppositions, he can affirm the guilt of the ghost he leaves behind in them, only at the risk of then being haunted by that very ghost. We are reminded of the paradox with which "The Ends of Man" closed: there is a strong complicity between staying *in* the house of Being and leaving it. And the Nietzschean dance outside the door becomes an ever more remote possibility, as "active forgetting" is haunted by the recurrence – the remembering – of the ghost that refuses to be left behind inside the house.

It appears that the Heideggerian tactic is a kind of sacrificial speech act – when the word *Geist* is used, either with or without quotation marks. In both cases, there is a rejection of an "other" on Heidegger's part: either he refuses (by putting quotes around the word) the "forgetting of Being," a gesture that leads to the use of the word *Geist without* quotes, or he opposes biologism through the direct use of *Geist* without quotes. It seems that the *act* of quoting, with or without quotes, is a function of sheer repetition: it is an oppositional but also founding act that can only be reiterated, reimposed, and can itself only be opposed through its repetition (a repetition which nevertheless precludes that opposition). Thus "spirit" can only be repeated by spirit – and Derrida's gesture of reading, which allows no affirmation of the specificities of metaphysical oppositions, only repeats Heidegger's complicity, his spirit, at the very moment it opposes it.

The ghost of *Geist* is temporalized: it can never be left behind in a metaphysical dyad, but instead it always precedes and contaminates the act of its imposition. Both strategies, it seems, are haunted by their inability to oppose nazism. On the one hand, the most one can do is put an oppositional term in quotes. In this way, the term will itself always be haunted by a complicity with metaphysics and the evil it seems to represent. There is no criterion of judgment provided, in any case, by Derrida for replacing spirit with a term that would be less complicitous. If spirit or "spirit" is contaminated, it is hard to see, then, how alternative terms that Derrida himself briefly suggests (E, 66) – "thought" and "action" (again in quotes) – are any less so. They carry with them a philosophical baggage that goes directly back to Sartrian existentialism, as Derrida himself makes clear when he writes of the "responsibilities" of "thought" and "action" that are necessarily "absolutely new" – as if the Sartrian program can be made new just by inserting the now thoroughly haunted quotation marks around a few selected words. If one could escape a complicity this easily, it would be a matter only of the choice of terms – of their semantic content as deconstructed philosophemes – that would determine an effective resistance. But, as we have already seen in "Plato's Pharmacy," such a thematic reading has never been a possibility for Derrida – in fact it implies the very type of straightforward opposition that he has consistently put in question.

There is a price to pay, then, for recognizing the irreducible complicity between opposing terms: one comes to be in complicity oneself with philosophical dyads, and with the larger culpability of metaphysics. One certainly cannot oppose those dyads: one therefore only quotes them, doubling them – and we have seen where Heidegger's too confident gesture of "citation" leads. In that repetition their complicity, and one's own, returns.

If on the other hand one does attempt to oppose certain ideologemes, as Heidegger himself did, one falls back into a logic of contraries that is identified by Derrida not only with Western philosophy but with a sinister Western culture in general: "And if, far from any desert, it [nazism] sprouted like a toadstool in the silence of the European forest, it did so in the shadow of the great trees, sheltered by their silence or their indifference, but in the same earth. I will not read off, I will not count the varieties of these trees which make up an immense black forest in Europe. For essential reasons, their presentation defies the space of my depiction [*l'espace du tableau*]. In their dense taxonomy, they are named religions, philosophies, political regimes, economic structures, religious or academic institutions. In short, what is called in a fairly confused way culture or the world of the spirit" (E, 179). By opposing the toadstool one shelters it, one is lost in the dense (*touffu*) underbrush of systems and modes that always amount to the same thing: the tangle of their taxonomy, the interconnections of philosophy with all other aspects of a profoundly complicitous European culture, allow for confusion, result in the blur of identity.

Opposition, like quotation, displacement, or deconstruction, results in a larger complicity: one is always already lost in the cultural black forest, the cave in which European onto-technology mechanically reproduces the fungoid "contradictions" of philosophemes – the dangerous shelter, in other words, of thought. It seems we have run into a double bind at the end of *De l'esprit*, one which Derrida would perhaps refuse to recognize but which seems unavoidable when we follow Derrida, if not Heidegger, to the end. Opposition and displacement are themselves doubles, haunting each other in an opposition that gives way to a vicious circle. Derrida himself has, in his reading of Heidegger, formulated most clearly the political haunting, and the political impossibility, of deconstructive reading.

Put another way, Derrida faces two different, opposed, but incompatible ways of being in complicity with a dangerously complicitous Heidegger. His first approach is to *refuse* Heidegger's gesture: Derrida must analyze the danger – to be avoided at all costs – of taking the quotation marks off the word *Geist*. What must be criticized, from this point of view, is the gesture of dropping the deconstructive marks that, at the very least (and even this gesture is potentially dangerous) only situate the "ghost" of the term in relation to a system. As soon as Derrida formulates this kind of critique, however, he himself must move beyond the strategy of situating the ghostly term: he must drop his own quotes and affirm the straightforward meaning of a philosophical gesture – even if that gesture is a thoroughly negative one. In order to analyze Heidegger's failure, Derrida must do something more than, or other than, miming systems. He can no longer only read Heidegger against himself, attributing a certain Heideggerianism to Heidegger's disciples (who did not know how to read) rather than to the complex movement of the text – his gesture in his reading of Plato, whom he opposed not only to the "Platonists," and to "Platonism" but to the entire movement of Western philosophy. Now he must have a certain distance from the object of his analysis, interrogating it from a position that is sure of itself, that can decisively indicate the problem. He must arrogate to himself the same kind of authority that Heidegger assumed when he freed *Geist* from its quotes, thereby giving it an unambiguous and efficacious, but also poisonous, status (in this sense Derrida returns Heidegger's "gift," his tempting cultural toadstool, with interest). Derrida can definitively affirm Heidegger the metaphysician and humanist's complicity with nazism only by himself entering into complicity with Heidegger, not on a political level, but on the level of the question – not the question of Being, but eventually that of the labyrinth in which the questioning of Heidegger's questioning throws him.

If one affirms the inevitability of this complicity, there is only one possibility, and this is the second option: to recognize, as Derrida himself did at least implicitly at the end of "The Ends of Man," that "France" is already Heidegger's Germany, that "man" is inscribed at the heart of Heidegger's project, that the dance outside the Heideggerian "house of Being" is not an escape from it. In this case, a similar recognition would entail not the confrontation with Heidegger, the attempt to criticize and reject the European philosophical forest and its fungi from the outside, but rather the affirmation that one is also in that labyrinthine forest, also condemned to move from tree to tree, miming each philosophical shoot, each religion, each term, and thus no doubt oneself providing shelter for noxious pale growths, themselves ghosts of one's own ghostly parodies – just as one recognizes that the forest is already inscribed in one's own project, that it is the internal death or limit both instituting and precluding it (its double "end"). In this way one ceases to confront Heidegger self-righteously on his own terms, one ceases to play his game – or, rather, one plays one's own game, "playing along" with Heidegger's while displacing his rules.

Confrontation inevitably means the establishment of a new philosopheme, the representation of a new coherent position to combat and expel the old. It too will then be just another tree in the forest, just another "house" from which suspect options must be expelled. When we, as philosopher-intellectuals, look around, affirming that we too are in the forest, that the only way to escape the complicity of opposition is by embracing the nonopposition of miming in the forest (which itself is a complicity), we can haunt our old position and engage in a syntagmatic, lateral movement from position to position, from tree to tree. Rather than the representation of a single position, we can now embrace a larger complicity, a mechanical movement in which we serially perform the positions of others. Now we, or the textual function that "we" have always already become, will be haunted by the old position and by each new position that we ourselves have haunted. We haunt the forest, and we in turn are haunted by it; the only way out is just that, into a complicitous confrontation that leads back in again. We will be forced to make hard choices, distinctions, and commitments, even if we are always again caught up in complicitous and duplicitous miming. The very inconsistency of a higher knowledge guaranteeing this or any miming – the not-knowing embedded in or devouring the knowledge of parody or the parodic knowledge – will ensure the at least occasional sincerity of commitments. There is representation and there is performance – each implied in, each making necessary, and each precluding, the other. Only one question remains: how long are we to continue to look forward to a *third* option, the dance of the Derridean overman just outside the forest?

9

De Man and Guilt

I am not given to retrospective self-examination and mercifully forget what I have written with the same alacrity I forget bad movies – although, as with bad movies, certain scenes or phrases return at times to embarrass and haunt me like a guilty conscience. – Paul de Man, Foreword to *Blindness and Insight*, second, rev. ed.

So it was the fact that Sartre wrote essays like L'Imaginaire, L'Etre et le néant, *which were technical philosophical books, while at the same time being a literary critic, at the same time being somebody who expressed strong opinions on political matters – that somewhat bicephalic dissent of the philosopher – had a very strong attraction; I don't think anybody of my generation ever got over that. We all somehow would like to be like that: it takes about a whole life to get over this notion.* – Paul de Man, "Interview with Stefano Rosso," in *The Resistance to Theory*

The knowledge of radical innocence also performs the harshest mutilations. – Paul de Man, *Allegories of Reading*

*

THE REVELATION came in 1987: the Yale literary critic Paul de Man as a young man had written book reviews for the leading Brussels newspaper *Le Soir* in the period 1940–42. This was the "Soir volé," the paper stolen by the Nazi occupiers and used as a prestigious vehicle for their propaganda.[1]

Many obvious questions arose, having to do above all with the links between the later, apparently apolitical or antipolitical method of reading and the earlier committed but politically and even personally disastrous commentary. Only a few years before, in the early 1980s, the same problem had surfaced when it became widely known that Maurice Blanchot, another critic whose work apparently precluded a conventional political "engagement," had written quite a few incendiary articles for a prewar right-wing review, *Combat*.[2]

In de Man's case, the "scandal" of the early articles spawned an entire volume of "responses," all of which attempted in one way or another to account for the curious relation of culpable engagement followed by seemingly innocent disengagement.[3] Was "deconstruction" tainted by its apparent connection with right-wing propaganda? Was it a mere continuation of the irresponsibility manifested in the earlier journalism? Or was de Man's later reputed quietism the result of an embarrassment (or shame) caused by his memory of the earlier writings? Amid the flurry of accusations, condemnations, newspaper articles, and radio reports (the first time, by the way, that the "mass media" had chosen to recognize Paul de Man's existence) one simple problem was overlooked: de Man was a European intellectual, whose orientation was formed at least in part by the pressures of political action. For him the initial question, in 1940, had been not whether to be politically committed but, rather, how to orient that commitment under very precise and brutal circumstances.

De Man never ceased to be a European intellectual. While it is true that he was greatly influenced after the war by the American New Criticism, I think it can be argued that his larger project remained essentially a revision of Heidegger.[4] That such is the case can be seen as early as 1955, when the article "Tentation de la permanence" was published in *Monde Nouveau-Paru*, and *Blindness and Insight* and later in *Allegories of Reading*. His version of temporality (as in the essay "The Rhetoric of Temporality," contained in the second edition of *Blindness and Insight*) is first Heideggerian and "phenomenological," and only then, and in addition, linguistic and rhetorical. It is in this sense that de Man belongs to the French tradition, even though he wrote in English, largely for an American academic audience. The theoretical bases of his work must be seen in conjunction with the French versions of Heidegger of the 1950s and 1960s – with Blanchot, Foucault, and Derrida – because he, like the French, and unlike American and German philosophers and critics of the same period, attempts to use Heidegger against himself, as an integral element in a thoroughgoing avant-garde critique of the signifying practices of Western, Socratic culture. In his later work he carries out his project by linking Heideggerian antihumanism and antisubjectivism to a precise and powerful version of rhetoric – just as Blanchot, Foucault, and Derrida tie it to versions of writing, language, and textuality. His project is, moreover, an original one, not just a recasting or transmission of the works of the European masters.

De Man's earliest journalistic writings, then, are fully in the European mold of the intellectual, and his later project, carried out in America, is really "French" in its brilliantly original recycling of Heidegger through the "linguistic turn." His work should first be considered in the French context and not in the American, which, at least before Derrida and de Man himself exerted their influence, for the most part entailed the consideration of Heidegger as a primarily "existential" thinker.

I

There are two types of readings of Paul de Man's *Le Soir* articles that should be, I think, avoided. The first is what I would call a naive Sartrian reading, which attempts to present all of de Man's later work as inherently "reactionary" because, at the age of twenty-one and twenty-two, he wrote newspaper articles, in a German-funded and controlled paper, that were clearly sympathetic to the changes taking place in the "revolutionary epoch" (as he calls it) in which he was living.[5] In this sure-to-be-played-out scenario, Sartre gets his revenge on de Man; the really important de Manian writings will not be read, but, as so often happens, de Man's "life decision" will be examined, his personal "choice" will be evaluated, and no doubt condemned. That the kind of analysis elaborated in *Allegories of Reading* does not lend itself easily (or at all) to use by ethicists, aestheticians, hermeneuts, or formalists will be attributed to the fact that de Man all along was "a Fascist." Above all, the argument will be put forward that his apparent elimination, for example, at the end of *Allegories of Reading*, of the possibility of a morally responsible subjectivity is proof, at best, of "moral idiocy," and, at worst, a simple refusal to come to terms with his own guilt.[6] The complexities of the text will be ignored, while biographical evidence will be sifted; moral evaluation will be issued, both of de Man "himself," and of "deconstruction." One need only read Sartre's biography of Baudelaire (or Genet, Mallarmé, Flaubert) to see where this kind of approach leads. The second tactic, equally misguided, and carried out with an equally clear conscience, will attempt "rhetorical readings" of certain of the 1941–42 articles, no doubt to show that they too can be "deconstructed," that de Man is not writing about the decadence of French culture, the role of the Jews in post-World War I literature, the "necessity" of the replacement of prewar individualism with the recognition of the tasks to be carried out in a German-occupied "postwar" Europe – he is "really" writing only about language itself, and the problems of rhetoric that go along with it.[7] This kind of approach – which many critics affirm when it is used by de Man himself in an analysis of, say, Rousseau's *Social Contract* – seems insufficient when we are talking about a writing practice that was, one could argue, inseparable from a larger policy of the intellectual "pacification" of a conquered, but (from the Nazi point of view) not entirely trustworthy, people.[8]

Are we, as readers of de Man, to be caught between these two poles, torn between a simplistic moral or political judgment of the young de Man and an uncritical acceptance of the later de Man's theory? How, in other words, can one talk about the seemingly inevitable political and social responsibility of the engaged intellectual (for this is what de Man was in 1941–42, and what he fervently resisted later), or of the thinker in general, while at the same time affirming, or at least taking seriously, an approach that seems to leave no possibility whatsoever for any kind of moral responsibility, individual conscience, or free subjectivity? If we can pose this question – the real *casse-tête* of contemporary theory – it will only be because we have recognized, first, that no simple dividing line can be drawn between de Man's *Le Soir* articles and, for example, *Allegories of Reading*. Many of the Belgian articles pose problems that are still being grappled with forty years later – and, even near the end of his life, de Man was positing a textual "machine" whose method of accounting for the production and excusing of guilt will suddenly be seen as a necessary (and also highly suspect) strategy when one recognizes the gravity of the implications of the writings that were kept secret for so long. My purpose in this chapter is not to put forward any moral evaluation or condemnation, but rather to follow, if only very briefly, the inscription of guilt in de Man's text – guilt as a theme, but also guilt as the very practice of writing itself – and the various problems that this inscription entails. I will not attempt to resolve the aporia (if one chooses to call it that) between ethical judgment and rhetorical reading but to stress the necessity and impossibility of the collaboration between these two options, in de Man's text itself. As we will see, both at a very early stage of de Man's career and at a very late one de Man rigorously excludes a political and moral responsibility – the gesture of political and moral interpretation and commitment (in an early article from 1942), the interpretation which itself imputes guilt (in a chapter from *Allegories of Reading*) – a move that, in the end, only forces him ever further into collusion with the very gesture he would refuse.

I want to examine first an article that appeared in *Le Soir* on 31 March 1942, a book review of the French translation of Ernst Jünger's *On the Marble Cliffs*.[9] Through this article, one can see quite clearly the problem de Man faced in writing a necessarily political article on a book that he maintained was rigorously apolitical.

De Man starts by presenting a theme that recurs often in his reviews: the French novelistic tradition, going back at least to Stendhal, was decadent; it promoted individualism, dry psychological and moral analysis, and it tended to display its own passionless, mechanical functioning. This decline is clearly associated with that of the French nation as a whole – a state of affairs that made the German conquest inevitable.[10] "Since Stendhal, the French novel is an explanatory work, a work of the intellect. It necessarily turns around a case, a problem, and its principle concern is to show, cog after cog, the complex mechanism that is made to function before our eyes."

The antidote to this decadence is, not surprisingly, German. De Man rather unconvincingly, given what he says elsewhere about the weakness of France before the war, says that he is presenting it without the least desire to judge the French tradition. If de Man often presents the French approach as leading to, or inseparable from, weakness, he usually sees the German as one of strength, affirmation, synthesis, collectivity, in and through literary style.[11] And if French fiction and criticism entails dry analysis based on concerns alien to the specific strength of literature – de Man strongly criticizes literary analysis that judges works of art on psychological or moral grounds – then German works will stress aesthetic form at the expense of "extraneous" concerns; "poetic meditation," and the search for "metaphoric and symbolic forms" will be preferred to the "lucid clarity of analysis" and "precision in expression."[12] This distrust of a literature or criticism that would perform the tasks of psychological, ethical, religious, or political argumentation is ratified by Jünger's *On the Marble Cliffs* – or at least it is upheld by de Man's presentation of that novel. For, according to de Man, this is not an intellectual work; there is no message, only the depiction of characters who are "symbols," carried along by "forces and irresistible aspirations." "One must not confuse this conception of the world, a field of battle between vice and virtue, of grandeur and baseness, with an insipid moralizing lesson. The work of Jünger is that of a poet and not a spiritual adviser." Indeed the novel, it would seem, is only a pretext for an "inspirational theme," a series of images of "sun, fire and blood."

De Man closely associates imagination, inspiration, and artistic form with an aesthetic fusion that is represented in the novel by images of violent conflict and death. Despite all the talk of "mythical" experience, however, and of the "frisson that comes from true art," one can see that de Man is also pulled in another direction: "form" here is nothing other than "pure narration." Narration, in other words, about narration itself – for what else could the elements in the novel "symbolize," if they do not "objectively" refer to anything, and if they, unlike the contents of the French novel, have nothing to do with "comprehension and judgment"?

It might seem that the young de Man is still in fairly safe territory here, arguing for an aesthetic self-reflexivity that the later de Man was to single out as just another "ideology."[13] But de Man's reading cannot remain purely aesthetic, and in that way it risks falling from a neat specularity into a most treacherous vicious circle. *On the Marble Cliffs* is not "inherently" aesthetic and apolitical; de Man's is a highly tendentious interpretation, and one that is also profoundly political. In fact the conflict between the "forces of Good and Evil" in Jünger's novel practically force on the reader an allegorical interpretation of the crudest kind: the Head Ranger (Evil) is, one is led to conclude, none other than Hitler himself; the two brothers who are working in their mountain retreat (Good) are easily interpreted as the elitist but impotent German intellectual opposition of the late 1920s and early 1930s. The novel is certainly suggestive as a thesis novel – so much so, in fact, that the Nazis prohibited its reprinting in the early 1940s. To argue that the novel is not political – and to suggest that Jünger is therefore innocent of carrying out a subversive political gesture – is itself already political.[14] De Man's refusal of the "extraliterary" is inseparable, at this early stage, from the profoundly political gesture of affirming an aesthetic quietude in the face of the Nazi "revolution" – all the more so, since Jünger's novel virtually forces itself on the reader as an allegory of precisely that kind of withdrawal and its consequences.[15]

De Man is caught in a paradoxical position: he affirms a severing of art and criticism from morality and politics, but his very affirmation is necessarily political. He can only reassert this depoliticization by discrediting his own (political) affirmation of it. Like the serpent biting its own tail, the more he denounces the engagement of the writer and critic, the more *engagé* he finds himself, and thus all the more vulnerable to his own denunciation. To quote the later de Man himself, he "has to reaffirm, at the end of his argument, the priority of the category against which his argument has been consistently directed" (AR, 245). That category, in the case of the article on Jünger at least, is a belief in the analogy between the aesthetic object (the self-reflexive literary work and the criticism that affirms it) and the realm of political and moral judgment.[16] (Indeed immediately after his discussion of Jünger's novel, de Man goes on to present, in a favorable light, two openly political books, one of which, *Agonie de la paix*, by Georges Suarez and Guy Laborde [1942], is a frank apology for the Nazi foreign policy immediately before and after the Munich crisis; the real culprits responsible for the war, according to the rather suspect narrative of Suarez and Laborde, were the French themselves, who, along with their Czech accomplices, from the Versailles treaty on unjustly attempted to weaken and contain the Germans.)

Put another way, the more innocent of writing a subversive thesis novel Jünger is, the more guilty of collaborating with the Nazis his writing becomes; in the same way, the more de Man asserts (via his proxy, Jünger) the innocence of his own writing in relation to any "extrinsic" morality or politics, the more guilty it too becomes. In this way de Man's criticism, rewriting Jünger's novel, becomes an allegory of the confrontation not so much of a mythical Good and Evil, but of the "pure narration" of the force of an incessantly reaffirmed innocence which is always betrayed at the moment of its positing, in and through its positing, but whose betrayal always necessitates its reaffirmation and reelaboration.

We can ask if the Jünger novel, as presented by de Man, is a purely self-referential aesthetic object after all. Its "pure narrative," its "battle between Good and Evil," which is conveyed by symbols, must in fact be seen as an allegory not only of its own form, or of a certain political or social conjunction, but of the bind in which de Man's own critical text finds itself. In its very innocence it affirms its guilt and vice versa; this procedure would seem to entail not a definitive representational closure but an open-ended repetition. De Man's writing can continue to excuse itself (as it does throughout these early articles) by arguing for an exclusively aesthetic role for the novel and criticism; the gesture after a while becomes both guilty and purely automatic – like the "cogs" of the French fiction to which de Man so strongly objects, but with which we can now see that his writing is in complicity.[17] And here we are faced with a question which, as any reader of the later de Man knows, comes to have an overwhelming importance: does the guilt – the moral category and the responsible subjectivity it implies – cause the author to excuse himself by repetitiously valorizing a nonmoral (or extramoral) writing? Or is the guilt a mere aftereffect of the exclusively mechanical positing of innocence? In other words, does the aesthetic writing that refers only to writing present an inner conflict between good and evil – between moral terms, in other words, like guilt or innocence – or does it present a kind of incongruous juxtaposition (which perhaps can be represented only through images of violence, of heated conflict, of mechanical operation or mutilation) of a purely automatic process of excuse making and the inevitably moral or psychological representation and judgment which interprets – and misinterprets – it? Given de Man's orientation even in his early writings, we would be forced to opt for the latter position – but then, if the novel is fully divorced from questions of morality, as he argues, why would it present a struggle between eminently moral, pre-Nietzschean categories such as good and evil? Those very terms, and this conflict, must be read as allegories of something else – of the "pure narrative" that is the mechanism of the text and the point of conjunction and rupture between the repetitive, mechanical excuse making and the guilt that is inevitably produced by it, and that serves only as a device through which the process can be known, and can continue.

Is this kind of argument, in the context of these early writings, objectionable? Most of us, de Manians or not, would probably say so; it is impossible to read these pieces without forming a negative moral evaluation of the young de Man's conduct. He certainly knew what he was doing; there was nothing mechanical or blind about it. He was evidently a highly intelligent and well-read reviewer, and his contributions could only lend prestige and credibility to a collaborationist paper. They were a small part of the German strategy to undermine opposition by funding or in other ways backing relatively sophisticated and reputable newspapers like *Le Soir*, or highly prestigious reviews like the *Nouvelle Revue Française*. But then the question returns: how can we come to any conclusion about de Man's responsibility, his "engagement," how can we evaluate him from a political and moral standpoint, while at least respecting the methods of analysis he has left us?[18] The answer, which will probably be troubling for many, is that de Man's later writings preclude the possibility of any moral or political critique or analysis of his early work. One certainly has the uncanny feeling when rereading them that certain pieces – such as the last two chapters of *Allegories of Reading* – were written in the shadow of the early articles (even with the expectation that those articles would one day be discovered), as extremely elaborate devices whose net effect is to defuse the very question of de Man's responsibility or guilt. The last chapter in particular can be read as an allegory of de Man's relation to his own responsibility: Rousseau's autobiography, in other words, can be read not only as an allegory of reading but as an allegory of de Man's reading of his own autobiography. But how can we see the last chapter of *Allegories of Reading* as autobiographical? Is there really any justification for this argument in de Man's text itself? Or is his text written in such a way that it forestalls such an argument?

De Man first considers the stolen-ribbon episode from the *Confessions* from the point of view of a reading oriented toward a critique or interpretation of desire. Such a reading, no doubt compatible with methods taken from psychoanalysis, is also suggested to anyone who has read the passages in the *Confessions* in which Rousseau indulges in his exhibitionistic tendencies. It is impossible not to associate the perverse pleasure Rousseau takes in his own exhibitionism (with Mlle Lambercier, for example) with the dialectic of desire implicit in the very writing of the *Confessions*. In other words, Rousseau himself, *in* his autobiography, suggests a method that will "uncover" his desire – and which he will inevitably affirm just as much as he affirms his "exposure" (in the act of exposing himself) by the various authority figures he presents in his text. Discussing this kind of approach early on in his chapter, de Man notes the "true" shame of Rousseau's destruction of Marion: Rousseau carries it out "in order to provide him[self] with a stage on which to parade his disgrace or, what amounts to the same thing, to furnish him[self] with a good ending for Book II of the *Confessions*" (AR, 286). This self-perpetuating structure entails a true *mise-en-abîme* in which "each new stage in the unveiling suggests a deeper shame, a greater impossibility to reveal, and a greater satisfaction in outwitting this impossibility."

The operative mode here is concealment; excuse making is always belated, occurring after the crime: "the excuse consists in recapitulating the exposure in the guise of concealment." Interpretation will involve a hermeneutics, a process by which the truth or the true meaning of the original guilt is revealed, freed from the many overlying strata of excuses. This logic is already implied by Rousseau himself in this episode; he says that he "accused Marion of doing what he wanted her to do"; in this way he exposes himself, or at least he exposes his own underlying (guilty) desire. De Man writes: "What seemed at first like irrational behavior bordering on insanity has, by the end of the [stolen ribbon] passage, become comprehensible enough to be incorporated within a general economy of human affectivity, in a theory of desire, repression, and self-analyzing discourses in which excuse and knowledge converge" (AR, 287).

This ethical model is also the model the reader cannot escape if he or she suddenly finds in this chapter a de Manian autobiographical resonance, a veiled confession not only of his "guilt," but of the structure of that guilt. After all, the very writing of a chapter – the final one of the book – in which the strategies of excuse making and the guilt that accompanies it are analyzed must seem, in the light of the articles in *Le Soir*, to be the same kind of self-lacerating movement that reveals in the act of creating an "impossibility to reveal," and that revels in the shame of "outwitting this impossibility." And, by this logic, the more de Man seems to be writing about a textual guilt, one that is an aftereffect of the automatic repetition of the speech act, the more he is simply covering his own guilt, the better to reveal it.

Of course de Man's main argument goes against the possibility of such an uncovering, and works to discredit it. But it must also be understood how de Man in effect shifts the guilt from the excuse-making author onto the reading that would interrogate the responsibility of the producer of excuses. De Man's argument rests on a quote from Rousseau's *Fourth Reverie*, which de Man interprets in this way: "Fiction has nothing to do with representation, but is the absence of any link between utterance and a referent" (AR, 292). Rousseau's affirmation of the harmless "pure fiction" – which is not a lie, since it "fails to concern justice in any way" – is associated by de Man with Rousseau's lie, in the *Confessions*, that Marion had stolen the ribbon. De Man thus links the notion of a "harmless" fiction with Rousseau's "unmotivated lie," when he accuses Marion only because she is the "premier objet qui s'offrit." De Man now quotes Rousseau against himself, noting a point in Rousseau's text when the latter does *not* claim to be acting because of hidden motives or desires but, rather, out of sheer impulse. Against the method of hermeneuts and psycho-analysts, and against Rousseau himself, then, de Man in this instance takes Rousseau's claim entirely seriously: there are unmotivated fictions, Rousseau's accusation of Marion was strictly a matter of random selection. One cannot delve into a "psyche" to uncover ever deeper and more thoroughly concealed motives, urges, and causes.

This kind of argument raises a problem that de Man readily recognizes, but for which he has an ingenious response. The inevitable objection is that the first kind of fiction, mentioned in the *Reverie*, is "harmless," has nothing to do with moral or legal evaluation, while the whole point of the stolen-ribbon episode is that Rousseau faced a kind of impromptu legal tribunal, lied, and thereby permanently injured his victim. The second kind of "fiction," while still perhaps unmotivated, is hardly harmless. De Man's response is simple: in the case where someone is injured by a fiction, the fault lies not with the "author" of the fiction – if such a term can even be used – but with the *misreading* of the lie, its interpretation along ethical or legal lines. Indeed, if Rousseau's judges had understood the lie correctly, they would not have been forced to choose between Rousseau's and Marion's versions of the theft. Judgment, the potentially dangerous ascription of innocence or guilt to a subject (or to the subject's "fiction"), is intimately tied to a misguided affirmation of the primacy of "referential meaning." "If the essential non-signification of the statement had been properly interpreted . . . they would have understood [Rousseau's] lack of guilt, as well as Marion's innocence. . . . *Not the fiction itself is to blame for the consequences, but its falsely referential reading.* As a fiction, the statement is innocuous and the error harmless; it is the misguided reading of the error as theft or slander, the refusal to admit that fiction is fiction, the stubborn resistance to the 'fact,' obvious by itself, that language is entirely free with regard to referential meaning and can posit whatever its grammar allows it to say, which leads to the transformation of random error into injustice" (AR, 292–93; emphasis added).

This does not mean, of course, that "pure fiction" can ever be simply separated from a "misguided reading" that is "resistance," that adds a referential (mis)interpretation, and that therefore imputes guilt: the moment of non-referential fiction, in other words, can never be isolated. ("It seems to be impossible to isolate the moment in which the fiction stands free of any signification; in the very moment at which it is posited, as well as in the context it generates, it gets at once misinterpreted into a determination which is, *ipso facto*, overdetermined" [AR, 293].) De Man notes that "empirical experience" also shows that "fictional discourse" and the "empirical event" always are caught in a kind of mutual interference: one can never decide between them, and thus one can "excuse the bleakest of crimes because, as a fiction, it escapes from the constraints of guilt and innocence," but, at the same time, one can "accuse" fiction, "the most innocent of activities," of "being the most cruel" (AR, 293).

It becomes clear already, at this stage of the argument, that the recognition of the "guilt" of the excuse (pure fiction is "the most cruel" of activities) is for de Man of a different status than its radical fictionality (its "lack of guilt," in other words, is not necessarily the equivalent, the symmetrical opposite, of a moral category like innocence). The awareness of the "guilt" of the excuse is only the "empirical" experience of an "empirical" event (de Man uses the word twice), but the very category of the "empirical" is itself associated with reference, truth-value, and all the terms that are compatible only with a "falsely referential reading." The reading of the fiction as "guilty," even while unavoidable, will, from de Man's perspective, never be anything other than false, a "misguided" reading. Indeed it is that very reading, according to de Man, that "is to blame" – that is guilty.

This is borne out by the rest of the chapter; the misinterpretation of the text – the excuse-making process that generates distortion and the necessary but deluded application of terms like "guilt" – is first shown by de Man to be represented in Rousseau's text (again in the *Fourth Reverie*) by the figure of bodily and textual mutilation. But mutilation implies a natural metaphor, the body as subject of mutilation (as well as a phenomenological approach on the part of the reader), and so the "threat remains sheltered behind its metaphoricity" (AR, 297). Mutilation and headlessness imply nothing more than the recognition of the undecidability of authorship, which "remains ensconced within the figural delusion that separates knowing from doing." Beyond this cognitive and self-referential model – the same one that would, finally, mandate a reading of a text and the author "responsible" for it as "guilty" or "innocent" – there is another: the machine. "The text as body, with all its implications of substitutive tropes ultimately always retraceable to metaphor, is displaced by the text as machine, and, in the process, it suffers the loss of the illusion of meaning" (AR, 298).

The possibility of meaning really is illusion, then; the excuse is generated not through a process of desire, which seeks to reveal by covering up – in other words, through metaphor and a system of tropes – but through a purely automatic process of positing, through the speech act: the performative and not the constative. This performative aspect of language is "anti-grav" (one imagines a word processor on autopilot drifting off into the void of space), operating like a grammar, with no necessary links to "human" purpose or intention, but also "entirely ruthless in its inability to modify its own structural design for nonstructural reasons" (AR, 294).[19]

The "resistance" – of theory – comes when the "machine's" effects are inevitably misinterpreted, as an aftereffect of the unavoidable imposition of the referential or cognitive moment. Guilt is an aftereffect of the inhuman process of excuse making: "It is no longer certain that language, as excuse, exists because of a prior guilt but just as possible that since language, as a machine, performs anyway, we have to produce guilt (and all its train of psychic consequences) in order to make the excuse meaningful. Excuses generate the very guilt they exonerate, though always in excess or by default" (AR, 299). There may be an excess or shortage of guilt, but clearly guilt, and the cognition that it implies, is both made possible ("any speech act produces an excess of cognition" [AR, 300]) and is precluded by the performative. In order for a text to "come into being" (an interesting turn of phrase, in which one can perhaps note de Man's "earlier" Heideggerian orientation), "the referential function had to be radically suspended" – otherwise "there would have been nothing to excuse since everything could have been explained away by the cognitive logic of understanding" (AR, 298). We can say, then, that the moment of the performative "machine" always has a kind of absolute priority, though it can never be "known" without the referential function of language, which itself "can never hope to know the process of its own production" (AR, 300) – but which nevertheless paradoxically and impossibly does so, in de Man's theory itself. The result is a "disjunction" between performative and cognitive, the "anacoluthon" or "parabasis" that implies "the sudden revelation of the discontinuity between two rhetorical codes" (AR, 300).

This presentation of de Man's argument in the last chapter of *Allegories of Reading* has been necessary, I think, because we must have some grasp of these arguments to see how de Man himself in his later work handles the problem of a "personal" guilt that follows from an earlier act. In fact, if we are as faithful as possible to de Man's reasoning on this point, we cannot justify even asking about the motives, desires, and responsibility of the (un)committed intellectual.

Our earlier impulse, to read the chapter on excuses in autobiography from *Allegories of Reading* as an elaborate autobiographical excuse for the articles in *Le Soir* (an excuse in the Rousseauian sense, where the compulsion and pleasure of revelation is inseparable from the labyrinthine game of repeated concealment), is checked by the argument in the closing section of the chapter itself. Indeed de Man is demonstrating there the fallacy of interpreting a text to uncover the originary guilt complex that underlies it. How can one even imagine an "autobiography" based on the revelation of a "guilt" that is only a function of a mechanical movement of positing (and not at all a "compulsion")? Under no circumstances are we justified in reading the chapter "Excuses" as autobiographical. There can be no consideration of an originary consciousness, subjectivity, or the recognition of a "personal" responsibility in de Man's model. Guilt is only a residue of the inevitable misinterpretation of the mechanized excuse-making process, a function of a misreading.

Yet it is difficult not to read this text as an autobiography, above all when de Man shows why this approach is "misguided." What better excuse for the early articles can there be than the fact that the performative "code" eliminates the possibility of a responsible subjectivity on the part of the author, as well as a coherent ethical stand on the part of the reader, and that the tendency to judge is based on an unavoidable misunderstanding of the operation of the textual machine? The author purchases his nonguilt, in effect, at the rather modest cost of proclaiming himself a necessarily misinterpreted mechanism. The more this kind of approach is presented, the more suspect it becomes (and it is implicit in all of de Man's later work, where poetics is given priority over hermeneutics); when we realize what de Man is excusing himself of (through his proxy, Rousseau), we do not want to accept his version of things quite so easily. Was Marion really just an arbitrary signifier, "the first word" that came into Rousseau's head? Does she really have no cause for complaint? Are there other victims in this story? Will they remain as silent as Marion, who is of importance only because she furnished a pretext for excuse making? Does what de Man says about Rousseau's (and Marion's) situation also apply to his own – that "the disproportion between the crime that is to be confessed and the crime performed by the lie adds a delirious element to the situation" (AR, 294)?

We are caught in a vicious circle. The more we recognize and affirm the power of de Man's arguments against an autobiographical subjectivity, and a personal responsibility, the more we recognize their significance for a (re)writing of his own biography, or autobiography. He has come up with the one excuse that really "works," that really gets him off the hook, precisely by no longer worrying about the point at which the excuse would intersect with the "cognitive level of understanding." And, following his logic, as soon as we consider de Man's own biography, and in any way try to "judge" him, it is our reading that is guilty, that inevitably ascribes guilt to a purely aleatory act, and sees de Man's larger argument, so rigorous, so irrefutable, as just another excuse. Our ascription of guilt is, however, necessary to the functioning of de Man's system, just as the glance of the outraged spectator or reader is necessary to any of Rousseau's gestures of shameful or embarrassing sexual or textual self-exposure. As soon as we accuse de Man of unjustifiably excusing himself, we are caught in his game, we are just another cog in his machine; now we are the ones who automatically provide the unavoidable "resistance to theory," ours is the bad reading that produces the guilt that always will be produced (and that projects it onto him). Ours is the cognitive, theoretical moment, the inevitable misinterpretation that is guilty when we misread de Man's text as guilty: it is the "falsely referential reading" that is "to blame for the consequences" (AR, 293).[20] Of course it is not a question here of a "personal" guilt on our part – one that somehow adequately characterizes our subjectivity. Instead it is our reading that bears the burden of the culpability of the affirmation of the primacy of personification (the attribution of a responsible consciousness and intention), judgment, reference, knowledge, and truth.

It might be objected that such misreadings are inevitable, that this kind of resistance is inherent in the process. The sheer performative "fiction" can never exist in isolation; there will always be a referential moment, a cognitive rhetoric, that interferes with it. While that may be true, it is clear that for de Man some readings are more misguided than others; his own text enjoys a greater level of self-reflexivity even when, and because, it "knows" that "there is never enough knowledge available to account for the delusion of knowing" (AR, 300). In other words, de Man's reading itself knows the futility of trying to know, to perform a reading that would "know" anything resembling a subject's true responsibility. In that way it is not as responsible – at least in the same way – as those misguided readings that would try to "uncover" and thereby know hidden causes or originary meanings and which, in that way, only produce more guilt. De Man's text is innocent of that delusion, at least. It knows about it.

We can see the progress de Man has made over the earlier dilemma he faced in his review of Jünger's novel. There, the more de Man asserted the innocence of writing – a removal from political "engagement," the affirmation of "pure narration" – the more guilty of political collaboration his text became. The continuous, automatic reassertion in different reviews of a lack of engagement through a higher aestheticism was itself a commitment.[21] De Man's defense of Jünger, seemingly guilty in the eyes of the Nazis for writing a compromising thesis novel, became the unavoidable, repetitious inculpation of his own text. In this early article we realize that de Man's inescapable guilt, such as it is, is never distinguishable from a repetitive, always rewritten and reposited will to innocence. In his chapter on Rousseau's *Confessions*, this model is inverted; de Man is now able effectively to affirm an innocence in practice, if not in principle (since he would reject the priority of an ethical vocabulary), by recognizing the inescapability of guilt. The "anti-grav" linguistic machine is beyond good and evil, to be sure, but at the same time its commitment/culpability is only an inevitable misinterpretation, a theoretical, referential, "resistance." Pure aesthetic withdrawal, pure narration (affirmed in the Jünger article), although already implicitly supplanted in the early articles by an unreflective, mechanical repetition, is now openly replaced by sheer fiction, by the inhuman process of an arbitrary positing and repositing of meaning.[22] Now any attempt to "blame" de Man, or to judge him, will fly back in the accuser's face; the reader-theorist's text is to blame when it attempts to establish a coherent, moral grounding for the determining of the innocence or guilt of the author or the autobiographical subject. The more we question the other's innocence, belatedly attempting to establish the criteria for determining an autobiographical innocence – in other words, the harder we work to establish the conditions of possibility for our own innocence – the guiltier our own reading becomes, and the more guilt our anthropomorphizing reading generates in order to "make the excuse meaningful" (AR, 299) and to assign a truth-value to a fundamentally arbitrary speech act. We suddenly realize that the ethical text is now repeating the bind in which de Man found himself in the early articles, when he too could only attempt to affirm his own and others' innocence through the guilty complicity of his own writing.

De Man and Guilt

But it is only through our paradigm of guilt – in which our own position doubles his guilt from the early articles – that we are able to perceive a guilt in de Man's later work: when we see his later texts, in other words, as doubling the guilt of the early ones by attempting to excuse them – and succeeding. In this larger view, the more de Man proves not so much his innocence as the absence of any possibility of subjective responsibility, the more suspect his arguments become – but, by the same token, from the de Manian perspective, the more suspect ours become as well. The guilt of his later writing is, then, merely a double of the earlier bind he found himself in, but one in which we too now find ourselves.

The only guilt that de Man's text can recognize is its own, when it affirms the guilt of the resistant reading. As we know from the essay "The Resistance to Theory," when the rhetorical reading knows itself *as* theory, when it is at its most referentially accurate, codifiable and teachable, it is then that it most resists itself *as* a theory of reading. "Nothing can overcome the resistance to theory since theory *is* itself this resistance" (RT, 19). In the same way, the text's certainty of the guilt of another reading (the inevitable statement that it is the *other* reading, the "falsely referential one" – and what theory, including de Man's, is not in the end "falsely referential"? – that must "take the blame"), the unavoidable prosopopoeia by which de Man's text determines another text's responsibility, can only be a recognition of its own guilt, its own responsibility (since it too is now in the business of issuing judgments);[23] it is the moment of rhetorical reading's strongest truth, its greatest self-knowledge and self-certainty as theory, the most definitive attribution of guilt to the other theory, but for that reason it is also the moment of its greatest "self-resistance," as de Man calls it – and self-betrayal.

This is perhaps the impossible final point in de Man's centerless labyrinth. De Man's text – but not de Man "himself" – will "have to take the blame" for determining the guilt of other (mis)readings that would ascribe guilt to subjectivities "responsible for" false writings, lies, ideology, propaganda, and so on – readings that would, in other words, ascribe guilt to de Man the subject, the "person," who determines that only texts, misreadings, can be guilty, and not subjects. De Man's writing as self-betrayal, as the always-repeated resistance to theory, is thus in profound complicity with all the "weak" (or "inattentive," etc.) readings that would strive for theoretical certainty and ascribe guilt, and that are also – but on a lower level – resistances to theory. De Man's theory knows more than they do, to be sure – as de Man says, "technically correct rhetorical readings . . . are irrefutable" (RT, 19) – but in its very certainty, in its more advanced knowledge, in its more accurate attribution of guilt, it is a more profound resistance, and it is thus in an ever-deeper complicity with all the other resistances. In its resistance to resistance, it is the most advanced resistance movement. Its affirmation in practice of the priority of accurate judgment, truth-value, reference – which allows it to argue in theory for the priority of the performative, with the generation of truth (and the determination of guilt and innocence) as an aftereffect, an inevitable misinterpretation, of the "fiction" of the speech-act – establishes de Man's text as a double of those (mis)readings that, perhaps naively, perhaps cynically, argue for the priority in principle of accurate judgment, truth-value, and cognition. The stable, full (self-)knowledge of de Man's text is the moment of its greatest deviation from the rigor of its project of reading, the moment in which it doubles all other theories. It is the necessary moment of self-awareness that the knowledge of the theory of rhetorical reading is not different in kind from all the other knowledges. De Manian knowledge, in other words, at the moment of truth in which it would most rigorously exclude, even purge, other methods – such as psychoanalysis, Marxism, and feminism, all of which depend on the priority of reference and an affirmation of the self-certainty and responsibility of individual (or collective) subjectivity – itself becomes indistinguishable from them, indeed automatically repeats them in their essential feature, their total resistance to a radically heterogeneous practice, to a method of reading that alone does "justice" to an unknowable and inhuman force: the performative, grammar, and so on.[24]

The most codifiable and truthful affirmation by rhetorical reading of an innocence that is not the symmetrical opposite of guilt is also the moment at which, inevitably, it will enter into collaboration with those methods that would accuse it, and the "author" behind it (and who is, in any case, today nothing more or less than a collection of texts), of guilty responsibility. The more de Man's writing "knows" its difference from other theories, the more it is certain of itself and its truth (it is "the universal theory of the impossibility of theory" [RT, 19]) – the more strongly it works, in other words, to expel them, and the more thoroughly it recognizes that they are "to blame" for the inevitable misreadings and ascriptions of guilt – the greater is its complicity with other guilty, truthful theories (which themselves always cast the blame on the Other), and the greater is its self-betrayal as well. If there is to be a "unification" of the different approaches in literary theory, then, it will take place not under the sign of a dialectical synthesis or a harmonious eclecticism, but in and through culpability, betrayal, and self-resistance: "literary theory is not in danger of going under . . . because the language it speaks is the language of self-resistance" (RT, 19–20).[25]

II

One can argue, however, that the later de Man does indeed have a way of countering the threat of fascism. It involves neither the recourse to an originary responsible self, nor the possibility of an adequate (self-)referential language, but a method of reading that demonstrates the complicity between an affirmation of such a self or language and all the "madness" of exclusionary messianism. In effect, history, tyranny, and historical guilt are generated by the kinds of misreading that would pretend to know or determine guilt (and thus do away with the guilty) and accede to the truth of social events. A fundamentally religious desire for a fully adequate language – that can be certain, can judge and predict – is the root of the problem.[26] One thinks of any number of passages in de Man's work; for example, the end of chapter 11 of *Allegories of Reading*, on Rousseau's *Social Contract*, where we learn that language's "promise of its own truth" – again the mechanical speech act – is necessarily misleading, and that, for this reason, "textual allegories on this level of rhetorical complexity generate history" (AR, 277). De Man is no doubt thinking of the French Revolution, and the Terror, much of which was justified, and even motivated by, various misreadings of the *Social Contract*. While de Man states here that this misreading is inevitable ("Just as any other reader, Rousseau is bound to misread his text as a promise of political change. The error is not within the reader; language itself dissociates the cognition from the act"), at other times he implies that through a rhetorical reading the temptation to misread "textual allegories" as authoritative demonstrations of political or ethical truth can be avoided – and the temptation of any personal allegiance to tyranny or terror can in that way be eliminated. For example, in one of his last published essays, "Hegel on the Sublime" (a reading of Hegel's *Aesthetics*), de Man closes with these remarks: "Hegel's *Aesthetics*, an essentially poetic discourse on art, is a discourse of the slave because it is a discourse of the figure rather than of genre, of trope rather than of representation. As a result, it is also politically legitimate and effective as the undoer of usurped authority. . . . Poets, philosophers, and their readers lose their political impact only if they become, in turn, usurpers of mastery."[27] Finally, in perhaps his bluntest statement, de Man, answering a question after his 1983 lecture "Benjamin's 'Task of the Translator,'" says of all attempts to link politics to a sacred or religious language and a totalizing messianic futurity: "that way madness lies" (RT, 103).

De Man's gesture here owes much to Heidegger; for Heidegger too there was a profound complicity between a rational humanism that would posit a stable "essence (or spirit) of man," a language that would be adequate in its representation of that essence, and the cult of technology that posits fully knowable, stable, and quantifiable entities. As I mentioned in the previous chapter, Heidegger was able to associate highly disparate political systems: American-style capitalism, Soviet communism, and (only after the war) nazism. All of these ignored Being, all instituted a kind of tyrannical mechanization and quantification. Heidegger, for that reason, had no way of accounting for the differences between, say, secular humanism – the ideology of advanced capitalism – and the racist ideology of nazism.[28] While de Man usually refuses to engage in a critique of technology, he does clearly associate any attempt to identify the word with the "natural object" or the sacred – or any attempt to see language as having a stable referential function, be it in relation to "external" objects or to subjectivities – as politically dangerous.[29] Secular humanism and messianic mysticism are both suspect for exactly the same reason. The only way we can avoid the "madness" of various fundamentally religious models which, through the misreadings they authorize, generate a kind of bad history, is by carrying out rhetorical readings.[30] Only then will politics and poetics merge, and another kind of history be apparent (see RT, 93).[31]

I do not intend to be critical of de Man on this point; indeed he may be right. But one must recognize the implications of what he is saying, especially in pieces like his lecture on Benjamin. As was the case for Heidegger, there is no way for him to distinguish (from within his method) between various doctrines: rational humanism and messianic religions of all stripes are all vulnerable to the same critique. And all, we can conclude, have mouthpieces – "committed" poets, philosophers, and literary critics – who are "usurpers of mastery."

This, then, would seem to be the answer to our earlier dilemma; if the very possibility of a responsible subjectivity is set aside in the later de Man, it is not to excuse a possible earlier guilty collaboration (with a messianic faith, if there ever was one); on the contrary, the later method alone allows an effective critique of de Man's early "commitment." De Man in his youth was also a usurper of mastery. Having recourse to an ethics based on respect for individual consciousness and its drives as an alternative to this collaboration can only be misguided, for humanistic ethics and the madness of messianic cults – be they Jewish or German – are in profound complicity.[32]

Many supporters of de Man – as well as his critics – might have difficulty in lumping together "religions" that are so different. I only want, however, to pose a problem that arises from reading de Man's text. If humanism and all its baggage – the rights of man, individual responsibility for crimes – are to be jettisoned, the question arises whether a new certainty will replace the comfortable old one of "the sacredness of the human person" (as Durkheim called it) that seemed to offer a bulwark of truth in the face of, but also necessarily in the midst of, an infinity of cultures and relativized truths. It is de Man himself, in some of his later pieces, who indicates the necessity of certainty in and through his own method. As we will see, in fact, de Man's certainty is directed precisely against the possibility of the "sacred." But how justifiable is that certainty? And what is its status?

We can now turn to the lecture "The Task of the Translator," in order to examine what seem to me to be a few problems. Much of the strength of de Man's argument here comes from the fact that he shows – or purportedly shows – that translators Harry Zohn and Maurice de Gandillac are "wrong" in their translations of Benjamin's essay. They are wrong specifically because they mistranslate in the crudest sense: Gandillac reverses the meaning on several occasions (RT, 80, 81), Zohn gets it completely wrong at least once (RT, 85), and so on. But in a larger sense what they "get wrong" is the basic orientation of Benjamin's article, in other words his version of translation, which they distort through mistranslations at certain key points. According to de Man, for Benjamin "What the translation reveals is that . . . alienation is at its strongest in relation to our own original language, that the original language within which we are engaged is disarticulated in a way which imposes upon us a particular alienation, a particular suffering" (RT, 84). Translation for Benjamin (in de Man's translation of his text), like literary theory, critical philosophy, and history, "undoes" a text that was never "done," that was never an original that was adequate to itself, "pure form," in the first place. "They [translation and the rest] relate to what in the original belongs to language, and not to meaning as an extralinguistic correlate susceptible of paraphrase and imitation. They disarticulate, they undo the original, they reveal that the original was always already disarticulated. They reveal that their failure, which seems to be due to the fact that they are secondary in relation to the original, reveals an essential failure, an essential disarticulation which was already there in the original" (RT, 84).

The original language, the *reine Sprache*, a "pure language" (RT, 90) which a mystic (or a reader of Benjamin like Gershom Scholem, who holds that Benjamin is a mystic) assumes is the pure self-adequation of form, a utopian language liberated from the contingencies of meaning, is presented by Benjamin, according to de Man, as fragmentary; the always already broken pieces of a translation do not add up to a whole and do not refer to a whole. The translation is a fragmentation of a fragmentation; it is not a fragmentation of an originary, mystical unity, a "sacred vessel." "What we have here is an initial fragmentation; any work is totally fragmented in relation to this *reine Sprache*, with which it has nothing in common, and every translation is totally fragmented in relation to the original. The translation is the fragment of a fragment, is breaking the fragment – so the vessel keeps breaking constantly – and never reconstitutes it" (RT, 91).

And this is precisely where the translations "get it wrong"; Zohn insists in his that there *is* a greater language, he stresses the "life" of the original, the birth pangs of the translation – whereas Benjamin's text, as de Man has it, stresses exactly the opposite: "The translation belongs not to the life of the original, the original is already dead, but the translation belongs to the afterlife of the original, thus assuming and confirming the death of the original" (RT, 85). The translators, in other words, mistranslate when they imply that there *is* an original mystico-linguistic totality, that there is a sacred. De Man's argument is thus built on a paradox: the faithful translation does not convey or represent the unitary "original," and its pure form, but rather "undoes" it; the unfaithful translator betrays the original by implying that the original can be faithfully translated, reconstituted, and "brought to life."

The certainty of de Man's argument is based on the possibility of a faithful translation – which his own argument, doubling Benjamin's by translating it (both into English and into its own critical language) argues against. It is through this certainty that de Man can justify his refusal of a larger mystical or sacred politics, based on the synthesis of messianism and the political dialectic (RT, 92–93). Instead, de Man affirms a politics that is inseparable from poetics, that refuses any teleological totalization.

De Man is not advancing "his own" argument here – he is a "philologist, not a philosopher," as he tells an interviewer (RT, 118) – but is affirming, through his own (correct) translation, that of another (Benjamin). He translates it by fragmenting it, disarticulating it, establishing in relation to it a "metonymic, successive pattern" rather than a "metaphorical, unifying pattern" (RT, 90). It is important to grasp that de Man ascribes much importance to this (impossible) faithfulness to Benjamin's "original"; the correct translation refutes those translators who would characteristically and erroneously present, via Benjamin, the possibility of a faithful translation – who, in other words, are in complicity with those who would hold (and here one should recall de Man's chapter on the *Confessions*) that a fiction really does represent, that a correct judgment really is possible, that a unitary subject really is responsible for its acts and meanings.

I do not want to attempt to argue against de Man's position, or "disprove" it. Rather I would only point out that, in the piece on Benjamin at least, it is based on a total belief in the empirical possibility of the correctness of a translation – so much so that Zohn and Gandillac, rather shockingly, are called "inhuman" because they get it all wrong (RT, 98–99). Of course the latter statement is off the cuff, and ironically refers to a much more important use of the word "inhuman" – a description of the deanthropomorphized operation of grammar. Nevertheless it represents a problem: not that de Man has contempt for other, less capable or less careful translators (who cares?), but that, in order to be effective, de Man's argument must *definitively* eliminate the possibility of the other, mystico-political, reading. There is absolute certainty on de Man's part – but necessarily based on the least reliable source: translation. De Man will never admit that there might be a certain ambiguity in the text as it relates to his own reading. And yet there is: even setting aside the egregious errors, or the dumb ones, it is clear that Zohn and Gandillac, in their necessarily "free" translation, sometimes provide possible readings, ones that are at least as plausible as de Man's. (A totally "literal" translation would be, as de Man recognizes, incomprehensible – like Hölderlin's translation of Sophocles.) The clearest example of possible readings appears on page 85 of de Man's article; de Man criticizes their translation of *Wehen* as "birth pains" and *Nachreife* as "maturing process." These might not be the only possible translations of these terms, but they are at least possible, as any German-English dictionary will show. Just as possible, in fact, as de Man's "death pains" and "afterlife." De Man, in other words, wrongly associates a simple mistranslation, an error (as when Zohn or Gandillac leaves out or adds a "not") with a reading that may or may not be correct but that disagrees with his. His empirical certainty having to do with a clear mistranslation is made to carry over onto a certainty concerning the "error" of a different interpretation of the text, which happens not to agree with his.

De Man himself is not necessarily wrong. The "correct" translations, however, on which the certainty of his argument depends, are themselves tendentious – as are, moreover, all translations. De Man's translations become "correct" only in light of a reading that has already been determined. A "free" translation – any translation – will necessarily ignore certain syntactical irregularities and peculiarities of vocabulary or style if they violate the overall implicit interpretation of the translator, and it will highlight others, if they conform to it. Yet de Man will accept the "free" translation only if it backs up his own interpretation, even if in its very freeness it ignores some things and underscores others: "The faithful translation, which is always literal, how can it also be free? It can also be free if it reveals the instability of the original, and if it reveals that instability as the linguistic tension between trope and meaning" (RT, 91–92). It can be free, then – it can make sense – only if it rigorously conforms to de Man's own approach. Yet de Man himself admits, in the question-and-answer session that follows his lecture, that there are elements in Benjamin's piece that escape him, that openly defy his "free" translation, and have yet to be accounted for: "Whenever I go back to this text, I think I have it more or less, then I read it over again, and again I don't understand it. I again see a messianic appeal" (RT, 103).

On the basis of translation itself, de Man is not justified in simply rejecting the mystico-political version of Benjamin's text. And the impossibly but necessarily faithful translation – in this case a double of de Man's own critical method – is all he has to rely on. His approach, after all, is based not on some larger philosophy or method but on philology and on close reading. There is, then, ambiguity, and Zohn's and Gandillac's metaphorical and messianic version cannot be excluded outright. Through translation, de Man is not capable of attaining – or usurping – a mastery that will enable him to definitively exclude other readings: humanist, mystical, messianic-political, or whatever. He cannot always guarantee himself the certainty that would enable him to exclude them.

My remarks should not be seen as a defense of rational humanism, or of some type of formalism linked to a mystical or sacred knowledge. But what is the status of certainty in de Man's own text? Why should we accept his version as being "irrefutable" and "totalizing (and potentially totalitarian)," as he puts it in "The Resistance to Theory" (RT, 19)?[33] He would argue, for example, that he "assume[s], as a working hypothesis . . . that the text knows in an absolute way what it's doing" (RT, 118). Yet in order to grant the text that certainty, and to deprive himself of a transcendent knowledge in relation to it, he must also assume that he is certain that the text knows something that it was never admitting before. Why was the *Social Contract* misread (and bad history generated) for over two hundred years? Why are there all these mystical readers of Benjamin? Because de Man can be certain that he, for the first time, can "translate" the text correctly? And if he cannot? If there is still another justifiable reading? If there is ambiguity? Above all (as in the famous example of Archie Bunker's bowling shoes [AR, 9–10]), if "it is impossible to decide by grammatical or other linguistic devices which of the two meanings . . . prevails" (AR, 10)? In the case of the translation of Benjamin's essay, one reading, we might say, is "metonymic," the other (bad one) "metaphorical," but the undecidability remains.

De Man, in choosing the example of the bowling shoes, has a perfect foil: Archie Bunker, of the old television series "All in the Family," is the archetypal political reactionary who "misreads" and therefore creates a certain oppressive history. But in doing so, he is the double of the de Man who insists on certainty from his translations, who would read a sentence one way and peremptorily refuse another reading, which perhaps can be justified (or at least, even if only in a few instances, cannot be ruled out).

It is the "decidability" of the de Manian text, then, that I would like to question. What if it is not tenable? What if his text "really" is an allegory for something else? What if de Man really "knows" what he is doing and it has as much to do with allegories of reading as Rousseau's *Confessions*, in de Man's reading of it, has to do with the revelation of guilt of an autonomous subject?

It may be, in other words, that there really is not "enough knowledge available to account for the delusion of knowing" (AR, 300); that the knowledge of de Man's text is founded on a kind of "not-knowing," an abyss into which it cannot keep from falling. This abyss might not be simple disarticulation, or textual "death" of some sort, but instead the very knowing, the very certainty, through and with which the text must identify "not-knowing" in order to establish itself as knowing, as certainty. Moral judgment, perhaps, and the problem of subjective responsibility – along with the sacred and political commitment – are perhaps not positive terms but negative ones, logical anomalies or aberrations from the impossible point of view of de Man's method, moments which cannot simply be arbitrarily lumped together and definitively excluded. Rightly or wrongly, for good or ill, they will always assert their difference from each other, and, from the space to which they have been relegated, take their revenge. And their revenge will consist in the fact that in order to exclude them the de Manian text is forced to partake of precisely the same exclusionary logic by which sacred – and sacrificial – knowledge is itself constituted. It will be forced to double them, be as fundamentally arbitrary in its exclusions as they are, thereby entering into complicity or collaboration with them in its (unsuccessful) attempt to purge them: their return from the realm of exclusion is always certain. In this sense indeed the notion of the commitment of the philosopher or critic through socially engaged writing – and all the other versions of a "not-knowing" – will certainly take about a whole life, and beyond, to get over.

De Man in any case clearly rejects the possibility of a critical work – a translation – that can refer back to a Kantian *reine Sprache*, a "language that would be entirely freed from the illusion of meaning – pure form, if you want" (RT, 84). Such a reference would in fact be a kind of self-reflection by which the translation, through its very (partial) transmission of that originary form, represents its own formal integrity. It is the possibility of such a pure unity of language that de Man refuses, both in and through Benjamin. The "original" – the text to be translated, as well as the originary (sacred) language of which all texts are imperfect copies – is never a unity, but a disjunction: "The movement of the original is a wandering, an *errance*, a kind of permanent exile if you wish, but it is not really an exile, for there is no homeland, nothing from which one has been exiled. Least of all is there something like a *reine Sprache*, a pure language, which does not exist *except* as a permanent disjunction which inhabits all language as such, including and especially the language one calls one's own" (RT, 92; emphasis added).

An implicit equation is established by Gershon Scholem between the language of pure form and the "broken vessels" of the Kabbalistic tradition, which are restored – and along with them, the "original Being of things" – by the coming of the messiah (RT, 90).[34] In other words, in this kind of reading the possibility of an originary "pure speech" is also the necessity of the sacred, and of the "sacrificial, dialectical, and elegiac gesture" by which historical loss is overcome. De Man counters that, for Benjamin, the translation, and the original, are not "fragments of a greater language, just as fragments are part of a vessel" (as the Zohn translation has it) – are not, in other words, parts of a larger whole – but that "fragments are fragments, and that they remain essentially fragmentary" (RT, 91).

The impossibility of the pure speech is inseparable from the impossibility of the sacred, of a sacrificial representation (and victim) that adequately conveys or retransmits the divine presence, and so forth. It is also identified by de Man with history, which in turn is linked, through Benjamin, with the "separation and the acting out of the separation of the sacred from the poetic": "*Reine Sprache*, the sacred language, has nothing in common with poetic language. . . . It is within this negative knowledge of its relation to the language of the sacred that poetic language initiates" (RT, 92).

It would seem that the "poetic" is the language of indefinite fragmentation, and disjunction, which de Man noted in the previous paragraph that I quoted. It should be stressed, however, that de Man did not simply eliminate the possibility of the *reine Sprache* there in the same way that he rigorously opposes it to poetic language. Instead, he writes that the "pure language . . . does not exist *except* as a permanent disjunction." This is not to say, in other words, that the *reine Sprache* has simply been eliminated. Benjamin, in using the term, has displaced its meaning; the *reine Sprache* now, according to de Man, is exclusively a grammatical function, "completely devoid of any semantic function whatsoever, a purely technical linguistic language" (RT, 97). But the distance between such a language and one of "pure form," "entirely freed from the illusion of meaning" (RT, 84) starts to seem fairly minor, especially in light of de Man's ambiguity concerning the status of this *reine Sprache*. What does it mean to say that this language "does not exist except as a permanent disjunction"? Does this mean that the "originary" pure form must now be read as an abyssal fragmentation, or that that fragmentation is simply another version of pure form? That to affirm the broken – and always again breaking – vessel rather than the whole (or reassembled) one is just to affirm one version of form over another? If that is the case, can we say that de Man is ever able to escape a strict formalism? And, from within formalism, how can one definitively valorize one version of form (the ever-fragmenting fragment) over another (the whole, the totality)?

This problem carries over to the sacred. If the *reine Sprache* is associated with (or identified as) the sacred language, then what is to keep us from concluding that, far from dismissing the sacred, or sacred language (as he seems to do) de Man is now simply redefining the sacred: it is the "permanent disjunction which inhabits all language as such." Indeed, after all the sound and fury mounted against the sacred, sacrifice, and the messianic, de Man himself recognizes that what he affirms in Benjamin could still be called the sacred: "it [the *reine Sprache*] would be purely limited to its own linguistic characteristics. You can call that divine or sacred, if you want, but it is not mysterious in that sense, I think, though it is paradoxical in the extreme" (RT, 97). (The sacred, we learn, is now simply not mysterious – but when was "mystery" ever presented as the main component of the sacred, either by de Man himself or by his presumed opponents?)

In this sense, de Man himself might not be so far after all from the Bataille who associates a secular religious experience more and more with the very necessity and impossibility of the act of translating the (secular) sacred in language or writing (see Bataille's *Inner Experience*, for example). But what is most important is that the de Manian formal sacred – his version of the fragmented vessel – is itself still engaged in the sacrificial act of exclusion – although now this gesture comes to inhabit "the language one calls one's own."

Excluded, of course, is the possibility of the traditional inside/outside opposition, of the recemented, recomposed vessel that contains and excludes.[35] De Man's very rigor in excluding the faulty translations that validate the integrity of the vessel – that validate the sacred and flirt with the messianic – is itself sacred in that it is inseparable from an exclusion of the sacred. The more rigorously de Man's text eliminates the sacred, closing itself as fragmented vessel *against* the sacred – and thus also eliminating the role of the intellectual (a certain Benjamin or his avatars) as the apostle, the vessel, of a new messianism – the more purified the de Manian version of form becomes: fragmentation will inevitably be identified with the integrity of form if it is fully affirmed in opposition to form (hence the ambiguity of de Man's own formulation, where the "pure language . . . does not exist *except* as permanent disjunction"). The rigor of the impossibility of the pathos of exclusionary form itself acts as exclusion: in this way, sacrificial logic is returned to in and through the very act of the exclusion of sacrifice. The more the sacred in its various avatars (such as its secularized and anthropomorphized representative, the intellectual) is purged, the more it is embraced: rhetorical reading is locked in the infinite repetition of this act.

In this context, one thinks of the problem of the teacher of literature, or the literary critic, as de Man presents it in the short article "The Return to Philology." De Man's philological project follows the procedure first elaborated by Reuben Brower in the famous introductory course "The Interpretation of Literature" (HUM 6) at Harvard in the 1950s. This course, in which de Man served as a teaching assistant, required students "to begin by reading texts closely as texts and not to move at once into the general context of human experience or history. Much more humbly or honestly, they were to start out from the bafflement that such singular turns of tone, phrase, and figure were bound to produce in readers attentive enough to notice them and honest enough not to hide their non-understanding behind the screen of received ideas that often passes, in literary instruction, for humanistic knowledge" (RT,

23). De Man cites the influence of Brower as a determining one partly for polemical reasons but also, and above all, to stress the purely technical nature of his project.[36] If the critic or teacher is attentive to the "philological or rhetorical devices of language" (RT, 24), as Brower was, he or she is not engaged in the affirmation of the "ethical function of literature." According to de Man, it is not at all clear that "aesthetic values can be compatible with the linguistic structures that make up the entities from which these values are derived" (RT, 25); the task of the critic, his or her *Aufgabe*, is therefore to read critically – and eventually to read Kant critically – thereby putting into question the easy unification of "cognition, desire and morality in one single synthetic judgment" (RT, 25). The literary critic, like the good student in HUM 6, eschews traditional humanistic methods of interpretation and "cultural excellence" that, "in the last analysis, are always based on some form of religious faith" (RT, 26). History, ethics, aesthetics, all those inspirational sources for undergraduates and their teachers – and all of which are regularly extracted by them from literary texts – will be ruthlessly purged. They are, after all, totally extraneous to literature; such readings pull literature in the direction of other specializations – not only history (and politics), but ethics, and therefore morality and religion. For de Man it is time to end the chaotic situation in which English departments become "large organizations in the service of everything except their own subject matter" (RT, 26).

Their own subject matter, it seems, is nothing other than this rigorous reading of texts, of the constative against the performative and vice versa, of figure against grammar and vice versa. If we could leave de Man at this point, there would be little to which one could object. The role of the critic is a rigorously technical one (if not a technocratic one), distinct from that of others – historians, aestheticians, ethicists, humanists in general – which are all fundamentally "religious." Literary study now is an autonomous discipline, "critical in the full philosophical sense of the term" (RT, 26), if not scientific. At last we know what we are doing as literary critics, and we know as well what others do in their specializations.

The problem lies in the fact that de Man is presenting his project here with a certain false modesty. Those other "religious" disciplines are precisely the ones that will be called into question by rhetorical reading. Such readings are performed not just on "literature" (whatever that is), but on all genres of texts: one need only recall *Allegories of Reading*, which includes chapters on philosophical works (Nietzsche), social and political ones (Rousseau's *Social Contract*), protopsychological or psychoanalytic ones (Rousseau's *Confessions*), as well as novels and poetry. De Man even makes the point that the problems he is concerned with in Rousseau cross over and render pointless the traditional genre classifications of his works (social theory, novels, autobiography). We cannot say, then, that rhetorical reading, having found its niche in the literature departments of the academy, would "respect" the autonomy of all the other "religious" disciplines. On the contrary, it would call their legitimacy into question; just as the boundaries between Rousseau's social theory and his fiction are irrelevant, so too the boundaries between history and ethics will be expendable. Rhetorical readings of works commonly read in departments of sociology, anthropology, history, or philosophy will be carried out, and the humanism of those disciplines will, presumably, meet the same fate as that of the slipshod humanism within literary studies. History will inevitably be purged not only from the study of literature but from history itself. The conflict of the faculties as interpreted by de Man will end not (as in Kant) in the direction of the university – and of the other disciplines – by philosophy, but will find its resolution – its end of history – in the absorption and expulsion of all disciplines by rhetorical reading. This absorption will not, however, be the digestive process – or the synthetic movement – of idealism but will be a kind of repetitious and radical autopurgation of rhetorical reading by itself. With all other disciplines deconstructed, rhetorical reading, and the university along with it, will continue to turn on itself, continuously reading itself against itself, always again analyzing its resistance to itself, the inevitable delusion of the certainty of its own readings.

This academic dystopia (or utopia, depending on one's point of view), the stuff of Walter Jackson Bate's worst nightmares, bears more than a little resemblance to the Terror (which inevitably excludes the "idea" or "thought") as analyzed by Paulhan. We need not condemn or applaud de Man for putting forward, directly or by implication, such a scheme; he himself recognizes that "the institutional resistances [to it] are probably insurmountable" (RT, 26).[37] It is only a certain version of one side of the Terror (grammar), one that is an inevitable component of any Rhetoric, discourse, or social/academic model. Of interest here instead is the figure of the teacher or critic that de Man's dys/utopia implies. In the end, all is excluded from the de Manian pedagogy except the pure act, and power (based on the certainty of the method), of reading. The fundamentally religious intellectual – who *represents* (humanity, a class, or whatever) – is replaced by the reader, the critic, who *acts*; the reading is an act of purgation by which all "extraneous" disciplines are eliminated from literature and from themselves. In this way the de Manian critic purges his own authority as an intellectual while at the same time affirming his own omnipotence in the very act of his own autopurgation. This power will always again be affirmed in the necessary and repetitious act of its purgation, since the strength – the force – of the purgation will inevitably be misread (or mis*represented*) as intellectual authority.

For this reason one cannot say that it is mere "institutional resistance" that prevents de Man's thorough cleaning of the academic house. Once again, the "resistance to theory" is "in" the theory itself; more important for the never *simply* excluded social implications and consequences of rhetorical reading, however, is the fact that, just as the rigor of de Man's exclusion of the sacred (or the religious) is itself the final instance of the sacred, so too the act of purging the function of the intellectual in de Man's academic model – the intellectual's authority and representative capacity – is itself an instance of the power, and finally the authority, that is inseparable from the intellectual function. The de Manian critic is always again an intellectual – a priest of the secular sacred – at the moment he or she sacrifices all pretensions to the religion of humanism. As such the de Manian cannot simply escape the unavoidable social and ethical ("religious") questions – such as the question of what exactly it is that the intellectual "represents" – that he or she incessantly eliminates, not only from the intellectual function and from the university, but from society as a whole. The intellectual, after all, always represents *something*, no matter how minimal or negative, and that something implies distinctions, qualifications, and oppositions to be taken seriously within the realm not only of metaphysics but of society as represented by metaphysics.

10

Sur Bataille:
Nietzsche in the Text
of Bataille

The rending question of this book. – Georges Bataille, *Sur Nietzsche*

*

IN THE SECOND part of this book, I posed the question of the moment of commitment, subjectivity, and representation in a number of authors who are best known for their refusal, or critique, of such categories. This is not to say, of course, that one can somehow discover hidden away in their texts – perhaps under a false bottom – a secret message affirming the necessity of revolutionary action or the coherence of a society founded on humanistic principles. Instead, I have tried to demonstrate, in these writers, the necessity of the valorization of an oppositional political stance (Blanchot and Derrida), of a moment of the coherent subject (Foucault), and of the cathartic-sacrificial-speculative mechanism (de Man). Such terms are not dominant in these texts, of course, but they work there, making possible the very affirmation of an all-pervasive textuality they subvert. From Foucault to de Man, we can even see a development – in the direction of an always more sophisticated deconstruction of the very possibility of a positive message or mission – whose always-receding goal is nevertheless put in question by the very strategies on which it depends. The question now is this: can one posit a text in which the movements I charted in part 1 – the establishment of a moment of sacrifice, knowledge, and social unity made possible and undermined by the impersonal movement of the performative and textuality – and part 2 – textuality established and undermined through the necessity of a constructive knowledge and subjectivity – are both, together, *known* in the fissures of the project of a single "writer"? Could such a knowledge itself even be conceived or represented? To consider this problem in more detail, we must turn to the curious labor of Georges Bataille.

More than any other of the figures examined in this book, except perhaps Blanchot, Bataille presents the reader – and the potential critic – with a dilemma. Are we to *repeat* what Bataille has already written, appropriating aspects of a coherent "theory of waste"? This might have a certain value if we are applying those theories to other texts or political constructs. If, however, we return to read Bataille, it seems unlikely that we can formulate anything about "spending without return" (*dépense*) that will be more incisive than what Bataille himself wrote. At best we can summarize or schematize.[1] Yet summaries or schemas will be the inevitable result if we approach Bataille's writings as a kind of homogeneous body of work. Is there in fact one Bataillean "theory"? To my knowledge, no such unity has ever been demonstrated.

Another approach dismisses (overtly or covertly) any possibility of a Bataillean "totality," only to privilege certain aspects or periods of Bataille's work over others. *Tel Quel* in the early seventies, for example, stressed certain of Bataille's political texts from the thirties which, in some ways, are quite compatible with a Maoist dialectic.[2] The problem with readings of this kind is that, in stressing a single period, the critics who would appropriate Bataille ignore his subsequent writings, which might, in fact, be critiques of the positions they themselves are using. They ignore the possibility of an effective Bataillean critique of their own positions.

Both of these approaches neglect the specificity of texts within Bataille's oeuvre. If Bataille is a repetition of both Hegel and Nietzsche (as Denis Hollier and Jacques Derrida have argued), the interrelation of periods and positions in Bataille must be seen from both a dialectical and a transgressive point of view.[3] This interrelation will be dialectical in the sense that succeeding positions attempt to take into account the failures of preceding texts and try to work out successfully new positions. On the other hand, it will be transgressive to the extent that the new positions taken will not attempt to be correct formulations of an absolute knowledge but, rather, of a not-knowing, an impossible "durable orgasm" (as Bataille refers to it in "The Pineal Eye"). The position of the commentator will then both be necessary and untenable. Necessary because an overview will reveal a coherence in Bataille's works that up to now has remained unexplored (and will remain so if the oeuvre is seen simply as a collection of texts that present a unified theory), and untenable to the extent that the awareness or self-reflexivity of this development will reduce it to the status of a simple dialectic, conflating it with Hegel and entirely losing Nietzsche in the process. Bataille himself was "aware" of this problem, not in relation to a commentary on his works, but in the possible interrelation of his texts as a dialectic leading to a simple endpoint. It became necessary for him to confront any dialectical movement, no matter how transgressive, with another series, or side, of texts that would work to forget "actively" that dialectic. That very forgetting, in its all-pervasiveness, would therefore seek to devalorize any systematic reading of Bataille. Ironically, however, that process of total forgetting (which constitutes the major intervention of Nietzsche in Bataille) has its own dialectic of development, which indicates the necessity of our critical intervention.

I

We must separate two main periods (whose interest for us is less historical than conceptual) in Bataille's rewriting of Nietzsche. The first period can roughly be associated with his founding of and involvement in the Acéphale group, ending with the beginning of World War II. The second starts at the beginning of World War II, and culminates in *Sur Nietzsche* (written in 1944, published in 1945). In an unfinished preface (written in 1960) to *Guilty* (*Le Coupable*), Bataille recalled the crisis that ended the Acéphale project: "I had spent the preceding years with an untenable preoccupation; I had resolved, if not to found a religion, at least to head in that direction. What the history of religion had revealed to me gradually excited me. . . . And even though such a whim might seem utterly stupefying, I took it seriously."[4] In another manuscript, written about the same time, "I even find a little pleasure in evoking the bitter memory of the faddish notion that I had some twenty years ago, of founding a religion. I want to make it clear now that my stalemate, the fact of which appeared more clearly to me with each passing day, is the origin of this *Summa* that today is on the point of being completed. It was at the very moment that my efforts proved to be vain that I started *Guilty*. (It was consequently with *Guilty* that, on September 5, 1939, I started this disconnected work)" (OC, 6:370).

The dream of a "religion" – and of a community inseparable from one – collapsed at the outbreak of the war. A war that, needless to say, made the individual heterogeneity of a subversive group or community seem petty – especially after June 1940.[5] The war is now a kind of heterogeneity in itself, not the result of a tissue of political compromises and violations like those condemned by Contre-Attaque but, rather, the destructive force of a tornado or some other natural disaster.[6] Bataille is not now forced somehow to affirm or create a heterogeneity of mobs or violence. He is forced inward – he is alone – the "outer world" *is* heterogeneity, as in the case of the noise of the battle between Germans and Americans in Bataille's area: "If there is any grandeur in these noises, it is that of the *unintelligible*. They suggest neither the murderous nature of the projectiles, nor the immense movements of history, nor even a danger that is coming close" (OC, 6:178).[7] Of course external events play their role in an "inner emigration," and Bataille's was only one of many during the war. What interests us, however, is the logic that dictated the turn from "community" to "impossible individuality."

Nietzsche was the centerpiece of the Acéphale project, and to understand what happens to Nietzsche in the switch from Acéphale to the *Summa atheologica* (which is composed of *Inner Experience* [*L'Expérience intérieure*] [1943], *Guilty* [1944], and *Sur Nietzsche* [1945]), a clear picture of the Nietzsche of Acéphale must be grasped.[8] Nietzsche (and Nietzsche as "overman" [*surhomme*]) in Acéphale is, first of all, not clearly separable from a mythic entity, a chthonic earth deity, or a gnostic archonte: "The acéphale mythologically expresses the sovereignty committed to destruction and the death of God, and in this the identification with the headless man merges and melds with the identification with the superhuman, which IS entirely the 'death of God.'"[9]

This headless god is associated with the *surhomme* of Nietzsche and with the position of time as an imperative object and as explosive liberty of life. A time that is radically outside construction and utility (and hence outside the time of Hegel's dialectic) and which is associated by Bataille with the impossible time of the eternal return. The article "The Obelisk," which is contemporaneous with the Acéphale writings, bears this out: "The *toxic* character of the 'return' is even of such great importance that, if it were for an instant set aside, the formal content of the 'return' might appear empty. . . . And the audacious act that represents the 'return' at the summit of this rending agony only wrests from the dead God his *total* strength, in order to give it to the deleterious absurdity of time" (VE, 220).

Despite this impossible time, the projected rebirth of gnosticism will take place on a cultural level. Implicitly opposing the Contre-Attaque position, this gnosticism will be outside of any conceivable political formulation (this "'Dionysian' truth cannot be the object of any propaganda," [OC, 1:489]). The only vehicle left, it would seem, is the religious or mythical one. But the *acéphale* (the mythical figure) is a *critique* of any religious position, since it represents nothing other than "the death of God." The *acéphale* in turn is inseparable from the *surhomme*, and together they are identical to:

NIETZSCHE DIONYSOS

The critical phase of the decomposition of civilization is regularly followed by a recomposition, which develops in two different directions: the reconstitution of religious elements of civil and military sovereignty, tying existence to the *past*, is followed or accompanied by the birth of free and liberating sacred figures and myths, *renewing* life and making it "that which frolics in the *future*," "that which only belongs to a *future*." (VE, 206)

Nietzsche "himself" becomes "*acéphale*/Dionysos," but what does this multiheaded mythical entity represent? In the first quote we examined, the *acéphale* was "committed to destruction" (VE, 199). It was primarily being put

forward as an entity that represented sheer negativity. That toxic destructive-
ness was in turn associated with an eternal return that was not related in any
way to a constructive movement of time, or to the possibility of fixing time in a
religious eternity or in a secular end of history. Once "toxicity" was manifested
on a social plane, however, history would nevertheless end, at least the positive
notion of history put forward by Hegel: "the fall of the return is FINAL" (VE,
220). Already another time scheme – another (Nietzschean) history and finality – crosses the temporal model of Hegel. A kind of antihistory (manifesting
itself historically) is therefore proposed. But how does this deleterious time
make itself known in the life of society, and what does it promise for the
future?

This is where "Nietzsche Dionysos" attempts to advance a solution. It first
mentions the "regular decomposition" of a society that manifests itself in two
different "directions." One of these is the "reconstitution" of a civil and military society. This is the process outlined in two of Bataille's essays written in
the early thirties, "The Old Mole and the Prefix 'Sur' in 'Surhomme' and
'Surrealist'" (VE, 32–44), and "The Psychological Structure of Fascism" (VE,
137–60). In these essays, an initially heterogeneous tendency is presented as
being immediately reappropriated by the very bourgeois forces that it had
threatened. Society's "excess" is channeled not into nonproductive orgiastic or
sacrificial waste, but is instead rerouted back into the military for war or (as in
the case of the surrealists) into the aesthetic as a mode of cultural domination.
The heterogeneous-become-homogeneous is characterized by elevation: the
Nietzschean "*over*man" ("*sur*homme"), the *sur*realist, the Roman imperial eagle that flies over, and holds in contempt, all it has conquered, the sadistic
Fascist dictator who "stands tall" above and before the crowd, and so on. The
acéphale is specifically meant as a mythical figure whose very headlessness will
counteract such dangerous fantasies (and practices) of altitude and leadership.
People need myth, and the myth of the *acéphale*, which will overwhelm decadent (mythless) bourgeois democracies, is the only one that can adequately
counter the repressive myths of race, leadership, and hard, constructive labor.
Bataille (in "Nietzsche Dionysos") thus postulates a movement through which
the reappropriation by civil or military forces is "followed or accompanied by
the birth of sacred figures and myths." This second possible direction is disclosed by "figures" that are seen as "renewing" and which "only belong to a
future," and it is associable as well with the "toxicity" mentioned elsewhere in
connection with the mythic, acephalic figure. The appearance of these figures
is the irruption of the eternal return – of a toxic time – in the time of conservation and renewal.

We should first note the uncertainty as to the nature of the temporality
proposed in Bataille's formulation. The "or" of "followed or accompanied by"

is important, for it indicates a lack of clarity concerning the positioning of the "sacred figures." Will they disrupt any new civil-military regime? Or will they merely follow it, stepping into a gap caused by its self-destruction? Finally, how "toxic" will they be if they are only agents in a "renewal" of society?

The paradox of a historical "antihistory" is thus accompanied in the Acéphale texts by an ambiguity as to the position and nature of that terminal stage of antihistory. If it "regularly" follows the "decomposition of a civilization," how can it be "final" or "belong only to a future"? How can it break away definitively (and be nothing but destruction) if it is always again recomposition? Does it indeed follow the stage of reappropriated negativity or does it occur at the same time? If it follows, does it break away from or destroy that previous stage – or does it merely complete it? If on the other hand it occurs at the same time, how can it be an epoch that is radically different and "final"?

A similar uncertainty applies to the problem of myth. In the "Nietzschean Chronicle," just before "Nietzsche Dionysos," Bataille writes: "Nietzsche set aside, for good reason, the word religion which alone lends itself to a confusion almost as unfortunate as that between Nietzschean Dionysianism and fascism" (VE, 206). As long as an antimyth representing the death of God can be separated from a traditional, appropriated mythology, Bataille can argue that Nietzsche and eventually Bataille's own sect escape being a religion. The very notion of an acephalic figure, however, is the conjunction of a concept that is totally outside any anthropomorphic model ("headlessness" representing not only the death of God but also the lie of signification, grammar, authority, and any notion of the elevated "human") with what is, nevertheless, an anthropomorphic *figure* – one endowed with a human form, if not a head. One could argue that, rather than being any sort of toxicity or destruction, this mythological figure represents in fact a reinsertion of toxicity into a comprehensible human model. This contradiction – the antimythical myth – is compounded by the temporal nature in which it is framed. The "death of God" implies a prior existence of God. Was his existence then a mere fiction, now definitely discredited, or will he return? Was at least the mythical (or fictional) representation of a coherent God necessary? That representation would, in fact, be a religion, and its existence would be compatible with a "civil and military" civilization ("the reconstitution of religious elements of civil and military sovereignty"). Once this problem is introduced, the uncertainty we saw in the problem of an "antitemporality" returns as well. Will the definitively antimythical myth replace religion? If so, will that antimyth be part of a "recomposition"? Will it follow or be contemporaneous with a different type of myth? If it is contemporaneous, how will it guarantee its autonomy from the "civil and military" myth? Will it not in fact lend itself (if it is not autonomous) to reappropriation by fascism? Will another "critical phase" have to be posited later in which that myth (as "recomposition") is in turn "decomposed"? Once again we have a contradiction (antimythic myth) accompanied by uncertainties as to its social and historical execution.

Perhaps this explains the indecisiveness of the (nonpolitical) political activity undertaken by the Acéphale group.[10] How does one go about organizing a mythologically oriented sect that would nevertheless bring about a sweeping change in society? It was necessary to avoid conventional political moments – Stalinism because it leads to a new "Caesarism" (VE, 209), fascism because it represents a violent social "effervescence" that is immediately "put back to work."[11] The Acéphale group had ritual meetings in a woods outside Paris, where lightning and its penetration into the earth (symbolic of blinding light on high and its rending fall to earth) were revered.[12]

All this was an attempt to inscribe socially and temporally movements that were impossible, that radically exceeded categories such as utility and temporality. The *surhomme*, the will to power, and Dionysos, were seen as terms worth establishing in opposition to the political and social dead end of the 1930s. The problem – and the uncertainty – was to be found in their implementation. Bataille hoped that somehow the fervor of a human sacrifice performed by the Acéphale group would unleash a heterogeneous force that would cause society to erupt.[13] How that transformation was to take place was never clear; in any case, Acéphale was unable to find a victim, or a sacrificer, or both.[14]

We know that this "religious" movement breathed its last in September 1939 (OC, 6:484). When the problem surfaces again, in "Le Rire de Nietzsche" ("Nietzsche's Laugh") (OC, 6:307), a transitional text published in 1942, the *surhomme* is affirmed, but the *acéphale*, the mythic "deity" around which a sect established itself, has been dropped. The experience is now a *personal* one.[15] It involves an individual's radical ("inner") experience, and the experience of Nietzsche is posited in relation to that. The *surhomme* is less a mythical entity than it is the individual seeker, who is also the narrator. The experience – which is the writing – of the narrator (rather than society) has become the place of the *surhomme*, the point of the positing of the will to power: "What I am here and now is summonsed to be possible: what I am is impossible, and I know it: I put myself at the height of the impossible: I render the impossible possible, or at least accessible. The virtue of non-salvation is *first* to give salvation, not to make it the endpoint but the springboard of the impossible. The eternal return opens the abyss, but is the summons to leap. The abyss is the impossible and remains so but a leap introduces into the impossible the possible that it is, willed to the impossible from the first without the slightest reserve. The leap is the overman [*le surhomme*] of Zarathustra, and the will to power. The slightest cutback and the leap would not take place" (OC, 6:313).

The role of the *surhomme* is to "leap," an activity in the possible that some-how makes the "impossible" attainable. ("But if I pose the possible at the outset, really at the outset? By this I only open the way to the impossible" [oc, 6:313].) The "impossible," being beyond the human will, cannot be reached through activity. This is the province of the slave of Hegel's dialectic. Instead, a certain state can be reached *through* the volition, through purposeful activity. Then, beyond that, the abyss will open up to the overman (who is also the narrator): "First of all, I succeeded in making a great silence inside myself. That became possible just about each time I wanted it. In this silence, often dull and exhausting, I evoked all possible lacerations. Obscene, laughable, funereal representations followed one other" (oc, 6:299).[16]

The activity of the overman consists therefore of a purposeful activity, the preparation for the mystical but secular inner experience through the "leap." The leap (of disbelief, not of faith) is not the experience but only an unavoid-able preparation, which cannot bridge the abyss. The experience itself is *one individual's*, and it is at least related to certain meditative practices. Yet this meditation is not on any anthropomorphic deity, nor is it the communal and disciplined activity of the Zen monk (see Bataille's comments in *Sur Nietzsche* [oc, 6:90–91]). It is the purposeful activity of an individual who distrusts (or laughs at) organizations or sects because they impose a form, a discipline, because they make a project of the experience. On the other hand, Bataille's goal in this text is to act only to the extent that he contemplates what radically escapes purpose and coherence. As soon as the discipline of the *surhomme* becomes discipline as such, attention is diverted from obscenity and destruc-tion. It will then be led away from what will enable – or cause – this figure to explode beyond its limits, to "be" heterogeneity, expenditure, etc. Attention, in that case, is focused merely on another project, albeit a "mystical" one.

This project remains in some ways similar to the Acéphale effort, but it is also an implicit critique of it. Any sect will impose an external, goal-oriented discipline on the experience itself. The experience in "Nietzsche's Laugh" is still reached by an activity, to be sure, but the latter is a simulacrum of a disastrous, mortal, or obscene event (such as the execution of the Chinese man by dismemberment [see oc, 5:139]) that can offer no comfort or social rein-forcement. And once the social element drops away from the question of the radical experience (along with the notion of a project, a teleology), the tem-poral aspect, the interrelation of the radical experience and *time* (which is constituted by work), withers away as well. In fact we see that the final activity is not of the slave but of the springboard, whose rebound (which "causes" the leap into the impossible) is outside the time of preparation and anticipation.

In order to grasp the difference between the Acéphale position and that of "Nietzsche's Laugh," it is perhaps first necessary to understand Bataille's use of the word "impossible" in that essay. In "The Summit and the Decline" (the second part of *Sur Nietzsche*), the problem of the "radical experience" is retained. In *Sur Nietzsche*, as we will see shortly, the notion of constructive effort is criticized even more systematically than in "Nietzsche's Laugh." It is worth noting in the following quote from *Sur Nietzsche* how the terms "impossible" and "inaccessible" are used:

> Like Kafka's castle, the summit in the end is only the inaccessible. It escapes from us, at least in that we continue to be human, to speak.
>
> The summit is not "what must be attained," the decline "what must be suppressed."
>
> Just as the summit is only, in the end, inaccessible, the decline, from the beginning, is inevitable. . . .
>
> The summit in essence is the place where life is impossible to the limit. (oc, 6:57)

The summit here represents the kind of experience Bataille was attempting to reach in "Nietzsche's Laugh." Working for the summit causes it to elude one's grasp. At the same time the very act of grasping is human. To attain it, then, we must cease to be thinking, speaking human beings. But if we are not human, then what are we?

Two alternatives to the human in Bataille are the animal and the dead. Neither simple animality nor simple death, however, are what Bataille means here by "the summit." One is at the same time human, consciously acting and still recognizing interdictions, *and* not human (not a speaking, acting, conscious subject). One is somehow human and dead (or human and an animal, like Bataille's erotic subjects) at the same "instant." This experience is "impossible" according to a logic that forbids contradiction, and from that point of view, it is "inaccessible."

If the summit were simply inaccessible, if it definitively could not be experienced, Bataille would not be justified in writing about it. The important point comes, in fact, when he admits that the "inaccessible" is accessible, the impossible is possible: "I only attain [the summit], to the very feeble extent that I do attain it, in spending my forces without counting" (oc, 6:57–58).

The contradiction between human and nonhuman, between thought and animality, is the impossible, which must somehow be experienced and which for this reason must be possible. "What I am here and now is the totality of the possible. What I am is impossible. . . . I put myself at the height of the impossible" (oc, 6:313). This is a second-order possible, however, in that it indicates a reaching of the impossible not through work – the slave's labor – but through some process that succeeds in escaping work. Only to the extent that it escapes the possible of labor, language, and finally the civil/military and religious state, does the impossible become *possible*.

Where does this leave the Acéphale position? The very stress that Bataille places on the possibility of the impossible in "Nietzsche's Laugh" indicates a problem in the earlier Acéphale version of Nietzsche. We saw that there was a contradiction in those earlier positions – one that might be associable with a certain kind of impossibility. A temporality outside of time and an antimythic myth are, in fact, identical to the nonhuman human experience put forward in "Nietzsche's Laugh." The problem lies not in resolving these contradictions, of appropriating their negativity – but rather in exacerbating them. How can one affirm the negativity of the impossible relation – how can that negativity be torn from an abstract, uncertain manifestation, and its concrete, *possible* manifestation be seen (without at the same time denying its impossible status)? In this light, the Acéphale positions had to be left behind for the simple reason that the implementation (the possibility) of their impossibility was uncertain – it remained largely theoretical. It could not be experienced for the evident reason that Bataille himself could not determine how the coercive totalizing nature of a social entity (be it communism, fascism, democracy, or any theocracy ever created) could at the same time embody a "toxicity" and an "empty" "destruction." His only model was eventually a regressive one: the return to the destructive rituals and human sacrifice of "primitive" cultures. Yet there was no mechanism for preventing the inevitable appropriation of violence that took place in those cultures, nor were there ways, in Bataille's project, of applying a "primitive" model to "modern" society. Bataille, in other words, could no longer see the simple inversion of Durkheim – the affirmation of an irrational secular sacred and of sacrifice as the death of "man" and of the disciplined and disciplinary collectivity – as offering a viable alternative to a Durkheimian version of democratic humanism. Finally, incapable of projecting a concrete social manifestation of radical negativity on a social plane, and uncertain of guaranteeing it (and indeed uncertain whether a guarantee of the permanence of the experience was necessary or not), Bataille replaced the social model with a personal one. An idealized, empty impossibility, "minor" to the extent that it was immediately appropriable by fascism or official religion (its negativity risking the destruction of nothing) was succeeded by an – at least provisionally – "major" impossibility, whose negative force could actually be experienced, if only alone in one's room.

1939, 1942: a crisis occurs in Bataille's Nietzsche. We saw in Bataille's pre-1939 Nietzsche some remnant of constructive temporality opposed to abyss (eternal return), rite and myth opposed to the absence of God. Now the tables are turned: the sect has been disbanded, the experience itself transpires in a time that is not the simple result of a project but is its unplanned and instantaneous offshoot. The end is only a springboard, perhaps leading to something that eludes the control of the subject and that then acts on and against him. The impossible becomes possible only to the extent that the possible plays its part (and is thus retained) and then falls away, is forgotten, leaving only the impossible. On the rebound, the springboard catapults the subject somewhere else, outside of subjectivity. The violence of this act is independent of human volition and signification.

But to what extent is the invocation of Nietzsche in this context justified? Can a rereading of Nietzsche justify a movement from a collective model to a personal one? And to what extent is contemplation (even if it is of *horror*) still an activity? Is the impossible in fact still only a function – a product – of the possible?

II

A brief consideration of a few of Nietzsche's texts themselves, specifically those dealing with the social implementation of the overman (*Übermensch, sur-homme*) might be useful at this point. It is pertinent to recall here that the Acéphale group saw as a major aim the refutation of the Fascist reading of Nietzsche and the denial of Fascist ideology as a continuation of Nietzsche's thought.[17] We recall also the refusal of Acéphale to take part in the politics of compromise (or just plain "politics," which was seen as a synonym). Nietzsche himself, however (in his own text) was forced to posit a social – if not political – version of the overman. Although space does not permit an in-depth study of Nietzsche here, we might point to a few of his texts in which a certain problem appears. For example: "There is a need to prove the importance of a countermovement to an ever more economical expenditure of human existence, and to an ever more narrowly confined machinery of interests and realizations. I designate this a countermovement insofar as it is a discharge [*Ausscheidung*] of a luxurious excess [*Luxus-Überschuss*] of humanity; in it a stronger, more elevated type must step into the light. This type must have other conditions of formulation and conservation than the average man. My concept, my metaphor [*Gleichnis*] for this type is, as is known, the overman."[18]

In opposition to the settling of accounts and the equalization by the man of interests and *ressentiment*, the overman is capable of affirming himself in relation to luxury and waste (excess). Bataille at certain points (in "The Old Mole" and in the texts of Contre-Attaque) reversed this Nietzschean devalorization of the slave. In those texts, the proletariat or the mob (the distinction is somewhat blurred) was portrayed not as a force of conservation, production, and peaceful socialization (Hegel's slave) or as one of revenge (Nietzsche's) but, rather, as an embodiment of sheer waste and destruction. The mob decapitates the king, but not out of revenge. In this act of destruction or discharge in which the embodiment of excess – the king – is himself wasted, prevented from becoming homogeneous, the revolutionary mob is seen to be closer to a Nietzschean "sacrifice of the notion of God itself" than is a Nietzschean social elite that would inevitably become a tool of the homogenizing bourgeoisie. Realizing, however, that simple mob negativity was not clearly separable from fascism (see OC, 7:461: "If one wants to understand what was true [in Contre-Attaque], in spite of the radically contrary intention of this paradoxical Fascist tendency, one must read *The Red Carnation* by Elio Vittorini"), Contre-Attaque disintegrated in 1936. Acéphale, founded later that year, sought to avoid *that* trap of fascism and embraced a more straightforwardly Nietzschean version of heterogeneous social forces. The only problem was that following the Nietzschean text more closely led to certain other problems. The *surhomme*, seen on a social level (as a social force) separated from an incarnation as the proletariat, tends to rise to the status of a figure for the privileged elite.

To continue our consideration of this passage of Nietzsche: "In the era of this diminution and adaptation of human beings to a specialized utility, there is a need for an inverse movement, the creation of a human being who synthesizes, totalizes, and justifies, for whom this mechanization of humanity constitutes an understood, agreed-upon being. This being can be used as a base [*Untergestell*] on which he can invent his higher form of being. He especially needs the rivalry between the masses of the 'equalized' and the feeling of distance in relation to them: he stands on them, he lives off them. This superior form of aristocratism is that of the future" (F, 150).

The "higher form of being" in its social and temporal manifestation, the overman, is possible only through the support of the "mechanization of humanity." The overman, however, "synthesizes, totalizes, and justifies." His reign, while not stopping technologized utility, the inevitable leveling of the slave and the bourgeois, nevertheless gives it a new purpose and grandeur; utility is now tied to the "excess of force" that justifies humanity and gives it its meaning:

> There is the need to dig a trench, the need for distance, for hierarchy. . . .
> This equalized species, as soon as it is realized, will need a justification: this lies in serving a higher, sovereign kind which stands upon the equalized ones; only if it is based on those can it raise itself to its task [*Aufgabe*].
> Not only a race of masters whose task will be completed with governing, but a race having its own sphere of life, with an excess of force for beauty, courage and culture . . . it is an affirmative race which can accord itself every great luxury. (F, 105)

In order for there to be waste there has to be accumulation and work; the instant of rupturing (transgression, heterogeneity) requires a moment, a stage, a sense of coherence (interdiction, homogeneity) that is ruptured. The problem is this: what form will the future have? What form is the interdiction to take? And the transgression?

Although the latter terms are foreign to Nietzsche's text (they come instead from the Nietzschean anthropology that Bataille derived from Durkheim and Mauss), a problem still appears. In the texts we have cited, the work of the slave continues to be seen as a necessary moment. The mastery of that moment is radically different. Unlike the bourgeois who can offer no meaning for the process of work, the overman affirms life (and therefore "justifies" and "totalizes" it) rather than worrying about its waste or expenditure. The rationalization for the mechanization of life has therefore passed from an ideology whose main concern is governing to another ideology (or "sphere of life"), which gives it a more affirmative meaning – but at the same time that mechanization (the fully rationalized moment) itself has not changed. We are not at this point criticizing Nietzsche for not taking up the task of changing it. Why should he? If he were to change it, he would become involved in the settling of accounts, the overman himself would be caught up in a task – and in so doing he would lose sight of the affirmative life of luxurious excess that constitutes his higher form of being. By not questioning the form that that mechanization takes, however, the overman does not radically change life. He does not question the rationalized forms he has inherited from his predecessor. He is therefore a continuation of his predecessor's rule. In isolating himself from the realm of production and rationalization, the overman has created an exclusively abstract realm that cannot be tainted by considerations such as what form the moment of sense or mechanization (or interdiction, recuperation, etc.) should take.

This argument begins to look familiar: it is Bataille's critique of the eagle, the surrealists, in "The Old Mole," and his critique of the Fascists in "The Psychological Structure of Fascism."[19] In those writings, however, the homogeneous world of the workers (as Nietzsche would have it) was not considered as such, but rather as a heterogeneity in relation to the formerly heterogeneous but now fully homogeneous masters. The nobles, the leaders, the surrealists, initially heterogeneous in their escape or separation from the day-to-day world of production and use, simply establish a new realm that is homogeneous within itself – a transgression which cannot be transgressed and which thus becomes interdiction (in a similar context, Bataille writes of the necessity of "transcending transcendence" [oc, 6:173]). Indeed, "The Old Mole" contained one of the few disparaging references to Nietzsche in Bataille (ve, 39). (The article draws correspondences between the *surhomme* and the idealist surrealists, and the association of Nietzsche with both positions.) But the consequences of "The Old Mole" can be seen in the positions of the Contre-Attaque group, in the affirmation of sheer revolutionary (mob) negativity. The violence of "Contre-Attaque in the street" was established entirely against forms of rational compromise, with the perhaps inevitable result that that violence was eventually seen – both by Bataille and by his opponents – as "paradoxically" related to fascism. And Acéphale, too, as we have seen, ran the risk of fascism.

It seems that we are caught in a vicious circle from Acéphale to Contre-Attaque and back. But there might be a way out. This would be to consider the moment of rationalization as heterogeneous in relation to the hierarchical overman, but that heterogeneity could remain so only if, paradoxically, it interrogated its rationalized status. Once it shuns (as does Nietzsche) that rationalization, it is removed from the threat of identification with that rationalization (or work, social formation, and so on) – but only at the risk of itself becoming a "paradoxical fascism," a fully homogenized heterogeneity. The status of the rationalizing sphere must itself be rationalized and criticized, then, in light of its relation to the "sovereign kind." By this I mean that a heterogeneous activity can be precisely the investigation of the other, homogeneous, side (or part). The forms of that side are not neutral and their reformation and destruction is a function of a radical heterogeneity that develops itself through a self-critical, dialectical process. If we admit a gulf separating these two realms, we must nevertheless posit their manner of interaction and mutual transgression. That development through transgression (and the critique of the specific forms of the homogeneous) will become clear when we examine, in the next section, the transition from "Nietzsche's Laugh" (1942) to *Sur Nietzsche* (1944).

It might be objected that Nietzsche himself ironizes or deconstructs the overman. Bataille was fond of what has been called the "laughing Nietzsche": "Neither say yes nor no to reality, unless it is only from time to time, in order to tap it with your toes, like a good dancer . . . stick a comic tail onto the most sacred things."[20]

If Nietzsche ironizes his own status as a philosopher (or even as overman) (as in *Ecce Homo*, "Why I am a Fatality": "I require no 'believers'; in my opinion I am too full of value to believe even in myself and I never address myself to the masses. I am horribly frightened that one day I will be canonized"), he can only ironize (or "waste" in a kind of intellectual potlatch) what he has already established as the truth. That is, he can risk only the stable model of a social order in which those who affirm life, who reject the "decline" of the morality of the slave, will be separated in a hierarchy from the "masses." (*Ecce Homo* also contains the vision of a political prophet whose works will inspire a war that establishes an era of the overman: "The concept of politics will then be elevated entirely into the realm of spiritual warfare. . . . Only from my time will politics on a large scale exist on earth.")[21]

At this point, the analysis of the problem of the "homogeneous part" shifts – as it did in "The Old Mole" – from the rationalized life of workers to the idealized realm of the overman itself. We can perceive now in Nietzsche (at this level of the analysis), not the overman radically going beyond the realm of the "masses" – the opposition of heterogeneous luxury to homogeneous work – but instead the opposition of heterogeneous irony to the homogeneous but necessarily ironized doctrine of the overman. The question now is, by what criteria is this homogeneous moment to be established? ("what possible can be introduced into the impossible?" [OC, 6:310]). Even if it *is* ironized, what are the criteria for judging the acceptability of a given homogeneous "part" that enters into relation with a heterogeneous "part"? All versions of the homogeneous are, after all, not identical; Bataille himself recognized this even before the war when, for example, he favored democratic over Fascist regimes.[22] Nietzsche can laugh at himself, but how can we make any determinations of the acceptability, not of the laughter or ironization (or deconstruction, which fulfills the same function) itself, which we affirm, but of what he is laughing at *within his text*?[23] Put another way, how does one determine which philosophy, which dialectic, is to be deconstructed? Is there a dialectic of dialectics to be (or that always already are) deconstructed? How does one "move" from dialectic to dialectic (if only within a vicious circle)? Where does a Nietzschean history stand within the history of deconstructed histories? And Hegel? And Bataille?

III

We have already seen Bataille's dilemmas in first positing a purely destructive proletariat overman (in Contre-Attaque), and, in recognizing the limits of that, being forced to develop a more conventionally mythological Nietzsche (in Acéphale) that would go beyond both a political (leftist) dead end and a co-optation by a Fascist "Nietzsche." This latter Bataillean Nietzsche reaffirmed "sect" (as opposed to "mob"), reaffirmed "myth" and "rites" (but not "religion"), which would be opposed to a somehow "effective" political action. To be merely political was to "compromise." Although Acéphale as well saw its acts as a turning point of history, they were not seen in a political sense – they were not associated with class struggle. Contradictory relations therefore appeared between "myths" and elements that destabilized or escaped myth, and between "time" (associated with the constructive development of history) and a "future" in which a radical break with history would appear. The "impossible" relations that characterized Bataille's position on Nietzsche in the late 1930s are associable with community, its formation and social change. At a certain point (after 1939) he dropped them: the mythical *surhomme* and his community were no longer an acceptable manifestation of a homogeneous moment that impossibly conveyed its own undermining.

I posed, at the end of the last section, a question concerning the criteria for determining acceptable homogeneous "sides" in oppositions of this type. Bataille, when he again wrote on Nietzsche after the beginning of the war ("Nietzsche's Laugh"), dropped the social, mythic, and temporal aspects of Nietzsche. We inferred that he did so because a simple homogeneity (or abstract impossible) always devolved out of the posited heterogeneity. Nietzsche, by 1942, had become, then, an exclusively "internal" component of Bataille's project, outside of the social, temporal, or mythical moments in which he would inevitably play a stabilizing role. In that transitional text of 1942, there was still a certain clinging to terms associated with the Acéphale mythology, such as *surhomme* and "will to power," but by then the only possible act was an individual contemplation of horror that would, in turn, and without the subject's effort, lead him or her out of any planned action or individuality. Horror itself was still a function of a goal-oriented "contemplation." Nietzsche, in "Nietzsche's Laugh," was the manifestation of a useful activity and still embodied a possible in relation to an impossible. Nietzsche at that point was not entirely heterogeneous: he was an instance of homogeneity, rather than being the most general force of heterogeneity or (major) impossibility. Nietzsche (in Bataille) after 1942 breaks away from his moorings in possibility (the contemplation of horror) because they indicated a point where the laughing Nietzsche had to take himself seriously. Giving this form (of effort, of "method of meditation") to Nietzsche would simply make him another possibility.

The final transformation in Bataille's Nietzsche occurs in 1944–45 with the writing and publication of *Sur Nietzsche*. The reason for the collapse of the Acéphale group can be seen clearly in Bataille's approach to Nietzsche in *Sur Nietzsche*. Through *Sur Nietzsche* we can understand the criteria for evaluating the homogeneous "part" in a text (such as Nietzsche's, or Bataille's) that thematizes or represents heterogeneity.

The "solution" is quite simply to strip Nietzsche of the homogeneous part that haunted Bataille throughout the 1930s and into the 1940s. We read in *Sur Nietzsche*:

> The weakness of Nietzsche: he criticizes in the name of *moving* values whose origin and end – evidently – he could not grasp.
>
> To grasp an isolated possibility, having a particular end, which is only for itself an end, isn't this in the end to risk oneself?
>
> It might be that the interest of the operation is in the risk, not in the chosen end.
>
> The narrow end is lacking? Risk will nonetheless order one's values.
>
> The overman or Borgia sides are limited, vainly defined, in the face of possibles having their essence in the going beyond of oneself.

(*This takes nothing from the upheaval, the great wind, upsetting all the old satisfactions.*) (OC, 6:119–20; emphasis added)

A full reversal from Acéphale has taken place: it is now the overman who is subject to criticism. The experience of "excess" entails going beyond oneself and beyond the limits of oneself. If, for example, sexual experience is the rupture of the limited being that constitutes the self, the formulation of a limited, adialectical "being" that is an end in itself, then any attempt at fixing the self's stable identity (as in the case of the overman) will miscarry.

In *Sur Nietzsche*, above all, Bataille seeks to avoid defining or limiting the nature of this experience. The very project of the *Summa atheologica* is the embodiment of this distrust of formulation, of limiting the text itself to a single mythology or to an internal or external teleology ("Working badly, in disorder, is the only way, often, of not becoming a function" [OC, 6:154]). It was the writing of the first part of *Guilty* (the first book written of the *Summa*) that led Bataille away from the goal of starting a religion (which he could no longer differentiate, to his own satisfaction, from a sect), or away from a coherent mythology and community – away, in short, from a *project*.[24]

What replaces the overman? (Or, put another way, how can the overman be left empty, while the experience of impossibility remains a possibility, or at least more than an empty impossibility?) We recall that, earlier, the *acéphale* (the mythical personage, who was associated with the *surhomme*, Dionysos, and Nietzsche) was seen as an embodiment of the "death of God." Within the "death of God" there must still be a moment of God. A limit – the existence of God – had still to be posited, in order to be transgressed. That violation must somehow be incessant (but not "permanent" or "stable"), since once God was "definitively" transgressed, a new "proof" – of his death – would merely replace him. Already before 1939, Bataille, in "The Labyrinth" (VE, 171–77; written 1935–36), presented a Christ in the moment of death: "The universal God destroys rather than supports the human aggregates that raise his ghost. He himself is only dead, whether a mythic delirium set him up to be adored as a cadaver covered with wounds, or whether through his very universality he becomes, more than any other, incapable of stopping the loss of being with the cracked partitions of ipseity" (VE, 175).

Christ is stripped of the accretions of morality and knowledge – the aspects of Christianity that Nietzsche criticizes in the *Genealogy of Morals*. All that remains is a "universal" dying God. The essence, then, of Christianity is seen not as redemption or as eternal life but as a universalized death and destruction. This is the kernel of Christ, so to speak, anterior to his "reversal" and elevation as the source of all interdiction. At the same time, Christ as nothing but a bloody cadaver is still "universal." This implies an advance over the "primitive" religions that Bataille presented via Mauss and Caillois. Those religions, as we see in "The Notion of Expenditure," were limited by the fact that they were dependent on a given local area's version of "potlatch" (ritual waste and destruction) (see VE, 120–23). The chief could be intensely hated for his abuses of potlatch by the "miserable" natives, who are impoverished by his waste. To that extent, the greedy and jealous nature of the secular or religious leaders was just as pronounced as the jealousy (the homogenizing tendency, the selfishness and hypocrisy concerning waste) of the bourgeoisie – only the primitive chief was more open about his waste. Just as in the case of the bourgeois, then, the chief could misunderstand the process he was acting out; he could see it as nothing more than an aid to his power. Potlatch was still a localized, piecemeal, individualized operation, not universally seen as a total waste. The advantage of Christ as a sacrificial victim, then, is that he is "universal" not in "saving" people but rather in that he *is* waste – permanent, absolute waste for all, a waste that is definitive and eternal (to the same extent that the "eternal return" was "final"). Christ's death is not limited by specific events of a single ritual or sacrificial (destructive) event. Christ disrupts social forms and does not solidify them; he is the embodiment of potlatch *in general*. In that sense he separates heterogeneity from primitive rituals and from the possible homogenization that would accompany their diversity. Christ is "a monster lightly taking on many crimes" (VE, 177) but *not* a monster redeeming them. Unfortunately, like the "primitive" practitioners of potlatch, Christ, on assuming his purely heterogeneous position, was immediately transformed into a homogeneous force. This homogenization is the church and organized "religion."

Christ therefore represents a progress over the earlier religions. His transgression takes fragmented versions of sacrifice and potlatch, which could easily be misrepresented as having to do with personal power and gain, and transforms them into a universal. But in the act of enforcing the universality of Christ's sacrifice, Christianity makes it more abstract and therefore easily appropriable. Christianity "forgets" sacrifice's true nature, just as the chief forgets that of the potlatch over which he presides.

How to combat this process of the institution of homogeneity in place of the instance of the heterogeneous? The answer in *Sur Nietzsche* is the confrontation of Christianity with Nietzsche. Bataille quotes Nietzsche:

And moreover we want to be the inheritors of Christian meditation and penetration.

. . . to go beyond all Christianity by way of *hyperChristianity*, and not to be content with merely undoing it.

We are no longer Christian, we have gone beyond Christianity, not because we have lived too far from it, but too close, and above all

278

because we have come out of Christianity; our simultaneously more severe and more delicate piety today forbids us from still being Christian.[25]

Nietzsche is the splitting or tearing apart of Christ. He is "hyperChristian," even *more* Christian than the Christians who merely participate in a morality of *ressentiment* and salvation. "Christ" or "God" is only a destabilizing force that breaks open any coherent or rationalized social, political, or productive (philosophical) system: "God tearing apart the night of the universe with a cry [the *Eloi! lama sabachtani?* of Jesus] – isn't this a summit of malice? God himself, addressing himself to God, cries 'why have you abandoned me?' In other words, 'why have I abandoned myself?' Or more precisely: 'What is going on? Have I forgotten myself to the point where I am risking myself?'" (oc, 6: 151).

Nietzsche goes beyond an elimination of the state of doubt on the part of Christ. Christ's followers somehow forget his doubt – and he is reappropriated within a homogeneous temporal and social order, within an absolute knowledge. Nietzsche splits the worshiped Christ and becomes more like Christ – hyperChrist – to the extent that Nietzsche remembers himself, remembers forgetting or doubt, does not allow himself to be reappropriated the way Christ was.

But Nietzsche, in the very act of remembering, of guarding himself from being reappropriated as Christ was (in avoiding a morality of the slave or producer), sets himself up as an alternative Christ, establishes a new kind of formalized knowledge on the basis of the necessity of that remembering, of that self-reflexivity. Nietzsche is then appropriable (in one way or another) by the Fascists – as the Bataille of Contre-Attaque and Acéphale became aware. This is a Nietzsche who takes himself seriously. Nietzsche thus had to be split, just as Christ was. In the preface to *Mémorandum*, a collection of Nietzsche quotes compiled by Bataille at about the same time as *Sur Nietzsche* was written, Bataille states: "The distance of sovereign men from the masses can – and in my opinion *must* – have nothing in common with political differences separating classes during the feudal epoch. Moral liberty wins (it wins in liberty) in self-effacement, in lightening, in profound immanence. This goes against Nietzsche's insistence and the useless worry he had about new political authorities" (oc, 6:251).

Bataille, who often stated that there was no "possibility" of his being an "original" philosopher ("nothing is more foreign to me than a personal mode of thought") and that he had nothing to "add" to Nietzsche, in fact takes something away from him.[26] He suppresses Nietzsche's suppression of luck (or the forgetting of Nietzsche's forgetting). In emphasizing force, Nietzsche is still emphasizing a unitary power: the willful establishment, high on the hierarchy, of the overman, to the exclusion of others. Bataille states in a post-humous note of *Sur Nietzsche*: "The limit of Nietzsche: assigning a form to luck: it is necessary to gamble: and to accentuate the part of the future – exaggeration of 'passéism' – it is impossible to predict in advance the forms of sovereignty" (OC, 6:425).

This passage contains a condemnation of a dialectic that would attempt to predict a future and posit a human will – a will to power; Bataille, rewriting Nietzsche, subtitles *Sur Nietzsche Volonté de chance* (will to luck) and therefore posits a will that is outside the sphere of human activity – a will that is not "human" but simply an instance of chance, an activity that cannot be used to form. Luck usurps power's power: redefining will as chance, the earlier spring-board of "Nietzsche's Laugh" is implicitly criticized, since the leap there was still linked to an *activity* – even though the latter was a simulacrum of pure chance. Here simulacra or forms are not enough: it is chance itself that is at stake.

Bataille splits Nietzsche apart and plays him against himself, as Nietzsche did Christ. *Why* one side of Nietzsche is so firmly tied to a reactionary history is of little interest to Bataille. In the notes to *Sur Nietzsche* he states: "many contemptuous thoughts have a meaning in relation to the poverty of 1880" (OC, 6:425). Bataille must be to Nietzsche what Nietzsche was to Christ. Nietzsche broadens (universalizes) the death of God (Christ's death) into a death of *all* totalities (morality, philosophy, etc.). Bataille broadens the death of all totalities into a death of Nietzsche. Bataille must be "hyperNietzsche" or *Sur Nietzsche* (or *surnietzsche*). He must strip away the last retrograde totalities that Nietzsche affirms. Nietzsche then becomes sheer death, rupture, or chance in which any positive "side" is removed from the "impossible" relation "inter-diction/transgression."

Bataille is the culmination of a "historical" process that goes from primitive cultures through Christianity and then through Nietzsche. Each stage is an advance over the earlier – a preserving (of the element of loss, of hetero-geneity) and a negation (of each succeeding form, which in the end falls back into homogeneity). Nietzsche (stripped of his aristocratic side) for Bataille by 1944 is, then, an exclusively heterogeneous moment, refusing compromise with any established order, never dealing with any philosophy before laughing at it twice, sacrificing the very notion of God itself.

"Bataille," going beyond Nietzsche, is the expression of this total rejection of a rationalized, dialectical, homogeneous moment. *Sur Nietzsche* embodies this rejection in its contingent writing. At the same time, however, this *develop-ment* or progression in heterogeneous moments implies a certain temporality. Each "sacred" moment is a progression over the last.[27] Each stripping of a new phase in the series (potlatch, Christ, Nietzsche, Bataille) presents a new configuration in unity with a heterogeneity that in turn must be stripped on a higher level. "Stripped" in the sense of stripping clothes *and* skin – for the rupture of limits through eroticism and violence is central to Bataille's notion of the sacred. What is stripped always remains essentially the same – heterogeneity *à l'état pur* with no affiliation with any homogeneous form. If this is a dialectic, it is a stripped dialectic; the endpoint is not the effacement of some negativity and its "sublation" in a positivity (in which the negativity is given its meaning and in which its action of negation ceases) but, rather, a telos from which the positive (stable social, cultural) forms have been removed and all that remains is negativity in its raw formlessness. This impossible endpoint and relentless negativity, strangely, is made possible by a self-reflexivity – by the *awareness* that the previous forms of heterogeneity had somehow been compromised. "Bataille," the endpoint of this development (the guarantor of this purity, turning it back on Nietzsche himself), is the "awareness" of the "compromise" of Nietzsche. But any awareness on Bataille's part will itself be a compromise, a betrayal of the integrity of the Bataillean Nietzsche's radical negativity.

For that reason, we must establish two separate moments within Bataille: Bataille's Nietzsche and Bataille as *surnietzsche*. Bataille's Nietzsche is the flayed version of Nietzsche, freed from his political anachronisms; Bataille as *surnietzsche* is the author of the autobiographical journal in which that flaying takes place. Bataille is the text that posits the relations of the series that extends from potlatch to *surnietzsche*, but which does so *problematically*. In other words, we can deduce the final moment of this dialectic, but at no point does Bataille directly state – or become clearly, self-reflexively aware of – his own position in that dialectic. "Nietzsche," then, in Bataille is a radical self-forgetting, a loss; "Bataille" is the agent of that loss, just as Nietzsche is the agent of the "loss" to Christianity, the remembering of the definitively unrecuperable loss. At the same time, though, Bataille is problematically an awareness or remembering of that loss, its positioning at the end of a temporal chain.[28] "Bataille" is a radical break at the end of history ("history" being here the history of forms of rejection of previous homogeneity – heterogeneity freeing itself from any ties to homogeneity), affirming loss or expenditure and beyond any homogeneous manifestation. But since Bataille is both the narrator and *surnietzsche*, eccentric to the pure negativity of "Nietzsche," there will always be a traitorous minor dialectic; this development cannot be kept out of the text that is Bataille (since *Sur Nietzsche* is a kind of empty autobiography, an oblique chronicle of Bataille's experience in occupied France). This dialectic – or development of forms of heterogeneity to its final, most radical state – is glossed over, *forgotten*, by the state of Nietzsche, the intensification of that state that Bataille effects. This state is "major" – in the sense that it (problematically) forgets or ignores (as the "masters" in Nietzsche have "forgotten" the *ressentiment* of the slave – hence its *major* aspect) the problem of that development, and its status as endpoint. The dialectic is minor, since it is a stripped teleology already, culminating not in any knowledge but in simple squandering. This stripped-down dialectic – which corresponds to the purely textual *community* Nietzsche/Bataille ("my book is this community" [oc, 6:33]) – though minor, nevertheless disrupts the purity of the heterogeneity that was for Bataille "Nietzsche."[29] That minor disruption, and major affirmation, are what can go under the name "Bataille."

Bataille's Nietzsche (and its minor dialectic) is not, however, the only side of Bataille's oeuvre.[30] Another one, a different kind of reflection between a dialectic and forgetting, that of Hegel/Marx, is associable in the post-1939 writings with the progressive social dialectic of the three-volume *Accursed Share* (1949–54). (It is important to stress that, although *The Accursed Share* was written after the war, the project itself was started in 1941 – under the title "La Limite de l'utile" [The limit of the useful]. Thus it is contemporaneous with the *Summa atheologica*.) While "Nietzsche" is first cut down to a relentless negativity, then reinscribed as "Bataille" and "acquires" another (minor) dialectic, another side of Bataille is also evident. This is the "Hegelian" and "Marxist" side which goes beyond and parodies Hegel and Marx. It entails a major historical dialectic, but also a minor "active forgetting." Bataille *is* Hegel/Marx.

These two sides of Bataille – Nietzsche and Hegel/Marx – do not result in a higher textual synthesis (or do so problematically, perhaps only here, in my own writing). In fact, they constantly risk and transgress each other, each denounces the lie of the other.[31] Yet at the same time each is contaminated by the other, each contains a residue of the other. Already in *Sur Nietzsche* Bataille poses the necessity of a project such as that of *The Accursed Share* while refusing to carry it out. He recognizes, in advance, the alteration that the *The Accursed Share* project would work on the *Summa atheologica*, precisely by externalizing it: "Insidiously, I have wanted to show what external significance my question could take. I must, it is true, recognize that situated in this way – on the plan of economic calculations – the question loses in acuity what it gains in completeness. It is, in fact, altered" (oc, 6:60).[32]

Free of any positivity, "Nietzsche" in Bataille becomes a philosophically coherent radical negativity that can enter into relation with and defy any positivity that the text can present to it, rendering that positivity, and the text itself, incoherent. It will not, however, mistake a homogeneous simulacrum of itself for the heterogeneity of its own process – except, of course, when it takes its own heterogeneity to be somehow untainted by a mere homogeneous simulacrum.

11

Hegel's Return

I

HEGEL in Bataille's text must be seen in the larger context of French Hegelianism of the 1930s: the reading of Hegel – and above all the reading of the master/slave dialectic – is carried out by Bataille, following Kojève (the Kojève of the *Introduction to the Reading of Hegel*), from an "anthropological" point of view. In order to read and rewrite Hegel, Bataille takes up again a number of fundamental Hegelian themes – labor, production, slavery, expenditure, the end of history, absolute knowing, "not knowing" (*le non-savoir*), and reinscribes them in another text, a text that is not blind to the importance of questions that Hegel could not *see*.

First we should consider "The Notion of Expenditure," first published in 1933.[1] In it, Hegel is not mentioned, but we can note the constellation of terms that are taken from the master/slave dialectic: mastery, slavery, the thing (that is, the product), freedom, and, above all, *death*. Bataille's "master" (the chief) does not produce, but he "consumes" products – through potlatch, the rite studied by Mauss in his *Essay on the Gift*. Products, even those made by slaves (or the poor) are not *destroyed* by them. Unlike Hegel's slave, Bataille's slave does not gain mastery through the production of things; for Bataille it is the act of production – sad but necessary – that is the very indicator of slavery. In this *overturning* of Hegel, social power is associated exclusively with destruction. For the first time, but not for the last, Bataille mimes Hegel in the very act of overturning him: he valorizes what Hegel rejects. The mastery associated with a fiery consumption is more fundamental than the production of life's necessities.

The result, however, is not the simple affirmation of exploitation and slavery demanded by the master. The master, according to Bataille (following Mauss) establishes his power, which depends on the quantity of products that he is able to destroy. (The poor man, possessing nothing, is powerless: he can destroy nothing. Sometimes he is even the possession, the slave, and it is he that is destroyed: Bataille notes the "slaughter of slaves" among the rites of potlatch.) But the master is blind; he does not see the importance and the consequences of his destruction.

The consciousness represented by the point of view of Bataille – a parody of Hegelian reason – sees the blindness of the master. But for Bataille the "liberation" of the slave is associated not with his work but with his own destructive acts. The dialectical *Aufhebung* has it that the slave gains his mastery, such as it is, *as* a laborer (as laborer he alone masters negativity), whereas the "nonlogical difference" valorized by Bataille, at the end of "The Notion of Expenditure," implies the slave's mastery through the liberation of raw destruction. That is the class struggle: the slave becomes master when, fully conscious, he can destroy and derive an ecstatic pleasure from his destructive acts; he destroys the masters – in other words the bourgeoisie – in a social potlatch, the revolution. Class consciousness for Bataille is the (slave's) consciousness of the social and even physical necessity of destruction: all the different types of expenditure – cultural (games, rituals), social (wars, revolutions), and sexual (orgies, perversions), will be, in the future, the work of slaves, that is, of the proletariat.

Implicit in "The Notion of Expenditure" is the idea of an "absolute knowing" and of the end of history. After the recognition of expenditure, and after the revolution, man will be conscious of his most fundamental urges – and then, at that point, nothing fundamentally new can ever take place. But perhaps the exclusion of the problem of the end of history at the end of "The Notion of Expenditure" reveals a difficulty in that essay: how will this Bataillean endstate be different from the other end of history, that of Hegel? By recognizing this radical negativity, it would seem that Bataille risks the simple recuperation of expenditure. What, in fact, is the relation between the Hegelian end of history and the future foreseen by Bataille? Can there be an absolute knowing of expenditure? What will be the utopian existence of man *after* the revolution predicted by Bataille?

One can find a proposed solution to this problem in the letter to Kojève written by Bataille in 1937.[2] Bataille puts forward there, in fact, two negativities: one would be linked to Hegelian action ("doing") – in other words, useful activity – the other would follow the end of Hegelian-Marxian history and would be an "unemployed negativity." Thus there would be a Hegelian end of history, followed by an after-end, a supplement to the end.

But the utopian question reemerges: what would this after-end be? Bataille finds the answer to this question in his own person: "[I am] precisely this 'unemployed negativity' (I couldn't define myself with more clarity)" (L, 123). This second kind of negativity requires, moreover, another type of consciousness. This recognition of negativity has a paradoxical status: it has nothing to do with artistic productions because in art negativity is simply "made objective." Now the objectification of art – its reification, if you like – is the opposite of this movement of sheer negativity that strips art of its significance and usefulness. Another possibility is religion but, as we know, religion always results in a simple "putting to work" of negativity: the sacred becomes a function of the state, of a Christian "Good," and so on. In both art and religion, therefore, negativity "is not 'recognized' *as such*" (L, 124).

Where, then, is negativity, unadulterated by art or religion, recognized as such? Only, it seems, in the person incarnating it, Bataille himself. But because this negativity is "unemployed," its incarnation is absolutely and radically insignificant, an "abortion"; if the person of Hegel incarnates the truth of his system, Bataille, on the other hand, is, finally, *nothing*; like the rent at the summit of existence, Bataille the superfluous *is* the negativity that is "void of content." This negativity is not even sin. And, at the end of the letter to Kojève, Bataille is not optimistic. He can do nothing, for it is impossible to propound a doctrine of sheer, empty negativity. "He [i.e., Bataille] confronts his own negativity as if it's a wall. However uneasy he feels about this, he knows that after this nothing can be ruled out, since negativity has no more outlet" (L, 125).

Absolute knowing reaches its end – and this is the solution this letter puts forward – but this end is possible only because there is, rigorously, nothing; paradoxically, we cannot even speak of Bataille, since the person of Bataille is an objectification as well. Here is a dead end if there ever was one. The recognition at the summit – at the end of history, at the moment of absolute knowing – is overturned and becomes a full recognition of empty negativity ("full" because this recognition does not deceive itself with art or with religion – which would call this negativity "sin"). And then the malaise, the wall – or the madness of Hegel, when he "recognizes" this nonrecognizable negativity.

Bataille tried to escape this problem by posing, in *The Accursed Share*, a counterhistory of civilizations in which this negativity was not "recognized" but at least, was manifested in a dramatic and overwhelming way (by the Aztecs, Tibetans, etc.). Bataille implies, at the end of *The Accursed Share*, a utopia (but he does not use that word for it) in which negativity would somehow – impossibly – be recognized and carried out in society – but, unfortunately, and necessarily, perhaps, Bataille stops there, and he does not reveal to us the forms that this negativity will (or should) take.

The problem is to know what will happen at and after the end of history, on the personal level, but especially on the social plane. The project of Bataille is in this respect utopian, even if he does not (and, as we have seen, cannot) give details concerning a future life or society. He nevertheless proposes the consideration of the question that finally has perhaps a greater connection with the Wittgenstein of the *Tractatus* than with Mauss: when I know everything, when society knows everything (when society has been perfected), what can I do and know? And the most fundamental question: what can I write when writing, by its very nature, is fundamentally tied (as a project) to the history that has just ended and not to the future that radically escapes from this history and its end? As in Wittgenstein, perhaps the only word possible in the future for Bataille will be *silence*.

But to understand what happens to absolute knowing, we must read a text that appears in *Inner Experience*, and is entitled simply "Hegel." This section was written a few years after the letter to Kojève. Here Bataille takes up again the expression used by Jean Hyppolite in his translation of the *Phenomenology of Mind*: *le non-savoir*, "not-knowing." In fact Sartre used the term as well, and a study of the ramifications of this term in French philosophy of the 1930s, 1940s, and 1950s would easily fill a book. But we should note that for Hegel, this opposition between knowing and not-knowing in tragedy resides in a single person. Hyppolite, in a footnote to "The Esthetic Religion," writes: "the opposition between knowing and not-knowing which is found within each person gives rise to two distinct divinities, Apollo and the Furies. But, as Hegel is about to show, Zeus is the unity of the substance that expresses the relation between these powers."[3]

This opposition between knowing and not-knowing in a single, higher and tragic person (such as Zeus) becomes, in the "Hegel" section of *Inner Experience*, a struggle within the *ipse* that mimes Hegel – in other words, within Bataille "himself." As in the letter to Kojève, Bataille starts with the presupposition that knowing and history have been completed, have reached their end, in a circular manner: "The *Phenomenology of Spirit* is made up of two essential movements that complete a circle: the completion by degrees of self-consciousness (of the human *ipse*) and the becoming all (the becoming God) of this *ipse* completing knowing (and in this way destroying particularity in itself, thus achieving the negation of itself, and becoming absolute knowing)" (IE, 108).

Through a circular process, the completed *ipse* becomes God. Bataille, however, sees this absolute knowing as a limitation, rather than as a completion. "*Circular absolute knowing is definitive not-knowing*. Even supposing that I were to attain it, I know that I would know nothing more than what I know now" (IE, 108). If he "mimes" God, Bataille will see "no longer an unknown, but an unknowable." Circular absolute knowing is defined in relation to not-knowing; it needs this not-knowing, this unknowable, this necessarily excluded "share." Knowing depends on not-knowing, but it does not recognize it, or rather it does not formulate a certain question. Bataille, miming Hegel, supposing that he is God (that he is the completion of absolute knowing), parodies Hegel, and overturns him. He adds something to Hegel, he becomes his supplement, because, "knowing everything," he knows that there is still a question: "Why must there be *what I know*? Why is this a necessity?" (IE, 109). Put another way, this metaquestion, this supplement, asks, why is the exclusion of not-knowing definitive? This question cannot be answered in and through knowing, because not-knowing is not an unknown, susceptible to investigation and understanding, but is instead a priori unknowable.

God (or Bataille), knowing everything, knows that doubt remains. It is a much more caustic doubt than that of Descartes, since it is directed at absolute knowing *when it is completed and necessarily accepted.*

The mime, the clown, adds something to what he reincarnates and imitates. One cannot simply be Hegel: one reincarnates him in rewriting him. This surplus value is the writer's questioning and doubting *ipse*, which, in a circular movement, continues "beyond" the final point of Hegel: there is first completion of self-consciousness, then the becoming-all of this *ipse* completing knowing, and finally, and simultaneously, a third movement which is a "nonlogical difference." This is the heterogeneous existence of absolute knowing that poses a supplementary question: "why must there be what I know?" In this "moment," absolute knowing incessantly overturns and automutilates, as it recognizes an unrecognizable negativity, the excessive question that must be excluded in order for knowledge to constitute itself in the first place. This third movement leads, then, to another circle, a vicious circle, or, put another way, to an eternal return. The existence of a heterogeneous "me" breaks the closed circle of knowing – one thinks here of the article "The Labyrinth," written in 1935 but rewritten and included in *Inner Experience*: there as well it is a question of the *ipse* being that is heterogeneous, and man "is a particle inserted in unstable and tangled groups" (IE, 84). At the summit of the pyramid of existence, there is God, who dies: like the *ipse* beings that are always "insufficient" in relation to the larger grouping, God at the summit becomes the very principle of insufficiency. This lack in being is repeated by the man (or by the victim) in his necessary but impossible independence from that larger grouping of *ipse* beings, society.

In "Hegel," the figure Bataille refers to is the circle, not the pyramid. But the problem is the same. The completion of the circle – the being of the philosopher who is God – is radically *insufficient.* The existence of the writer is heterogeneous: because of a radical doubt (a function of the absolute knowing that sacrifices absolute knowing), in fully completing and incarnating absolute knowing this existence deviates from it: "Knowing is in no way distinct from myself. *I am it*, and it is existence that I am. But this existence is not reducible to it: this reduction would require that the known be the end of existence, and not existence the end of the known" (IE, 110). The known is lost in a particular (and thus a nonrepresentative, nontotalizing) existence and, with it, the straightforward function of the philosopher: Hegel, if he "knew," would have been a madman (or, put another way, God, if he "knew," would be a pig).[4] Knowing, finally, is the knowledge of that which cannot be known (its exclusion makes possible the closed circle of the known), the incessant recuperation of the definitively unrecuperable. The improbable and specific existence of the "philosopher" (Bataille *as* Hegel) is this knowing of not-knowing (and vice versa).[5]

Bataille uses a metaphor of the circle: the eye. The ocular sphere – which is, moreover, an image one "sees" often in the text of Bataille, charged with an erotic power (*Story of the Eye, The Pineal Eye*, etc.) – has a blind spot that makes vision possible (exactly like not-knowing, which makes knowing possible). This spot is at the basis of vision, and guarantees it: but when vision gazes at itself and considers its own act of vision (when vision sees itself), it sees only the blind spot – and it loses itself in that blindness. Of course Bataille is not writing here (literally) of vision, but of questioning and understanding: when understanding understands itself, "sees" itself, the circle is broken, because it "sees" its blind spot, the questioning of not-knowing. "To the extent that one envisages in the understanding man himself, I mean an exploration of the possibility of being, the spot absorbs one's attention: it is no longer the spot that is lost in knowing, but knowing in the spot. Existence in this way closes the circle, but it cannot do so without including the night which it escapes only to reenter. Just as it went from the unknown to the known, it must fall back from the summit into the unknown" (IE, 110–11).

The known – the "fabricated," the product of the labor of the slave – is overturned at the summit, but we should note above all here the new circle: knowing must know *everything*, including the unknown which, at the end of history, remains definitively unknowable. Thus in order to constitute itself, the known sinks into not-knowing. The result is the parody of circular (dialectical) thought: "circular agitation," the undecidable movement that is outside the productive time of the dialectic – and that is situated between absolute knowing and the not-knowing that is both necessary for its constitution and radically heterogeneous with it. This circular agitation is associated not with labor, knowing, and rest but with "desire, poetry, and laughter," which cause life to "slide" in the direction of the unknowable.

If rest is impossible – and if not-knowing always implies the fall into ecstasy and night – not-knowing will never have the possibility of being knowing. In other words, not-knowing will never be able to be studied or explored as a psychological or social phenomenon: it is not not-knowing that is explored, but "it is the night that explores me" (IE, 111).

Perhaps we see here Bataille's distrust of the petite bourgeoisie, which one finds in his writings of the 1930s ("The Sorcerer's Apprentice," "The Practice of Joy before Death," etc.). In this text we do not have the "wall" or the "malaise" that we find at the end of the letter to Kojève: here it is a question of an agitation, of a laceration that is both metaphysical (between knowing and not-knowing) and physical ("poetry, laughter, ecstasy"). "Hegel" ends with an evocation of a state of hebetude, but this state is not the result of the experience of not-knowing; on the contrary, it is the weakness that results from a return to the "satisfaction" of the life of knowing. "Short of dying of them, one sneaks away from them [i.e., poetry, laughter, ecstasy] like a thief (or as one sneaks away from a girl after making love) dazed, stupidly thrown back into the absence of death: into distinct knowledge [*connaissance*], activity, and labor."

This rather inglorious end takes us back to the beginning of "Hegel," and thus inscribes a circle, since the text begins, in fact, in knowing and in the surplus-knowing that follows from it ("I know that I would know nothing more than what I know now"), a surplus-knowing that is inseparable from the agitation of the knowing of not-knowing.

The essay, however, describes another circle. And it is possible to conclude that Bataille's not-knowing results, finally, neither in death, nor the wall, nor for that matter in the hebetude of "distinct knowing." Perhaps we cannot ask, with Bataille, What is not-knowing in general? – but we can ask, on the other hand, "What is the not-knowing *of this text*? What is its blind spot, the position or problem that it is incapable of thinking or posing? Miming Hegel, Bataille isolated the not-knowing of Hegel's text, and it is, finally, thinkable, if not livable: it is ecstasy, laughter, poetry. Sartre's objection, as we know, was that this not-knowing belongs simply to the domain of science, that is, to psychology and sociology. And as science, of course, Bataille's project left much to be desired.

It is obvious, I think, that *The Accursed Share* and other Bataille projects of the postwar period put forward theories that aspire to a scientific rigor and value. But how does one attain a general validity while starting with "a malaise," "a wall," or "a circular agitation"? How does one start with a state "without rest" and end with observations having a practical value for the comprehension (and safeguarding) of the future of the human race (as in the last chapter of *The Accursed Share*)? How does one base a historical investigation on a theory that questions the labor of knowing?

First we must recognize that *The Accursed Share* and all the other studies by Bataille that make use of the "human sciences" (sociology, psychology, anthropology, history) are fully Hegelian and, consequently, betray not-knowing. They give us a model of history, of the end of history (at which time the tendency to expend will be recognized), and so on. If we suppose that writings like *The Accursed Share* are such a betrayal, then we can see that a text like "Hegel" makes this betrayal possible – a betrayal that is, moreover, necessary.

It seems, in fact, that there is a circulation between knowing and not-knowing in the text "Hegel." This circulation is indicated on a thematic level at the end of the text: the subject (the writer), falls back, dazed, into work, activity, and knowing. His labor, furthermore, was necessary in order to carry out the writing of the text. "Written" within not-knowing, this text would only be a scream, or silence – thus by virtue of its very existence as a coherent text it violates not-knowing and it situates itself back in knowing.

We have seen the paradoxical situation in which absolute knowing incessantly is overturned and falls back into not-knowing when it is constituted *fully* as knowing. That is the circular agitation Bataille writes of; knowing is repetitiously lost in night. Knowing can finally *know* only in and as not-knowing. I would maintain, however, that the wheel can turn a little more; given that knowing can be overturned and lost in not-knowing (when it recognizes, and knows, a definitive not-knowing), I would suggest that not-knowing can be overturned and lost in knowing (this in fact has been implied all along in the notion of circular agitation), and not only on the thematic level, simply represented in the text (which is what we see at the end of the "Hegel" section with the feeble return to "knowing, activity, and labor"). An overturning of this text, on the other hand, implies its nonlogical opposite, its unthought, that which it has to expel in order to constitute itself – here, a practical doctrine (which is not isolated in the *ipse* of the writer), even a *science* of not-knowing. In the final analysis, knowing implies a dialectical advance: not-knowing can be overturned and lost in knowing, but this will be a (necessarily dialectical) knowing that is conscious of the phenomenon of not-knowing, that recognizes it, that studies its effects in the world (and which, consequently, betrays it). The "Hegel" section turns around this textual blind spot. This spot is the instability of the text implied by the parodic nature of not-knowing. If not-knowing is parodic it implies, again, a circulation, a return. And if "circular absolute knowing is definitive not-knowing," the text, which cannot guarantee not-knowing in a stable way (satisfaction and stability, we should recall, are simply the work of knowing), cannot hope to eliminate this parody: "circular not-knowing is definitive knowing." Language is parodic (this is one of the lessons of *The Solar Anus*), and it cannot stop the repetitious overturning of terms that it itself had seemed to establish in such a serious way. In other words it cannot guarantee, in the end, the rigorous difference between not-knowing (and its "circular agitation") and the knowing that still remains knowing while fully *recognizing* not-knowing. (We should note, in addition, the instability of terms in the text, such as "knowing" ["I know that I would know nothing more than I know now"] and "end" ["this reduction would require that the known be the end of existence, and not existence the end of the known"].)[6]

The blind spot of this text – the point at which it cannot read itself – lies therefore in the fact that its oppositional structure is more unstable than the text would be able to recognize and that, consequently, there *is* a stable doctrine of not-knowing: not-knowing is absorbed by knowing, just as much as knowing is absorbed by not-knowing. This is a double "truth" that "Hegel" cannot *see* if it is to be a demonstration (and a valorization) of not-knowing. But the text "Hegel" depends on the finality of not-knowing *as* not-knowing, and it must try to be rigorous – otherwise, it will fail and will simply fall back into what it had moved to avoid at all cost: a Hegelian absolute knowing. In fact the doctrine (the knowing) of this not-knowing, unthought here but formulated elsewhere, is not the wall or silence, or circular agitation, but a science, a constituted knowing that must lead, finally, to the formulation and comprehension of what will take place at and after the end of history, a knowing not only of the human *ipse* but of society: history and anthropology. This doctrine (this knowing and not-knowing that labors in the world) cannot be seen in "Hegel" (and it betrays this text, even though it is generated out of it), but it can be seen very clearly in other works by Bataille – such as *The Accursed Share*. It is another kind of parody of Hegelian absolute knowing, this time carried out clearly on the social and historical level (in the analysis of the historical and social manifestations of not-knowing).

The Accursed Share, of course, is the violation of the idea that the night cannot be explored. The stability of this project is the betrayal of circular agitation (but, for that matter, circular agitation betrays the stability of Bataille's anthropology). Bataille's text is not simple. Instead, it has two sides: a Hegel side, in which not-knowing is overturned and falls into knowing (*The Accursed Share*), and a Nietzsche side, in which knowing is overturned and falls into not-knowing, in an incessant and circular agitation (in other words, in the eternal return) (this side, more nihilistic and personal, can be associated with the *Summa atheologica*, which includes *Inner Experience*). And – can it be recognized? – between these two sides there is a circular agitation. We see the generation of both sides in the "Hegel" section of *Inner Experience*.

II

From the first there is a problem in any attempt to posit a new era, society or state "at the end of history." Bataille, in his letter to Kojève, writes of the liberation of negativity, and of the various forms it will take when history is over. But what does it mean for negativity to be "out of a job"? Unemployment seems to imply a new "steady state," a new mode of operation that can take place in a straightforward way: the revolution is completed (or will be in the near future, which, Bataille implies, is the equivalent of that completion), negativity no longer goes to blow up bridges or fight the Fascists in the street: now it manifests itself as lovemaking, gambling, and other forms of (necessarily acceptable) potlatch. At least at the end of *The Accursed Share* Bataille implies that some state, perhaps some avatar of the no longer fully capitalist American one (which engages in the biggest potlatch of all, the Marshall Plan), will direct this unemployed destruction, making sure it does not veer in the direction of warfare or sadistic, repressive violence. The problem is this: how can one propose, let alone predict or wager on, a period after the end of history, since that "end" would also imply the end of temporality itself – the end, in other words, of the very possibility of a before and after?

One response would be to argue that all the Bataillean manifestations of "unemployed" negativity take place not after the end of history but at that moment. From this perspective, the end is not superseded, but only opens out to an infinite series of repetitious instants. This is another version of the meeting of Nietzsche and Hegel: the culminating moment of the dialectic, the absolute knowing of Kojèvian Marxism, opens out into, knows, and is doubled by the proliferation of the eternal return. Bataille, in fact, in the letter to Kojève, seems strangely unconcerned about the actual facticity (if we can call it that) of history's end: in the original version of the letter, Bataille pointedly ignores temporality: he "assumes" that the end is upon us now, even though the final stage is still to come, and he is even indifferent to the outcome, whether it be fascism or communism.[7] Not only are the details – such as the difference between these two very different social and ideological models – overlooked, but they are passed over *because* the temporality of the end of history is of no consequence. "It will come" is the same as "it is upon us now": the details that would affirm the certainty of the coming of the end are irrelevant (if the "end" is already here, those details, strictly speaking, are not essential). As soon as the end is posited and announced in a speech act, its coming is certain; we are living in that certainty, that knowing – and so we are living in the end now. There is no temporality in the end: it is already the end in the repetitious instant in which the end's necessity is proclaimed.

This model itself, however, is still a temporal one: one must, at some point, declare history to be at an end. Time is split in two: there is the time of time, and the time at the end of time. But if we consider Bataille's statement a little more carefully, we realize that even this latter time is made problematic. If negativity can be left without a job, then it is in no way identifiable with the dialectics of history: it lends itself to a dialectical movement, but it is not reducible to it. If negativity is posterior to temporalization, then it will be anterior as well: violence in a sense predates the movement of history, of time, because it will generate it, "open its possibility" (without it there would be no history, no time) without being identifiable with it or subordinated to it. Once we have said this, however, we face the same problem: if a "posthistorical" era literally makes no sense ("post" itself implies the continuation of history), then an anteriority to history is equally absurd: that anteriority, by virtue of its coming before, will itself always already be historical. There is only one other way of considering negativity: at each instant of the dialectic, at each articulation point, negativity is both subordinated to historical development and different from it, radically unredeemable, making history possible through the *Aufhebung* but also escaping the all-powerful incorporation it generates. That generation itself is not simply "in time"; like the negativity from which it is inseparable, it is both in time and radically different from it – but it is above all not atemporal, since atemporality implies a time to which it is opposed. Negativity in this version is not opposed to time; such opposition would indicate only the replacement of one time by another (even if it is an "antitime"), a "posthistory." Bataille's negativity instead accompanies the dialectic, doubling it, opening the space of its oppositions, miming it, repeating it, while differing from it. Haunting it. Here one thinks of Derrida's version of Bataille's Hegelianism: "In the course of this repetition a barely perceptible displacement disjoints all the articulations and penetrates all the points welded together by the imitated discourse. A trembling spreads out which then makes the entire old shell crack" (RGE, 260).

It should be stressed that negativity is never simply separable from time. It is always implied in time, in its movement and in its "beginning" and "end." For this reason, negativity is the limit at the heart (or hearts) of the dialectic, at all its points of articulation: at the same "time," as Bataille stressed in the "Hegel" section of *Inner Experience*, negativity always again reasserts itself at the end of history, at the moment of completion (which is also a circular movement, the rejoining of the origin) – it always again succeeds and swallows the movement and culmination of history.

Negativity is always out of a job, even at the moments in which it is most intensely employed. It lends itself to employment (Bataille would say that it prostitutes itself), making possible the completion of whatever task is at hand – the opposition of terms, the resolution of a contradiction – but it is not reduced or reducible to that utilization. It leaves only its ghost in the dialectic. It is the limit at the heart of the job, the job's origin and end, "end" in this case meaning both goal (the end of history for Bataille is nothing less than the freeing of negativity from the clutches of the dialectic) and death, the violent end of time, the mechanical repetition of the apocalypse at every moment of history.

Hegel's Return

It was fairly easy to imagine an end of history in the Kojèvian sense, which amounted to very little other than the ceasing of wars and revolutions and the development of human potentials in a progressive, rational, and egalitarian society, in which the desire of each person is recognized by every other. Bataille's "posthistory" in his 1937 letter seemed only to be a variation on that: the negativity of festivals and lovemaking would replace the productive, historical, but potentially cataclysmic, violence of war. But the function of negativity that I have been discussing disturbs this easy model: a straightforward implementation *in society* of a violence that mimes every articulation point of the dialectic is difficult if not impossible to imagine. Nevertheless it must be stressed that Bataille fully intended his writings to "change society": his discussion of the Marshall Plan at the end of *The Accursed Share* makes this clear enough.[8] And yet a violence that is inseparable from the movement of history would indicate that this end is always here, that any effort to enforce a program at or after the end is beside the point. But what then of the clearly utopian or at least reformist tendencies in Bataille?

Perhaps one could argue that Bataille's tactic from the first was to shift the scene from the establishment of the community to the doubled figure of the intellectual. We have seen this already in the letter to Kojève, where the writer himself, Bataille as Hegel, comes to be the embodiment of the impasse at the end of history, "standing before his negativity as before a wall." The intellectual alone in his or her particular, nonuniversal "existence" can parody the philosopher – can become the philosopher's clown and ghost – thereby in some way "being" the negativity that dogs the movement of history, that is history's end at every instant of its development. In fact, Bataille the intellectual is split in two: there is Bataille as Nietzsche, the *surnietzsche* I discussed in the previous chapter, the textual instance tending toward "not-knowing" through a movement of sheer negativity, of incessant "stripping," differing, or rewriting; this Bataille is itself (or himself) doubled by another which, as we have seen, arises out of the "not-knowing" of the circular action of not-knowing in the dialectic. This second Bataille is Hegel, the transgression of Bataillean-Nietzschean textual transgression, the night in which not-knowing itself is lost, the figure of the writer who mimes Hegel by taking seriously a project in which not-knowing is instituted in society – an intellectual, in other words, who sees expenditure, laughter, and sexuality as inseparable from the motors of history, who foresees an end of history in which the domination of sheer negativity will somehow be clearly established.

But the figure of the intellectual is in any case never separable from that of the community: Bataille as Nietzsche is part of a community as well: that of the textual community Bataille/Nietzsche. The movement of reading is the *communauté inavouable*, as Blanchot calls it, the community of those who have no community.[9] The Hegelian community, on the other hand, is one that would turn away from textuality, toward a larger movement – even toward a state that somehow manages a surplus that, strictly speaking, cannot be recognized. Thus there are two radically opposed Bataillean communities, just as there are two Bataillean intellectuals: one written under the sign of Nietzsche, the other under Hegel/Marx. This duality of Bataille's project, in one sense, is no different from the split we have seen running through French intellectual activity in general in the twentieth century: there is a side that embraces discontinuity, negativity, and the movement of the text, or rhetoric – all of these being presented typically in terms of sacrifice or the sacred – over that of a stable social grouping or project; conversely, there is a side that affirms the necessity of a represented and representable consciousness, a political task, a historic mission – often made possible through a sacrificial gesture or logic – along with an economic program, established against an "inward-turning," "aestheticizing" textual movement. And, as was the case with every one of the authors I have discussed in this book, Bataille was unable to keep either side from constituting and contaminating the other: Bataille as Nietzsche is already dependent on a dialectic (albeit of stripped forms), a movement that is teleologically oriented; Bataille, as Hegel, is generated out of not-knowing, the eternal return of the fall into labor, history, and referential language.

Bataille, however, goes beyond the authors we have studied – and in this respect his project is unique – in that he refuses to attempt to subordinate one side to another, to confine safely textuality within a social movement (as the intellectual's message, his praxis linked with useful sacrifice, etc.), or society within the textual (here one thinks of de Man's characterization of history as generated out of misreading). Instead, the two options remain at war, each insubordinate to the other, each already undermining while instituting the other. At the impossible moment of "awareness" of this radically sundered and incoherent project, the figure of the intellectual is crucial (just as, in another way, the intellectual was indispensable to the coherency of Durkheim's system). In a final footnote to *The Accursed Share*, Bataille writes:

> It will be said that only a madman could perceive such things in the Marshall and Truman Plans [i. e., the fundamental tendency to expend rather than conserve: potlatch, sacrifice, etc.]. I am that madman. In the very precise sense that there is the choice of two things: either the operation will fail, or the madman will arrive at the *self-consciousness* I speak of, because reason, being consciousness, is fully conscious only if it has for an object that which is not reducible to it. I apologize for introducing considerations here that refer to a precise fact: that in other respects the author of this book on economy is situated (by a part of his

work) in the line of mystics of all times (but he is nonetheless far removed from all the presuppositions of the various mysticisms, to which
he opposes only the lucidity of *self-consciousness*).[10]

We see in this remarkable passage a return of the circularity that characterized the "Hegel" section of *Inner Experience*. Reason is self-aware when it
"loses itself in the night," or, as Bataille puts it here, if it has as its object
something that "is not reducible to it." But Bataille does not write that it is a
question of reason losing itself in madness: rather it is the madman (the writer,
Bataille himself) who arrives at *self-consciousness*, at the reason of his madness.
The movement goes in both directions, then, from reason to madness – and
the accomplishment of madness through reason – but also from madness to
reason, to self-recognition – and the accomplishment of reason *in* madness.
Hegel is lost in laughter, eroticism and (most important) Nietzschean textuality; Nietzsche's madman recognizes himself in the very madness of a potlatch – the Marshall Plan – that is the highest historical reason, and that will
save mankind from a nuclear holocaust (that will, in other words, enable it to
distinguish good potlatch from bad).

The Bataillean intellectual is dual, both the highest embodiment of the
reason of society and the state and, at the same time, a madman who repetitiously betrays the state in the very act of fulfilling it – whose senseless revolt
against that fulfillment can only be another instance of fulfillment.[11] Bataille
clearly shows in the above quote – without necessarily being aware of it – the
fundamental duality of his project. The madman who attains self-consciousness is not at all the same as the philosopher – Hegel – who attains the highest
knowing and the lowest stupidity in not-knowing. In one case reason (the
dialectic) arrives at its end (in the double sense of that term) in and through
unreason; in another, that of the madman, unreason – exemplified in the
various historical instances of social excess analyzed in *The Accursed Share* –
arrives at a higher reason through analysis (Bataille's own writing). It is almost
as if we are staring at the same process from two different, and radically incompatible, perspectives: in the "Hegel" section of *Inner Experience*, we see the
movement from knowing to not-knowing; here, at the end and in a footnote
of *The Accursed Share*, we see the movement in a very different direction, from
not-knowing to knowing.

It should be stressed that the movement of circulation between these two
texts entails more than the apparently purely thematic movement from knowing to not-knowing and back; above all, it is a question of writing practices
that defy and defeat each other, but which at the same time are necessary to, as
well as implied in and by, each other. In the case of *The Accursed Share*, the
writing is coherent, but it leads to, and ends in (as Bataille himself informs us)

a madness that is established by, but that also necessarily swallows, self-consciousness – the very movement sketched out in the "Hegel" section of *Inner Experience*. In the case of *Inner Experience*, however, the writing is radically incoherent – fragmented, self-defeating, scattered – but it entails, in spite of itself we might say, the movement to higher reason through not-knowing that we have examined (in the first part of this chapter) in the "Hegel" section, and thus to the project, and the writing, of *The Accursed Share* itself. And the circulation continues; *The Accursed Share* ends, as we see in the above quote, in a parenthesis within a footnote, a parenthesis which proclaims nothing other than the larger project of *Inner Experience*: the effort to liberate the sacred text "from all the presuppositions of the various mysticisms." The effort, in other words, to write a sacred text that will be the end of sacred texts, a mystical doctrine that recognizes the necessity of the absence of all coherent mystical doctrine, the "lucidity of a *self-consciousness*" that is the recognition of the death of that very self-consciousness. Such a project inevitably implies the broken, incoherent, yet obsessive and exhaustive writing of *Inner Experience* – the textuality of the impossibility of the text as doctrine. The circle of writing is in agitation: from the coherency of *The Accursed Share* to the violence of *Inner Experience*, and back again – and back again once more. The "sense" of Bataille's project is implicated in the "senselessness" of writing, and vice versa. These two sides are impacted in each other not just on a thematic level (the Nietzschean madman attains Hegelian reason, Hegel is revealed to be Nietzsche in his madness, etc.) but in the writing practice of the doubled text itself. This is not (or not exclusively) a dialectical circularity. No higher knowledge is attained in or through it: Bataille himself, the authorial function, nowhere professes or obtains an awareness of this movement in or through his radically fissured oeuvre, in the space of communication between *The Accursed Share* (Hegel) and the *Summa atheologica* (Nietzsche). The negativity of this circular agitation is not so much in opposition to historical reason as it is its "nonlogical difference."

Bataille, unlike all the other secular clerics whose writing I have examined in this book, openly puts forward the duality of his project. Unlike on the one side Nizan, Drieu, or Sartre, and on the other Paulhan, Blanchot, Foucault, Derrida, or de Man, Bataille never attempts to subordinate the radicality of his writing to a coherent social consciousness and dialectic, or vice versa. These two possibilities are implicated across the strata of his text, each in turn finding its origin in the other, and at the same time disrupting the other, openly, without any effort on the author's part to reduce or expel what, at a given moment, is the other.

Must one then still maintain that Bataille "knows" more than the other authors do? Clearly not: such a knowing would merely bind the "sides" of his text together in a neat opposition, thereby establishing a higher knowing to which other secular clerics might rise. As we have seen, at no point does Bataille proclaim this as his project; instead, the two sides are simply "there," giving themselves, so to speak, and there is no plan to undo the chiasmus and subordinate one project, one figure of the cleric, one writing, to the other. The two sides can cross, but this very crossing, unremarked by Bataille and even working against his argument (why would one read a work on economics written by a madman?), indicates the extent to which one stratum is implied in the other. The madman can replace the "philosopher," the "economist": the figures are interchangeable, but they are also incompatible. Or, put another way, any knowing of the difference between the two figures, and the two textual sides with which they are related, itself must end in a night of not-knowing. Yet the difference cannot not be noted: just as the madman usurps the position of the philosopher, so too the philosopher always again rises from the remains of the madman. And so on to infinity: Bataille *is* this knowing of not-knowing, and this not-knowing of knowing – incessant war, circular agitation.

Is there any way out of this vicious circle? Put another way, is there any way to avoid what would seem a dead end, a wall – the intellectual as embodiment of the community (textual or social) but also as the figure of the not-knowing, the mutilation or betrayal of the very social "organism" and "consciousness" that he both founds and guarantees? It is tempting at this point to turn to Heidegger, or at least a certain Heidegger: perhaps the vicious circle can be replaced by the hermeneutic circle, not-knowing can be incorporated into a larger, positive notion of finitude, one that allows one to grasp one's own (albeit limited) place in history and to evolve one's own personal but also (and above all) collective project.

   This problem has dogged French criticism in recent years, and perhaps it is the contemporary version of the split that, in the 1930s or 1940s, divided Lange from Bloyé (in Nizan's *Trojan Horse*), or the Sartre of *What Is Literature?* from the Bataille of *Inner Experience*. It is, in a word, the bind between a repetitious, fragmented, and seemingly inward-turning avant-garde writing or rhetoric, and an outward facing, sensible, progressive social project that would perhaps retain the lesson of a transgressive language, but only while subordinating it to (as Foucault called them) "specific practices" and "everyday struggles" in the world – to the realm of the "nondiscursive," in other words. Certainly Foucault has been caught on the horns of this dilemma, but so have, in other ways, Derrida and de Man. The chimera of the positive project will no doubt continue to haunt French theory – as will the other chimera, that of writerly writing on writing. In any case, as we have seen throughout the second part of this book, any attempt to "replace" one model with the other (Foucault), or somehow to coordinate the two (Derrida, especially in his later writings on education and on Heidegger), is problematic, to say the least.

In recent efforts, the Hegel/Nietzsche combination has simply been replaced by Heidegger. Such is the strategy of Jean-Luc Nancy's recent book, *La Communauté désoeuvrée.*[12] In Nancy's view, which he elaborates through a kind of dialogue with Bataille, the community is not a work, an oeuvre, nor an instrumentality or myth: it is not the result of the means to a larger social unification, as Durkheim had hoped. Rather, it is a grouping of singularities that are brought together precisely through the recognition of their own mortality, their own limitation and singularity: *"The totality is itself the play of articulations.* That is why a whole [*un tout*] of singularities, which certainly is a whole, does not close on them in order to raise them to its power: this whole is essentially the opening of singularities in their articulations, the line [*le tracé*] and the flutter [*le battement*] of their limits" (CD, 188).

As was the case with Derrida and Lacoue-Labarthe, Nancy is also answering Heidegger here, showing how a community, founded not on the destruction of singularity and the subordination of limitation to a higher totem or fetish (as was the case with nazism) but on the affirmation of singularity and the deconstruction of monocephalic power, can be derived from Heidegger's work itself. In this way Nancy's essay looks back to the Bataille of the prewar Acéphale period, or to early essays by Bataille such as "The Obelisk" and "The Labyrinth," but also across to other contemporary French Heideggerians who would defend Heidegger from himself, such as Jean-François Lyotard.[13] Nancy, however, can carry out such an effort only by simply refusing the "Hegel" side of Bataille (a position which implies a critique of Derrida's reading of Bataille; see CD, 62–63), and, in a classic Heideggerian move, by criticizing Bataille for his retention of a progressive "subjectivity" (CD, 60–61): "For Bataille, as for us all, a thought of the subject thwarts a thought of the community" (CD, 60).

This faithfulness to a Heideggerian refusal of subjectivism, and no doubt humanism, nevertheless leads to problems. As we have seen, the most interesting subjectivism in Bataille is his valorization of the figure of the textualized intellectual, the *surnietzsche,* or Bataille as the knowing Hegel at the moment of his loss in the not-knowing of his own system. This is, in other versions, the secular shaman of "The Sorcerer's Apprentice"; L'Abbé C., the cleric who incarnates not God's law but madness and perversion; Troppmann (in *Blue of Noon*), the betrayer of the regime he would establish, and so on. The intellectual at the end of history for Bataille is the figure who is the necessary complement of the community, its completion, its servant, its incarnation, its totem, its victim. The community cannot be thought outside of the intellectual subject that fulfills and violates it. This is the Bataille who clearly is rewriting the Hegelian tradition, via Durkheim and Kojève. To *eliminate* Hegel and the subject from the problematic of the community, however, as Nancy attempts to do, leads not so much to the accomplishment of a Heideggerian community as to another, more resolute, version of Hegelianism. Nancy writes: "The myth of the writer is interrupted: there is a scene, an attitude, a creativity of the writer which are no longer possible. What will have named itself 'writing,' and what is called 'writing,' will have had, as a task, precisely, making them impossible. And consequently making impossible a certain type of literary and communal foundation, uttering and accomplishment: finally, a politics" (CD, 172).

As in Foucault, this "interruption" of the writer is a definitive elimination of the old-style intellectual who embodies, speaks for, represents, and leads: the secular cleric. But such a simple elimination *in practice* cannot be carried over directly into theory.[14] (Nancy, again like Foucault, sees the effects of the classical intellectual as harmful.) An elimination *tout court* smacks of a sacrificial and speculative logic of expulsion and closure. Instead, the intellectual resurfaces as the "disappearance of the writer." The clerical function is now exclusively the *retrait* of that function, its self-erasure:[15] "The interruption of the myth of the writer is not the disappearance of the writer. It is above all not 'the death of the last writer' as envisaged by Blanchot. . . . It is what prints, through interruption, the withdrawal [*retrait*] of its myth: it is not the author, nor a hero . . . but it is a singular voice (a writing: this can be, as well, a way of putting it . . .). And this singular voice, resolutely and irreducibly singular (mortal), is so in *common*: so one can only be 'a voice' ('a writing') in *common*. The literary experience of the community takes place in singularity. . . . The word [*la parole*] is communal [*communautaire*] to the extent of its singularity, and singular to the extent of its truth of community [*sa vérité de communauté*]" (CD, 173).

It seems that Nancy's final position as regards the writer is itself double: either in practice the traditional writer is expelled, withdrawn, or in theory he is singular in his communal existence and communal in his singularity. The former position, although impracticable, is eminently speculative, and the latter does not seem that far from a Hegelian Durkheim: it was, after all, the singularity (individuality) of the intellectual for Durkheim that guaranteed his position as a spokesman of – or the truth of – the community; conversely, the community for Durkheim could only be a collectivity of individualities. No doubt Nancy would object that "singularity" is a long way from the "individuality" or the "person" – Nancy's term is used to avoid the subjectivizing connotations of the latter two terms, and to circumvent any possible fall into a pre-Heideggerian humanism – but the fact remains that singularity for Nancy functions in relation to the community in exactly the same way that individuality does for Durkheim. It is the very limitation, the uncommonness, that everyone has in common – and that therefore serves as the basis, the foundation, for the community. It seems that the further we flee from a sacrificial logic of the excluded or the exemplar, and from a concomitant social grouping dependent on representative but individual or singular intellectuals, the closer we are to these traditional options.

Escaping Hegel, then, seems to lead only further back into a dialectic, or into a method (like Durkheim's) which itself is dependent on a Hegelian knowing and state – as Derrida himself argued.[16] Bataille recognized this, and his Heideggerianism, his recognition of a fatal negativity that mimes the dialectical articulation points of history, opening their possibility while transgressing them, never serves simply to eliminate the state at the end of history, or the intellectual's (self-mutilating) function at its end – nor does it attempt to efface the vicious circle in which Hegel and Nietzsche are locked at that "end," which is inscribed at every negative moment *in* history. Bataille's Heidegger is "himself" caught between Hegel and Nietzsche. Heidegger for Bataille is not only the negativity that generates philosophical oppositions without being reducible to them. He (or it) is also the impossibility of the very book that Bataille is writing – its *impensé*, so to speak, the rigorous truth that the book (*Inner Experience*) is unwriteable, that it cannot be formulated as a coherent position, in relation to the community or anything else.[17]

At the "end" of the French history of the intellectual – as Heidegger folds back into Sartre (Ferry and Renaut) or Durkheim (Nancy) – the figure of Bataille remains: impossibly crossing the options of Hegel and Nietzsche, "society" and "textuality," the intellectual and the death of the intellectual; he is the "wall" against which any thinking of the intellectual collides – and against which he "himself" collides.[18] He is the violence and the incoherence of any future attempt to formulate, adequately, the function of the intellectual. Yet the figure of the secular cleric is itself necessary, and it cannot be escaped, try as we might; at this end of history, which is also the end of the history of the intellectual, we face the eternal return of this collision against Bataille's "wall," this incessant embrace of Hegel and Nietzsche at the "final" moment of auto-mutilation.

Notes

INTRODUCTION

1. A spate of books has appeared very recently, all of which touch on either the crisis of higher education, the crisis of the intellectual, or both. Some are essentially positive about the potential (if not the actual) role of the educator or intellectual, particularly those books of a Foucauldian or Derridean cast, such as Paul Bové's *Intellectuals in Power: A Genealogy of Critical Humanism* (New York: Columbia University Press, 1986), or Samuel Weber's *Institution and Interpretation* (Minneapolis: University of Minnesota Press, 1987). Others seem more pessimistic – and highly critical of the role of the academic as conceived by Bové or Weber – either because of their culturally conservative outlook (see Allan Bloom's *The Closing of the American Mind* [New York: Vintage, 1987]) or because of their somewhat disillusioned radicalism – see Russell Jacoby's *The Last Intellectuals* (New York: Basic Books, 1987). Finally, some authors apparently just don't much like intellectuals (despite the obvious fact that they are intellectuals themselves): such is the case with Paul Johnson and his *Intellectuals* (New York: Harper and Row, 1989). It is worth noting that of such works, only those highly, even venomously, critical of intellectuals or academics make it to best-seller status – this has been the fate of the Bloom and Johnson books. Other, more serious and challenging works – such as the Bové and Weber books – seem inevitably fated to be read only in extremely limited academic circles. This is no doubt due to the fact that two versions of the intellectual – the academic and the journalist – have, for various reasons, never been very closely allied in the United States: this is especially true now, because the mediating intellectual-journalist, conversant in both ab-

struse philosophical, political, and literary debate and in the methods of writing for the *grande presse* has, as Jacoby would remind us, largely become extinct here. The astonishing (to me, at least) hostility of many journalists (writing in the *New York Times, Newsweek,* the *New York Review of Books,* etc.) to recent critical trends (Derrida, de Man, Foucault, Baudrillard above all) is also quite fascinating; a very interesting book could be written, using a sociological and historical approach, to analyze this rather freakish split between prestigious mass circulation periodicals on the one hand and contemporary critical movements on the other (it is certainly not to be found – at least not with this level of *ressentiment* – in England, France, or Germany).

2. See the essays by Michel Foucault that I discuss in chapter 7: "Intellectuals and Power" (hereafter I P), in *Language, Counter-Memory, Practice: Selected Essays and Interviews,* ed. D. F. Bouchard, trans. D. F. Bouchard and S. Simon (Ithaca, N.Y.: Cornell University Press, 1977); "Truth and Power" (hereafter T P), in *Power/Knowledge: Selected Interviews and Other Writings, 1972–77,* ed. and trans. Colin Gordon (Brighton: Harvester Press, 1980). Jean-François Lyotard's most notable statement on this topic can be found in *Tombeau de l'intellectuel et autres papiers* (Paris: Galilée, 1984).

3. The "new class" approach has been followed by Alvin W. Gouldner in his book *The Future of Intellectuals and the Rise of the New Class* (New York: Continuum, 1979).

4. See, on this topic, Richard Hofstadter's famous work *Anti-Intellectualism in American Life* (New York: Knopf, 1964).

5. One of the very first, if not the first, critic to analyze and denounce Stalinism *from the left* was Boris Souvarine, an exiled Russian Communist. In the early 1930s he edited in Paris *La Critique Sociale,* to which Georges Bataille, among others, contributed. *La Critique Sociale* ceased publication in 1934, about the time *Partisan Review* was founded as an organ of the New York chapter of the John Reed Club, an eminently correct Communist organization for young writers and artists.

6. For an overview of the history of the American intellectual, see the excellent *Intellectual Life in America: A History,* by Lewis Perry (Chicago: University of Chicago Press, 1989). While Perry presents any number of avatars of the intellectual in America – ministers, educators, journalists, etc. – one looks in vain for one with the centrality and authority of the European literary-philosophical figure. A characteristic American intellectual is one whose work itself points away from the authority of the intellectual and toward a purely pragmatic capacity called, for example, "intelligence," which can be measured in a "quotient" and developed in a practical way. See Perry, *Intellectual Life,* pp. 344–52, and 374. The Dewey-inspired doc-

trine of the "useful intellectual" can be contrasted to the Sartrian "committed intellectual": the former utilizes his or her "intelligence" as a tool in the service of state- or industry-sponsored programs; the latter, at least in principle, retains a critical and self-reflexive distance.

7. On the role of the *Bild* and *Bildung* in personal and philosophical formation, and their ties to a rhetoric-based theory of education, see the fascinating book by John H. Smith, *The Spirit and Its Letter: Traces of Rhetoric in Hegel's Philosophy of "Bildung"* (Ithaca, N.Y.: Cornell University Press, 1988).

8. See, for example, Georges Bataille's use of the word "agonistic" ("involving rivalry and struggle") in his essay "The Notion of Expenditure" (in *Visions of Excess: Selected Writings, 1927–39*, ed. Allan Stoekl, trans. Allan Stoekl with Carl Lovitt and Donald M. Leslie, Jr. [Minneapolis: University of Minnesota Press, 1985], p. 123; hereafter VE. It should be stressed that Bataille does not mean "struggle" here as a synonym for a dialectical opposition (as in the master/slave dialectic in Hegel's *Phenomenology*) – nor do I.

9. On the "République des lettres" as an institution that transcends traditional political distinctions, and on the French language itself as a rational vehicle which allows access to a higher aesthetic and ethical realm, see Priscilla Parkhurst Clark, *Literary France: The Making of a Culture* (Berkeley: University of California Press, 1987), esp. chaps. 2, 5, 6, and 7.

10. Quite often a sociology of the intellectual operates largely to discredit the actual content of the intellectual's writings. Such is the case especially with Pierre Bourdieu's work in, for example, *Homo Academicus* (Paris: Minuit, 1984). The limitations of Bourdieu's approach can be seen even more clearly in a book by one of his followers, Anna Boschetti: *Sartre et "Les Temps Modernes": Une Entreprise intellectuelle* (Paris: Minuit, 1985). Boschetti's book gives a kind of social-historical account of the rise of Sartre after the World War II. She astutely points out that quite consciously Sartre maneuvered to eliminate intellectual opposition, marginalizing both other, competing critics, and, above all, the prewar generation. Hence the hegemony of *Les Temps Modernes* in the 1940s and 1950s. Unfortunately, in all this the actual content of Sartre's work, the validity and/or the coherence of his positions, is largely ignored, since its importance has been downgraded. Sartre's entire project becomes just another "habitus," like a style of clothing or decor, which proved the right formula for a certain generation and class facing the early stages of the cold war and the decline of French temporal power in the world. Another sociological work, less polemical in its orientation, is Jean-Louis Fabiani's *Les Philosophes de la république* (Paris: Minuit, 1988). This work, dealing with the

late-nineteenth-century role of the Ecole Normale Supérieure and other institutions and rituals of professional formation, provides interesting insights that could very well be followed through in an analysis of the school's decisive role in the period 1920–60 – the period, in other words, in which Sartre, Althusser, Foucault, and Derrida, among many others, passed through its doors. Fabiani, in any case, gives some interesting insights into the direction such an inquiry might take in his last chapter, "D'une fin de siècle à l'autre."

Some works do not attempt any great level of theoretical sophistication in their analyses of the sociological question of the intellectual; in their very naïveté, they are more useful, I think, because they continue to respect, and address, *what* was being written, as well as *who* was doing it. Such is the case with *Les Intellectuels en France, de l'Affaire Dreyfus à nos jours*, by Pascal Ory and Jean-François Sirinelli (Paris: Armand Colin, 1986), a valuable source book for an understanding of the larger trends, fads, and passions that have swept the French intellectual scene in the last hundred years. The bibliography is especially good.

11. In this sense my project moves in the opposite direction from that of someone who would write exclusively on the American intellectual, of whom there has never really been a definition that makes sense (other than the purely empirical one of the technician of power in a think tank or "kitchen cabinet"), or whose definition (other than in the ad hoc or purely pragmatic sense) is always situated on the infinitely receding horizon.

12. One thinks here above all of the article "Philosophe" in the *Encyclopédie*, which was in fact written not by Diderot but by the rhetorician Dumarsais. Already in this article we see an emphasis on reason as a replacement for Christian experience or grace, and in this sense Durkheim's inspiration clearly came directly from the Enlightenment theories of the *honnête homme*. We read in "Philosophe," for example, that "Reason is to a philosopher what grace is to a Christian. Grace impels the Christian to act, reason impels the philosopher." (The unstated problem here, as it would be later for Durkheim, lies in the coordination of the force or energy of the act with the static representations of reason.) We also find this characteristic statement in "Philosophe": "One might say that [the philosopher] looks on civil society as a divinity on earth: he offers incense and honors it with probity, with a painstaking devotion to his duties and a sincere desire not to be a useless or troublesome member of society" N. S. Hoyt and T. Cassirer, eds. and trans. *Encyclopedia: Selections* [Indianapolis: Bobbs-Merrill, 1965], pp.283–89).

13. See, in this context, Marianna Torgovnick, *Gone Primitive: Savage Lives, Modern Intellects* (Chicago: University of Chicago Press, 1990).

14. W. S. F. Pickering, *Durkheim's Sociology of Religion* (London: Routledge and Kegan Paul, 1984), notes that, after the war, none of Durkheim's associates or followers maintained the master's emphasis on religion. Pickering notes that "within [his] *équipe* Durkheim was unique in his enthusiasm for things religious. In this sense he was without parallel and none of his colleagues possessed the enthusiasm for religion which we have suggested he had" (p. 508).

15. On the topic of Bataille and Durkheim, see my article "1937: The College of Sociology Is Founded," in *A New History of French Literature*, ed. Denis Hollier (Cambridge: Harvard University Press, 1989), as well as the end of chapter 1, below.

16. See, for example, Bataille's novels *Story of the Eye* and *L'Abbé C.*

17. "A day comes when the pen is forced to stop, and the writer must then take up arms," says Jean-Paul Sartre in *What Is Literature?* trans. B. Frechtman (Cambridge: Harvard University Press, 1988), p. 69; hereafter WIL.

18. It would be naive at this point to attribute this breakdown of the Durkheimian scheme to historical factors alone – the post–World War I malaise, the economic and political crisis of the 1930s, etc. As we will see, the political/historical explanation itself depends upon the tacit acceptance of a certain model of what Roland Barthes has dubbed the "writer" – who is only a shard of the larger, impossible, figure of the intellectual. This "writer" sees historical factors as the determining ones. Conversely, attributing the fragmentation of Durkheim's anthropological/sociological model exclusively to a split in rhetoric – between the performative and the constative, for example – itself limits us, this time to the activity, and ultimately to the method of analysis, of Barthes's "author." My point all along in this book will be that, writing after Durkheim, one cannot choose between, or give priority to, the constative (which entails the political and the historical) or the performative (language/rhetoric), the knowledge and representation of the intellectual, or his mad, or mechanical, act.

19. See Clark, *Literary France*, chap. 6.

20. Roland Barthes, "Authors and Writers" (hereafter AW), in *Critical Essays*, trans. Richard Howard (Evanston, Ill.: Northwestern University Press, 1972), p. 144. It should be noted that Howard's translation of these two terms is loose in the extreme: I use them here only for convenience' sake, to remain in conformity with his widely read version. In fact in the original French, "author" is not *auteur* at all but *écrivain*, and "writer" is not *écrivain* but *écrivant*. The latter is a Barthesian neologism, the present participle ("writing") used as a noun. The point is that the *écrivant* is using writing as a means, not an end – his or her activity is "transitive." One should bear in mind that, in French, the present participle is used to

indicate one activity carried out at the same time as another (as in the sentence "While walking, we ran into our friends"). The *écrivant*, too, while doing one thing (writing), carries out another task ("While [or by] writing, we fight for the proletariat, etc."). Thus a much better translation than "Authors and Writers" would be "Writers and Writings" – but that would lead only to another confusion, because the word "writing" does exist in English as a noun (it means a "text," an *écrit*). See "Écrivains et écrivants" in Barthes's *Essais critiques* (Paris: Seuil, 1964), pp. 147–54.

While Barthes associates (using Howard's terms) the "author" with the priest and the "writer" with the "clerk" (or the intellectual), I would consider them to be both variants of the post-Durkheimian intellectual. In any case, the link between "clerk" (or "cleric") and priest is clear enough; for Benda, for example (in *The Betrayal of the Clerks*), the clerk, ideally, is devoted to eternal, absolute principles, as is, we would add, at least in principle, the priest.

21. I refer here to Paul de Man's reinterpretation of the theory of the speech act, most notably elaborated in the last two chapters ("Promises" and "Excuses") of his book *Allegories of Reading: Figural Language in Rousseau, Nietzsche, Rilke, and Proust* (New Haven: Yale University Press, 1979); hereafter AR. I will be referring, explicitly or implicitly, to these important chapters throughout this book; my chapter on de Man (chap. 9) contains a critical reinterpretation of "Excuses." It is worth noting that de Man himself, in maintaining the distinction between "reference" and "performance" is in the end simply giving another, much more sophisticated, version of Barthes's dyad of "writer" and "author," and, ultimately, of Sartre's "committed literature" and "poetry." This distinction runs like a fault line through postwar criticism and is fundamental to my approach in this book.

22. See Barthes's "Death of the Author," in *Image, Music, Text*, ed. and trans. Stephen Heath (New York: Hill and Wang, 1977), pp. 142–48. In this essay, Barthes conceives of the subject as a grammatical function rather than as an ontological presence or existential agent: "Linguistically, the author is never more than the instance writing, just as the I is nothing other than the instance saying I: language knows a 'subject,' not a 'person,' and this subject, empty outside the very enunciation which defines it, suffices to make language 'hold together,' suffices, that is to say, to exhaust it" (p. 145).

Barthes's conception of the subject here as an "empty" linguistic or grammatical function clearly anticipates Paul de Man's conception of a performative rhetoric as an "anti-grav" machine-grammar, arbitrarily and violently positing meaning (see the last chapter of *Allegories of Reading*). A similar, and contemporaneous, "emptying" of subjectivity and meaning can be found in Foucault, Blanchot, and Derrida (see the chapters devoted to these authors, below).

23. Of course one could explain this shift historically, by citing the decline of the French Third Republic, the breakdown of the apparent (and fragile) consensus which, after the Dreyfus affair, seemed to promise at least the possibility of the implementation of Durkheim's goal of a thoroughly secular state, bolstered by a lay religion and clerisy. But to ascribe this shift entirely to historical causes is to take sides with the "writer" (and especially the "committed" "writer") against the "author." As I hope will be clear by the end of this Introduction, due to the fundamental impossibility of any coherent *Bildung* of the contemporary intellectual, the writing "I" of this book is incapable of deciding between "writer" and "author," is indeed torn between these sides – not because of a contingent inability to choose between them, but because of their rigorous necessity and incompatibility, on the level of rhetoric *and* on the level of history.

24. There is a strain in the de Manian approach that would simply *eliminate* the mimetic, the anthropological, the cathartic, etc., despite the fact that, for de Man at least, the moment of representation, deluded as it may be, can never be eliminated, or even simply differentiated from the performative act. For an example of this antimimetic bias, see the critique of mimesis in Lacoue-Labarthe, in the chapter "Hölderlin and the Greeks," in Andrzej Warminski's book *Readings in Interpretation: Hölderlin, Hegel, Heidegger* (Minneapolis: University of Minnesota Press, 1987), pp. 39–41.

25. One thinks here of the case of the totem in Durkheim (analyzed in chap. 1, below): it can be both that which institutes the clan and that which represents it. These two functions are both necessary and incompatible.

On the inseparability of the performative (or the "material") and the constative in de Man, see Cynthia Chase's excellent chapter "Giving a Face to a Name: De Man's Figures" in her book *Decomposing Figures: Rhetorical Readings in the Romantic Tradition* (Ithaca, N.Y.: Cornell University Press, 1986), pp. 82–112. See esp. p. 105: "the text's materiality cannot be isolated as such or as an origin, although it is the condition of possibility of any text." It should also be stressed, though, that if the "material" moment cannot simply be isolated from its representation, then that representation too is necessary, and it too is the "condition of possibility of the text." If the performative is always belated, it is belated precisely in relation to the constative; in excuse making, for example, no matter how mechanical the performance of the speech act, it is always a response to the (erroneous) imputation of guilt. The referential reading is always in error, perhaps, but it is also always a precondition of the act of which it is always again the misinterpretation, just as the act (the excuse) is the precondition of the false judgment. These two "sides," then, are inextricable, but radically incompatible.

26. Maurice Blanchot, "Literature and the Right to Death" (hereafter LRD), in *The Gaze of Orpheus and Other Essays*, ed. P. Adams Sitney, trans. Lydia Davis (Barrytown, N.Y.: Station Hill, 1981), p.51.

27. As we will see throughout the second part of this book, one of the most characteristic gestures of authors – such as Foucault, Derrida, and de Man – who would affirm a mechanical writing or rhetoric over a utilitarian and denotative prose is the maintenance of Heidegger's critique of humanism and subjectivism, which, in one of its best-known and influential formulations, was directed against Sartre himself (*The Letter on Humanism*). This critique is also directed, of course, against metaphysical oppositions in general, one of the most notable of which is the "human/inhuman" or "culture/nature" dyad.

28. Blanchot is perhaps referring here to the literary "terrorism" analyzed by Jean Paulhan in his book *Les Fleurs de Tarbes* (Paris: Gallimard, 1973), one version of which holds that all writing, contaminated by rhetorical devices and clichés, must disappear before the "meaning" that it represents or transmits. See chap. 6, below.

29. Maurice Blanchot, "The Gaze of Orpheus" (hereafter GO), in *The Gaze of Orpheus*, p.103. Translations have been modified.

30. Philippe Lacoue-Labarthe, "The Caesura of the Speculative" (hereafter CS), trans. Robert Eisenhauer, in *Glyph* 4 (Baltimore: Johns Hopkins University Press, 1978), pp.57–84.

31. Georges Bataille stresses the role of representation and theatricality in sacrifice in his essay "Hegel, la mort et le sacrifice," in *Deucalion* 5 [Neuchatel: La Baconnière, 1955]; see esp. pp.32–34.

32. On this subject (the link between catharsis as a literary mechanism, catharsis as a medical strategy, and catharsis as the motor of ritualized sacrifice) see René Girard, *La Violence et le sacré* (Paris: Grasset, 1972), pp.396–409.

33. The duality of political betrayal/impotence which undoes any possibility of political correctness, and behind which lurks a larger problem of the duplicity of language and the temptation of a utopian expenditure, is the subject of my earlier book, *Politics, Writing, Mutilation: The Cases of Bataille, Blanchot, Roussel, Leiris, and Ponge* (Minneapolis: University of Minnesota Press, 1985).

34. All of Bataille's efforts in the period 1937–39, when he directed the College of Sociology, clearly were aimed at the reinstitution of a sociology that

would, far better than Durkheim had done, account for the role of "sacred" violence in society, while at the same time sparking a renewed experience of the sacred in moribund bourgeois societies. On this period, see Denis Hollier's anthology *The College of Sociology, 1937–39*, trans. Betsy Wing (Minneapolis: University of Minnesota Press, 1988). The "left" and "right" distinction I mentioned is developed most fully by Bataille in his lecture "Attraction and Repulsion II," on pp. 113–24 of *The College of Sociology*; the problem of the priority of "left" over "right" is discussed on p. 123.

35. Such a Bataillean sociology of the intellectual should be sharply distinguished from Roger Caillois's attempt at putting forward a "Sociologie du clerc" (his essay, under this title, can be found in his book *Approches de l'imaginaire* [Paris: Gallimard, 1974], pp. 61–69). Though Caillois was associated with Bataille in the College of Sociology, his "cleric" is a member of a hierarchical, quite antidemocratic "order." Bataille's intellectual was never so politically unambiguous, and that is what makes him or her so interesting.

36. This is the overall plan of Vincent Descombes's influential book *Le Même et l'autre: Quarante-cinq ans de philosophie française, 1933–78* (Paris: Minuit, 1979).

37. There seems to be, after the Foucauldian fete of the late sixties and early seventies, and after the resigned quietism and anomie that has followed it (and after the inevitable disillusionment with Mitterand-style socialism), a desire on the part of a number of French critics to return to a more progressive, engaged, and conventionally politicized social model. Such is the case, for example, with Jean-Michel Besnier and Jean-Paul Thomas, as evidenced in their book *Chronique des idées d'aujourd'hui: Eloge de la volonté* (Paris: PUF, 1987). Michel Surya's review *Lignes*, founded in 1988, also displays a strong desire – or nostalgia – for the more straightforward leftist political task of the intellectual.

38. On the question of the fictionality of the speech act, see Derrida's essay on J. L. Austin, "Signature, Event, Context," in *Margins of Philosophy*, trans. A. Bass (Chicago: University of Chicago Press, 1982).

39. Jean Baudrillard, *America*, trans. C. Turner (London: Verso, 1988); hereafter A.

1. DURKHEIM AND THE TOTEM ACT

1. If Durkheim's influence is all-pervasive in France (more often, it seems, in a negative rather than positive way) the same can certainly be said of the United States. American sociology – the problems it sets itself, the solutions it is willing to accept – would be unthinkable outside of the ground

rules laid by Durkheim. See, on this topic, the introductory chapter of Ernest Wallwork's *Durkheim: Morality and Milieu* (Cambridge: Harvard University Press, 1972). It is interesting to note, though, that while the French seem to have picked up on the resonances of Durkheim's emphases on religion, violence, and the sacred (this is true above all of Bataille, Foucault, and their followers) the Americans have virtually ignored this area. One looks in vain in their writings for any stress upon moral enthusiasm as a rational version of religious ecstasy, the role of the teacher as secular priest, the centrality of sacrificial ritual, and so on.

2. Throughout this book I will often use "he" or "him" as a generic pronoun to refer to "the human person," "the intellectual," "the sovereign," "the cleric," etc. This is by no means meant to indicate that these figures are exclusively male; I do it only for simplicity's sake ("he or she" and its variants become extremely cumbersome when repeated often). Indeed one can just as easily imagine female as male incarnations of each of these figures. Moreover, the sacred and its relation to gender is an important question – in a very specific way, the female victim is a central figure in Bataille, of course, and the sacredness of menstrual blood is always given by anthropological writers of Durkheim's era (and before) as a prime example of the force of mana. The problem of gender, while not explicitly posed in this chapter, is nevertheless one that is very worthy of development – especially since so many anthropologists (Durkheim, Mauss, even Bataille in his own way) ignore the larger implications of gender differentiation in their analyses of the sacred.

3. See, for example, Michel Foucault's "What Is an Author?" in his *Language, Counter-Memory, Practice*, pp. 113–38, and, most characteristically, Lyotard's *Tombeau de l'intellectuel*.

4. See Emile Durkheim's *Le Suicide* (1987; Paris: PUF, 1985), esp. chap. 5, "Le Suicide anomique." Anomie in modern Western societies, it seems, is above all the result of the absence of coherent goals and meanings provided by society as a whole: the individual must provide his own, and in so doing he inevitably posits ends that seem to be of benefit to him alone and that pit him against all other members of society. Since he does not exist in isolation, however, but as a member of society, these orientations can only be ephemeral. Individual and purely "utilitarian" activity, in fact, can never lead to fulfillment, and the growing frustration of the individual as he chases will-o-the-wisps inevitably leads to suicide. "One is avid for new things, for unknown pleasures [*de jouissances ignorées*], but which lose all their flavor after they have been experienced. From that point on, one is without the strength to withstand the least setback" (*Le Suicide*, p. 285).

5. Emile Durkheim, *The Elementary Forms of the Religious Life*, trans. J. W.

Swain (1912; London: George Allen and Unwin, 1927); hereafter EF. I have considerably modified many of the quotations.

6. Robertson Smith was the author of the influential *Religion of the Semites* (1889), a work that strongly influenced Durkheim's own theory of sacrifice.

7. Auguste Comte, in *The System of Positive Polity* (New York: B. Franklin, 1967), had put forward the need for a lay religion that would provide society with the hierarchy and mythology it stood to lose with the demise of Catholicism. Durkheim's objection to Comte was that his "religion" was posited arbitrarily; Durkheim, on the contrary, wanted to show the *necessity* of a rational morality (seen to exist already, albeit in a mystified form, in "primitive" societies and, finally, arrived at scientifically through the analysis of ethnological findings) that would satisfy basic social needs without having recourse to any kind of obscure symbolism. There are other crucial differences: Comte stresses "intellectual" progress, while for Durkheim intelligence is inseparable from its grounding in social integration, which is actually *more* developed in "primitive" societies. Comte does see "traces" of the earlier "stages" of man in the latter – the theological conceptions continue to manifest themselves in the metaphysical stage – but for Comte the metaphysical transcends itself in the "positive." The point, then, is to go beyond the "theological traces" as much as possible and not to recognize their inherent truth and permanence. Finally, while Comte, like Durkheim, stresses the preeminence of the individual, for the former it arises only at the later stages of cultural evolution, whereas for Durkheim religion symbolizes from the first the interaction of individual and society, an interaction that is universally valid but which has been lost and must be rediscovered by modern anomic societies.

Durkheim was, in fact, writing in the wake of a long tradition of social reformers who saw the need for a secular religion that would replace the irrationality of Christianity while retaining its good points (for Durkheim, this was above all the Christian stress on the autonomy and sacredness of the soul): besides Comte, Jean-Jacques Rousseau and Henri Saint-Simon were key figures of this tendency. See Pickering, *Durkheim's Sociology of Religion*, esp. pp.481–85; Robert Nisbet, *The Sociology of Emile Durkheim* (New York: Oxford University Press, 1974), pp.158–60; and D. G. Charlton, *Secular Religions in France, 1815–70* (London: Oxford University Press, 1963).

8. Emile Durkheim, *Moral Education*, trans. E. K. Wilson and H. Schnurer (1902–3; New York: Free Press, 1973), p.9; hereafter ME.

9. Durkheim stresses that the teacher, as conduit for his higher morality, must be possessed by it in a way that, perhaps, elevates him above the

Notes to Pages 35–38

"profane." In this way he will be closer to human personhood than those who are content with mere jobs. This idea is at least implied in the following quote, from *Education et sociologie* (1922) (Paris: PUF, 1985), p.68: "It is the high idea of his mission that colors so easily the word of the priest, for he speaks in the name of a god [*sic*] in which he believes, to which he feels closer than the profane crowd [*la foule des profanes*]. The lay teacher can and must have something of this feeling. He too is the organ of a great moral person that transcends him."

10. The image of society as a hierarchical organism composed of cells, which is most alive when its cells are most intensely in contact, seems to be a commonplace of much French social thought; one thinks of Teilhard de Chardin, to be sure, but also of Bataille in such essays as "Le Labyrinthe" (although Bataille is attempting to disarticulate this metaphor in the very act of recycling it). In Durkheim, see chap. 5 of *Les Règles de la méthode sociologique* (1895; Paris: PUF, 1986): "the degree of the coalescence of social segments best expresses the dynamic density of a people" (p.113).

11. Emile Durkheim, "Individualism and the Intellectuals" (1898; hereafter 11), trans. M. Traugott, in *Emile Durkheim: On Morality and Society* (Chicago: University of Chicago Press, 1973), p.48.

12. Emile Durkheim, "The State" (hereafter s), in *Durkheim on Politics and the State*, ed. Anthony Giddens, trans. W. D. Halls (Cambridge: Polity Press, 1988), p.46. The translations have been modified. The essay was first published in *La Revue Philosophique* 4 (1958): 433–37.

13. At one point, in fact, Durkheim recognizes that many forms of expenditure in ritual are not subject to reason, that they occur senselessly. Toward the end of *The Elementary Forms*, he writes of a kind of "fusion" of consciousnesses that takes place when people are gathered in ritual. "Life stirred up in this way enjoys such a great independence that it displays itself sometimes in pointless events, lacking any usefulness, for the pleasure of affirming itself alone" (EF, 605). This trace of another reading of ritual appears for an instant, then is gone, passed over; its consequences, if fully considered (it is doubtful that they could ever be "grasped") would put the whole enterprise of *The Elementary Forms* in jeopardy.

14. On page 297 of *The Elementary Forms*, Durkheim in fact stresses the exclusionary nature of socially accepted ritual representation: "It [the accepted representation] tends to repress the representations that contradict it, it keeps them at a distance; it commands, on the other hand, acts that realize it, and this is done not through a material coercion or through the perspective of a coercion of this type, but through the simple radiation of the mental energy within it." It should be stressed, however, that for Durkheim sacrificial ritual is not primarily oriented toward the generation of the

314

community through arbitrary expulsion (catharsis), scapegoating, and so on. Durkheim's model is, instead, one of exchange and reflection, whereby both individuals and community gain by the movement of sacrificial distribution within a closed circle; we have to do here not with violent ostracism and social expectoration but with peaceful incorporation and appropriation. Telltale passages like the one above, however, indicate that something very different underlies Durkheim's peaceful and natural sacrifice-exchange. They are the trace of the totem act that can never be successfully effaced: "The very violence with which society reacts, by rebuking or even materially repressing dissident efforts, strongly demonstrates the ardor of communal conviction, and contributes to the reinforcement of its dominance" (EF, 297).

15. Claude Lévi-Strauss, "Introduction à l'oeuvre de Marcel Mauss" (hereafter I), in Mauss's *Sociologie et anthropologie* (Paris: PUF, 1983). This collection, which originally dates from 1950 (as does Lévi-Strauss's essay), also includes Mauss's *Outline of a General Theory of Magic*.

16. The resonance of these characterizations of language in the writings of subsequent theorists is worth noting; one thinks of the "sliding signifier" in Lacan, de Man's statement that there is always a "surplus" of guilt over (and generated by) the excuse, "supplementarity" in Derrida, etc.

17. Pierre Bourdieu, *Ce que parler veut dire* (Paris: Fayard, 1986); hereafter PVD. It should be noted that for Austin the performative is always tied to a force that is put in opposition to meaning and that cannot simply be subordinated to meaning. As he notes on p. 100 of *How to Do Things with Words* (Oxford: Oxford University Press, 1962): "I want to distinguish force and meaning in the sense in which meaning is equivalent to sense and reference, just as it has become essential to distinguish sense and reference within meaning."

18. I should stress, however, that this emphasis on the double priority of *both* the speech act and the referential moment is my own; de Man, and his followers, always ultimately privilege the moment of the performative, the force of the act, etc. I would argue, however, that an attentive reading of de Man – reading de Man against himself, so to speak – would authorize the double priority of these terms. See my comments on de Man in the Introduction.

19. The published translation misses this double use of the word *rudimentaire*. See the French version in *Revue Philosophique*, p.436.

20. Durkheim saw the German Empire as an example of how *not* to unify a people around a collective ideal; see his *L'Allemagne au-dessus de tout: La Mentalité allemande et la guerre* (Paris: A. Colin, 1915).

21. On the question of sacrificial exchange as a circle, see Rodolphe Gasché's

article on Marcel Mauss, "L'Echange héliocentrique," *L'Arc* 48 (1972): 70–84.

22. In his discussion of the difference between the "person," whose autonomy is impersonal, having nothing to do with selfish (and ultimately anomic) motives, and the isolated subject, Durkheim, invoking Kant, sees "individuation" as based on mere contingency: "[Human reason] is the mind's power to raise itself above the particular, the contingent, the individual, in order to think in the form of the universal. . . . Individuation is not the essential characteristic of the person. A person is not only a singular subject distinguished from all the others. He is, beyond this and above all, a being to whom is attributed a relative autonomy in relation to the milieu with which he is most immediately in contact" (EF, 271). Durkheim nevertheless uses the terms "individual" and "individualism" any number of times – as in, most notably, his discussion of sacrifice ("society only exists and lives in and through individuals" [EF, 347]). What first seems a fairly rigorous distinction between the selfless and universal "person" and selfish and arbitrary "individualism" (and even "the individual") seems to break down later in *The Elementary Forms*. This slippage in terminology is only a trace of a much larger inability to distinguish definitively a healthy, equal exchange between person and society from the sickly and malevolent force of the imposition of purely individual or arbitrary goals and meanings.

2. NIZAN, DRIEU, AND THE QUESTION OF DEATH

1. See Susan Rubin Suleiman's book *Authoritarian Fictions: The Ideological Novel as a Literary Genre* (New York: Columbia University Press, 1983) for in-depth analyses of a number of *romans à thèse*, including those of Nizan (she analyzes *The Trojan Horse* on pp. 102–18), Maurice Barrès, Louis Aragon, Drieu, and others. Suleiman associates the "authoritarian" message of these novels with their supposedly authoritarian style. Thus as the extreme example of "readerly" texts they tend to be fundamentally totalitarian, and their actual political positions (of Left or Right) come to seem almost irrelevant. In their form, they are reactionary; in opposition to them, presumably, we can pose "writerly" modernist texts, or at least open-ended realist novels, which allow the reader a good, democratic choice in the establishment of meaning (see, for example, her comments on pp. 242–43). Suleiman is willing to grant in her penultimate chapter that some thesis novels in fact problematize their meaning, but her general approach still stands. (Her discussion in that chapter of Paul Nizan's first novel, *Antoine Bloyé*, is nevertheless excellent: she points out that Nizan in

several key passages was incapable of insulating the working class from a totally meaningless, "bourgeois" death; see pp. 216–23.)

It should be noted that any easy distinction between the Barthesian "readerly" and "writerly" – as in the case of Sartre's equivalent distinction between "committed literature" and "poetry" – can never, in any case, be rigorously maintained. Ross Chambers, in his book *Story and Situation: Narrative Seduction and the Power of Fiction* (Minneapolis: University of Minnesota Press, 1984), points out that even "readerly" texts of the nineteenth century, which seem to limit severely the range of possible interpretations, still make possible (like a democratic regime, we might say, authorizing limited dissent) a certain range of interpretations on the part of the reader, "opening up interpretive options while simultaneously programming them, determining a narrative situation without imposing a single interpretation of the narrative content" (p. 35).

In the situation analyzed here, however, I would argue that there is neither a relatively simple opposition between readerly and writerly (Suleiman), nor is there a kind of liberal democratic cohabitation (Chambers); instead, the joining of the two, if we can call it that, is characterized by vicious circularity and violent betrayal.

2. See the chapter "Politics, Mutilation, Writing," in my book *Politics, Writing, Mutilation*, pp. 3–21.

3. See especially Julien Benda, *La Trahison des clercs* (Paris: Grasset, 1927).

4. For a classic example of this, see the description of Dr. Parrottin's pseudo-Cartesian heuristic method as it is described in Sartre's *La Nausée*: after taking his young followers to the point at which they doubted even the very right of the bourgeoisie to lead, the obstetrician Parrotin then caused them to doubt a little more. But they cannot doubt their own reason (for reason is the foundation of their doubt), and they suddenly find themselves back at the belief in their own superiority, which is now grounded in reason. See *La Nausée*, in *Oeuvres romanesques*, ed. Michel Contat and Michel Rybalka (Paris: Gallimard, 1981), p. 104; hereafter OR.

5. See Paul Nizan's *Les Chiens de garde* (Paris: Gallimard, 1965), pp. 42–43.

6. Major texts in this renewed interest in German thought and phenomenology are Alexandre Kojève's lectures on Hegel from the 1930s, *Introduction à la lecture de Hegel* (Paris: Aubier, 1947); Jean Wahl's *Etudes Kierkegaardiennes* (Paris: Aubier, 1938); and the first translation (by Henri Corbin) of Heidegger in French, "Qu'est-ce que la métaphysique," which appeared in *Bifur* 8 (1930) – a translation which was not as faithful as one might have wished but whose vocabulary anticipates (and clearly influenced) writers such as Sartre, Blanchot, and Bataille.

7. Paul Nizan, *The Trojan Horse*, trans. Charles Ashleigh (London: Long-mans, 1937), p.139; hereafter TH. All translations have been modified.

8. It is no coincidence that Sartre intended to title the last (uncompleted) volume of *Les Chemins de la liberté*, *La Dernière Chance* (The last chance). In that novel, we were to see men, under the Occupation and at the Liberation, giving their lives meaning through collective action. (Fragments of this work have recently been discovered; they appear in OR, 1585–1654; see Chapter 4.)

9. The reader will note the virtually nonexistent role women play in this novel of liberation. All collective action is male, and even phallic (one thinks of the penetrating writing that sullies the "virgin" surface of the white walls when Bloyé and his comrades carry out their first revolutionary gesture). Here it is Berthe who plumbs the depths of revolutionary defeatism; later Catherine, another worker's wife, dies the meaningless death par excellence as she bleeds to death, alone, after an abortion. One could argue that in this novel the real sacrificial victims are not so much the workers slain by the bosses but the women: they are the victims not only of the capitalists but of the novelist himself, who does not foresee any contribution they might make to the struggle, and who portrays them (as in the cases of Berthe and Catherine) as unwitting accomplices of the reactionaries: Berthe is a defeatist, and Catherine aids the bosses in their desire to limit the ever-growing numbers of workers. It would even appear that revolutionary solidarity is aided by the exclusion of women: the heroic moments portrayed in the novel are lived not at home, where the men are with their wives, but in the streets, where they are with other men, be they Fascists or Communists. One could also say that, to the extent that the violence against the virginal white wall is a kind of metaphoric violence against women, the bond between the male workers is strengthened. One sees a virtually identical kind of "male bonding" in Sartre's wartime novels, especially *Le Sursis* and *La Mort dans l'âme*.

10. One can speculate that Nizan's portrait of Sartre as a hapless misanthrope must have hit home: already in *Le Mur* (*The Wall*) (1939) we see a greater politicization on Sartre's part (this becomes clear in the story "Enfance d'un chef" ["Childhood of a Leader"]). After Nizan's death in 1940 Sartre set himself the task of writing a series of novels about the growing commitment of an intellectual (Mathieu Delarue) just before and after the defeat of 1940. It is almost as if Sartre set himself the task not only of defending his friend's memory (which was defamed by the French Communist party, because Nizan had resigned his membership after the Hitler-Stalin pact of 1939) but of reincarnating Nizan in his own person, embodying a "committed" philosophical stance while retaining the primacy of the question

of Being. Sartre clearly thought that Nizan's break with the Communist party indicated a refusal of Stalinism and an openness to Sartre's existential problematics of individual responsibility. If that were the case, then there would be no difference between Sartre and a fantasmatic Nizan, Nizan as he would have been had he lived: Sartre is politicized, Nizan is more open to the fact of individual freedom and responsibility. Sartre clearly worked out, on a fictional plane, his fantasy of this Sartre/Nizan conjunction, perhaps the ultimate "group in fusion" – or example of male bonding. The fragments of *Drôle d'amitié* and *La Dernière Chance* (see n.8, above) also show this imaginary Sartre/Nizan fusion: the joining of first Vicarios (a dissident Communist who, like Nizan, broke with the party in 1939) and Brunet (a hard-line Communist) and then, after Vicarios's death, the joining of Brunet and Mathieu (an independent leftist intellectual, modeled on Sartre himself).

11. It is rather astonishing that Sartre remained Nizan's friend after the publication of *The Trojan Horse* (even if he came to recognize that there was a certain truth in Nizan's depiction of Lange). Seeing Sartre's "perception" as a kind of voyeuristic, nihilistic X-ray drive is, to say the least, not a very subtle reading of Roquentin's vision of "contingency" in the Jardin public in *La Nausée*. Nevertheless, it is interesting to note that two major aspects of Lange's experience in *The Trojan Horse* came to be major concerns for Sartre after Nizan's death: first, of course, is Lange's bad faith (he seems to disdain fascism, refusing to recognize that he is, indeed, a Fascist himself) – Sartre, in *L'Etre et le néant* (*Being and Nothingness*) (1943), based much of his philosophical method on an analysis of bad faith; second, the excitement of the crowd into which Lange is drawn just before he fires his pistol, and the loss of his individual, critical will when he is swept away, prefigures Sartre's concern with the "group in fusion" in *La Critique de la raison dialectique* (*The Critique of Dialectical Reason*) (1960).

   In one area, of course, Nizan's portrait is accurate: Sartre, like Lange, always refused to recognize "false bottoms," and his later attempts at rethinking Marxism and psychoanalysis in the light of a fully responsible subjectivity were dependent on that refusal.

12. On p.236 of *Le Cheval de Troie* we are told that the ties between the workers are actually stronger (*des rapports autrement puissants*) than the "hasards du destin et du sang," because they are the result not of chance (as in a family), but of group unification through common sacrifice. (The English translation [p.244] misses this nuance.)

13. This – with the remarks that follow – is a thesis that is unavoidable when the novel's larger thesis is examined critically.

14. And especially, perhaps, against women (see n.9, above, and n.16, below).

15. A. W. Gouldner, in his excellent book *Against Fragmentation: The Origins of Marxism and the Sociology of Intellectuals* (New York: Continuum, 1985), sees Marxism not only as a philosophy of human liberation, but (above all) as a doctrine of a new social order created by a "new class" of technocratic and rationalist intellectuals – a social order which will, not coincidentally, make possible these clerics' own career advancement and prominence.

16. No doubt this episode is meant to convey the idea that abortion is anti-social and reactionary. Aragon's thesis novel from the same period, *Les Cloches de Bâle*, conveys a similar message. It would seem that while the men are dying, thereby giving meaning to their own lives and unifying the community, the women are having abortions and therefore decimating the community.

17. Lange's movement from one system (labyrinth) to another is also a labyrinth, but, because it is open-ended, it can be comprehended only by another one – and so on to infinity.

18. One of the best books to chart Drieu's fascism in his writing (as opposed to a strictly biographical representation of his politics) is Julien Hervier's *Deux individus contre l'histoire: Ernst Jünger, Pierre Drieu La Rochelle* (Paris: Klincksieck, 1978). Hervier also begins a task of great importance: setting the relatively neglected but important author Ernst Jünger in a larger literary and philosophical context. The other important name with which Jünger should be linked is Martin Heidegger. (See chap. 9, below, for a discussion of Jünger's *On the Marble Cliffs* in the context of Paul de Man's "wartime journalism.")

19. Pierre Drieu La Rochelle, *Gilles* (Paris: Gallimard, 1973), p.673; the translation is my own.

20. See Pierre Drieu La Rochelle, *Fragments de mémoires, 1940–41* (Paris: Gallimard, 1982).

21. Pierre Drieu La Rochelle, "Les Evènements de Février," in *Socialisme Fasciste* (Paris: Gallimard, 1934).

22. For an inventory of groups on both the Left and Right that attempted to rethink the role of the individual, politics, and labor in this period, see Jean-Louis Loubet del Bayle's book *Les Non-conformistes des années trente* (Paris: Seuil, 1969). Another group that Loubet del Bayle does not mention, but which was important on a theoretical level if not on a social or political one, was Georges Bataille's Acéphale group. See his writings from this period (1937–39) in the first volume of his *Oeuvres complétes* (Paris: Gallimard, 1970).

23. During the same period, however, Georges Bataille was attempting to evolve a party of "effervescent" revolt that would not be Fascist, anti-Semitic, or controlled by big business (indeed, as Bataille saw it, "efferves-

cence" was inimical to the absolutism of fascism). See the Acéphale writings, referred to in n.22, above.

24. See especially the concluding pages of "Mesure de l'Allemagne" in Pierre Drieu La Rochelle's *Socialisme fasciste* (Paris: Gallimard, 1934). See also "Nietzsche contre Marx" in *Socialisme fasciste*. Bataille was carrying out a very similar reading of Nietzsche at the same time as Drieu, but he attempted to dissociate Nietzsche from his Fascist exponents (see "Nietzsche et les fascistes" in the first volume of Bataille's *Oeuvres complètes*).

25. The establishment of an equivalence between one who collaborates with Germans and one who does so with Americans is an obvious way for a Fascist to escape guilt: he can (wrongly) claim that everyone collaborates, and that one Occupation is as bad as another. Céline, in his postwar novels (such as *Féerie pour une autre fois*), puts an added twist on this: in his version, everyone is a collaborator, and the same people collaborated first with the Germans, then with the Americans. Underlying the changing allegiances (and the changing way Céline himself is viewed: first he is a hero, then a traitor) is the unchanging nastiness and mendacity of the people.

26. Pierre Drieu La Rochelle, *Les Chiens de paille* (Paris: Gallimard, 1964), p.111; hereafter CP. Translations are my own.

27. This self-destruction of *Les Chiens de paille* should not be taken as a mere manifestation of Fascist ideology – or of the decline of Fascist ideology. Indeed the characterization of pure intellectual activity as "decadent" and the desire to posit a "third force" that recognizes the limitations of the orthodoxies of Left and Right, and that attempts to go beyond them through an experience of collective enthusiasm, sacrifice, madness, or deviancy, can be seen in writers of various ideological orientations: Artaud, Bataille, Genêt, even Sartre, and more recent French authors like Sollers (and recent theorists like Deleuze and Baudrillard). While other, earlier novels by Drieu are clumsily ideological – one thinks of *Gilles* – *Les Chiens de paille* is relentless in its demystification of the possibility that any novel can serve as a simple vehicle for a doctrine or for a simple, efficacious sacrifice. Perhaps the strongest Fascist element in *Les Chiens de paille*, aside from the foul residue of his anti-Semitism, is Drieu's decision to interpret what we would see as a final textual self-sacrifice as cause for cynicism and apparent despair, rather than as something to be affirmed with a certain Nietzschean strength (the latter strategy has been that of Drieu's acquaintance, Maurice Blanchot).

28. As we have seen, the logic of sacrifice can be put to work for reactionary or revolutionary ends by groups of the Right or the Left.

29. This is true of novels such as Blanchot's *Le Très-Haut* and Bataille's *L'Abbé C.* (See chap. 2 of my *Politics, Writing, Mutilation.*)

3. THE PERFORMANCE OF *NAUSEA*

1. On desire and recognition in Sartre, see Judith P. Butler's *Subjects of Desire: Hegelian Reflections in Twentieth-Century France* (New York: Columbia University Press, 1987), chap. 3.

2. Immanuel Kant, *Critique of Judgment*, trans. J. H. Bernard (New York: Hafner Press, 1951), pp. 91, 83; hereafter CJ.

3. Jean-Paul Sartre, *Nausea*, trans. Lloyd Alexander (New York: New Directions, 1964), p. 133; hereafter N.

4. Throughout *Nausea* a certain strain of Nietzscheanism is evident: in this view, it is man who makes sense out of nature by conveniently naming things, creating systems of metaphors that are useful for his survival but which bear no necessary relation to the way things "really" are. Even logic itself, which grounds science, is not eternally valid but is only an arbitrarily posited, contingent device tailored to man's peculiar needs. See Nietzsche's "On Truth and Lie in a Nonmoral Sense," in *Philosophy and Truth: Selections from Nietzsche's Notebooks of the Early 1870s*, ed. and trans. D. Breazeale (Atlantic Highlands, N.J.: Humanities Press, 1979), pp. 79–97.

5. It is important to stress here that the portrait of the jerks and humanists together constitutes, on the part of Sartre, a thoroughgoing critique of both the unofficial and the official ideology of the Third Republic. Most of the jerks that Roquentin investigates (such as Parrottin and Blévigne) were influential local "leaders" in the period immediately following the debacle of the Franco-Prussian war and the Commune; they were primarily concerned with the guarantee of the rights and privileges of the haute bourgeoisie under the new republic. Humanism, of course, represented an equally influential strain of republicanism during this period; this model, on the surface opposed to the ideological reign of the jerks, promoted egalitarianism and the reestablishment of rationalism as a kind of state religion (which would be taught in the public schools). It is no coincidence that Roquentin confronts both jerks and the humanist (the Autodidact) in public places, since both forms of republicanism were attempts at mastering and making sense of the potentially chaotic secular "public sphere" (and since public places were the equivalent, for a secular morality, of the sacred space of a church). Appropriately enough, Roquentin confronts the jerks in a "privileged" public space (the art gallery) and the Autodidact in a more humble one (the municipal library) – and he "experiences" the Nausea in a space in which *all* social groups can, or are supposed to, come together: the public park.

6. The greatest exponent of an educational mission to propagate morality was of course Durkheim; see his *Moral Education*. The only doctrine that the Autodidact is able to disseminate is one of obscenity and fragmentation.

7. The reader is referred to Brunschvicg's two-volume masterwork, *Le Progrès de la conscience dans la philosophie occidentale* (Paris: Alcan, 1927). See his discussions of consciousness in Kant, sections 149 (pp. 306–8) and 165 (pp. 339–42) especially. Sartre's reliance on the term "consciousness" in the short article on intentionality in Husserl ("A Fundamental Idea in Husserl's Phenomenology: Intentionality" – see n. 8, below) underscores the fierce rivalry between the younger philosopher and his resented master. Paul Nizan also launched into a violent attack on Brunschvicg and his colleagues, but Nizan's critique was more overtly political; see *Les Chiens de garde* (1932; Paris: Gallimard, 1965).

8. Jean-Paul Sartre, "Une idée fondamentale dans la phénoménolgie de Husserl: L'Intentionalité," reprinted in *Situations I* (Paris: Gallimard, 1975), p. 38; hereafter, IH. Translations are my own.

9. There is a reactionary, even sexist side to Sartre that has not been sufficiently analyzed. One essay that does treat it is "Holes and Slime: Sexism in Sartre's Psychoanalysis," by Margery L. Collins and Christine Pierce, in *Women and Philosophy: Toward a Theory of Liberation*, ed. Carol C. Gould and Marx Wartofsky (New York: Putnam, 1976), pp. 112–27. I am grateful to Alice Y. Kaplan for referring me to this article. "Digestive" gooeyness is usually associated, especially in the novels, with weak-willed, manipulative women and homosexuals (see *The Age of Reason*, the first volume of Sartre's *Roads of Freedom*). In the essay on Husserl, Sartre contemptuously dismisses the neo-Kantian "protoplasmic" philosophy as one in which "everything is done by compromise" (p. 40). One has to remember that this essay was written in 1939, not exactly a good year for the democratic regimes that valued compromise.

   For an interesting analysis of the significance of the distinction between the sticky and feminine "immanent" and the hard and masculine "transcendent" (which nevertheless does not broach the political overdetermination of this distinction), see Serge Doubrovsky's article "Phallotexte et gynotexte dans *La Nausée*: 'Feuillet sans date,'" in *Sartre et la mise en signe*, ed. M. Issacharoff and J.-C. Vilquin (Lexington, Ky.: French Forum, 1982), pp. 31–55.

10. The tendency on the part of readers of *Nausea* often seems to be to assume that what Roquentin "sees" in the park (the tree-root, etc.) is radically different in kind (hence a "revelation," "unveiling") from the modes of perception and representation employed by the jerks/humanists. See, for

example, "Les Parcours de l'aventure dans *La Nausée*," by Sandra Teroni-Menzella (in *Etudes Sartriennes* 1, no. 2 [1984]: 57–74), where it is a question of a "dévoilement" (p.70), despite the fact that Roquentin's discovery is situated by Teroni-Menzella entirely within an "adventure," and "Roquentin et le langage naturel," by Gerald Prince, in Issacharoff and Vilquin's *Sartre et la mise en signe*, pp.103–13, where we learn (on p.110) that what Roquentin perceives is the "véritable nature du monde." I want to argue precisely the opposite: that Roquentin's vision, like that of his enemies, depends above all on metaphor; in that sense his vision, and theirs, are in complicity. This similarity is stronger than any difference.

A number of critics, however, have noted the resolutely metaphorical nature of Roquentin's nauseous vision of the world: Christopher Prendergast, in his article "Of Stones and Stories: Sartre's *La Nausée*" (in *Teaching the Text*, ed. S. Kappeler and N. Bryson [London: Routledge and Kegan Paul, 1983], pp.56–72), discusses this problem at some length, and cites some other critics (including Fredric Jameson) who have grappled with it. See also Dominic La Capra's discussion of *Nausea* in his book *Rethinking Intellectual History: Texts, Contexts, Language* (Ithaca, N.Y.: Cornell University Press, 1983), pp.203–8. La Capra states at the end of his discussion of *Nausea*: "Some small residue of meaning is always there in the world already, however far back or deep down one goes in trying to get to its root."

11. Here once again we think of Nietzsche's "On Truth and Lie in a Nonmoral Sense." We could add that, while Nietzsche sees an army, a hierarchy, of metaphors, Roquentin sees swarming replication; this does not mean, however, that Roquentin's metaphors are any less human, any less arbitrary or fixed.

It is important to recognize that, for Roquentin, this mendacity of metaphor and abstraction is central in all facets of life – perception, narration, societal formation, philosophical argument. For this reason it seems to me somewhat off the mark to stress the differences between conceptual thought and metaphorical language in the vision in the park, as Rhiannon Goldthorpe does in chap. 1 (on *Nausea*) of *Sartre: Literature and Theory* (Cambridge: Cambridge University Press, 1984).

12. I am quoting from the Hazel Barnes translation of Jean-Paul Sartre, *Being and Nothingness* (New York: Washington Square Press, 1966), pp.28–29.

13. Descombes very effectively criticizes Sartre's conception – or lack of conception – of the "in-itself" in his book *Le Même et l'autre: Quarante-cinq ans de philosophie française, 1933–78* (Paris: Minuit, 1979), pp.64–70.

14. Peter Brooks, in the context of a discussion of the role of adventures in *Nausea*, makes the point that narrative itself is fundamentally indissociable

from (depending on, and acting as) metaphor. See *Reading for the Plot: Design and Intention in Narrative* (New York: Vintage, 1984), p.91.

15. Donald Pease, "Sublime Politics," *boundary* 2 12/13 (Spring/Fall 1984): 264.

16. Peter Caws, *Sartre* (London: Routledge and Kegan Paul, 1984), p.117.

17. I am referring here to the notes for a "Factum sur la contingence" that Sartre wrote about 1932. These fragments can be found in OR, 1678–86. See esp. p.1685: "The possible is a category of thought preparatory to the necessary because in the necessary there is choice, elimination. But in the contingent: no elimination. That which exists leads to that which exists and leads to it without this being necessary; the link between them is also contingent. The relation between two existing facts cannot therefore be either from principle to consequence or from means to end. It is a transformation without rigor from one fact to another fact. It does not possess the power to affirm itself, nor to exist as such, it slides out of the subject. From the passage from one state to another state there is too much [*il y a trop*]. Disorder, monotony, sadness" (my translation).

18. See the last two chapters in de Man's *Allegories of Reading*: "Promises (*Social Contract*)" and "Excuses (*Confessions*)." On the impossibility of keeping promises, see chap. 2 of J. Hillis Miller's *The Ethics of Reading* (New York: Columbia University Press, 1987).

19. Terry Keefe, in his article "The Ending of Sartre's *La Nausée*" (*Forum for Modern Language Studies* 12, no. 3 [1976]: 217–35) argues, on the basis of a close examination of evidence within the text, that Roquentin will go on to write another book, not *Nausea*. Keefe's position, it seems to me, is a bit too literal minded; the resonance of *Nausea* with Proust's *A la recherche du temps perdu* will always raise the question of the necessity of Roquentin's writing or rewriting *Nausea*, whether the internal evidence of the novel bears it out or not. In any case, Keefe's article contains an extensive list of articles that have maintained that *Nausea is* the novel that Roquentin goes on to write.

20. See the article by Rémy G. Saisselin, "Bouville ou l'anti-Combray," *French Review* 33, no. 3 (1960): 232–38.

21. Christopher Prendergast, in his essay "Of Stones and Stories: Sartre's *La Nausée*," p.71, poses an important problem concerning the overall project of *Nausea*: was Sartre *aware* that it was a paradox to carry out a critique of metaphor and adventure using metaphor and adventure? In asking this question, however, he already assumes a subjectivity that can know, reflect upon, and be responsible for its acts, etc. In other words, he is squarely back in the world of figurative language – and he is also begging the question (if a priori one cannot escape "fictions," Sartre was either lying to

us – he was ironic – or he was lying to himself – he was in bad faith; either way it amounts to the same thing).

4. THE IMPOSSIBLE CONCLUSION OF SARTRE'S
ROADS OF FREEDOM

1. In this chapter, I will give English titles to Sartre's works that are literal translations of the original titles. *Les Chemins de la liberté* has been translated as *The Roads to Freedom* – which has a different sense, I think, from the title I prefer: *The Roads of Freedom*. The third volume of the series, *La Mort dans l'âme* (*Death in the Soul*, but, as an idiom, *With a Heavy Heart*) was given first the title *Troubled Sleep* (!?) and then *Iron in the Soul*.

2. See the summary of the projected plot of the last volume of *The Roads of Freedom* in OR, 2104–5.

3. The fragments of *Drôle d'amitié* are in OR, 1461–1534; those of *La Dernière Chance*, OR, 1585–1654. The translations from these two works are my own (so far as I know, English translations have not yet been published).

4. The abandonment of *The Roads of Freedom* certainly did not cause Sartre to lose interest in the synthesis of the realms of subjective and objective, of individual initiative and political responsibility (or conformity). Instead, Sartre attempted to work the problem out on a theoretical rather than on a fictional level; this at least is the argument of Mark Poster, in his excellent book *Existential Marxism in Postwar France* (Princeton: Princeton University Press, 1975). According to Poster, the later Sartre pinned all his hopes not on a novel but on the theoretical work *The Critique of Dialectical Reason*.

5. This passage is taken from the Gerard Hopkins translation of *La Mort dans l'âme*, which is entitled *Troubled Sleep* (New York: Knopf, 1951). It has been slightly modified.

6. On the character Moûlu and his status as a scapegoat – and the role of eating and defecating in the sacrificial ritual in which Moûlu is caught – see George H. Bauer, "Just Desserts," in *Sartre after Sartre*, ed. Fredric Jameson, *Yale French Studies* 68 (1985): 3–14.

7. It appears that Sartre made very little headway on the project after this point; there exist, however, 233 pages of manuscript from this period that were sold at auction in 1959. They are now in the hands of private owners and are not available for inspection; they may contain additional fragments of *La Dernière Chance*. My statement here must therefore remain provisional pending the publication of this material. (See OR, 2106.)

8. See the second volume of Sartre's *Critique de la raison dialectique: L'Intelligibilité de l'histoire* (Paris: Gallimard, 1985), where Sartre discusses at

great length the interrelation of subjectivity, historical change, and the need for discipline in revolutionary activity. It should not come as a surprise that much of the book is devoted to an analysis of Stalin's praxis and to the necessity, and evil, of the cult of personality. See also Ronald Aronson's *Sartre's Second Critique* (Chicago: University of Chicago Press, 1987), an excellent explication of this unfinished work.

9. On the distinction between figurative and performative rhetoric – between a language of truth and speech acts – see the last two chapters of Paul de Man's *Allegories of Reading*.

10. It is worth noting in this discussion that Sartre himself never officially recognized a distinction between language as performance or act and language as representation. On the contrary, he actively attempted to conflate the two. See, for example, *What Is Literature?* (trans. B. Frechtman [Cambridge: Harvard University Press, 1988]), where we learn (on p. 38) that the engaged writer both knows that (to cite Brice Parain) "words are like loaded pistols" (if the writer "speaks," he "fires") – that writing, in other words, is an act – and that "the writer has chosen to reveal the world and particularly to reveal man to other men" – that writing is a depiction of the (humanistic) truth.

11. One thinks here of René Girard's analysis of sacrificial violence in his book *Violence and the Sacred* (Baltimore: Johns Hopkins Press, 1978) – but we should note that, in applying this kind of critique to Sartre, we are only turning it against its author, since Girard's model itself is taken from the kind of interpersonal dynamics sketched out by Sartre in works such as *No Exit*.

12. This story, the last and most fully developed in the collection *The Wall* (*Le Mur*) – and the one that points most clearly to Sartre's later political concerns – may be found in OR, 314–88.

13. Drieu La Rochelle, as firmly rooted in his times as Sartre was, followed exactly the same model but reversed one of the terms: for him, the homosexual/feminine/surrealist figure was on the Left, while the hard-bitten man of action was a Fascist. See, for example, his novel *Gilles*.

14. My discussion of the scapegoating method used against Moûlu is inspired by the Girardian feminist readings to be found in Eve Kosofsky Sedgwick's book *Between Men: English Literature and Male Homosocial Desire* (New York: Columbia University Press, 1985). It should be stressed that for Sedgwick the term "homosocial" implies a bond between heterosexual men, usually accomplished through the scapegoating and exclusion of a woman.

15. This point is inspired by Sedgwick's discussion of homosexuality on pp. 5–11 of *Between Men*.

16. This observation was made very early on in a book review, by Roger Nimier, of *Death in the Soul* (see OR, 2021).

5. SARTRE'S *CRITIQUE OF DIALECTICAL REASON*

1. Jean-Michel Besnier, in conversation with the author. The reader is referred to Besnier's article on the *Critique* in the *Dictionnaire des oeuvres politiques*, ed. François Chatelet (Paris: PUF, 1986). See also Besnier's remarks on Kojève in chaps. 2 through 6 of part 1 in his *La Politique de l'impossible: L'Intellectuel entre révolte et engagement* (Paris: La Découverte, 1988).

2. See, in this context, Judith P. Butler's analyses of the role of desire and transparency in the dialectic, from Hegel via Kojève to Sartre, in the first three chapters of her book *Subjects of Desire: Hegelian Reflections in Twentieth-Century France* (New York: Columbia University Press, 1987). Also see part 2 (on Kojève) of Michael S. Roth's *Knowing and History: Appropriations of Hegel in Twentieth-Century France* (Ithaca, N.Y.: Cornell University Press, 1988).

3. Jean-Paul Sartre, *The Critique of Dialectical Reason*, trans. A. Sheridan-Smith, ed. Jonathan Rée (London: NLB, 1976), p. 261; hereafter CDR. I have modified all translations in order to remain closer to Sartre's terminology and syntax. (*Ordination*, for example, is translated as "ordering.")

4. This is an example of a somewhat imprecise use of terminology on the part of Sartre; in the *Critique*, "group" is usually used in a precise sense: it refers to the group in fusion, not to the serial *collectif* or *rassemblement*.

5. On the practico-inert, see Dick Howard's discussion of it in his book *The Marxian Legacy* (London: Methuen, 1977), p. 166: "Because of its paradoxical nature, its lack of univocal signification, Sartre speaks of matter as *practico-inert*. The etymology of the term indicates its dialectical origin: it is the product of plural individual *praxis*, but in the inertia of exteriority it has lost the translucidity of that *praxis*. The active passivity of the practico-inert is at the root of alienation." Howard notes that not only can objects be considered to make up the practico-inert: so too can language and "cultural artifacts." Finally, as "products and producers, inhuman and human at once," even men are caught up in it.

6. One is struck, at this point and often in the *Critique*, by the apparent circularity of scarcity and seriality. As in the quote I am discussing here, seriality is evidently a function of scarcity; you wait in line, compete with others, because there is a scarcity of seats (or anything else). Seriality results from scarcity. On the other hand, when Sartre first discusses scarcity (CDR, 200–10), it is clear that things are not scarce "in themselves" but only in relation to the *collectif*, in which individuals are competing: "In

fact, scarcity as tension and as a field of forces is the expression of a quantitative fact (more or less rigorously defined): a given natural substance or manufactured product exists, in a determined social field, in an insufficient number given the number of group members or inhabitants of the region: *there is not enough for everyone*" (CDR, 204). In good dialectical fashion Sartre can argue that scarcity, produced by men and the competition between them, returns (as the practico-inert) to generate ever more seriality. It is an endless cycle, and neither scarcity nor seriality can be said to be prior.

On one level, at least, Sartre, in the *Critique*, refuses the possibility that "matter," or its scarcity, can be seen as radically external to human signs or life: "where finally is matter, in other words Being that is totally lacking in signification? The answer is simple: it appears *nowhere* in human experience. In whatever period of History one finds oneself things are human to the precise extent that men are things; a volcanic eruption can destroy Herculaneum: it is, in a certain way, man who gets himself destroyed by the volcano; it is the social and material unity of the city and of its inhabitants which gives, in the human world, the unity of an event to what, without men, would perhaps dissolve in a limitless and meaningless process" (CDR, 247).

Still, there is a problem. To what extent does the inertia of the practico-inert itself escape man and his intentions? To what extent is it foreign to him? As soon as Sartre starts to present a "Being" that is radically resistant to man's goals, that is always external to them and that thwarts them, he is back at the problem that we saw facing Roquentin in *Nausea*: to what extent is the "in itself," the "contingent" level of existence that is radically external to human consciousness, simply meaningless in any philosophical discussion? The problem can be seen in the very fact that many Sartre commentators continue, obstinately, to see "scarcity" as an irreducible phenomenon, a necessity that is radically external to man and his world of signs. For example, Fredric Jameson, in *Marxism and Form* (Princeton: Princeton University Press, 1974), writing of the consistency of Sartre's approach in *Being and Nothingness* and the *Critique*, states: "Just as lack, as an abstract way of characterizing human existence, takes place in a world arbitrarily characterized as contingent, whose essential structure, with respect to man, is *facticity* (that is to say, incommensurability with human thought and human existence, or, in the terminology of a more literary existentialism, absurdity or meaninglessness); so, in these new concrete terms, in which man's emptiness takes the form of *need*, the resistance of the world to man is now defined in terms of *scarcity*. For scarcity is precisely the unanalyzable starting point, the contingent datum, of the world in which we exist. Unintelligible in itself, simply a fact to which we cannot assign any metaphysical significance whatsoever, it nonetheless is the framework in which we must act, and conditions and alienates our acts and projects even in their very conception" (232–33).

But if scarcity is "unintelligible in itself," how can it be a framework for our acts? How can we enter into any kind of relation with it? How can it be the starting point for any kind of coherent philosophy? Jameson's linking of such earlier terms as contingency and facticity with scarcity only underscores the problem: can the notion of scarcity – or the seriality that is always linked with it, from scarcity's very first appearance in the *Critique* – make any more sense, finally, than the supposedly radically "contingent" experience of Roquentin in the park? Yet it is clear enough that Sartre always needs a bedrock scarcity as a kind of absolute underlying his system; after all, people can be "alienated" from themselves and their products – reified, in other words – only if they are capable of inadvertently producing a level of Being which, if only momentarily, radically escapes their desires and meanings, not to mention their knowledge or consciousness.

Thus commentators are justified in reading the later Sartre as espousing the same kind of radically exterior, antihuman contingency that can only be read as Roquentin's fallacy in *Nausea*. Without this bedrock level of Being as resistance, as the alien or alienated, Sartre's entire philosophy, early or late, makes no sense at all. So it is no surprise that, in his last purely philosophical work, the projected second volume of the *Critique*, Sartre unambiguously returns to a radically external and contingent level of existence. Ronald Aronson, in his book *Sartre's Second Critique* (Chicago: University of Chicago Press, 1987), notes at one point: "The possibility that a cooling of the sun would end history from the outside (not from within, as in the case of a nuclear holocaust) throws into sharp relief the fact that our human projects take place in a universe which is indifferent to them and are conditioned by forces which are *on principle* unknowable and uncontrollable. . . . Our every act is marked by a kind of impotence. This is the limitation of practical beings living in a material universe they did not create and which is on principle indifferent to them. If this limit defines praxis-process from the *outside*, it also does so from within" (198).

7. For a typical example, see CDR, 635: "The practical unity of the group and the free pledged inertia of its members are reflected back to it as the inorganic passivity of a pure physical or human materiality retaining on itself and in the exteriority of its parts the false unity of the seal." Sartre also writes, in the same paragraph, of the results of the group's action as "imprinted in inorganic matter."

8. This definition is taken from the *American Heritage Dictionary of the English Language*, s.v. "ordination."

9. For an extensive exposition of the speech acts of address by which a speaker gets the attention of his audience, maintains it, passes it on – and by which the audience indicates its consent, interest, lack of interest, desire to speak, and so on, see Mary Louise Pratt's *Toward a Speech Act Theory of Literary Discourse* (Bloomington: Indiana University Press, 1977), pp. 100–51.

10. There would seem to be a weakness in Sartre's theory here, or at least a problem if he hoped to account for the mass manipulation of groups under fascism (or under a demagogic bourgeois regime that borders on fascism). The model of radio listeners can account for the passivity of societies in the face of tyranny, not the mobilization of groups. If Sartre's narrative "I" is worried about individuals in those groups somehow being convinced by the radio speaker's lies, and then effectively carrying out the speaker's commands, he is clearly mistaken. The action in concert of the listeners can be directed only against the possibility of action in concert.

11. One thinks – is indeed forced to think – here of the glueyness of Roquentin's experience of the Nausea, which is also a kind of serial impotence (or a vision of a universal seriality, in which the subject is implicated).

12. We see here the final stage of Sartre's thinking of the Nausea. The serial *rassemblement* is, like the melting and revolting objects that Roquentin confronts in the public park, a random collection of "objects" (or reified individuals) which are both gelatinous (they are held together only by the "glue" of their own weakness and isolation) and opened out to an Other, through the pitiful escape of whatever substance they have momentarily managed to accumulate. The great difference is that in *Nausea* Roquentin (or the reader through Roquentin) was still grappling with the nature of this facticity: was it an attribute of nature? Were "things in themselves" contingent? Or was it the result of the intervention of an inevitably human language (and figurative rhetoric)? Some of the uncertainty on this score remained, as we have seen, as late as *Being and Nothingness*, where it was still unclear whether the *en soi* was a brute materiality untouched by human intervention, or whether it was the petrified residue of subjective action in the world. The *Critique* seems (at first, at least) to resolve this problem: seriality is a social phenomenon, one of the weakness of people and of the failure of a certain practice of language and speech acts. If materiality reflects, transmits, and imposes this seriality, in the form of scarcity or absence (the lack of seats on the bus, the absent speaker on the radio), it is only because it carries, as the practico-inert, a "seal," the product of human labor, which nevertheless escapes direct human control (and indeed it then

reifies the human). As I have mentioned in n.6 (above), however, this "humanization" of contingency is itself open to question.

13. For a useful extended explication of the theory of the group in fusion, see Joseph S. Catalano's *A Commentary on Jean-Paul Sartre's "Critique of Dialectical Reason"* (Chicago: University of Chicago Press, 1986), pp. 165–78.

14. The term "shifter" is discussed in chap. 9 of Roman Jakobson's *Essais de linguistique générale*, vol. 1 (Paris: Minuit, 1963). Jakobson points out that "each shifter possesses a general, proper signification" (p. 179, my translation). Thus "I," "here," "now" are not simply interchangeable; they *do* have a meaning. But that level of meaning is, we would point out, generally, tautologically true, and thus empty, nothing more than a grammatical function; "I" in general applies to everyone, "here" to everywhere, "now" to any time at all, etc. This kind of "meaning" of these general terms is to be found exclusively in the grammatical roles they play in sentences. Jakobson goes on to note a second kind of meaning: "In reality, the only thing that distinguishes shifters from all the other constituents of the linguistic code is the fact that they necessarily refer back to the message" (p. 179, my translation). Thus "I" takes on its full meaning when I use it to refer to a specific person, who is otherwise indicated in my message (i.e., I can refer to myself with the word while speaking, or can indicate myself by name elsewhere in a text). What happens, however, when the "message" is ephemeral, a function of a momentary conjunction (a "here") that disappears as soon as it arises? (This would seem to be the case in the situation described by Sartre, where each "now" and "here" is immediately followed by another, as is each "I," the preceding "heres," "nows," and "I's" always disappearing back into the crowd.) In that case, the shifter's meaning is of the first type noted by Jakobson; it is exclusively an empty term, referring not to any plenitude of subjectivity or experience (the "meaning" of the "message") but to its differential function within a syntactic movement. In this way, the Sartrian shifter comes very close to the "degree zero" phonemes that Lévi-Strauss associates, in his interpretation of Mauss, with mana (see n.16, below). Finally, we should note that the "meaning" of Sartre's shifters, in Jakobson's second sense, when they are fixed on the pages of the *Critique*, is only that they refer to their larger absence of definite meaning (thus their determinate meaning, as codified in the book, only affirms their larger absence of determinate meaning, their emptiness).

15. Of course Sartre himself at no point in the *Critique* writes this sentence; I am arguing here that "I am here now" is the only thing that can be said (or written) after the revolutionary *mot d'ordre* becomes a pure shifter, valid only for me here now (which is also for everyone everywhere anytime).

16. In Hegel's *Phenomenology*, it should be recalled, sense certainty is possible only through the "here" and "now." One only need recall the discussion of the attempt to grasp the absolutely certain – but absolutely differing and deferred – moment of presence, through the use of a shifter. Hegel writes: "They [the proponents of the immediate certainty of sense-data] have in view this piece of paper on which I write *this*, or rather I have already written it; but what they have in view they do not say. If in an effectively real way they wanted to say this piece of paper, which they have in view, and if they wanted to say it properly, then that would be impossible because the sensible here which is in view is *inaccessible* to language which belongs to consciousness, to the universal in-itself. During the effectively real attempt to say it, it would break down" (Jean Hyppolite's translation of the *Phenomenology*, 1:91).

The "here" and "now" can only be "indicated," and they are inseparable from their indication; but as soon as they are indicated, they are no longer "here" and "now." They are in the past. The "now" is always in the past, "it has no truth of being" (1:88). As Hegel says, "The now and the act of indicating the now are constituted in such a way that neither the one nor the other is an immediate Simple, but is a movement that has in it a number of moments" (1:88).

Thus for Hegel the reality and its "indicator" – the shifter – are inseparable from the universal only in that "here" is really "everywhere," "now" is really every moment that passes and that is indicated, but always after the fact. "If we determine more exactly the thing as this piece of paper, then each and every paper is a *this piece of paper*, and I have still said only the universal" (1:91–92). In the same way, each day is composed of an infinity of "heres" and "nows" – the resulting "universal," which is all that can be said, is nothing more than an immense aggregate of elements – and is certainly not a fusion, or a movement toward fusion, in a Sartrian sense. (If anything, it is the very impersonal and arithmetic collection of ciphers that the group in fusion is meant to overcome.)

The importance of recalling Hegel here is not to "correct" Sartre but only to observe that Sartre, in order to base a dialectic on this fundamental experience of the "here" and "now," would at least have to take into account, and refute, Hegel's version of the self-differing shifter and its non-synthetic ("universal") agglomeration in the "Sense Certainty" section of the *Phenomenology*. He does not do this. The very first chapter of the *Phenomenology* is, then, the unthought of Sartre's *Critique* – what, in other words, Sartre must forget in order to conceive the group in fusion.

17. The reader will recall our discussion, in chap. 1, of Lévi-Strauss's characterization (in the "Introduction à l'oeuvre de Marcel Mauss," in Mauss's

Sociologie et anthropologie, p.L) of the empty phonological term as a version of "mana" – a kind of mathematical sacred.

18. On the problem of Hegel's version of "sense-certainty" and its "example" on the page, see Paul de Man, *The Resistance to Theory* (Minneapolis: University of Minnesota Press, 1986), chap. 3, esp. p.42 (hereafter RT), and Warminski, *Readings in Interpretation*, chap. 7.

19. It is worth recalling that for Lévi-Strauss (see n.14, above) these elements with a "zero symbolic value," like mana, are capable of resolving otherwise insoluble antinomies, such as "force and action, quality and state . . . abstract and concrete . . . omnipresent and localized" ("Introduction à l'oeuvre de Marcel Mauss," p.L). These last two opposed terms in particular are the ones that Sartre is resolving through his revolutionary "commands": the "orders" are both as particular as they can be, yet they are abstract, even universal (because empty); and, as we have seen, they are both localized and omnipresent in the group. This very evanescence of the shifter guarantees its manalike force – which itself is nothing other than a function of a differential series of terms, the grammar of the text in which those shifters play a role (the *Critique* itself).

20. Section B of vol. 2 of Sartre's *Critique*, pp.198–348, can be read, in fact, as a long and not very convincing apology for the Stalinist purges of the 1930s.

21. I am thinking, of course, of the section in Hegel's *Phenomenology* – "Absolute Liberty and Terror" – that presents the violence of the French Revolution as a necessary moment in the movement of History. For Kojève above all this necessity became the basis for a Marxist version of Hegel, in which the man of destiny – the Napoleon figure of the twentieth century – was none other than Stalin himself (see, in this context, Besnier's Introduction to his *Politique de l'impossible*).

22. As Sartre says in a footnote to a footnote (CDR, 244–45), "certain moments of the dialectic are capable of being expressed by an algebra; but the dialectic itself, in its real movement, is beyond any mathematics."

6. PAULHAN AND BLANCHOT

1. See, for example, Pierre Klossowski, *Nietzsche et le cercle vicieux* (Paris: Mercure de France, 1967); the "Hegel" section of Bataille's *L'Expérience intérieure* (see chap. 11, below); etc.

2. Julien Benda, *Exercice d'un enterré vif* (Paris: Gallimard, 1946), p.92.

3. Paulhan's rhetorician, as we will see, is very much devoted to the possibility of meaning and truth through style and the skillful use of seemingly artificial clichés and figures of speech. In this sense he or she is a full-fledged member of the traditional French *République des lettres*, which

unites literate and literary people through a higher, eminently rational culture that transcends political oppositions (on this *République*, see Clark, *Literary France*). Paulhan in fact was editor of the *Nouvelle Revue Française* during the 1920s and 1930s, a period in which it tried to maintain the unity of such a *République* in the face of total political fragmentation. During this period, the NRF published writers of the far Left (Aragon, Nizan), the far Right (Drieu La Rochelle), the equivocating Left (Gide), the rationalist Left (Benda), the mystical Center (Daumal), etc. This extremely fragile balance was destroyed, of course, in 1940, with the occupation of the NRF by the Germans, and the editorship of Drieu. The *Nouvelle Nouvelle Revue Française*, reestablished in the mid-1950s, was never able to assert the République in as convincing a way, and it was therefore incapable of playing the hegemonic role that it had enjoyed in the prewar period – a role whose prestige, ironically enough, the Nazis had recognized in 1940, and which they had attempted to turn to their own purposes.

4. Jean Paulhan, *Les Fleurs de Tarbes* (Paris: Gallimard, 1973), p.63; hereafter FT. Translations are my own.

5. Jean Paulhan, *Lettre aux directeurs de la Résistance* (Paris: J. J. Pauvert, 1968); hereafter LD. Translations are my now.

6. Jean Paulhan, "La Demoiselle aux miroirs," in *Jacob Cow le pirate, ou si les mots sont des signes* (Paris: Tchou, 1970), p.58.

7. Here one thinks above all of Bataille's analysis of the monstrosity of the sun and its worshipers: see the brief article "Rotten Sun" in *Visions of Excess*, pp.57–58.

8. Jean Paulhan, "Le Don des langues" (hereafter DL,), in *Oeuvres complètes* (Paris: Cercle du livre précieux, 1970), 3:406. Translations are my own.

9. Paulhan makes a similar point in a 1939 essay he read before Bataille's College of Sociology group: "D'un langage sacré" (in *Cahiers Jean Paulhan, vol. 2, Paulhan et le Madagascar* [Paris: Gallimard, 1982]), p.335. In this piece Paulhan argues that the proverb becomes "clear" by *not* being examined. Its meaning, its "clarity," is imminent, a function of a contrast, a difference, that separates it from the words and meanings that surround it. The state of distraction of the speaker of the proverb – who ignores the obvious fact that the proverb "literally" means nothing – enables the proverb to become clear, even radiant, if the speaker and his interlocutor gaze "a little bit beyond" it (i.e., beyond its literal meaning).

10. Jean Paulhan, "La Rhétorique avait son mot de passe" (hereafter RSM), in *Jacob Cow le pirate*, p.115. Translations are my own.

11. Paulhan argues in another work, however, that the layman in a way is more aware of the arbitrariness and rules – the "wagers" – of language, than is

the intellectual; see *Les Incertitudes du langage* (Paris: Gallimard, 1970), pp. 182–83.

12. The venomous response by Louis Martin-Chauffier that immediately followed the publication of the *Lettre aux directeurs* in 1952, and the ensuing debate between Paulhan and Martin-Chauffier, is provided in an appendix to the Pauvert edition.

13. Paulhan's "Comment la littérature est-elle possible?" (hereafter CLP) can be found in Blanchot's *Faux pas* (Paris: Gallimard, 1943). Translations are my own.

14. That distinction, as we saw in the previous section, is better conceived as the difference, within rhetoric, between meaning and syntax, reference and grammar. It is by no means certain that Paulhan was simply a slave to his own Rhetoric (i.e., the maintenance of the traditional opposition between thought and matter), or that Blanchot has – or is capable of, within the parameters of his method – a more advanced "awareness" of what is at stake in Paulhan's version of Rhetoric. This is not meant as a negative judgment of Blanchot, but only as a "recognition," on my part, that the logic of Blanchot's approach might preclude the possibility of a straightforward "higher level" of knowledge.

15. For another Blanchotian rewriting of Paulhan's "reading/writing" amalgam, see "La Facilité de mourir," in *L'Amitié* (Paris: Gallimard, 1971), pp. 172–91.

16. In the same way, language itself always both eliminates and conveys its subject. See, on this topic, the last page of Blanchot's article "Recherches sur le langage" (on Brice Parain's *Recherches sur la nature et les fonctions du langage*) in *Faux pas*: "My word is both an affirmation and a negation of the intelligible world, an affirmation and a forgetting of the principle of contradiction" (p. 108).

17. Maurice Blanchot, *Le Livre à venir* (Paris: Gallimard, 1973), p. 132, quoted in Vincent Kaufmann, *Le Livre et ses adresses: Mallarmé, Ponge, Valéry, Blanchot* (Paris: Meridiens Klincksieck, 1986), p. 192; hereafter LA. Translations are my own.

18. Maurice Blanchot, *La Communauté inavouable* (Paris: Minuit, 1983), pp. 31–32; hereafter CI. Translations are my own.

19. Maurice Blanchot, "Où va la littérature," in *Le Livre à venir*, pp. 301–2, quoted in LA, 196.

20. Maurice Blanchot, "Les Intellectuels en question," *Le Débat* 29 (Mar. 1984).

21. Propaganda, in fact, which called for a wave of terror that would do away with a "more or less secret association of uncourageous politicians who scare people, and capitalists without ability on a national level, who defend

their profits." Blanchot's terror before the war is one of fierce vengeance and violent retribution directed against the leaders of the Popular Front; at one point he calls for a "storm that will overwhelm in order to awaken [the people]." This terror, in other words, is the very type that Paulhan hoped to control through grammar. See Blanchot's "Terrorisme, méthode de salut public," in *Combat* 7 (July 1936). (It should be noted, at the same time, that Blanchot in one of these articles condemns most figures of the Right as well: "imbeciles who understand nothing and clever profiteers who are looking for an alibi" ["Le Caravansérail," *Combat* 10 (Dec. 1936)]. In this light, it becomes easier to understand his later refusal of a partisan terrorism, and his attempt to shelter the violence of writing from the "imbecility" of *all* political expediency.)

7. FOUCAULT AND THE INTELLECTUAL SUBJECT

1. Luc Ferry and Alain Renaut, *La Pensée 68: Essai sur l'anti-humanisme contemporain* (Paris: Gallimard, 1985); see esp. pp. 160–64.

2. Both Hubert Dreyfus and Paul Rabinow's *Michel Foucault: Beyond Structuralism and Hermeneutics* (Chicago: University of Chicago Press, 1982) and John Rajchman's *Michel Foucault and the Freedom of Philosophy* (New York: Columbia University Press, 1985) argue that about 1970 there was a profound change in the orientation of Foucault's work: in general, the earlier, "archaeology" period was concerned exclusively with the analysis of discourse and did not recognize any realm outside of the movement of language. The second, much more overtly Nietzschean period, that of "genealogy," still concerns itself with a critique of subjectivity, but now it recognizes an extradiscursive realm of power, resistances to power, in short a social sphere in which struggle can take place.

3. An English translation of Foucault's "A Preface to Transgression" (hereafter PT) is to be found in Foucault, *Language, Counter-Memory, Practice*, pp. 29–52.

4. This is Heidegger's position in his *Nietzsche* (Pfüllingen: Neske, 1961). For an analysis of Heidegger's version of Nietzsche, see Christopher Fynsk's *Heidegger, Thought, and Historicity* (Ithaca, N.Y.: Cornell University Press, 1986), pp. 55–103.

5. By stating that Foucault was deeply influenced by Heidegger, indeed that he is involved in a project of rewriting Heidegger, I mean that Foucault, like Heidegger, is, first of all, engaged in a critique of humanism, and specifically of French humanism (Sartre, especially). This critique follows from Heidegger's "Letter on Humanism," which, it should be recalled, was expressly directed against Sartre's (approximate) usage of Heideggerian themes and vocabulary while, at the same time, putting forward the

un-Heideggerian thesis that "existentialism is a humanism." In this anti-humanism, Foucault is very much the contemporary of other philosophers of the 1960s, such as Deleuze and, especially, Derrida. Foucault follows Heidegger in a second way as well: his appropriation of the critique of technology. In works like *Discipline and Punish*, Foucault is specifically concerned with "technologies of the self," the production of the (humanist) subject through the use of various technical devices and strategies. In the later Foucault, then, there is a wholly original melding of Heidegger's critique of humanism and his critique of technology. (The rethinking and problematizing of technology, on the other hand, has never been a major concern of Derrida, except perhaps in his relatively recent writing on telephonic transmission in *La Carte postale*, or in his critique of the technical function of the university in the essay "The University in the Eyes of Its Pupils" – Deleuze, on the other hand, has devoted much of his time to rethinking the nature and function of the machine in relation to the organism.)

6. It was Kant who, according to Foucault, stressed that "the limits of knowledge provide a positive foundation for the possibility of knowing" (*The Order of Things* [*Les Mots et les choses*], trans. A. Sheridan-Smith [London: Tavistock, 1970], p.317; hereafter OT). This "analytic of finitude," as Foucault calls it, always supposes that "man's being will be able to provide a foundation in their own positivity for all those forms that indicate to him that he is not infinite" (OT, 315). Such "forms" include the necessarily limited elements, both "outside" man (the empirical environment, conditions of labor, etc.) and "inside" him (unconscious drives, hidden motives) that "make him up." For a good discussion of the analytic of finitude, see Dreyfus and Rabinow's *Michel Foucault*, pp.30–43.

7. See Heidegger's *Über "Die Linie"*: "Man does not only stand *in* the critical zone of the line. He himself, but not he for himself and particularly not through himself alone, *is* this zone and thus the line. In no case is the line, thought of as a symbol of the zone of complete nihilism, like something impassible lying before man" (in *The Question of Being*, trans. W. Kluback and J. T. Wilde [New York: Twayne, 1958], p.83).

8. For Derrida and the double sense of "end," see his essay "The Ends of Man," which I will discuss in the following chapter. The word *être* in French, uncapitalized, is often used in philosophical works in the Heideggerian tradition to mean "Being" (*étant*, on the other hand, is "being"); while the English translation of Foucault's essay has "being," it could just as easily read "Being."

9. Foucault stresses the connections between the loss of subjectivity (or subjective authorship), repetitive self-reflection and self-transgression, and

the text as an infinitely positing and retranscribing machine (which thematizes, in various novelistic situations, nothing other than this very process), in his analyses of Raymond Roussel's novels. See his book *Raymond Roussel* (Paris: Gallimard, 1963).

10. Michel Foucault, "Language to Infinity" (hereafter LI) in Foucault, *Language, Counter-Memory, Practice*, p.54. Translations have been modified.

11. Indeed Blanchot himself stresses the importance of Foucault's revision of Sartre, the valorizing of seriality in the face of Sartre's critique. See Blanchot's *Michel Foucault, tel que je l'imagine* (Montpellier: Fata Morgana, 1986), p.27.

12. Michel Foucault "La Pensée du dehors," *Critique* 229 (June 1966), 523–46; hereafter PD. Translations are my own.

13. Of course Foucault would distinguish between a representation that (like the enucleated eye in Bataille) focuses on the void, that reflects its own death to infinity, that "refers to itself and is folded back on a questioning of its own limits" (PT, 44), and a speculative or self-reflexive movement that "was intended . . . to still itself in a silence where the infinite Word reestablished its supremacy" (LI, 59). It should be noted, however, that for a rigorous Derridean critic like Rodolphe Gasché (in *The Tain of the Mirror*) this distinction does not hold; from his perspective, the infinitely reflective avant-garde movement of intertextuality, the *mise-en-abîme*, etc., is itself situable within the traditional "metaphysics of reflection."

14. For an analysis of the profound connections between sacrificial logic and the philosophical project, see Philippe Lacoue-Labarthe's important essay "La Césure du spéculatif" ("The Caesura of the Speculative" [CS]) in his book *Typographies II* (Paris: Galilée, 1986).

15. Michel Foucault, "What Is an Author?" in Foucault, *Language, Counter-Memory, Practice*, p.117.

16. Jacques Derrida, "From Restricted to General Economy: A Hegelianism without Reserve" (hereafter RGE), in *Writing and Difference*, trans. A. Bass (Chicago: University of Chicago Press, 1977).

17. As Derrida says about his own approach, "I am not sure that the dialectic is not, in certain cases, the most ample and resistant umbrella against undecidability" (in the discussion following his paper "La Question du style," in *Nietzsche aujourd'hui?* Colloque de Cérisy, 1972 [Paris: 10/18, 1973], p.292).

18. See n.24, below.

19. "Contemporary" is what Pamela Major-Poetzl calls the new epoch in her discussions of the various epistemes analyzed in *The Order of Things*; see her *Michel Foucault's Archaeology of Western Culture: Toward a New Sci-*

ence of History (Chapel Hill: University of North Carolina Press, 1983), pp. 191–95.

20. It is worth noting that, fiercely opposed as he was to Sartre in so many ways – Sartre, after all, clung to a notion of consciousness, or man, and to a dialectical model of history – Foucault nevertheless shared with Sartre a desire to undo radically any science or philosophy that posited a hidden or unseen other in relation to the personal or collective conscious self. But Sartre's critique of psychoanalysis in *Being and Nothingness*, and his alternative to it – "existential psychoanalysis" – recognized nothing more than a bad faith in the symptoms of the neurotic, a refusal to recognize the implications of one's own acts, and to take responsibility for them. In this, of course, Foucault was radically opposed to Sartre, for a critique of "bad faith" implies only another morality and another conception of the self, which now must assume an even greater honesty with, or transparency to, itself. (See chap. 2, above, for a discussion of Paul Nizan's version of the Sartrean critique of "false bottoms," and the inevitable reemergence of the false bottom in Nizan's own work.)

21. As Pamela Major-Poetzl writes in *Michel Foucault's Archaeology of Western Culture*, "For Hegel the unthought was the *an sich*; for Marx it was alienated man; for Schopenhauer it was *das Unbewusste*; and for Husserl it was the 'inactual.' In every case an effort was made to reconcile man to his double, that is, to integrate thought with being" (p. 190). For an overview of the Foucauldian critique of dialectical thought (in Hegel and Marx) see Werner Künzel's *Foucault liest Hegel: Versuch einer polemischen Dekonstruktion dialektischen Denkens* (Frankfurt am Main: Haag und Herchen, 1985).

22. It should be stressed, however, that an affirmative Heideggerian reading of Nietzsche is also necessary; as Christopher Fynsk remarks in *Heidegger*, such a reading must recognize "the possibilities that open when the foundation of the modern period is brought into evidence, circumscribed by a limit that necessarily marks the relation to an outside" (p. 60). At the end of the history of philosophy, Nietzsche at least enables us to pose the question of philosophy's foundations, its impossible exterior. I would argue that Foucault, however, never recognizes this ambivalence of Nietzsche for Heidegger; rather he tends to conflate Nietzsche and Heidegger (the Heideggerian critique of humanism and technology is largely related to Nietzsche or to a Nietzsche-Deleuze amalgam). For an excellent interpretation of Heidegger's critique of Nietzsche, see Michael Zimmerman, *Heidegger's Confrontation with Modernity: Technology, Politics, Art* (Bloomington: Indiana University Press, 1990), esp. pp. 168–73.

23. From the perspective of this quote, the Other would seem to assert itself, in Foucault's view, not through a dialectical procedure by which it, or the

unthought, is brought to the surface, but through an eruption of force. In this way this quote looks forward to Foucault's later (genealogical) writings, where knowledge is inseparable from, and is a kind of aftereffect or function of, power. Even if this is the case, however, the only way this eruptive Other can be recognized, and distinguished, from the (false) Other in a dialectical relation, is through the higher knowledge at which Foucault arrives through his book *The Order of Things*. Only that knowledge can serve as a guarantee of the integrity of the power or force of this Other – else the Other would be in danger of being confused with an Other that can be dialectically appropriated. In this way power is still an aftereffect of knowledge, and not vice versa.

24. Rajchman correctly notes, on p. 24 of *Michel Foucault*, the importance of the virtually Hegelian "we" (i.e., the figure of Foucault himself as author) as the developing consciousness of writing itself: "As is often the case, the figure referred to as 'we' traces a circle of interpretation. The book is written from 'our' modernist perspective, but also tells the story of how our perspective 'necessarily' emerged."

25. Dreyfus and Rabinow, in *Michel Foucault*, like Rajchman, also stress the Foucauldian "turn" away from the analysis of discourse to a rather mysterious "nondiscursive" realm, which is never really defined. Is this realm somehow outside discourse? What does that mean? Is discourse's limit, then, to be safely maintained outside it as well, as in the classical period? How will the genealogical project differ from the classical era in this respect?

26. Rajchman, *Michel Foucault*, p. 36.

27. *Discipline and Punish* tends to focus on the objectification and production of the subject through the imposition of power by means of the apparatus (the model of the panopticon), whereas the first volume of the *History of Sexuality* stresses the disciplines and techniques of the self-formation of subjectivity (the examination of conscience in both its religious and psychoanalytic modes).

28. Michael Foucault, "Nietzsche, Genealogy, and History" (hereafter NGH), in *Language, Counter-Memory, Practice*, pp. 139–64. The French version of this article is in *Hommage à Jean Hyppolite* (Paris: PUF, 1971), pp. 145–72.

29. It should be noted, however, that a certain nostalgia remains in Foucault's later work for the society of the violent, sacrificial spectacle championed by Bataille (and, in a tamed version, by Durkheim himself), along with the concomitant condemnation of bourgeois utility and sterility. For example, in *Discipline and Punish*, the Greek and Roman model of the arena, in which the unified crowd looks at the unique spectacle, is seen to be re-

placed by the "panopticon," in which a unique and all-powerful spectator is able to gaze with impunity upon the impotent crowd. Foucault represents this historical shift as something of a loss: "With spectacle, there was a predominance of public life, the intensity of festivals, sensual proximity. In these rituals in which blood flowed, society found new vigor and formed for a moment a single great body. The modern age poses the opposite problem: 'To procure, for a small number, or even for a single individual, the instantaneous view of a great multitude.' . . . Our society is one not of spectacle, but of surveillance; under the surface of images, one invests bodies in depth; behind the great abstraction of exchange, there continues the meticulous, concrete training of useful forces" (Michel Foucault, *Discipline and Punish*, trans. A. Sheridan [New York: Vintage, 1979], pp. 216–17).

30. It should be noted, however, that for Sartre the technician can become an intellectual only by becoming aware of the contradictions of his function (he uses his tools – science, logic – to arrive at the conclusion that what he is required to do, the role he is required to play, *as* a technician or teacher, is a lie, an instance of a mendacious ideology, etc.). The (self-)awareness of the intellectual in contradiction is thus the awareness of a universal contradiction of bourgeois society; Sartre writes: "Even though, *in order to be real*, this realization [*prise de conscience*] must operate, for the intellectual, *first* on the level of his professional activities and his function, it is nothing less than the unveiling of the fundamental contradictions of society" (*Plaidoyer pour les intellectuels* [Paris: Gallimard, 1972], p. 41). Thus for Sartre when the purely technical worker recognizes the contradiction of his own position and engages in a struggle (i.e., becomes a specific intellectual, in Foucault's sense), he is still reflecting a larger, universal, contradiction. Foucault's approach is clearly meant as a critique of this Sartrian position; his specific intellectual, also a technician who recognizes the limitations and implications of his narrowly circumscribed function, does not represent any higher movement or social truth.

31. This characterization of Foucault is not meant to be an ad hominem criticism but a factual statement concerning the role he plays in French society – a role that is *functionally identical* to the one played by thinkers that Foucault himself dubs "universal" (most notably, Sartre).

32. On a number of occasions Foucault said that his works were not meant to display a general truth, that they were meant only to be a "tool box" from which each specific intellectual was free to take whatever he or she found useful. This statement, however, can itself be the product only of a universal intellectual: just as Foucault, as a universal intellectual, proclaims his own death, so too he officially announces, in and through his universal

text, the death of the universal text: from now on (in general), books cannot be generally valid, they can only be tool boxes, etc.

8. DERRIDA AND THE CRITICAL QUESTION

1. See Rodolphe Gasché's book *The Tain of the Mirror: Derrida and the Philosophy of Reflection* (Cambridge: Harvard University Press, 1986). See esp. part 2, "On Deconstruction," where Gasché presents quite clearly not only the links between Heidegger's and Derrida's projects but also the points at which Derrida's effort is a revision and critique of Heidegger.

2. Jacques Derrida, "Plato's Pharmacy" (hereafter PP), trans. B. Johnson, in *Dissemination* (Chicago: University of Chicago Press, 1981); the quotations of Mauss are on pp.131–32 n.56. The essay dates originally from 1968. Translations have been modified.

3. Marcel Mauss, *The Gift: Forms and Functions of Exchange in Archaic Societies*, trans. I. Cunnison (New York: Norton, 1967), p.61; hereafter EG. The original version, *Essai sur le don*, first published in 1923, is in the collection *Sociologie et anthropologie* (Paris: PUF, 1983).

4. On this point, Bataille's project can be seen to follow quite directly from Mauss's. Both the essay "The Notion of Expenditure" (1932) and the concluding chapter of *La Part maudite* (*The Accursed Share;* 1949) stress the necessity of a reform of modern capitalism through the introduction of a deleterious, but also inevitably beneficial, ritualized gift giving. Bataille in the late 1940s saw the American Marshall Plan for the reconstruction of Europe as the first historically significant modern manifestation of this tendency to "spend without counting."

5. See Jacques Derrida, "Différance" in *Margins of Philosophy*, trans. A. Bass (Chicago: University of Chicago Press, 1982), pp.1–28.

6. Derrida often uses the French term *propreté* in a way that does not lend itself to easy translation in English. Implied in the word *propre* is not only "proper" and "clean" but also "one's own," the sense of possession. All these meanings imply interiority, presence to or possession of oneself, the expulsion of the alien, etc.

7. A way that is, one might add, suspect as a mode of reading; doesn't Derrida's approach here, while perhaps justified given the deconstruction of the outside/inside distinction, nevertheless border on free association?

8. Here, no doubt, is another echo coming from the ghost of Heidegger: it is a Latin expression, the expression of Latinity (and the concomitant forgetting of Greek), that would posit stable *étants* in the place of *différance*, of the radicality of the *pharmakon*, of – why not, at this point? – Being.

9. These, of course, were the objections to the intellectual that Durkheim

responded to in his essay "Individualism and the Intellectuals." See chap.
1, above.

10. On infrastructures in Derrida, see Gasché's *The Tain of the Mirror*,
pp.142–53 and pp.177–251.

11. See the discussion of Lévi-Strauss's "Introduction à l'oeuvre de Marcel
Mauss," in chap. 1, above. Derrida's version of Plato's *pharmakon* is clearly
a rewriting of Lévi-Strauss's version of Mauss's version of mana; like
mana, the *pharmakon* has a kind of "zero symbolic value"; it is, in Lévi-
Strauss's words, a "sign marking the necessity of a symbolic content that is
supplementary to the one already filling the signified." Like Lévi-Strauss's
mana, the *pharmakon* is not a term in a group (of opposing terms), but it is
part of an "available reserve" that can fill in at any moment, coordinating
and mimicking available terms while exceeding them. In this way it calls
attention to the incoherency or emptiness of opposing terms in the very act
of coordinating them, establishing their stabilized positions and resolving
their (unresolvable) differences.

Derrida differs from Lévi-Strauss, however, in that he refuses to posit a
higher human "mind" whose functioning is illustrated by the study of such
elements as mana or the *pharmakon*. Indeed his work is elaborated against
the possibility of such a humanism.

12. Jacques Derrida, "The Ends of Man" (hereafter EM), in *Margins of Philosophy*, pp.116–17. All translations have been modified. The essay was originally published in 1968.

13. One should recall that Sartre himself had refused (after initially accepting)
an invitation to give a series of lectures at Cornell University in 1965; this
was meant as a gesture of protest against the ever-increasing American
presence in Vietnam. Derrida, then, both associates Sartre's philosophy
with the very imperialism that Sartre was protesting when he refused to
lecture in America, and at the same time justifies his own lecturing in the
United States.

14. It is unclear whether or not Derrida means to affirm, at this point, that
Sartre was responsible for the rise in interest in the Hegelian dialectic in
France in the post–World War I period (the other, unnamed, target here is
Lacan: Derrida writes of the "desire and insistence of the Other"): if he
does wish to imply this, the main target would then have to be not Sartre
but Kojève. "Sartre" then is only a metonym for French philosophy from
Kojève to the later Sartre (up to, roughly, the publication of Sartre's *Critique* in 1960). After this, as we see later in "The Ends of Man," there are
another set of false Heideggerians, those affirming a complete break with
consciousness and subjectivity (here Foucault is the hidden referent).

15. Derrida writes: "But no matter, as concerns the question I would like to

ask, that such and such an author has read such and such a text poorly, or simply not at all, or that he remains, as concerns systems of thought he believes he has surpassed or overturned, in a state of great ingenuousness. This is why we shall not concern ourselves here with any given author's name or with the title of any given work" (EM, 119). By not naming his "adversaries," Derrida is himself able to avoid having to read specific texts that purportedly misread Hegel, Heidegger, and Husserl. As we have seen in the case of Foucault, some misreadings themselves are liable to problematize the very humanism that they reenact in their attempted escape. Derrida's silence is also a way of passing over the many connections between his own antihumanism (if one can call it that) and, for example, Foucault's. One should recall, of course, that there are texts in which Derrida directly confronts Foucault, most notably "Cogito and the History of Madness," in *Writing and Difference*.

16. See Derrida's essay "La Question du style."

17. Jacques Derrida *De l'esprit: Heidegger et la question* (Paris: Galilée, 1987), p. 14; hereafter E. Translations are my own.

18. Philippe Lacoue-Labarthe's important *La Fiction du politique* (Paris: Christian Bourgois, 1987). Lacoue-Labarthe would specifically avoid using the term "Holocaust," because he objects to its overtones of "sacrifice" (see *La Fiction du politique*, pp. 80–81). According to Lacoue-Labarthe, a too-easy identification of "Auschwitz" with sacrifice only works to normalize it, thereby presenting it as a manifestation of a "psycho-pathology" that the "free" world can smugly distance itself from. In addition, this move would deny the specificity of the Shoah: it is a gesture, then, which plays into the revisionist's hands, by presenting the murder of the Jews as "just another" example of racial or ethnic hatred, albeit on an unheard-of scale. Lacoue-Labarthe himself recognizes, however, that "on another level" one might indeed have to speak of sacrifice in this instance, which would entail reconsidering the "anthropological notion" of sacrifice itself (p. 81).

Certainly for Derrida a recognition of the sacrificial aspect of the Shoah cannot be avoided, although he never considers it in these terms. From the first, as we have seen in "Plato's Pharmacy," deconstruction undoes a sacrificial model of exclusion or opposition, identified with Western speculative (and specular) philosophy from its beginnings (see in this context above all Lacoue-Labarthe's essay "The Caesura of the Speculative"). And Derrida, at the end of *De l'esprit*, considers nazism not as an isolated event in Western cultural history, but as a mushroom (or toadstool) that could only grow in the shelter provided by the "Black Forest" of European philosophies. From this perspective, then, nazism, whose very raison d'être was the murder of the Jews, is just another, particularly noxious, version of "speculative" philosophy.

19. The later sections of *De l'esprit* are concerned with Heidegger's postwar readings of Georg Trakl.

20. The clearest exposition of Heidegger's goals in embracing nazism (and analysis of the opportunism of his gesture) can be found in an article published over forty years ago: "Le Cas Heidegger," by Eric Weil, first appeared in *Les Temps Modernes* in 1947; reprinted in *Lignes* 2 (1988): 139–51.

21. Derrida has analyzed the problem of the act as foundation of the university and its project in two important texts: "Mochlos ou le conflit des facultés," *Philosophie* 2 (Apr. 1984): 21–53, and "The Principle of Reason: The University in the Eyes of Its Pupils," *Diacritics 13* (Fall 1983): 3–20. "Mochlos" especially links the problem of the origin of reason to the violence of the speech act: "The origin of the principle of reason, which is also implied in the origin of the university, is not rational. The foundation of a university-institution is not a university-event" (p. 50). In "The Principle of Reason," interestingly enough, Derrida joins this analysis of the origin of the university's reason to a critique of technocracy and technologism that owes much to Heidegger.

22. This quote is not a translation of the translation in *De l'esprit* (p. 60) but rather the passage as it is rendered by Karsten Harries in Martin Heidegger, "The Self-Assertion of the German University," *Review of Metaphysics* 38 (Mar. 1985): 474–75.

23. This gambit is to be found in Victor Farias's controversial book *Heidegger et le Nazisme* (Paris: Verdier, 1987), a work that, despite its shortcomings, has caused many, especially in France, to take seriously for the first time the question of the larger political implications of Heidegger's work (and, perhaps more important, the political implications of the work of *French* Heideggerians, such as Foucault, Lyotard, and Derrida himself). It should be stressed, however, that Derrida's book, *De l'esprit*, published about the same time as Farias's (late 1987) was not written as a refutation of it but as a continuation of an investigation that Derrida, along with Lacoue-Labarthe, has been carrying out for a number of years. See, in this context, Derrida's other recent essays on Heidegger, "Geschlecht: Différence sexuelle, différence ontologique," and "Geschlecht (II): La Main de Heidegger," both in *Psyché: Inventions de l'autre* (Paris: Galilée, 1987), pp. 395–452. For an excellent critique of the Farias book, see Jean-Michel Palmier's "Heidegger et le National-Socialisme: A propos du livre de Victor Farias," *Lignes* 2 (1988): 152–82.

24. Again, one must recall that Derrida's polemical point here is directed in

large measure against many of the younger generation of French philosophers (such as Luc Ferry) who would advocate a return to some form of secular humanism and to a revalorization of the subject, as a kind of reaction to the "pensée 68" (Derrida himself, as well as the hidden interlocutors of "The Ends of Man," such as Foucault, Deleuze, and Lacan). The return to a humanism after a half-century of "totalitarianisms" might not be so easy after all. Luc Ferry and Alain Renaud's book *Heidegger et les modernes* (Paris: Grasset, 1988), brought out only a few months after *De l'esprit*, criticizes Derrida in no uncertain terms (see the section entitled "L'Interprétation derridienne," pp. 99–120) for this identification of biologism and humanism: according to them, humanism is precisely opposed to any positive characterization of the human, and thus it will be opposed to any racism (pp. 15–19). Ironically, Ferry and Renaut can oppose Derrida only by arguing for a reinterpretation of Heidegger that is nothing other than a return to Sartre! (See pp. 203–4, where they invoke Sartre's *Existentialism Is a Humanism*.) One has the definite impression that the French debate concerning humanism has, in the last forty years, moved in a perfect (or vicious) circle.

25. For more on Heidegger's politics in context, see especially Jeffrey Herf's *Reactionary Modernism: Technology, Culture, and Politics in Weimar and the Third Reich* (Cambridge: Cambridge University Press, 1984).

26. Heidegger, quoted in Richard Wolin, "Recherches récentes sur la relation de Martin Heidegger au National Socialisme," *Les Temps Modernes* 495 (Oct. 1987): 83, and in Lacoue-Labarthe, "La Fiction du politique," p. 58. My translation.

27. Richard Wolin does argue this point at the end of his article "Recherches récentes."

28. A similar strategy characterizes Derrida's reading of the debate between Heidegger and Meyer Shapiro concerning Van Gogh's shoes, in "Restitutions of the Truth in Pointing" in *The Truth in Painting* (Chicago: University of Chicago Press, 1987). Derrida points out the "pairing," the complicity between Heidegger and Shapiro; both are looking for the same thing, asking the same questions. Heidegger associates the shoes with the peasant, Shapiro with the city dweller, but, Derrida writes, "At all costs [the] size/pointure must be found, even if this 'subject' is not the same one for both parties. They are in agreement, that's the contract of this tacit institution, to seek for one, or to pretend to seek for one, given that both are certain in advance that they have found it" (*The Truth in Painting*, p. 282). One is justified in wondering, though, whether Derrida's reading of Heidegger's "Origin of the Work of Art" is any more effective in combating Heidegger's politically suspect "Black Forest" ideology than Shapiro's.

29. Heidegger, "The Self-Assertion of the German University," p. 474, emphasis added.

30. Derrida's orientation is shared by Lacoue-Labarthe who, in *La Fiction du politique*, states quite clearly: "Nazism is a humanism to the extent that it rests on a determination of the *humanitas* that, in its eyes, is more powerful, in other words more effective, than any other" (p. 138).

9. DE MAN AND GUILT

1. De Man's articles from *Le Soir*, along with those from a number of other sources, both in French and in Flemish, have been collected in Paul de Man, *Wartime Journalism*, ed. W. Hamacher, N. Hertz, T. Keenan (Lincoln: University of Nebraska Press, 1988). The French articles in this volume have not been translated.

2. Calling it the same problem is, of course, an oversimplification: Blanchot himself was engaged in various political projects of the Left in the 1950s and 1960s, most notably opposing the war in Algeria and the institution of De Gaulle's Fifth Republic in 1958. In addition, Blanchot wrote a number of brief articles that seem to indicate an affirmation, with reservations, of Marxism; see, for example, "Sur une approche du communisme," and "Les Trois paroles de Marx," in *L'Amitié* (Paris: Gallimard, 1971), pp. 109–17. See Jeffrey Mehlman, "Blanchot at *Combat*: Of Literature and Terror," in his *Legacies of Anti-Semitism in France* (Minneapolis: University of Minnesota Press, 1983).

3. W. Hamacher, N. Hertz, and T. Keenan, eds., *Responses: On Paul de Man's Wartime Journalism* (Lincoln: University of Nebraska Press, 1989); the first part of this chapter appeared originally in this work.

4. On Heidegger and de Man, see my article "De Man and the Dialectics of Being," *Diacritics* 15 (Fall 1985), 36–45.

5. See, for example, the opening paragraph of de Man's review of Drieu La Rochelle's *Notes pour comprendre le siècle*, in *Le Soir*, 2 Dec. 1941.

6. I am referring to the by now famous *Newsweek* article, "Deconstructing de Man's Life" (15 Feb. 1988, p. 63), where the phrase "moral idiocy" is used. At least those who decry de Man's gesture in *Allegories of Reading* should face the fact that they are opting for a return to a moral notion of subjectivity; rather than simply slinging accusations, they are then obliged, it would seem, to come to terms with the problems of such a formulation, which is by no means self-evident. Whose or what notion of subjectivity are they affirming? Sartre's? Someone else's? Upon which texts are they basing their arguments? How can we read those texts? Responsible subjectivity or consciousness is not a concept that we can all agree on simply because the authority of *Newsweek* is behind it, nor is it, at this late date, a

term that we can straightforwardly affirm as a given, without argument and with a clear conscience.

7. See Paul de Man, "Les Juifs dans la littérature actuelle," *Le Soir*, 4 Mar. 1941.

8. If one refrains at this point from hastily judging or morally evaluating de Man's actions, or at least resists as much as possible the tendency to do so, one should nevertheless try to grasp the larger political implications of his writings of 1941–42. This is not such an easy task.

It should first be noted that the Nazis, at least in Belgium and France, took intellectuals very seriously, and valued their cooperation. In the eyes of the Germans, any writer who published with Gallimard, for example, was collaborating, even if the contents of his book did not in any way celebrate the Occupation. (Many French authors of the period, however – including Sartre, Camus, Simone de Beauvoir, Blanchot, Bataille, Ponge, Paulhan, and Brice Parain – managed to convince themselves that, while publishing in the NRF was unacceptable because the editor [Drieu La Rochelle] openly excluded Jews, publishing a book with Gallimard, the publisher of the review, was still all right. The Germans, however, never recognized this fastidious distinction; they in fact took the opposite view, that publishing with Gallimard was *equivalent* to being in the review.) Authors who published their work from June 1940 to August 1944 were demonstrating that intellectual life was continuing under the Nazis, that it was possible to cooperate with them at least to the extent that one dealt with a firm that necessarily excluded Jews and Communists. Gallimard – and most other publishers of the period – were bringing their books out with the official approval of the censor, they were able to obtain precious paper, and so on. They could never have operated if the Germans had seen their books as being in any way inimical to the Occupation. See, on this topic, the biography *Gaston Gallimard*, by Pierre Assouline (Paris: Balland, 1984), esp. pp. 263–362, and *Paris allemand*, by Henri Michel (Paris: Albin Michel, 1981), pp. 334–39.

The same clearly applied to the press – journalism and book publishing – in Belgium. De Man was one of the literary and cultural critics of the most influential French-language Belgian newspaper, and he reviewed, and hence promoted, the books that the Nazi-approved houses were publishing. It is no coincidence that many of the books he reviewed were French translations of German works; one of the policies of the authorities – which publishers like Gallimard were happy to go along with – was to finance the translation and diffusion of "apolitical" but respectable German literature, including modern authors (such as Jünger) and the classics, as a way of burnishing the somewhat tarnished image of German culture.

An important part of de Man's job at *Le Soir*, then, was to argue for, and exemplify, a Francophone opening of French culture to German influences; see, in this context, the end of the review of F. Sieburg's *Dieu est-il français?* (28 Apr. 1942). (De Man, of course, was also during this period a French translator of German authors, such as Paul Alverdes and A. E. Brinckmann; Brinckmann's book, *Esprit des nations: France-Italie-Allemagne* [Brussels: La Toison d'or, 1943], itself is a call for cultural collaboration between European "peoples" – German "spirituality" is presented in this work as a higher synthesis that justifies and saves, through negation, the lesser tendencies of French "rationalism" and Italian "sensualism.") On the importance of *Le Soir* as a collaborationist paper, see *Contribution à l'histoire de la résistance Belge*, by George K. Tanham (Brussels: Presses Universitaires de Bruxelles, 1971), pp. 118 and 157–59.

With all this said, it should be stressed that de Man's "collaboration," such as it was, should be sharply distinguished from that of the Brasillach or Céline variety. Although, at least for a while, he clearly supported the "revolution," or at least saw it as a fait accompli, in a number of instances his notion of "collaboration" amounts to little more than a nonxenophobic communication between cultures; see, for example, his Flemish review of Ernst Jünger's work ("A Great Writer: Ernst Jünger," *Het Vlaamsche Land*, 26–27 July, 1942). De Man writes in this article: "[A writer] systematically impoverishes himself, he refuses to make use of that which constitutes the vital force of our European culture, if he, allegedly in order to remain true to his own people, does not want to become acquainted with that which comes into being elsewhere."

We should also note that de Man gave favorable reviews to two literary publications that were known, under the Occupation, to be forums for dissent and even resistance: *Messages*, a French-Belgian review that published surrealists such as Eluard and other writers, including Sartre and Bataille (*Le Soir*, 14 July 1942); and *Das Innere Reich*, a German literary review with a conservative Christian orientation, many of whose contributors had been executed by the end of the war (*Le Soir*, 20 Apr. 1942).

9. A coincidence: the translation is by Henri Thomas, the French novelist and author of the roman à clef that, rumor has it, recounts de Man's early experiences in the United States, *Le Parjure* (Paris: Gallimard, 1964).

10. The reader can compare the favorable image that de Man presents of German literary practice (as in the article "Regards sur l'Allemagne" [3 Aug. 1941]) with the negative one he usually has of French authors, even right-wing ones. See, in the latter case, the review of Robert Brasillach's *Notre avant-guerre* (12 Aug. 1941); Drieu's *Notes pour comprendre le siècle* (2 Dec. 1941); Henride Montherlant's *Le Solstice de juin* (11 Nov. 1941),

and so on. These reactionary French authors are guilty, in de Man's view, of many of the sins of French literature in general: elitism, "cérébralité," Parisian stylishness, individualism (see "La Littérature française devant les événements" [20 Jan. 1942]), the preaching of morality, and (related to the often abstract or mechanical didacticism) the attempt to hold forth on topics beyond the competence of the writer. (This latter accusation has been a staple of right-wing attacks on intellectuals at least since the Dreyfus affair.) The few French authors who escape these tendencies (such as Jean Giono) are seen as exceptions that confirm the rule.

11. See de Man's other review of a work by Jünger, "Jardins et routes" (23 June 1942). It is interesting to note that when de Man wrote on Jünger for a French-speaking audience, he made a sharp distinction between the cold and analytic French tradition and the mythic and vital German one, whereas, when he wrote on the same book, *On the Marble Cliffs*, for a Flemish audience ("A Great Writer: Ernst Jünger," *Het Vlaamsche Land*, 26–27 July 1942) he explicitly modified his position: in an argument reminiscent of those to be found in A. E. Brinckmann's *Esprit des nations*, de Man argues that Jünger's novel is a kind of higher synthesis between French "rational humanism" and German "mythical romanticism." Why the change? Perhaps de Man decided that the French audience needed to have its own tradition demystified before it could see the literary value of Jünger's somewhat obscure novel; on the other hand, the Flemish, who would be only too happy to reject the French tradition, would benefit from the eclecticism implied in a view of Jünger's work as an affirmation of what was best in the French tradition. At this late date it is pointless to speculate about what de Man "really" believed; throughout his writings of this period, he affirmed both the valorization of German "myth" over French "reason," *and* a synthesis of those "conflicting" traditions. In any case, as we see in Brinckmann's book (see n. 8, above), these two positions themselves are not necessarily mutually exclusive; in pseudo-Hegelian fashion, one can argue that the "higher," German synthesis (in this case Jünger) both negates a manifestly inferior French tradition and, in transcending it, incorporates it.

12. De Man's strongest early statement on the topic of literary judgments based on psychology or morality is in the article "Sur les possibilités de la critique" (2 Dec. 1941). In fact on this point he never wavered; near the end of his life, in "The Return to Philology," he was still maintaining, as the most basic gesture of his approach, the refusal of a criticism that would play an ethical, moral, or "religious" role.

13. See, for example, de Man's critique of H. R. Jauss's use of this approach in the article "Reading and History," in RT, 69.

14. Maurice Blanchot, in the essay "Une Oeuvre d'Ernst Jünger," in *Faux pas* (Paris: Gallimard, 1943), pp. 287–92, makes a point very similar to de Man's: Jünger's novel should not be seen as a thesis novel. No doubt Jünger himself, perhaps for very practical reasons, maintained the same thing. Such fervent arguing that the novel should *not* be read in a political light only underscores the fact that it so easily lends itself to such a reading; it also incites one to question the motives behind the flat refusal of a political interpretation.

15. Jünger's novel, however, much like the Martin Scorsese film *Taxi Driver*, has an ironically "happy" ending, which can be interpreted naively, but is all the more disturbing when read as a "fairy tale" that cannot begin to keep its promise, and knows it.

16. This is precisely why de Man, in the early articles, criticizes authors like Montherlant or Drieu, who stray beyond their competence and assume that there is some referential or analogical connection between the literary text and political reality.

17. When he does argue in favor of a history, it is one of aesthetic forms and solutions. Here de Man was probably influenced by Marcel Raymond (see the article "Criticism and Literary History" [*Het Vlaamsche Land*, 7–8 June 1942] for a discussion of Raymond's *De Baudelaire au surréalisme*).

18. I am thinking here not so much of the blind respect of the disciple as of the respect of any careful reader who would necessarily take the arguments of the text he or she is analyzing seriously, and follow them as far as they will go – thereby, perhaps, as Derrida would say, reading the author against himself. Not to do so inevitably leads to much of the simple-minded commentary that has proliferated in our most highly respected magazines and newspapers since the de Man "scandal" broke: cheap accusations, guilt by association, etc.

19. De Man's problematizing of the "humanity" of the grammatical machine here no doubt owes much to a Foucauldian dehumanization of the Lévi-Straussian structuralist-mathematical model of a differential language (in, for example, *Les Mots et les choses*). Beyond this, however, there is an echo of Heidegger's discussion of the machine, and its defamiliarization, in *Being and Time*. But while Heidegger tends to conflate humanism and technology (they are in complicity through a mutual forgetting of Being), de Man in some ways sees a radicalized technology – the "anti-grav" machine, grammar – as radically opposed to the human, subjectivity, etc.

20. Interestingly enough, de Man's gesture here is very close to Rousseau's who, at the end of book 4 of the *Confessions*, also shifts the blame onto the reader; if the reader finds Rousseau blameworthy, that is certainly not the fault of the autobiographer: "By relating to him [i.e., the reader] in simple

detail all that has happened to me, all that I have done, all that I have felt, I cannot lead him into error. His task is to assemble these elements and to assess the being who is made up of them. The summing-up must be his, and if he comes to wrong conclusions, the fault will be of his own making" (Jean-Jacques Rousseau, *Confessions*, trans. J. M. Cohen [Harmondsworth: Penguin, 1954], p.169).

21. Even when de Man posits a "synthesis" between committed writing and a pure aestheticism – as in his article "Paul Alverdes et sa revue 'Das innere Reich'" (20 Apr. 1942) – it is clear that the two sides come together only in order to remain completely separate: "And as, in addition, expression is a form whose beauty consists in an eternal value, *independent of the contingencies of the hour*, one can imagine the merit that this creation assumes" (emphasis added).

22. Of course we can discern a "middle period" in de Man's work where this repetitive positing was already evident; one thinks of articles such as "Intentional Structure of the Romantic Image" and the last page of the book review of J. Hillis Miller's *The Disappearance of God* in *Partisan Review*, Fall 1964. At this point what would later be presented as a result of the mechanical functioning of the machine-grammar is still presented in a Heideggerian terminology of "temporality."

23. On prosopopoeia in de Man, see Cynthia Chase, *Decomposing Figures: Rhetorical Readings in the Romantic Tradition* (Baltimore: Johns Hopkins University Press, 1986), chap. 4.

24. There is a moment in the chapter on "Excuses" when a feminist reading suggests itself – and which de Man explicitly avoids; we are clearly not to interpret Rousseau's singling out of Marion as his victim as having anything to do with the fact that she is a woman. "In the spirit of the text, one should resist all temptation to give any significance whatsoever to the sound 'Marion'" (AR, 289).

Clearly, the last chapter of *Allegories of Reading* is directed against the possibility of a psychoanalytic reading, just as the second to last, on Rousseau's *Social Contract*, is directed against the possibility of a historicist or Marxist one. No matter what some of his followers might say, for de Man there was never any possibility that any of these methods could be "coordinated" with his own. Instead, his method definitively excludes them.

25. While de Man asserts, in "The Resistance to Theory," that his theory subsumes other, weaker or less complete ones (grammar, semiology, reference, reading-avoidance, etc.) (RT, 19), it is clear that certain ones – Marxism, psychoanalysis, feminism – are explicitly eliminated; this is made clear in the last two chapters of *Allegories of Reading*. One can argue that de

Man's method can constitute itself only through this rigorous exclusion-expulsion.

26. Since de Man's death, this argument, used as a response to "historicists" emboldened by the discovery of the articles in *Le Soir*, has constituted much of the defense of "rhetorical reading" (by critics such as J. Hillis Miller).

27. "Hegel on the Sublime," in Mark Krupnick, ed., *Displacement: Derrida and After* (Bloomington: Indiana University Press, 1983), p.153. One is struck in this passage by the sudden and incongruous stress placed on "politics" and "legitimacy." If indeed "language itself dissociates the cognition from the act" (as de Man puts it in the earlier chapter on Rousseau's *Social Contract*), how can de Man later claim to speak authoritatively in any way about the legitimate political sphere?

28. Derrida, interestingly enough, has a similar problem when he attempts to analyze Heidegger's allegiance to nazism. It is when the quotation marks come off the word *Geist*, according to Derrida, that Heidegger's thought enters into complicity with Western metaphysics, humanism, and hence nazism. How one is to distinguish between, say, Christianity, humanism, and nazism is a question that this approach cannot hope to answer. See my discussion of this problem in the preceding chapter.

29. See, for example, his review in *Le Soir* of Giono's suggestively titled *Le Triomphe de la vie* (24 Mar. 1942) and his remarks on Heidegger in "Tentation de la permanence," in *Monde Nouveau-Paru* 93 (Oct. 1955), 49–61. But one should recall, on the other hand, his statement in his *Le Soir* review of *Dieu est-il français?* by F. Sieburg (28 Apr. 1942): "Americanism offers us the edifying spectacle of the danger inherent in submitting everything to technical requirements."

30. Here one should consider de Man's arguments in the short essay "The Return to Philology" (RT, 21–26) in conjunction with those presented in the lecture on Benjamin's "Task of the Translator." In the first essay, the target is primarily the garden-variety secular humanism that serves as the ethical (or, as de Man would have it, "religious") underpinning for what passes as the teaching of literature in the United States; in the second, it is a messianic and politicized Jewish mysticism that would seem to have little to do with American humanism. Yet both are to be avoided, and for largely the same reasons.

31. Characteristically, de Man holds that this other history will be one of translations. When one does not "give in to everything that would go in the other direction," when one refuses the ethical and the mystical, "at that moment translation occurs." Translations in this sense are the real events of

history, and they, it seems, generate a larger history almost as a by-product (see RT, 104).

32. It should be stressed that de Man, at the end of his life, describes messianism as "madness," but it is precisely the messianism of the Jewish tradition, and not the German, that is in question (see RT, 103).

33. De Man also states, in the same article: "They [that is, de Man's own readings] are, always in theory, the most elastic theoretical and dialectical model to end all models and they can rightly claim to contain within their own defective selves all the other defective models of reading-avoidance, referential, semiological, grammatical, performative, logical, or whatever" (RT, 19). This is a dubious statement, and one that merits some analysis. While it is certainly true that de Manian readings often pit a formalistic reading (based on an analysis of grammar or syntax) against a referential one that entails some version of the self-reflexivity of literary language, or vice versa, one would be hard-pressed to find one that starts from, and includes, say, a Marxist reading, or a feminist one. Such approaches are set aside a priori by de Man as bastard or imperfect versions of a fully self-referential literary model. Whether this exclusion is legitimate or not is a question that de Man's approach itself apparently cannot answer. It does not concern itself with the question of which approaches are to be "contained" within rhetorical reading, and which (like Gershon Scholem's [or Benjamin's] messianic-political, or Rousseau's proto-psychoanalytic) are simply to be excluded. This problem is, however, certainly worth considering. Why, for example, should we assume that a materialist model of knowledge (as in Marxism) can simply be collapsed into an idealist model of referential self-reflexivity? Here again it is a basic Heideggerian orientation in de Man that should be analyzed.

34. De Man here relies on a reading of Benjamin's "Task of the Translator" by Carol Jacobs ("The Monstrosity of Translation," MLN 90 [1975]) that, against Scholem, interprets the broken fragments of the mystical vessel not as "matching" but as "following" one another.

35. Again, one should recall here de Man's Heideggerianism: this critique of the traditional oppositions of metaphysics, and above all that of sacrificial exclusion/inclusion, is clearly related, not only to Heidegger's analysis of "metaphysics," but to Derrida's rewriting of Heidegger (see the preceding chapter, on Derrida, and particularly the strategies of "Plato's Pharmacy").

36. De Man's article was originally published in the *Times Literary Supplement* as a response to critics of deconstruction such as Walter Jackson Bate of Harvard; de Man's polemical gesture is thus to confront them with "one of their own" (Brower himself was a New Critic at Harvard), in that way demonstrating that they have misread both the genesis and the stakes of

his, and their own, project. De Man does not stress, of course, the influence on his project of other writers less palatable to the Harvard English department: Heidegger, Bataille, Blanchot, etc.

37. There would seem to be more than a little self-scapegoating or self-victimization on de Man's part here; he appears to be attempting to provoke nothing less than his own ostracism by and from the entire (professional) community of humanists when he puts forward a project so uncompromising, and so uncompromisingly hostile to the current state of affairs in academia, that it (and finally he) will be rejected out of hand by everyone except his own devoted followers.

10. SUR BATAILLE

1. Alain Arnaud and Gisèle Excoffon-Lafargue's *Bataille* (Paris: Seuil, 1978) is an example of this approach.

2. See Jean-Louis Houdebine, "L'Ennemi du dedans," and Julia Kristeva, "Bataille, l'expérience et la pratique," both in *Bataille*, ed. Philippe Sollers (Paris: 10/18, 1973).

3. Denis Hollier, "De l'au-delà de Hegel à l'absence de Nietzsche," in *Bataille*, ed. Philippe Sollers (Paris: 10/18, 1973); "Le dispositif Hegel dans la bibliothèque de Bataille" *L'Arc* 38; and Jacques Derrida, "From Restricted to General Economy." A text that deals with Nietzsche in Bataille is Jacques Chatain, *Georges Bataille* (Paris: Seghers, 1973). Chatain's approach, however, both conflates very different texts by Bataille and separates them without seeing any internal significance or motivation behind that separation.

Hollier's essay, "De l'au-delà de Hegel," while presenting a convincing model of a Bataillean repetition compulsion (the repetition Hegel/ Nietzsche) has some difficulties in explaining the modalities of the notion of community in Bataille (pp. 103–4). Once again, attention to the specificities of texts would help explain what otherwise appears to be an arbitrary valorization on Bataille's part of either an antisocial or individualistic conception of communication, or a more generalized concern with political entities or secret societies (community).

4. Georges Bataille, *Oeuvres complètes* (Paris: Gallimard, 1970), 6:369; hereafter OC. All translations are my own.

5. In this chapter, the terms "heterogeneity" and "homogeneity" will be used in a specifically Bataillean sense. The clearest exposition of these terms is to be found in the essay "The Psychological Structure of Fascism" (VE 137–60). Homogeneity refers to utilization, production, and above all to the conservation of limits: "Production is the basis of a social *homogeneity*. *Homogeneous* society is productive society, namely, useful society. Every

useless element is excluded, not from all of society, but from its *homoge-neous* part. . . . According to the judgment of *homogeneous* society, each man is worth what he produces; in other words, he stops being an exis-tence for itself; he is no more than a function, arranged within measurable limits, of collective production (which makes him an existence *for some-thing other than itself*)" (VE, 138). This homogeneity can refer to personal and psychological limits (and personal activity) as well as social. Hetero-geneity is thus any element or force that serves to break open those limits, that introduces elements that cannot be reappropriated by either personal or social utility: "heterogeneity defined as non-homogeneous supposes a knowledge of the homogeneity that delimits it by exclusion" (VE, 140).

6. Contre-Attaque was the political group Bataille founded in 1935 with a number of surrealists, including André Breton. It was short-lived, dis-banding when Breton accused Bataille of "surfascisme." Unlike the Acé-phale group of 1936–39, Contre-Attaque still saw itself as politically of the Left, and therefore in some sort of collusion, no matter how difficult, with French Marxists. Acéphale, on the other hand, was conceived as being completely above, or beside, conventional politics, including the Sorelian Marxo-anarchism of Contre-Attaque.

7. See OC, 6:147: "A wave of airplanes arrives, the siren . . . no doubt it's nothing, but once again everything is at risk."

8. Translations of *Le Coupable* and *L'Expérience intérieure* have recently ap-peared: see Georges Bataille, *Guilty*, trans. Bruce Boone (Venice, Calif.: Lapis Press, 1988), and Georges Bataille, *Inner Experience*, trans. Leslie Boldt (Albany: State University of New York Press, 1988), hereafter IE.

9. Georges Bataille, "Propositions," in VE, 199.

10. On the difficult question of Bataille's politics, two books are of great value: Francis Marmande's *Georges Bataille Politique* (Lyons: Presses Universi-taires de Lyon, 1985), and Jean-Michel Besnier's *La Politique de l'impossi-ble: L'Intellectuel entre révolte et engagement* (Paris: La Découverte, 1988). Both books give an excellent overview of the history (and contradictions) of Bataille's politics from the 1930s through the 1950s. On Acéphale in particular, see Marmande, pp. 59–69, and Besnier, pp. 25–37 and 113–61. As should be evident from its title, Besnier's book is concerned, from a different perspective, with the problem addressed by all my current work.

11. In this context, see Bataille, "The Psychological Structure of Fascism." Bataille in the end saw Contre-Attaque as, ironically enough, a reappropri-ation of negativity (in the form of a "paradoxical fascism") – the very thing Contre-Attaque had sought to avoid by positing a nondirected mob vio-lence (perhaps inspired by Georges Sorel's "myth of the general strike"). As an alternative to the "politics" of Contre-Attaque (which nevertheless

saw the mobs actively revolting against political institutions, making the mobs themselves participators in a political process), Bataille organized Acéphale, which was to substitute the experience of the negativity of myth and sacrifice to that of mob violence: "Contre-Attaque having dissolved, Bataille decided immediately to form . . . a 'secret society' which would turn its back on politics, and which envisioned nothing more than a religious end, but an anti-Christian one, a Nietzschean one" ("Fragment from an Autobiographical Sketch," in OC, 6:485).

12. Georges Bataille, "Instructions pour la 'rencontre en forêt'" ("Instructions for the 'Meeting in the Forest'") (OC, 2:227), gives a clear idea of the kind of rituals planned by Bataille for his co-conspirators in Acéphale.

13. Roger Caillois, "The Collège de Sociologie: Paradox of an Active Sociology," Sub-Stance 11, no. 12 (1976): 63.

14. Ibid., p.61. Caillois gives a strong portrait of the Bataille of this period, though very negative due to the conflict between the two over the nature of the gift in "primitive" cultures.

15. Although Bataille first introduced a practice of meditation before an ecstatic or horrible image in the fifth (and last) issue of Acéphale (see VE, 235–39) that is, in early 1939, at that time this practice was still associated with a "church" and "war." The war was to take place not only within and against the subject ("I myself am war") but also between the members of the sect and those who would attempt to crush it – presumably the Fascists.

16. This text is from "L'Amitié" ("Friendship"), whose writing was for Bataille the decisive factor in his break with the idea of forming a "secret society" or "sect."

17. See, for example, Bataille's exposure of a Fascist reediting of Nietzsche that turned him into an anti-Semite (VE, 183–84).

18. Friedrich Nietzsche, Nietzsche-Werke, vol. 8:2 (Posthumous Fragments, 1887) (Berlin: De Gruyter, 1974), p.150; hereafter F. Translations from Nietzsche are my own.

19. In a more general sense, the critique of "utility" and technology is at the center of twentieth-century German debates concerning modernity and the relation of democracy to the experience of modern life. One thinks in particular of Heidegger ("The Question concerning Technology"), Benjamin ("The Work of Art in the Age of Mechanical Reproduction"), Jünger (The Worker), Oswald Spengler (The Decline of the West), Fritz Lang (the film Metropolis), etc.

20. Nietzsche, Mar.–July 1888, quoted in Bataille, Sur Nietzsche, in OC, 6:78.

21. Friedrich Nietzsche, Ecce Homo (Berlin: De Gruyter, 1969), pp.363, 364.

22. At least he favored them to the extent that he argued for the necessity of

the democracies' resistance to Nazi expansion. At the same time, however, Bataille saw the failure of democracies to respond actively and firmly (as evidenced by the accords reached at Munich in Sept. 1938) as a symptom of the inevitable "devirilization" of society brought on by "bourgeois individualism." See, for example, Bataille's "Declaration of the College of Sociology on the International Crisis," in Hollier, *The College of Sociology*, pp.43–46.

23. I do not mean to imply that ironization and deconstruction are somehow equivalent, but only that deconstruction, exactly like Nietzsche's ironization, finds itself in a "parasitical" position in relation to an established philosophy, metaphysics, etc. – or, as Bataille would put it, in relation to an established philosophical homogeneity. But how does it happen that certain homogeneities, and not others, are "spent" in the game of intellectual potlatch? This is certainly a question that writers like Derrida seem to avoid: in Derrida's work, the choice of text to be deconstructed most often seems fully arbitrary. (No one has ever argued that there is a systematic program linking the various texts that Derrida deconstructs.) What I suggest in the next section of this chapter is that there is, in Bataille at least, an important homogeneity of homogeneities, a coherent dialectic of dialectics, that is inseparable from the movement of the systematic deconstruction of such dialectics. In that sense, the coherency of the (Hegelian) dialectic is never simply escaped in Bataille; it is affirmed at the very instant it is opened out.

24. Indeed *Sur Nietzsche* does work toward a climax, the liberation of Aug. 1944, but it is a climax that is outside the control of Bataille as he writes his journal – the events are contingent, they could have taken place otherwise, or not at all. As history, Aug. 1944 is a dubious endpoint (or "liberation"). Even if it is a culmination of sorts, it is not a stabilization but an experience of danger, gunfire, and peripheral involvement. It is less an end posited by Bataille – the narrator – than a springboard that he proposes in his journal through the very project of writing in wartime – which snaps back to catapult him beyond any telos he could have devised.

25. Friedrich Nietzsche, *The Will to Power*, 2:371, 374, 329, quoted in OC, 6:152. I have not been able to locate the early French edition of *The Will to Power* from which Bataille quotes, to verify his excerpts.

26. "Even more than the text of Volume One of *Being and Time* . . . Heidegger's inability to finish it by writing Volume Two underlines my similarity with [him]. . . . "I am not a philosopher" (OC, 5:217 n.).

27. The sacred, before its recuperation by organized religion, is for Bataille that which not only escapes all rationalized or even comprehensible societal or temporal forms but is indeed their rupture. See the essay "The

Sacred" (1939): "Christianity has made the sacred substantial, but the nature of the sacred, in which today we recognize the burning existence of religion, is perhaps the most ungraspable thing that has been produced between men: the sacred is only a privileged moment of communal unity, a moment of the convulsive communication of what is ordinarily stifled" (VE, 242).

28. Bataille's Nietzsche, as unadulterated "toxicity," criticizes Christianity not because it is the previous stage in any "dialectic" but only because "it is there" (or because "it is there" is precisely what it refuses).

29. Some would argue, unconvincingly, that this textual community is the *only* one of significance in Bataille: such is the position of Maurice Blanchot, in the first part of his book *La Communauté inavouable* (Paris: Minuit, 1983). The fact remains, however, that the textual community, as we have seen, is still dependent on, and is inseparable from, a "minor" dialectic that entails the going beyond of various necessary social – and hence communal – forms and activities (potlatch, the community of Christians, etc.). Moreover, the Nietzsche/Bataille community is never simply separable in Bataille from a post-Hegelian community that Bataille attempts to envisage on a political and cultural level; see his comments on the Marshall Plan, for example, at the end of *The Accursed Share*. It is clear enough from that discussion that, as late as 1949, he is still thinking in terms of larger social structures and their conflicts (nations, for example, and nuclear war), and not simply of rather tenuous groupings of absent and often dead readers and writers (the kind of collectivity that the later Sartre would have considered under the heading "seriality").

30. This reading of Nietzsche/Bataille seeks to push the notion of dualism in Bataille to its logical conclusion. Two other texts on this theme are "Le Matérialisme dualiste de Georges Bataille," by Denis Hollier, *Tel Quel* 25 (Spring 1966), and "Le Toit," by Philippe Sollers, *Tel Quel* 29 (Spring 1967), where the notion of "sides" (of a roof, of a text) is introduced.

31. Their coexistence is impossible: it is, in fact, the same impossibility that we saw working in "Nietzsche Dionysos" (VE, 206–7) – except now, of course, it is on a higher level – that is, the contents of the sides of the impossible relation have been made more coherent and comprehensive – they have come to include, for example, the thematization of the text itself and its processes (the text as *surnietzsche*, "community," etc.).

32. The reader at this point might object that the transgressive relation of the *Summa atheologica* to *The Accursed Share* is no less abstract than the contradiction between sheer toxicity and a new historical era that was characteristic of the Acéphale position.

This objection would be correct, up to a point. The abstraction would remain, but it would be on a higher level, so to speak, a level of greater particularity of texts and therefore of a greater (and at the same time more significantly problematic) self-reflexivity. To expect a simple "resolution" of this problem would be to call for a total return to Hegel. One postwar approach to this problem can be seen in a chapter of the last volume of the projected three-volume *Accursed Share, La Souveraineté* (OC, 8:365–74). It is arguable that one way of reading this chapter would be to see posited *within the impossible subject* (the subjectivity of the leftist intellectual) the contradiction: radical negativity (refusal)/social progression (affirmation).

This negativity would take place at the same *instant* as the positivity: in that sense it would be quite different from the Maoist dialectic (and the *Tel Quel* reading of it) in which the radical negativity is situated in a temporal, diachronic framework always overcome but always reasserting itself (the goal in any activity still being to overcome negativity to the greatest extent possible). Here, however, the affirmation and refusal would be embraced simultaneously, impossibly, *and with the guilt of betrayal*. The practical and material version of this? Since Bataille is dead, that is for us, his readers, to formulate or undergo.

11. HEGEL'S RETURN

1. Georges Bataille, "The Notion of Expenditure," in Bataille, *Visions of Excess*, pp. 116–29.

2. The second version of this letter (the one in *Le Coupable*), "Letter to X., Teacher of a Course on Hegel" (hereafter L), can be found in Bataille, *Guilty*, pp. 123–25.

3. Jean Hyppolite, in his French translation of G. W. Hegel, *Phénoménologie de l'esprit* (Paris: Aubier-Montaigne, 1941), 2:251 n.81. Translations are my own.

4. This formula ("Dieu, s'il 'savait', serait un porc") appears in the final footnote of Bataille's novel *Madame Edwarda* (OC, 3:31). It is a Hegelian rewriting of André Breton's somewhat naive blasphemy, "Dieu est un porc."

5. On the improbability of the writer's existence, see Bataille's essay "Sacrifices," in VE, 130–36.

6. See my discussion of Derrida's use of this double "end" in his essay "The Ends of Man," in chap. 8, above.

7. See the "Letter to X, Lecturer on Hegel," in Hollier, *The College of Sociology*, p. 90: "I grant (as a likely supposition) that, from now on, history is ended (with the exception of the denouement). But I see things differently (I do not attribute much importance to the difference between fascism and communism; furthermore, it seems not at all impossible that, a long time

from now, everything will begin again)." Note that Bataille is quite indifferent to the "actual" denouement; in effect, that denouement is *already* here.

8. See my comments on the Bataillean state at the end of history in *Politics, Writing, Mutilation*, pp. 101–2.

9. See Blanchot's *La Communauté inavouable*, p. 45, where Blanchot writes of the "anonymity of the book which is addressed to no one and which, through its relations with the unknown, institutes what Georges Bataille (at least one time) called "the negative community: the community of those who have no community."

10. I quote from *The Accursed Share*, trans. R. Hurley (New York: Zone Books, 1988), p. 197 n. 22. It should be recalled that this book was first published in 1949; it is a collection of articles that Bataille had written for his review, *Critique*, in the two or three preceding years.

11. On the betrayal by the Bataillean intellectual of his own *savoir absolu*, see chap. 6, "Betrayal in the Later Bataille," of my *Politics, Writing, Mutilation*.

12. Jean-Luc Nancy, *La Communauté désoeuvrée* (Paris: Christian Bourgois, 1986), hereafter CD. Translations are my own.

13. See Lyotard's *Heidegger et "les juifs"* (Paris: Galilée, 1988).

14. The theory/practice distinction which I suggest here would no doubt be rejected by Nancy himself as just another metaphysical opposition. Nevertheless, Nancy is clearly writing to proclaim, and through that speech act, to effectuate, a certain state of affairs in the world: the disappearance of the traditional intellectual. Thus he argues for the interruption of a certain figure or myth of the writer, who leaves his ghostly trace in Nancy's writing – in other words, in his theory. But the writer that Nancy does affirm will be found exclusively in the realm of theory precisely because his social function is impossible to distinguish from that of the writer Nancy is rejecting. (Nancy, I take it, is the sort of writer that he himself is valorizing; but Nancy does all the things the traditional intellectual did – he teaches in a university, publishes with prestigious publishing houses, organizes colloquia, writes in newspapers, even speaks for other people [withdrawing writers], etc.) Nancy's writer will be even more a myth, if that is at all possible, than was the traditional representative intellectual (there have been in the past, after all, intellectuals who actually did represent people, albeit perhaps with unfortunate results). Nancy's speech act proclaiming the interruption of the writer is effective only within the fiction of his own text.

15. Nancy, in using the word *retrait*, is doubtless referring to Derrida's use of it in the essay "Le Retrait de la métaphore," in *Psyché, inventions de l'autre*

(Paris: Galilée, 1987), pp.63–92. For a commentary on Derrida's essay that situates it as a rewriting of Heidegger, see Rodolphe Gasché's "Joining the Text: From Heidegger to Derrida," in *The Yale Critics*, ed. J. Arac, W. Godzich, and W. Martin (Minneapolis: University of Minnesota Press, 1983), pp.156–75.

16. See my discussion of Foucault's attempt simply to "escape" Hegel (or to "go beyond" him), and Derrida's critique of it, in the chapter on Foucault, above.

17. I quote (again) from *Méthode de méditation*, where Bataille writes: "Even more than the text of Volume One of *Being and Time* . . . Heidegger's inability to finish it by writing Volume Two underlines my similarity with [him]" (OC, 5:217 n.).

18. I refer to Ferry and Renaut's *Heidegger et les modernes*, which seems to call for a return to a Sartrian version and critique of Heidegger, as a counter to Derrida's.

Bibliography

Arnaud, Alain, and Gisèle Excoffon-Lafargue. *Bataille*. Paris: Seuil, 1978.

Aronson, Ronald. *Sartre's Second Critique*. Chicago: University of Chicago Press, 1987.

Assouline, Pierre. *Gaston Gallimard*. Paris: Balland, 1984.

Austin, J. L. *How to Do Things with Words*. Oxford: Oxford University Press, 1962.

Barthes, Roland. "Authors and Writers." In *Critical Essays*, trans. Richard Howard. Evanston, Ill.: Northwestern University Press, 1972.

———. "Death of the Author." In *Image, Music, Text*, ed. and trans. Stephen Heath, pp. 142–48. New York: Hill and Wang, 1977.

Bataille, Georges. *The Accursed Share*. Trans. R. Hurley. New York: Zone Books, 1988.

———. "Attraction and Repulsion II." In *The College of Sociology: 1937–39*, ed. Denis Hollier, trans. Betsy Wing, pp. 113–24. Minneapolis: University of Minnesota Press, 1988.

———. *Guilty*. Trans. Bruce Boone. Venice, Calif.: Lapis Press, 1988.

———. "Hegel, la mort et le sacrifice." In *Deucalion* 5. Neuchatel: La Baconnière, 1955.

———. *Inner Experience*. Trans. Leslie Anne Boldt. Albany: State University of New York Press, 1988.

———. *Oeuvres complétes*. 12 vols. Paris: Gallimard, 1970–87.

———. *Visions of Excess: Selected Writings, 1927–39*. Ed. Allan Stoekl, trans. Allan Stoekl with Carl Lovitt and Donald M. Leslie, Jr. Minneapolis: University of Minnesota Press, 1985.

Baudrillard, Jean. *America*. Trans. C. Turner. London: Verso, 1988.

Bibliography

Bauer, George H. "Just Desserts." *Sartre after Sartre*, ed. Fredric Jameson. *Yale French Studies* 68 (1985): 3–14.

Benda, Julien. *Exercice d'un enterré vif*. Paris: Gallimard, 1946.

———. *La Trahison des clercs*. Paris: Grasset, 1927.

Besnier, Jean-Michel, and Jean-Paul Thomas. *Chronique des idées d'aujourd'hui: Eloge de la volonté*. Paris: PUF, 1987.

———. *La Politique de l'impossible: L'Intellectuel entre révolte et engagement*. Paris: La Découverte, 1988.

Blanchot, Maurice. "Le Caravansérail." *Combat* 10 (Dec. 1936).

———. "Comment la littérature est-elle possible?" In *Faux pas*. Paris: Gallimard, 1943.

———. *La Communauté inavouable*. Paris: Minuit, 1983.

———. "La Facilité de mourir." In *L'Amitié*. Paris: Gallimard, 1971.

———. "The Gaze of Orpheus." In *The Gaze of Orpheus*, ed. P. Adams Sitney, trans. Lydia Davis. Barrytown, N.Y.: Station Hill, 1981.

———. "Les Intellectuels en question." *Le Débat* 29 (Mar. 1984): 3–28.

———. "Literature and the Right to Death." In *The Gaze of Orpheus*, ed. P. Adams Sitney, trans. Lydia Davis. Barrytown, N.Y.: Station Hill, 1981.

———. *Michel Foucault, tel que je l'imagine*. Montpellier: Fata Morgana, 1986.

———. "Une Oeuvre d'Ernst Jünger." In *Faux pas*. Paris: Gallimard, 1943.

———. "Où va la littérature." In *Le Livre à venir*. Paris: Gallimard, 1973.

———. "Sur une approche du communisme," and "Les Trois paroles de Marx." In *L'Amitié*. Paris: Gallimard, 1971.

———. "Terrorisme, méthode de salut public." *Combat* 7 (July 1936).

Bloom, Allan. *The Closing of the American Mind*. New York: Vintage, 1987.

Boschetti, Anna. *Sartre et "Les Temps modernes": Une Entreprise intellectuelle*. Paris: Minuit, 1985.

Bourdieu, Pierre. *Ce que parler veut dire*. Paris: Fayard, 1986.

———. *Homo Academicus*. Paris: Minuit, 1984.

Bové, Paul. *Intellectuals in Power: A Genealogy of Critical Humanism*. New York: Columbia University Press, 1986.

Brinckmann, A. E. *Esprit des nations: France-Italie-Allemagne*. Brussels: La Toison d'or, 1943.

Brooks, Peter. *Reading for the Plot: Design and Intention in Narrative*. New York: Vintage, 1984.

Brunschvicg, Leon. *Le Progrès de la conscience dans la philosophie occidentale*. Paris: Alcan, 1927.

Butler, Judith P. *Subjects of Desire: Hegelian Reflections in Twentieth-Century France*. New York: Columbia University Press, 1987.

Caillois, Roger. *Approches de l'imaginaire*. Paris: Gallimard, 1974.

Bibliography

———. "The Collège de Sociologie: Paradox of an Active Sociology." *Sub-Stance* 11, no. 12 (1976): 61–64.

Catalano, Joseph S. *A Commentary on Jean-Paul Sartre's Critique of Dialectical Reason*. Chicago: University of Chicago Press, 1986.

Caws, Peter. *Sartre*. London: Routledge and Kegan Paul, 1984.

Chambers, Ross. *Story and Situation: Narrative Seduction and the Power of Fiction*. Minneapolis: University of Minnesota Press, 1984.

Charlton, D. G. *Secular Religions in France, 1815–70*. London: Oxford University Press, 1963.

Chatain, Jacques. *Georges Bataille*. Paris: Seghers, 1973.

Chase, Cynthia. *Decomposing Figures: Rhetorical Readings in the Romantic Tradition*. Ithaca, N.Y.: Cornell University Press, 1986.

Clark, Priscilla Parkhust. *Literary France: The Making of a Culture*. Berkeley: University of California Press, 1987.

Collins, Margery L., and Christine Pierce. "Holes and Slime: Sexism in Sartre's Psychoanalysis." In *Women and Philosophy: Toward a Theory of Liberation*, ed. Carol C. Gould and Marx Wartofsky, pp. 112–27. New York: Putnam, 1976.

Comte, Auguste. *The System of Positive Polity*. 4 vols. New York: Burt Franklin, 1966.

De Man, Paul. *Allegories of Reading: Figural Language in Rousseau, Nietzsche, Rilke, and Proust*. New Haven: Yale University Press, 1979.

———. *Blindness and Insight: Essays in the Rhetoric of Contemporary Criticism*. 2d, rev. ed. Minneapolis: University of Minnesota Press, 1983.

———. "Hegel on the Sublime." In *Displacement: Derrida and After*, ed. Mark Krupnick, pp. 139–53. Bloomington: Indiana University Press, 1983.

———. *The Resistance to Theory*. Minneapolis: University of Minnesota Press, 1986.

———. *Wartime Journalism*. Ed. W. Hamacher, N. Hertz, and T. Keenan. Lincoln: University of Nebraska Press, 1988.

Derrida, Jacques. *De l'esprit: Heidegger et la question*. Paris: Galilée, 1987.

———. "Geschlecht: Différence sexuelle, différence ontologique," and "Geschlecht (II): La Main de Heidegger." In *Psyché: Inventions de l'autre*. Paris: Galilée, 1987.

———. *Margins of Philosophy*. Trans. A. Bass. Chicago: University of Chicago Press, 1982.

———. "Mochlos ou le conflit des facultés." *Philosophie* 2 (Apr. 1984): 21–53.

———. "Plato's Pharmacy." In *Dissemination*, trans. B. Johnson. Chicago: University of Chicago Press, 1981.

———. "The Principle of Reason: The University in the Eyes of Its Pupils." *Diacritics* 13 (Fall 1983): 3–20.

367

Bibliography

——. "La Question du style." In *Nietzsche aujourd'hui?* Colloque de Cérisy, 1972. Paris: 10/18, 1973.

——. "Restitutions of the Truth in Pointing." In *The Truth in Painting*. Chicago: University of Chicago Press, 1987.

——. "Le Retrait de la métaphore." In *Psyché, inventions de l'autre*. Paris: Galilée, 1987.

——. *Writing and Difference*. Trans. A. Bass. Chicago: University of Chicago Press, 1977.

Descombes, Vincent. *Le Même et l'autre: Quarante-cinq ans de philosophie française, 1933–78*. Paris: Minuit, 1979.

Doubrovsky, Serge. "Phallotexte et gynotexte dans *La Nausée*: 'Feuillet sans date.'" In *Sartre et la mise en signe*, ed. M. Issacharoff and J.-C. Vilquin, pp. 31–55. Lexington, Ky.: French Forum, 1982.

Dreyfus, Hubert, and Paul Rabinow. *Michel Foucault: Beyond Structuralism and Hermeneutics*. Chicago: University of Chicago Press, 1982.

Drieu La Rochelle, Pierre. *Les Chiens de paille*. Paris: Gallimard, 1964.

——. "Les Evènements de Février." In *Socialisme Fasciste*. Paris: Gallimard, 1934.

——. *Fragments de Mémoires, 1940–41*. Paris: Gallimard, 1982.

——. *Gilles*. Folio ed. Paris: Gallimard, 1973.

Durkheim, Emile. *L'Allemagne au-dessus de tout: La Mentalité allemande et la guerre*. Paris: A. Colin, 1915.

——. *Education et sociologie*. 1922. Paris: PUF, 1985.

——. *The Elementary Forms of the Religious Life*. 1912. Trans. J. W. Swain. London: George Allen and Unwin, 1927.

——. "L'Etat." *Revue philosophique* 4 (1958): 433–37.

——. "Individualism and the Intellectuals." 1898. Trans. M. Traugott. In *Emile Durkheim: On Morality and Society*. Chicago: University of Chicago Press, 1973.

——. *Moral Education*. 1902–3. Trans. E. K. Wilson and H. Schnurer. New York: Free Press, 1973.

——. *Les Règles de la méthode sociologique*. 1895. Paris: PUF, 1986.

——. "The State." In *Durkheim on Politics and the State*, ed. Anthony Giddens, trans. W. D. Halls, pp. 45–50. Cambridge: Polity Press, 1988.

——. *Le Suicide*. 1897. Paris: PUF, 1985.

Fabiani, Jean-Louis. *Les Philosophes de la république*. Paris: Minuit, 1988.

Farias, Victor. *Heidegger et le Nazisme*. Paris: Verdier, 1987.

Ferry, Luc, and Alain Renaut. *Heidegger et les modernes*. Paris: Grasset, 1988.

——. *La Pensée 68: Essai sur l'anti-humanisme contemporain*. Paris: Gallimard, 1985.

Bibliography

Foucault, Michel. *Discipline and Punish*. Trans. A. Sheridan. New York: Vintage, 1979.

———. *Language, Counter-Memory, Practice: Selected Essays and Interviews*. Ed. D. F. Bouchard, trans. D. F. Bouchard and S. Simon. Ithaca, N.Y.: Cornell University Press, 1977.

———. *The Order of Things*. Trans. A. Sheridan-Smith. London: Tavistock, 1970.

———. "La Pensée du dehors." *Critique* 229 (June 1966): 523–46.

———. *Power/Knowledge: Selected Interviews and Other Writings, 1972–77*. Ed. and trans. Colin Gordon. Brighton: Harvester Press, 1980.

———. *Raymond Roussel*. Paris: Gallimard, 1963.

Fynsk, Christopher. *Heidegger: Thought and Historicity*. Ithaca, N.Y.: Cornell University Press, 1986.

Gasché, Rodolphe."L'Echange héliocentrique." *L'Arc* 48 (1972): 70–84.

———. "Joining the Text: From Heidegger to Derrida." In *The Yale Critics*, ed. J. Arac, W. Godzich, and W. Martin, pp. 156–75. Minneapolis: University of Minnesota Press, 1983.

———. *The Tain of the Mirror: Derrida and the Philosophy of Reflection*. Cambridge: Harvard University Press, 1986.

Girard, René. *La Violence et le sacré*. Paris: Grasset, 1972.

Goldthorpe, Rhiannon. *Sartre: Literature and Theory*. Cambridge: Cambridge University Press, 1984.

Gouldner, A. W. *Against Fragmentation: The Origins of Marxism and the Sociology of Intellectuals*. New York: Continuum, 1985.

———. *The Future of Intellectuals and the Rise of the New Class*. New York: Continuum, 1979.

Hamacher, W., N. Hertz, and T. Keenan, eds. *Responses: On Paul de Man's Wartime Journalism*. Lincoln: University of Nebraska Press, 1989.

Hegel, G. W. F. *Phénoménologie de l'esprit*. Trans. Jean Hyppolite. Paris: Aubier-Montaigne, 1941.

Heidegger, Martin. *Nietzsche*. Pfüllingen: Neske, 1961.

———. *The Question of Being*. Trans. W. Kluback and J. T. Wilde. New York: Twayne, 1958.

———. "The Self-Assertion of the German University." Trans. Karsten Harries. *Review of Metaphysics* 38 (Mar. 1985): 470–80.

Herf, Jeffrey. *Reactionary Modernism: Technology, Culture, and Politics in Weimar and the Third Reich*. Cambridge: Cambridge University Press, 1984.

Hervier, Julien. *Deux individus contre l'histoire: Ernst Jünger, Pierre Drieu La Rochelle*. Paris: Klincksieck, 1978.

Hofstadter, Richard. *Anti-Intellectualism in American Life*. New York: Knopf, 1964.

Bibliography

Hollier, Denis. "De l'au-delà de Hegel à l'absence de Nietzsche." In *Bataille*, ed. Philippe Sollers, pp.75–96. Paris: 10/18, 1973.

———. "Le Dispositif Hegel dans la bibliothèque de Bataille." *L'Arc* 38.

———. "Le Matérialisme dualiste de Georges Bataille." *Tel Quel* 25 (Spring 1966): 41–53.

———, ed. *The College of Sociology: 1937–39*. Trans. Betsy Wing. Minneapolis: University of Minnesota Press, 1988.

Houdebine, Jean-Louis. "L'Ennemi du dedans." In *Bataille*, ed. Philippe Sollers, pp.153–91. Paris: 10/18, 1973.

Howard, Dick. *The Marxian Legacy*. London: Methuen, 1977.

Hoyt, N. S., and T. Cassirer, eds. and trans. *Encyclopedia: Selections*. Indianapolis: Bobbs-Merrill, 1965.

Jacobs, Carol. "The Monstrosity of Translation." MLN 90 (Dec. 1975): 755–66.

Jacoby, Russell. *The Last Intellectuals*. New York: Basic Books, 1987.

Jakobson, Roman. "Les Embrayeurs, les catégories verbales et le verbe russe." Chapter 9 in *Essais de linguistique générale*, vol. 1. Paris: Minuit, 1963.

Jameson, Fredric. *Marxism and Form*. Princeton: Princeton University Press, 1974.

Johnson, Paul. *Intellectuals*. New York: Harper and Row, 1989.

Jünger, Ernst. *On the Marble Cliffs*. Trans. Stuart Hood. Harmondsworth: Penguin, 1970.

Kant, Immanuel. *Critique of Judgment*. Trans. J. H. Bernard. New York: Hafner Press, 1951.

Kaufmann, Vincent. *Le Livre et ses adresses*. Paris: Meridiens Klincksieck, 1986.

Keefe, Terry. "The Ending of Sartre's *La Nausée*." *Forum for Modern Language Studies* 12, no. 3 (1976): 217–35.

Klossowski, Pierre. *Nietzsche et le cercle vicieux*. Paris: Mercure de France, 1967.

Kojève, Alexandre. *Introduction à la lecture de Hegel*. Paris: Aubier, 1947.

Kristeva, Julia. "Bataille, l'expérience et la pratique." In *Bataille*, ed. Philippe Sollers, pp.267–301. Paris: 10/18, 1973.

Künzel, Werner. *Foucault liest Hegel: Versuch einer polemischen Dekonstruktion dialektischen Denkens*. Frankfurt am Main: Haag und Herchen, 1985.

La Capra, Dominic. *Rethinking Intellectual History: Texts, Contexts, Language*. Ithaca, N.Y.: Cornell University Press, 1983.

Lacoue-Labarthe, Philippe. "The Caesura of the Speculative." Trans. Robert Eisenhauer. In *Glyph* 4. Baltimore: Johns Hopkins University Press, 1978.

———. *La Fiction du politique*. Paris: Christian Bourgois, 1987.

Lévi-Strauss, Claude. "Introduction à l'oeuvre de Marcel Mauss." In *Sociologie et anthropologie*, by Marcel Mauss. Paris: PUF, 1983.

Bibliography

Loubet del Bayle, Jean-Louis. *Les Non-Conformistes des années trente*. Paris: Seuil, 1969.

Lyotard, Jean-François. *Heidegger et "les juifs."* Paris: Galilée, 1988.

———. *Tombeau de l'intellectuel et autres papiers*. Paris: Galilée, 1984.

Major-Poetzl, Pamela. *Michel Foucault's Archaeology of Western Culture: Toward a New Science of History*. Chapel Hill: University of North Carolina Press, 1983.

Marmande, Francis. *Georges Bataille Politique*. Lyons: Presses Universitaires de Lyon, 1985.

Mauss, Marcel. *The Gift: Forms and Functions of Exchange in Archaic Societies*. Trans. I. Cunnison. New York: Norton, 1967.

Mehlman, Jeffrey. "Blanchot at Combat: Of Literature and Terror." In *Legacies of Anti-Semitism in France*. Minneapolis: University of Minnesota Press, 1983.

Michel, Henri. *Paris allemand*. Paris: Albin Michel, 1981.

Miller, J. Hillis. *The Ethics of Reading*. New York: Columbia University Press, 1987.

Nancy, Jean-Luc. *La Communauté désoeuvrée*. Paris: Christian Bourgois, 1986.

Nietzsche, Friedrich. *Ecce Homo*. Berlin: De Gruyter, 1969.

———. *Nietzsche-Werke*. Vol. 8:2. Posthumous Fragments, 1887. Berlin: De Gruyter, 1974.

———. "On Truth and Lie in a Nonmoral Sense." In *Philosophy and Truth: Selections from Nietzsche's Notebooks of the Early 1870s*, ed. and trans. D. Breazeale, 79–97. Atlantic Highlands, N.J.: Humanities Press, 1979.

Nisbet, Robert. *The Sociology of Emile Durkheim*. New York: Oxford University Press, 1974.

Nizan, Paul. *Les Chiens de garde*. 1932. Paris: Gallimard, 1965.

———. *The Trojan Horse*. Trans. Charles Ashleigh. London: Longmans, 1937. Originally published as *Le Cheval de Troie* (Paris: Gallimard, 1935).

Ory, Pascal, and Jean-François Sirinelli. *Les Intellectuels en France, de l'Affaire Dreyfus à nos jours*. Paris: Armand Colin, 1986.

Palmier, Jean-Michel. "Heidegger et le National-Socialisme: A propos du livre de Victor Farias." *Lignes* 2 (1988): 152–82.

Paulhan, Jean. "Le Don des langues." In *Oeuvres complètes*. Paris: Cercle du livre precieux, 1970.

———. "D'un langage sacré." In *Cahiers Jean Paulhan*. Vol. 2: *Paulhan et le Madagascar*. Paris: Gallimard, 1982.

———. *Les Fleurs de Tarbes*. Paris: Gallimard, 1973.

———. *Jacob Cow le pirate, ou si les mots sont des signes*. Paris: Tchou, 1970.

———. *Lettre aux directeurs de la Résistance*. Paris: J. J. Pauvert, 1968.

371

Bibliography

Pease, Donald. "Sublime Politics." *boundary* 2 12/13 (Spring/Fall 1984): pp.259–79.

Perry, Lewis. *Intellectual Life in America: A History*. Chicago: University of Chicago Press, 1989.

Pickering, W. S. F. *Durkheim's Sociology of Religion*. London: Routledge and Kegan Paul, 1984.

Poster, Mark. *Existential Marxism in Postwar France*. Princeton: Princeton University Press, 1975.

Pratt, Mary Louise. *Toward a Speech Act Theory of Literary Discourse*. Bloomington: Indiana University Press, 1977.

Prendergast, Christopher. "Of Stones and Stories: Sartre's *La Nausée*." In *Teaching the Text*, ed. S. Kappeler and N. Bryson, pp.56–72. London: Routledge and Kegan Paul, 1983.

Prince, Gerald. "Roquentin et le langage naturel." In *Sartre et la mise en signe*, ed. M. Issacharoff and J.-C. Vilquin, pp.103–13. Lexington, Ky.: French Forum, 1982.

Rajchman, John. *Michel Foucault and the Freedom of Philosophy*. New York: Columbia University Press, 1985.

Roth, Michael S. *Knowing and History: Appropriations of Hegel in Twentieth-Century France*. Ithaca, N.Y.: Cornell University Press, 1988.

Rousseau, Jean-Jacques. *Confessions*. Trans. J. M. Cohen. Harmondsworth: Penguin, 1954.

Saisselin, Rémy G. "Bouville ou l'anti-Combray." *French Review* 33, no. 3 (1960): 232–38.

Sartre, Jean-Paul. *Being and Nothingness*. Trans. Hazel Barnes. New York: Washington Square Press, 1966.

———. *La Critique de la raison dialectique*, Vol. 2: *L'Intelligibilité de l'histoire*. Paris: Gallimard, 1985.

———. *The Critique of Dialectical Reason*. Ed. Jonathan Rée, trans. A. Sheridan-Smith. London: NLB, 1976.

———. *Drôle d'amitié*. In *Oeuvres romanesques*, ed. Michel Contat and Michel Rybalka, pp.1461–1534. Paris: Gallimard, 1981.

———. *La Dernière Chance*. In *Oeuvres romanesques*, ed. Michel Contat and Michel Rybalka, pp.1585–1654. Paris: Gallimard, 1981.

———. *L'Etre et le néant*. Paris: Gallimard, 1943.

———. "Une Idée fondamentale de la phénoménologie de Husserl: L'Intentionalité." In *Situations I*. Paris: Gallimard, 1975.

———. *Le Mur*. 1939. In *Oeuvres romanesques*, ed. Michel Contat and Michel Rybalka, pp.211–388. Paris: Gallimard, 1981.

———. *Nausea*. Trans. Lloyd Alexander. New York: New Directions, 1964.

———. *Oeuvres romanesques*. Ed. Michel Contat and Michel Rybalka. Paris: Gallimard, 1981.

———. *Plaidoyer pour les intellectuels*. Paris: Gallimard, 1972.

———. *Troubled Sleep*. Trans. Gerard Hopkins. New York: Alfred Knopf, 1951. Originally published as *La Mort dans l'âme*.

———. *What Is Literature?* Trans. B. Frechtman. Cambridge: Harvard University Press, 1988.

Sedgwick, Eve Kosofsky. *Between Men: English Literature and Male Homosocial Desire*. New York: Columbia University Press, 1985.

Smith, John H. *The Spirit and Its Letter: Traces of Rhetoric in Hegel's Philosophy of "Bildung."* Ithaca, N.Y.: Cornell University Press, 1988.

Sollers, Philippe. "Le Toit." *Tel Quel* 29 (Spring 1967): 25–45.

Stoekl, Allan. "1937: The College of Sociology Is Founded." In *A New History of French Literature*, ed. Denis Hollier, pp. 929–35. Cambridge: Harvard University Press, 1989.

———. "De Man and the Dialectics of Being." *Diacritics* 15 (Fall 1985): 36–45.

———. *Politics, Writing, Mutilation: The Cases of Bataille, Blanchot, Roussel, Leiris, and Ponge*. Minneapolis: University of Minnesota Press, 1985.

Suleiman, Susan Rubin. *Authoritarian Fictions: The Ideological Novel as a Literary Genre*. New York: Columbia University Press, 1983.

Tanham, George K. *Contribution à l'histoire de la résistance Belge*. Brussels: Presses Universitaires de Bruxelles, 1971.

Teroni-Menzella, Sandra. "Les Parcours de l'aventure dans *La Nausée*." *Etudes Sartriennes* 1, no. 2 (1984): 57–74.

Thomas, Henri. *Le Parjure*. Paris: Gallimard, 1964.

Torgovnick, Marianna. *Gone Primitive: Savage Lives, Modern Intellects*. Chicago: University of Chicago Press, 1990.

Wahl, Jean. *Etudes Kierkegaardiennes*. Paris: Aubier, 1938.

Wallwork, Ernest. *Durkheim: Morality and Milieu*. Cambridge: Harvard University Press, 1972.

Warminski, Andrzej. *Readings in Interpretation: Hölderlin, Hegel, Heidegger*. Minneapolis: University of Minnesota Press, 1987.

Weber, Samuel. *Institution and Interpretation*. Minneapolis: University of Minnesota Press, 1987.

Weil, Eric. "Le Cas Heidegger." 1947. Reprinted in *Lignes* 2 (1988): 139–51.

Wolin, Richard. "Recherches récentes sur la relation de Martin Heidegger au National Socialisme." *Les Temps Modernes* 495 (Oct. 1987): 56–85.

Zimmerman, Michael. *Heidegger's Confrontation with Modernity: Technology, Politics, Art*. Bloomington: Indiana University Press, 1990.

Index

Index